FRANCE

BY

M. GUIZOT

AND

MADAME GUIZOT DE WITT

TRANSLATED BY ROBERT BLACK

IN EIGHT VOLUMES

WITH A SUPPLEMENTARY CHAPTER OF RECENT EVENTS
By MAYO W. HAZELTINE

ILLUSTRATED

VOL. VIII

NEW YORK
PETER FENELON COLLIER & SON
· M C M ·

TABLE OF CONTENTS—VOL. VIII.

LIST OF ILLUSTRATIONS

FRANCE

VOL. VIII

THE HISTORY OF FRANCE.

CHAPTER XIV.

THE DECLINE (1813).

IT was now more than seven months since Napoleon left France. He had been living in a distant country, almost without communication, isolated by the madness of his undertaking, and was now returning, condemned by human reason and divine justice. The rumor of his defeat had preceded him, though without unfolding the extent and gravity of his disaster.

On reaching Paris the emperor addressed a message to the Senate, in reply to their solemn professions of devotion:— "Senators, what you tell me affords me great pleasure. I have at my heart the glory and power of France, but my first thoughts are for all that can perpetuate tranquillity at home, and place my peoples forever out of danger of the distractions of factions and the horrors of anarchy. It is upon those enemies of the happiness of nations that, with the will and love of the French, I have founded this throne, with which, henceforward, the destinies of our country are bound up.

"Timid and cowardly soldiers ruin the independence of nations, but pusillanimous magistrates destroy the empire of law, the rights of the throne, and social order itself. When I undertook the regeneration of France, I asked from Providence a fixed number of years: to destroy is the work of a moment, but to rebuild requires the assistance of time. The greatest need of the State is that of courageous magistrates.

"Our fathers had as a rallying cry, 'The king is dead: long live the king!' These few words contain the principal advantages of the monarchy. I think I have deeply studied the disposition which my peoples have exhibited during the different centuries; I have reflected upon what was done at the various epochs of our history. I shall continue to consider them.

"The war which I am waging against Russia is a political war. I began it without animosity. I should have wished to spare her the evils she has done to herself. I might have armed against her the greater part of her population, by proclaiming the liberty of the slaves: a large number of villages asked me to do so. But when I learned the savage state of that numerous class of the Russian people, I opposed that measure, which would have devoted many families to death, devastation, and the most horrible torture. If my army has undergone losses, it is on account of the premature severity of the season."

Napoleon had recently had good reason to lay stress upon the advantages of an hereditary monarchy, anciently bound up with the memories and traditions of the nation. He was at the same time brought to estimate under its value the devotion of the magistrates to whom he had in his absence entrusted the government of the empire. He was leaving Moscow on fire, and beginning the series of battles which was to be concluded by his fatal retreat, when Paris, on its awakening, was terror-struck by a vague rumor that the emperor was dead. When the minds of all were disturbed, and news of a revolution was mixed with the general belief of a catastrophe in Russia, the discovery was made of a bold conspiracy, the arrest of the conspirators, and the falseness of the information which had alarmed the capital. But a little more and the daring attempt of a monomaniac had changed the form of government in France. For a moment or two General Malet and his accomplices were masters of the police, and of part of the garrison of Paris.

Claude François de Malet was born at Dôle, in 1754. He was a man of good family, and had served in the king's armies. Becoming a keen partisan of republican principles, he had fought with some distinction from 1790 to 1799, and was opposed to Napoleon's accession to power. Unsettled, ambitious, and daring, he soon became a conspirator; and after being twice arrested, he had been at the prison La Force for several years, when he conceived the idea of attacking the imperial power. His project was already in progress during the Austrian war of 1809. The police getting a hint of his plot, Malet was separated from his accomplices, Generals Lahorie and Guidal. In 1812 he succeeded in being transferred to an asylum in the faubourg St. Antoine, and there took up the broken thread of his conspiracy. When everything was prepared, he, on the night of the 22nd October, escaped from the garden of the asylum, and putting on his uniform of general officer, went immediately to the Popincourt barracks. There, under the name of General Lamotte, he announced to Colonel Soulier

who was in command of the 10th cohort of the national guard,
that the emperor had been killed by a musket-shot at Moscow,
on the 7th October; that the Senate having met secretly, had
decided upon restoring the republic, and had just appointed
General Malet to the command of the public forces in Paris.
He was provided with the copy of a "sénatus-consulte," and
his voice and appearance being full of authority, the colonel
had not the slightest suspicion, and had his troops drawn up
in battle-order in the barracks' quadrangle. Malet marched
immediately at their head to the prison La Force, and ordering
Generals Lahorie and Guidal to be set at liberty, made them
his aides-de-camp. He then ordered Lahorie to go to the house
of the minister of police and arrest the Duke of Rovigo, or, if
necessary, blow out his brains. Lahorie had formerly been
principal officer in Moreau's staff, a man of talent and honor,
deceived most probably by Malet, but originally a republican,
and with a strong personal antipathy to Napoleon. He had
formerly been in the army with Rovigo, whom he found in bed,
after forcing open the door of his room. "Surrender yourself!"
said Lahorie. "I like you, and have no intention of harming
you. The emperor is dead; the empire is abolished, and the
Senate has restored the republic." Savary protested against
this, declaring that he had received a letter from the emperor
on the previous evening; but Guidal coming to his friend's assistance, they both conducted to La Force the amazed minister, asking himself if it was not all a frightful dream. Pasquier, the prefect of police, was there before him, also arrested
at daybreak.

Frochot, prefect of the Seine, had not even been put under
arrest. More credulous than Savary, he received the false decrees of the Senate without reserve, and gave orders that the
Hôtel de Ville should be prepared to receive the provisional
government. A note from one of his assistants, with the words
"imperator fuit," prepared the way for Malet's daring attempt.
The colonels of the garrison at the same time received orders
to guard all the entrances to Paris.

Malet had himself gone to the house of General Hullin, the
military governor of the capital, who showed some astonishment, and asked to see the orders. "In your private room,"
replied Malet. As they entered, he fired a pistol at Hullin,
breaking his jawbone, and then locking the door of the room,
ran to the house of Doucet, chief of his staff. He was difficult
to convince, and understood by a hint from Major Laborde,

that the visitor was an escaped prisoner. At the moment when Malet was making ready to fire upon them, the two officers suddenly seized him by the arms, and threw him down. A few minutes later, the Duke of Rovigo was at liberty, as well as Pasquier. They ran to assist General Hullin; the accomplices or dupes were everywhere arrested. The victims of the daring attempt looked at each other, thunderstruck at the event which had just endangered their lives and the emperor's government. Paris, now reassured, laughed, and made fun of the police. "They have made a grand *tour de Force*," said the wits.

The conspirator and his accomplices in this one day's plot paid dearly for the anger and alarm of the great functionaries whom they had humbled. The Arch-chancellor Cambacérès had not been taken in Malet's net, but his customary moderation could not restrain Savary's vengeance, much less the military indignation of the Duke of Feltre. The three generals, the colonels, and their agents, were brought before a court-martial, presided over by General Dejean. "Who are your accomplices?" asked the judge, of General Malet. "The whole of France," replied the accused; "and you also, Dejean, if I had succeeded." When put on his defence he said, "A man who has undertaken to be his country's avenger, needs no defence; he triumphs or he dies." Fourteen prisoners were condemned to death, two only obtaining delay of punishment. "I die," exclaimed Malet to the soldiers appointed to shoot him; "but I am not the last of the Romans. I die, but I have made the enemy of the republic tremble." When Napoleon returned to Paris, Frochot, the prefect of the Seine, appeared before the Council of State, was deprived of his office, and compelled to leave Paris. "Frochot is an idiot," said the emperor, "but he is not a republican."

It was with as much annoyance as astonishment that Napoleon, at Dogoborouge, received the news of Malet's conspiracy, proving how precarious was the edifice which he had erected. "What!" he said, again and again, "did nobody think of my son, my wife, or the constitutions of the empire?" It showed him the uncertainty of human affairs. and the gulf ever open beneath his feet. Malet had not succeeded, and could not succeed; "but," says Rovigo in his memoir, "the emperor understood the danger better than any one else—not from what Malet had done, but from what had not been done by those whom he had invested with his confidence in the different branches of his administration." His anger and uneasiness caused by the conspiracy hastened his departure from Russia. "I am wanted in Paris," said he repeatedly.

It was the fundamental error in that constitution of the empire, so wisely combined and powerfully organized from an administrative point of view, that the government properly so called depended on a single will, and rested on a single person. In his immense states, which were strangers to each other in origin, interests, and language, Napoleon's presence was necessary, and his absence was felt by most disastrous results. His distance from Paris made Malet's daring attempt possible. By leaving his army, at the end of the cruel Russian campaign, he had delivered them up to the last extremity of despair. The disgust which he felt for the Spanish war, and the neglect with which he treated his lieutenants there, while despotically imposing his plans upon them, powerfully assisted towards the disasters by which we were pursued in that corner of the world. Marshal Suchet had indeed reduced Valencia, and been victorious at Albufera; on the 12th June, 1812, the battle which he gained before Tarragona put that important place in our power, and finally assured us the possession of Catalonia and Aragon. Yet these advantages did not compensate for our checks, and in particular they did not give to the command that unity which was necessary for success. Napoleon wished for it, but wished for it in his own hands; and now he had set out for Russia, and Lord Wellington was at the head of the English in the Peninsula. However displeased with his Portuguese and Spanish allies, he still succeeded in imposing his plans upon them, and the general direction of the war was entrusted to him. He pursued his operations with a steady and systematic firmness, which resisted the agitations and changes of policy which his country was then undergoing in her government. The English premier, Perceval, had been killed by a pistol-shot in the lobby of the House of Commons, without the motives of the crime having ever been discovered. His successors, less determined upon a warlike policy, had to contend against the increasing sufferings of the English population, as well as the well-founded dissatisfaction of the United States. War with the United States had just broken out, being solemnly declared by President Madison on the 19th May, 1812, and already some small engagements had taken place, and the English minister had quitted the United States, when the English cabinet at last agreed to withdraw the orders in

Council which, by unfairly shackling American trade, had been
the real cause of hostility between the two countries.   The
burden was heavy for England, and the position of her armies
in the Peninsula was becoming more difficult and dangerous;
but the faults of Napoleon was sufficient to restore the equilib-
rium.   Henceforward, the difficulties of England no longer
weighed decisively in the balance.   From one end of Europe
to the other the mad enterprises of Napoleon, and the reverses
naturally resulting from them, stirred up all the sovereigns
and peoples against the colossus now beginning to totter.

In January, 1812, Lord Wellington besieged Ciudad Rodrigo,
resuming the campaign on Spanish territory by an assault
which speedily gained him the place, and with the place
important supplies of ammunition and artillery.   The English
at once advanced against Badajos, to the great astonishment of
King Joseph's staff in Madrid, and of the Emperor Napoleon
himself, who maintained that as the English general was not a
madman he was certain to direct his efforts toward Salamanca.
On the 7th April, after repeated attacks, and at the expense of
great losses in his best troops, Wellington at last took our last
fortress on the Portuguese frontier.   Marmont's army was
now isolated and threatened, without the hope of being successfully assisted by the armies of the north, which were
occupied in guarding the places—or by the army in Andalusia,
which Marshal Soult made no exertion to bring to the assistance of his companions in arms.   Napoleon replied to Marmont's complaints: " He grumbles about the distances and the
difficulty of food; I shall have, in Russia, very different distances to go over, and very different difficulties to overcome
to feed my soldiers; well! we must do as we can."   The master's
difficulties brought no remedy to those of the servant.   In spite
of King Joseph's orders, henceforward appointed by his brother
to the chief command of the troops, no reinforcement had been
sent to Marmont.   Soult persisted in waiting in Andalusia for
the attack of the English, even after Wellington, on taking
Badajos, had brought back his forces to Fuente Guinaldo, in
the north of Portugal.   Generals Dorsenne and Caffarelli, who
held the command in the north of Spain, plainly refused their
assistance or made vague promises.   General Hill, however,
had advanced with 15,000 men upon the Tagus, and after
attacking the works and garrison which Marmont had prepared to defend the bridge of Almaraz, carried the bridge and
destroyed the fortifications.   Wellington commenced to march

towards Agueda, this time seriously threatening the province of Salamanca. He justly reckoned upon the discord and weakness of the government, and the jealousy which reigned among the military leaders. Unity of action in the French armies would have made his operation impossible. Yet he advanced, and Marmont, unable to resist alone, found himself compelled to evacuate Salamanca, leaving a garrison in the three fortified convents commanding the town. He withdrew first beyond the Tormes, and soon after beyond the Douro. The defenders of the convents kept Wellington for several days before their walls, but at last yielded; and on the 28th June the English occupied Salamanca. All Marmont's efforts were for the purpose of concentrating his forces, and Wellington's to prevent him from being assisted. An Anglo-Sicilian army occupied Marshal Suchet in Catalonia; and English squadrons, cruising in the Bay of Biscay, threatened the armies of the north with a disembarkation. King Joseph in vain issued orders to Soult; Marmont was obliged to measure himself alone with Wellington, against an English army equal to his own, assisted by Spanish and Portuguese troops. The marshal was both bold and conceited, but being conscious of the danger of his situation, he tried to restrain the enemy without joining battle.

Marmont's first movements were successful. He had recrossed the Douro, and the English general was compelled to retire gradually till in his turn he was protected behind the Tormes, nearer Salamanca; while the Marshal became hopeful of gaining a victory before the promised assistance could arrive. He took up position opposite the hills of Arapiles, about a league from Salamanca, fortifying the heights with its batteries of artillery. The situation of the English was becoming critical, when Marmont made a movement to outflank the enemy's right, and thus necessarily separated his left wing from the centre of the army. Wellington had left the heights which he occupied, and when he saw this movement begin he turned to General Alava, who commanded the Spanish auxiliaries, "I have them! My dear Alava, Marmont is lost!"

He was indeed lost; for the whole of the English army, in one mass, rushed like a torrent into the gap separating our two corps. The centre was keenly attacked, while General Maucune bravely met the enemy, and drove them back to the village of Arapiles. But the battle was engaged in hurriedly, without precise orders or general plan. Marmont was severely

wounded at the commencement of the battle, and also General
Bonnet on succeeding him in the command.   When General
Clausel, young and ardent but endowed with rare self-possession, was in his turn called to direct operations, he saw that
the importance of the advantages to be gained would not
justify the price they should cost, and ordered the retreat,
falling back behind the Tormes.   The English had suffered heavy
losses; but the consequences of the battle of Arapiles were
more serious than had been foreseen by either of the combatants.   Clausel recrossed the Douro and fell back upon Burgos,
being joined on the way by King Joseph, who was bringing
him, too late, a body of 13,000 men, the approach of whom he
had wrongly neglected to announce in time.   The campaign
was finished—unhappily finished.   Joseph withdrew towards
Madrid, but Wellington followed him in this movement.   The
army of the centre, the only resource of the King of Spain, did
not allow him to defend his capital, and he found himself
obliged to withdraw towards Valencia.   There he sent orders
to Soult to rejoin him, and abandon Andalusia.   A strange
suspicion had insinuated itself into Soult's distrustful mind as
to King Joseph's loyalty towards the emperor; and having
been informed of it by accident, the sovereign's first interviews
with the great military chief were so stormy as to still further
increase the difficulty of combining their military plans.

Meantime, Wellington had taken up his quarters at Madrid,
where the pride of the English officers, and the violence of the
Spanish democrats, frequently irritated the population.   They
had been accustomed to the kindness and winning ways of
King Joseph, who had thus almost become popular in his capital, and was well received when the English, after failing before the citadel of Burgos, were in their turn compelled to fall
back upon Salamanca.   The King of Spain had brought back
with him the army of the centre and that of Andalusia, and
effected a junction with the army of Portugal, which had been
rallied and re-formed by General Clausel.   Marshal Jourdan
urged him to march to Arapiles where Wellington was again
settled, in order to cut off General Hill's forces, then separated
from the main army.   The want of concord which always
reigned among the feeble king's advisers delayed that operation, and a different movement was attempted too late.   The
English withdrew without opposition, and the concentration
of the three great armies of Spain remained without any result.
Madrid was now covered by 24,000 men; but not a single place

was left us on the Portuguese frontier, and we had been obliged to evacuate Andalusia, and raise the siege of Cadiz.

In Spain, as well as in Russia, we were beaten. Europe was every day becoming emboldened against the conqueror, so long irresistible, but now at last beginning to gather the fruits of his wrong-doing—fruits which were also bitter for our country, successively engaged in senseless enterprises of which she was so long to bear the burden!

In his real mind, the Emperor Napoleon, as he left Smorgoni, wished for peace. He thought it necessary, but impossible to obtain without another grand display of his power. He was counting upon the remains of his army which were left behind. "I have 120,000 men," said he, to Abbé Pradt, as he passed through Warsaw incognito; "I am going to find 300,000 more; I shall lead them in three or four battles on the Oder, and in six months I shall be again on the Niemen. After all, I cannot prevent it from freezing in Russia!" Every post brought him news of a disaster more complete than the preceding. On General York's defection, he wrote as follows to the princes of the Rhenish confederation:—

"I flattered myself that I should have no new efforts to ask from my peoples; but that state of things has just been suddenly changed by the treason of General York, who, with the Prussian corps, 20,000 men strong, under his orders, has joined the enemy. On this occasion Prussia has given me the strongest assurances of her intentions, which I have reason to believe sincere, but which do not prevent her troops from being with the enemy. The immediate results of that treason are, that the King of Naples has had to retire behind the Vistula, and that my losses will be increased by those yet to be made in the hospitals of Old Prussia. A remote result may be a war in Germany. I have used all proper measures to guard the frontiers of the confederation; but all the confederate states ought, on their side, to feel the necessity of making efforts proportioned to the demands of circumstances. It is not only against a foreign enemy that they have to guard themselves; they have a more dangerous one to dread—the spirit of revolt and anarchy. The Emperor of Russia has appointed Baron Stein a minister of state: he admits him into his most intimate councils—him and all those who, aspiring to change the face of Germany, have long been trying to succeed by overthrow and revolution. I ought to expect that the confederate princes will not neglect their own interests and betray their own cause; they would

betray it by not assisting me by every means in their power,
or by not doing all they can to baffle the enemy's plans. They
would also betray it by not rendering agitators of every kind
powerless to injure, by allowing the public sheets to lead men
astray by lying news, or corrupt them by pernicious doctrines;
or by not anxiously watching what is preached, what is taught,
and whatever can in any way influence the public tranquillity."

That fermentation of men's minds which in France Napoleon
termed "ideology," and had violently attacked in a speech recently addressed to the Council of State, was characterized in
Germany, and especially in Prussia, by an ardent and patriotic
enthusiasm. For a long time the evils and humiliations undergone by Germany had kindled in men's hearts a deeply-
seated feeling, which secretly increased under the yoke of
silence. The disasters of the Russian campaign loosened their
bonds, and broke the seal which had been placed on every lip.
An explosion of hatred against France was everywhere manifested, with enthusiastic trust and admiration for the Czar,
though he had not fought, and had only allowed old Kutuzoff,
with the assistance of the cold, to triumph over an enemy come
to brave the deserts and formidable climate of his country.
Alexander hastened to Wilna, intoxicated by his triumph, no
longer modest and distrustful of himself, but eager to put himself forward as the liberator of Germany, welcoming all who
had fought against the French power, and laboring to rally
round him a new coalition. The thoughts of the enemies of
France were of course mainly directed to the King of Prussia;
no one had suffered as he had done by Napoleon's greedy ambition; no one was conscious amongst his people of a more ardent passion of vengeance. At Berlin, in spite of the presence
of our troops, the universal joy insulted our reverses, and
French soldiers had great difficulty in getting food. The same
sentiment burst forth throughout all Germany, together with
that idea of national unity which is easily produced in
the minds of conquered races by conquests and arbitrary
power.

The perplexity of King Frederick William was great. Still
convinced of Napoleon's preponderating power, he dared not
yet openly abandon him, but hoped to profit by our misfortunes so far as to obtain some improvement of his position. He
sent Hatzfeldt with his instructions to Paris, and backed up
his demands by increasing his armaments. In case his claims
were rejected, the King of Prussia gave it to be understood

that he should consider himself free from his engagements with France.

Austria was united to Napoleon's fortunes by closer ties, yet she also felt the thrill by which Germany generally was stirred. The Emperor Francis, as well as Metternich, began to modify their policy, hitherto more French than not, suited to the state of affairs and public opinion. Austria wished for peace; but while making the independence of Germany its basis, she also reckoned upon herself deriving several advantages. War preparations were begun in her states as well as in Prussia. Metternich, by skilful manœuvring, disseminated everywhere the idea of a German peace, and in France he laid stress upon the necessity for a glorious repose. Bubna was sent to Paris to offer for this purpose Austria's intervention with Europe.

In reply to the ideas thus communicated, Napoleon wrote to his brother-in-law, after much discussion in Council, and not without hesitation; at one time he thought of addressing himself to the Czar directly. Recapitulating the causes of his checks, he said,—

" In such a horrible tempest of cold, bivouacking became insupportable. The soldiers sought for houses and shelter in vain. That is how the Cossacks captured thousands. It is a fact that from the 7th to the 16th November the thermometer went down from ten degrees to eighteen, and even to twenty-two, and 30,000 of our horses in the artillery and cavalry died. I left several thousand artillery, ambulance, and baggage carriages, from the loss of horses. My losses were great, but the Russians cannot take any glory from the fact in any shape; I defeated them everywhere. I wished to enter into these details, not from military susceptibility, but because it seemed necessary in order that your Majesty might form a proper opinion of the present situation." This picture of our losses was succeeded by another of our resources, intended to impose fidelity through fear. "The necessary result of all this is, that I shall take no steps towards peace," continued Napoleon, " because the last circumstances having turned to the advantage of Russia, it belongs to her cabinet to take steps, if they understand the position of affairs. Nevertheless, I shall not object to those made by your Majesty."

Then, unfolding his plans respecting the projected negotiations, the emperor declared that he was ready to relax in favor of Russia the conditions of the peace of Tilsit, which hampered her commercial liberty; but that he could not yield up a single village of the grand duchy of Warsaw. With respect to England, he still adhered to the letter which he had written to Lord Castlereagh at the commencement of the Russian campaign, and which laid down the principle of the *uti possidetis.* He was, moreover, determined to make no concession with reference to the countries annexed to the empire by "sénatus-consulte;" they henceforth were part of France, such as the whole of Italy, Holland, and the Hanseatic provinces. Spain was to remain under King Joseph, the kingdom of Naples to Murat, and Prussia might obtain some increase of territory. Napoleon thought also of offering Illyria to Austria.

The concessions were illusory, and the display of pride imprudent and insolent. Beforehand, and by the conditions which he laid down, the emperor's conciliatory advances to Austria were useless; and the Duke of Bassano's bravado, in his correspondence with Metternich, aggravated still more his master's protestations. Napoleon undertook to put the seal to his provocations by his speech at the opening of the Legislative Body, on the 14th February, after an absence of more than a year from the political world:—

"Gentlemen—The war again begun in the north of Europe presented to the English a favorable opportunity for their plans; but all their hopes have fallen to the ground. Their army failed before the citadel of Burgos, and after suffering great losses was obliged to evacuate the territory of all the Spains. I myself entered Russia. The French armies were invariably victorious — at the fields of Ostrowno, Polotsk, Mohilev, Smolensk, Moskwa, Malo-Jaroslawetz. Nowhere were the Russian armies able to cope with our eagles. Moscow fell into our power.

"When the barriers of Russia were forced, and the powerlessness of her arms acknowledged, a swarm of Tartars turned their parricidal hands against the fairest provinces of that empire which it was their duty to defend. In a few weeks, in spite of the tears and despair of the wretched Muscovites, they burnt more than 4000 of their finest villages, and more than fifty of their most handsome towns, thus glutting their ancient hatred under the pretext of delaying our march by surrounding us with a desert. We triumphed over every obstacle. Even the burning of Moscow, where in four days the result of the labor and economy of forty generations was annihilated, made no change in the prosperous state of my

affairs. But the excessive and premature rigor of the winter
subjected my army to a frightful calamity. In a few nights I
saw everything changed, and I suffered great losses. They
would have broken my heart if, at such an important time, I
had been accessible to other sentiments than the interest, the
glory, and the future of my peoples.

"In view of the evils which have weighed upon us, the joy
of England has been great, and her hopes unbounded. She
offered our fairest provinces as a reward for treason; she laid
down as a condition of peace the dismemberment of this beautiful empire. It was, in other words, a proclamation of perpetual warfare. The energy of my peoples on so great an
occasion, their attachment to the integrity of the empire, the
love which they have manifested for me, have dissipated all
those chimeras, and brought back our enemies to a truer per-
ception of facts. It is with lively satisfaction that we have
seen our peoples of the kingdom of Italy, those of old Holland
and the united departments, rival the ancient French in their
zeal, and perceive that their only hope, futurity, and happiness, is in the consolidation and triumph of the great empire.

"The agents of England are propagating amongst all our
neighbors the spirit of revolt against the sovereigns. England
wishes to see the whole continent a prey to civil war and all
the terrors of anarchy; but Providence has marked herself to
be the first victim of anarchy and civil war.

"I have myself personally drawn up with the Pope a Concordat which puts a stop to all the difficulties which had unfortunately arisen in the Church. The French dynasty reigns,
and will reign in Spain. I am satisfied with the conduct of
my allies; I will abandon none of them. I shall support
the integrity of their states. The Russians will go back to
their frightful climate.

"I wish for peace; it is necessary for the world. Four
times since the rupture which followed the treaty of Amiens,
I have offered it in a formal manner. I shall never make any
peace except an honorable one—one suited to the interests and
greatness of my empire. My policy is not in any way mysteri-
ous; I have declared what sacrifices I could make. So long as
this murderous war continues, my peoples ought to be ready
for sacrifices of every kind; for a bad peace would cause us to
lose everything, even hope itself; and everything would be
compromised, even the prosperity of our grandchildren."

Europe was not deceived by the pacific declarations accompanied by such haughty manifestations; France was not deceived by them any more than the rest of Europe. The warlike preparations were on a vast scale. "If the great army had been drowned to the last man in recrossing the Niemen," wrote Bassano to Prince Metternich, "such is our martial superiority that we should not be any the less in a situation to recommence the campaign in the spring." A levy of 500,000 men had been decreed by the sénatus-consulte of January 11. It was composed of the contingent of 1813, already called into active service in the month of September, 1812, of the cohorts drawn from the first ban of the national guard, of 100,000 men called out from the four last classes of the conscription, and lastly, of the immediate enrolment of the contingent of 1814. This was not enough, and it was for France to respond by national enthusiasm to the impassioned ferment with which Germany was stirred up. First the great cities, then the departments, pledged themselves to supply the emperor with a certain number of cavalry ready mounted and equipped. An arbitrary tax was imposed by the prefects on the rich proprietors. Everywhere horses were requisitioned and well paid for; 27,000 fresh horses were in this way procured. Men were more difficult to find; the exigencies of military service had drawn from France its last resources. Compulsion was soon to be exercised towards families that until now had escaped conscription by means of pecuniary sacrifices. In the month of April there was a new levy of 80,000 men, from the six last classes of the conscription. In the departments an absolute authority was conferred on the prefects to call out from the gentry and middle class a certain number of young men who had hitherto kept aloof from the army through their opinions or through parental affection. From these, four select regiments were to be formed, under the appellation of guards of honor.

Dissatisfied and downcast, the upper classes were not deluded as to the necessity of the armaments which the Emperor Napoleon was preparing for war or for peace. The Senate voted without resistance the enormous levies demanded of it. The working classes, in the towns and in the country, saw themselves deprived of their natural supporters; anxiety grew into irritation. After the Russian campaign, to all mothers the death of their children seemed inevitable when they saw them called away for military service. Amongst the old wounded and invalid soldiers, more than one indignantly remembered how Napoleon had abandoned them at Smorgoni. "Wait till the emperor himself leads you to the army; and whilst you are waiting, stay at home," said they to the conscripts. At Paris, the women had more than once let their abusive outcries be heard. Outside France—in Holland, in the grand-duchy of Berg, in the Hanseatic provinces —there were outbursts of indignation, and a violent opposition to the conscription was manifested. " *Vive Orange!*" was everywhere the cry in the great towns of the Netherlands. The energetic repression of these movements was immediately commanded.

Napoleon was making preparations to leave France once more. For the purpose of contributing to the expenses of the war it was decided to sell a part of the communal domains, and to replace them with government annuities. This species of confiscation was likely to excite great discontent. The issue of a considerable quantity of paper money, necessary for the supply of immediate needs whilst waiting for the sales of the landed property to be effected, of course depreciated the banknote currency. Count Mollien, the perpetual minister of the Treasury, long resisted the adoption of this measure; he yielded at last, much against his will. "The emperor," says he, in his memoirs, "was thus retrograding towards the revolutionary practices which the public Treasury used to indulge in at the time of his advent to power, when no scruple was felt at substituting mere promises to pay for the real payments which had been guaranteed. His method of defining credit was this: *Credit is a dispensation from paying ready money*— forgetting that the first condition of credit is a free agreement between the borrower and the lender; and ruling himself by his definition, he concluded accordingly that, by the privilege of credit, the substitution of a simple promise to pay was, without any other condition, equivalent to an actual payment." Neither France nor the emperor had yet completely learned to abandon revolutionary processes; the transfer of the common lands was effected with ease, and without arousing much protest.

Napoleon sought at the same time to arrange other affairs, which had produced in his mind a feeling of alarm that does credit to his judgment. He was continuing to keep the Pope a prisoner, and had provisionally provided for the transmission of episcopal authority in his states. He still, however, felt impressed by the antagonist influence of this old man, so long isolated in a fortress, and whose endurance of oppression weighed upon all Catholic consciences. For several months past Napoleon had been desirous of bringing Pius VII. nearer to the centre of France, and he had had him transferred to that palace of Fontainebleau in which he had formerly received him, when the Pope crossed the Alps to perform the coronation of his devout son. On re-entering the royal residence the Pope saw himself again treated with the care and respect of which he had long been deprived; but to all this he appeared indifferent. He seemed crushed by the weight of his captivity. With difficulty could the prelates devoted to Napoleon rouse the Pope from his despondency, in order to discuss the ecclesiastical questions so closely connected with the repose of the Church. The method of canonical institution was taken as settled; Pius VII. appeared disposed to accept Avignon as his residence; he was resolute in refusing any establishment at Paris. The subject of the Church lands and bishoprics in the environs of Rome, in which the Pope was personally interested, still remained an open question. On arriving in France, Napoleon wrote to the Pope:—"Most Holy Father, I hasten to send to your Holiness an officer of my house, to inform you of the satisfaction I have experienced in hearing of your good health from the Bishop of Nantes, for during this summer I was for one moment much alarmed when I learned that you had been seriously indisposed. The new residence of your Holiness will enable us to see each other, and it is much on my heart to tell you that, in spite of all the events which have taken place, I have always preserved the same personal regard for you. We shall perhaps succeed in realizing the longed-for consummation of putting an end to the differences that exist between the State and the Church. As far as I am concerned, I am strongly disposed towards it; and it will depend entirely upon your Holiness. Most Holy Father, I pray God that He may preserve you for many years, in order that you may have the glory of re-settling the government of the Church, and that you may long enjoy the fruits of your labors."

A few weeks later the emperor suddenly arrived at Fontainebleau, so agitating the Pope that he could not recover his self-possession. "My Father!" cried the conqueror, on entering the room of the pontiff. Pius VII., without hesitating, responded by the name of son so familiar on the lips of priests: he, nevertheless, felt that there was a secret antagonism be-

tween the interests of his august visitor and his own. As soon
as the conversation turned upon important points, Napoleon
brought into play all the seductions of his manner and eloquence, in order to induce the pontiff to ratify the ruin of his
temporal power. Appealing to the religious sentiment which
was all-powerful in the mind of Pius VII., he set forth the
benefits that would result to the faith through a freedom from
anxiety as to those earthly possessions which had always been
to the Roman pontiffs a cause of embarrassment, and of disastrous concessions and transactions. The time was past for
the material power of the popes as sovereigns to have any
weight in the balance of European interests. Everything
around them was changed; religion alone remained un-
changed; it was necessary to disentangle it from every chain.
The Pope, free and independent at Avignon, endowed with a
revenue of two millions from the property already sold in the
Roman States, the possessor of all the domains still under se-
questration, should have reserved to him the appointment of
cardinals, and of the Roman bishops, whose sees should be re-
established, and the nomination to ten bishoprics in Italy or in
France at his choice. The canonical institution of the prelates
had been settled by the Council, with the consent even of the
holy father. The situation of the dismissed or disgraced
bishops should be provided for. The archives of the court of
Rome should be transported to the palace of the popes of
Avignon. The emperor did not even require a formal renunciation of the by-gone power of the Roman Church as regards
those territories which he had annexed to the empire. He accepted the formula which the Pope was willing to sign: "His
Holiness will exercise the pontificate in France, in the same
manner, and with the same forms, as his predecessors." The
question of residence was decided verbally. Pius VII. exacted
one final clause for the pious satisfaction of his conscience:
"The holy father submits to the above arrangements in consideration of the present state of the Church, and in the confidence with which the emperor has inspired him that his Majesty will entend his powerful protection to the innumerable
necessities of the Church in the times in which we live." The
Concordat was only to be published with the consent of the
cardinals, still dispersed or prisoners. The solemn deed was,
however, signed at Fontainebleau, January 25, 1813--a new
evidence of the blindness of men. A very few months were
to pass by before this edifice, so laboriously constructed, at the

cost of so many evil actions on one side, and after so much
conscientious hesitation on the other, was to crumble away.
Soon was the Pope to re-enter Rome, and the Emperor Napoleon to sign, even at Fontainebleau, the sorrowful act of his
abdication. No one foresaw the events that were preparing:
neither the simple faithful, rejoiced at seeing peace re-established in the Church, nor the majority of the counsellors of
the pontiff, anxious and uneasy at the concessions they had
granted, and who did not fail soon to excite in the mind of
Pius VII. the scruples which they themselves experienced.
Napoleon no longer troubled his mind about the matter; he
had obtained the result he wished for. Everywhere the circumstances were carefully reported, as affording fresh hopes
of that terrestrial peace perpetually promised to Europe, and
which, it was maintained, would even now be assured to it by
new and terrible combats.

For the first time during eight years, on hearing the news
of the disasters of the Russian campaign, Louis XVIII., constantly resident in England in a silent tranquillity that was
full of dignity, wished to remind Europe of his existence and
his claims, which seemed as if alike forgotten. He wrote to
the Emperor Alexander in favor of the 100,000 French prisoners detained in Russia. "Little does it matter under what
banners they have served," said he. "I see in them only my
children; I commend them to your Imperial Majesty. May
they learn that their conqueror is the friend of their father!
Your Majesty could not give me a more touching proof of
your sentiments for me."

The royal letter remained without reply. On February 1st,
Louis XVIII. published from Hartwell a manifesto explanatory
of his sentiments and his ideas—less liberal in its political sentiments than the declaration promulgated at Mittau in 1804,
more coaxing and encouraging as regards individuals and
their titles and dignities. The maintenance of the Code, *sul-
lied by the name of the usurper*, was amongst the promises
lavished upon the nation and the army. In response to the universal weariness, Louis XVIII. announced the intention of
suppressing the military conscription. The manifesto made
no stir, and the efforts put forth by a few agents of the prince
produced no result. It remained for the Emperor Napoleon
himself to replace the Bourbons on the throne, by the force of
his own faults and disasters.

Meanwhile, the sixth coalition against France was being

formed. The King of Prussia yielded at last to the irresistible movement which drew around him all his people. His propositions had been badly received at Paris. When Bubna returned to Breslau, whither Frederick William had transported his court, he found the prince resolved upon henceforth acting in concert with Russia, but still hesitating as to the method of effecting the transition from one alliance to the other. The Emperor Alexander was ready to furnish him with a pretext. Knesebeck, the Prussian envoy at his court, was ostensibly sent to ask for explanations from the Czar, with regard to the invasion of Silesia, and the authority which the Russians assumed over a foreign territory. It was easy to comprehend the secret object of his mission. The Prussians all knew it; their king was one with them in thought and feeling; he prudently waited till circumstances should compel him to act. The war-party were victorious at Kœnigsberg over the hesitating arguments of Kutuzoff. The Emperor Alexander was already at Kalisch; Wittgenstein was advancing upon Custrin and Berlin. The Prince of Schwartzenberg, adopting the conciliatory attitude of his government, retired towards Cracow without fighting. General Reynier had just fallen back upon the Elbe. The Viceroy of Italy followed him thither, and on March 4th he set out from Berlin towards Magdeburg, where he gathered together all the forces still scattered in Germany. His army numbered about 80,000 men, for the most part fatigued and dissatisfied. The effects of the Russian campaign had been disastrous for the *morale* as well as for the military force of the great army.

The King of Prussia was free; Berlin was evacuated. The joyful acclamations of his subjects recalled their monarch to his capital. He still lingered at Breslau, preparing his plans for a definite rupture with France, anxious to the very last moment, notwithstanding the significant measures he was every day taking. Everywhere the gentry, the students, and even the artisans, were rushing to enrol themselves in the service of their country. Marshal Blucher had just been called to take the supreme command of the armies. General York, whose trial had been formally commenced, was acquitted, and reinstated in his command. The Emperor Alexander was approaching. On March 15th he entered Breslau, accompanied by a brilliant staff. Baron Stein preceded his sovereign, happy in at length seeing his long-continued labors crowned with success, and Europe ready to unite her efforts against the Em-

peror Napoleon. At the same time (March 23rd) the Prince
Royal of Sweden wrote to his former chief: "I know how
favorably disposed towards peace are both the Emperor Alexander and the cabinet of St. James. The calamities of the
continent loudly call for it, and your Majesty ought not to put
obstacles in the way. Possessor of the grandest monarchy on
earth, ought you to desire ceaselessly to extend its limits, and
bequeath to an arm less powerful than your own the inheritance of never-ending wars? Will not your Majesty apply yourself to healing the wounds of a revolution of which there remains to France nothing but the remembrance of military
glory, and internal evils that are only too genuine? Sire, the
teachings of history repel the idea of a universal monarchy:
the sentiment of independence may be deadened, but cannot
be effaced from the hearts of nations. May your Majesty
weigh all these considerations, and truly turn your thoughts
towards a universal peace, of which the name has been pro-
fanated for the spilling of so much blood! I was born, sire, in
that beautiful France which you govern, and to its glory and
its prosperity I can never be indifferent; but, without ceasing
to indulge in good wishes for its welfare, I shall defend, with
all the faculties of my soul, both the rights of the people who
have called me to them, and the honor of the sovereign who
has deigned to adopt me as his son. In this struggle between
the freedom of the world and tyranny, I shall say to the
Swedes: 'I fight for you, and with you; and the good wishes
of all free nations will accompany our efforts.' In politics,
sire, there are neither friendships nor hatreds, there are simply
duties to be fulfilled towards the peoples whom Providence has
called upon us to govern. If, in order to succeed therein, one
is compelled to renounce ancient friendships and family affections, no prince who wishes to fulfil his vocation ought to hesitate as to the part he will take. As far as my personal
ambition is concerned, I admit that my ideal is a lofty one;
for it is to serve the cause of humanity, and insure the independence of the Scandinavian peninsula."

Bernadotte and Sweden were already bound by the conventions of Abo to act against the Emperor Napoleon. The King
of Prussia gave in his adherence to the coalition on the 28th of
February: on the 17th of March he declared war against
France. Our chargé d'affaires, St. Marsan, quitted Breslau;
several corps of Cossacks had already been thrown forwards
upon Hamburg and Lubeck. Prince Eugène found himself

compelled to abandon these places in order to protect Dresden. Hamburg was evacuated by the French authorities, menaced on all sides by the populace. The island of Heliogoland was occupied by the English. The King of Saxony, still faithful to Napoleon, but anxious and troubled on account of the sentiments prevalent among his subjects, inclined towards the mediatorial policy adopted by Austria. He quitted his capital, towards which the Russians were already advancing, and retreated into Bavaria. Dresden forthwith beheld the enemy appear before it. The Saxon troops were cantoned in Thurgau, refusing to unite in resistance to the French. Marshal Davout, resolute and harsh, immediately blew up the bridges over the Elbe, and put the city in a state of defence. Everywhere in Europe the conflagration was being ignited; Austria alone still sought to extinguish or to moderate it.

"In what way do you expect me to negotiate with England?" said Metternich to Otto, the French minister at Vienna; "your emperor proclaims that the French dynasty reigns, and will reign in Spain. How would you have me negotiate with Russia and Prussia, when you say that constitutional territories or dependencies of these allies—that is to say, the Hanseatic towns and the grand duchy of Warsaw—must remain inviolably alienated from them? Never should I be able to obtain the consent of Europe to such conditions. Why be so positive on points which it is impossible to defend? Peace is necessary for us; it is also necessary for you. For even in gaining victories (and you will need to gain many to make Europe what you would have it to be) the force of public opinion is not always to be resisted, and a consequent reaction is soon experienced. As for us, we shall merely have to choose: we are offered everything—everything. Do you understand? But we shall only desire those things which cannot be refused to us. We wish for an independent Germany, and for peace. We are thirsting for peace, and we wish to give it to the people who are demanding it from us."

The Prince of Schwartzenberg was sent to Paris in order to support, by his presence and advice, the sage councils of Metternich. He had formerly negotiated the marriage of Maria-Louise, that powerful bond by which the Emperor Napoleon expected to be able to keep Austria linked with his own fortunes. The Prince of Schwartzenberg was not disposed to sacrifice for any such cause his country's freedom of action. "The marriage! the marriage!" cried he one day, whilst arguing with Bassano. "Policy brought it about, and policy might undo it!" The Emperor Napoleon sent Narbonne to Vienna, for the purpose of sounding the Austrian court on the great projects which he was revolving in his mind, but which were based on a grave error. He thought Austria desirous of conquest, and ready to risk much for self-aggrandizement. The Emperor Francis, and his clever minister, were desirous of peace—peace at any price. They were prudently paving the way for it, caring little for the spoils of Prussia that were offered them, and which had only been for them a perpetual source of embarrassment and anxiety.

Peace was being negotiated at Vienna, whilst war was being prepared for at Paris. But every day the attitude of the Emperor Napoleon rendered the task of the mediators more difficult. Every day also, and by insensible degrees, Austria and the allied powers were becoming more closely united in opposition to the all-powerful master of France. The Prince of Schwartzenberg did not dare to announce it at Paris, but his master had determined not to furnish any troops for the war, and his alliance with France was becoming simply an armed mediation. The clever manœuvres of Metternich drew the King of Saxony away from Dresden. Under the pretext of guaranteeing his safety, this prince was induced to come to Prague, and to abandon the grand duchy of Warsaw, the disastrous gift of Napoleon to his ally. A secret convention was concluded at Kalisch between Austria and Russia. The Russian general Sacken was to march against the Austrian corps, who should give way before him, abandon Cracow, and retreat into Galicia, drawing in his train the Polish corps of Poniatowski. The Poles were to cross the States of the Emperor Francis without arms, free to resume them afterwards for the service of the Emperor Napoleon, wherever and however might be most convenient. The news of this arrangement reached Narbonne soon after his arrival at Vienna.

Metternich explained to the French envoy the bases upon which he believed it possible to establish peace in Europe. These were, the re-establishment of the intermediary powers in Germany, the evacuation of the Hanseatic towns, the abandonment of the chimera of the grand duchy of Warsaw, and the reconstitution of Prussia. "We shall have quite enough trouble," said he, "in preventing the affairs of Holland, Spain, and Italy, from being talked about. England will probably speak of them; and if she gives way as to Holland and Italy, she will certainly not give way as to Spain.   However, if you are reasonable in other respects, possibly we may be able to get you through that difficulty."   To these propositions Narbonne, reticent for awhile, soon replied by a proposition that Austria should take the principal part in the negotiations. She was to menace the allied powers with 100,000 men, and, if necessary, push them forward into Silesia.   Part of this province was to be assigned to her, whilst the Emperor Napoleon undertook to fight and overcome all the allied armies.   "And if the powers are willing to listen to our peaceful overtures, what proposals shall we make to them?" asked Metternich.   It was the part of the negotiator to bring about war, not peace. Narbonne kept silence.   "I am not yet acquainted with the conditions," he presently replied, "but suppose they were not such as you desire . . .?"   The Austrian minister, in his turn, was hesitating, not from indecision, but from a repugnance to letting his secret too soon escape from him.   He dwelt upon the good faith he was displaying towards France, and upon his admiration of the wisdom of the Emperor Napoleon. "But suppose my master thinks otherwise than you," rejoined Narbonne; "suppose he prides himself in not yielding the territories incorporated with the empire, and that he wishes to preserve to France all that he has conquered for it,—what would happen then?"   "It would happen—it would happen," replied Metternich, "that you would be compelled to grant to France that which she herself demands of you, that which she has a just right to demand of you after so many glorious efforts, that is to say, peace—peace with that just greatness which she has won with so much blood.   Her right to that greatness it does not enter into the mind of any one, even of England itself, to dispute with her."   "But in that case how do you understand the *rôle* of mediator?   Would you turn your forces against us?"   "Well, yes!" cried at last the minister, driven into a corner; "the mediator must be impartial. The armed mediator is an arbitrator who has in his hands the force necessary to make justice respected, it being well understood that all the favor this arbitrator can show will incline towards France . . ."   And as Narbonne turned aside with a humorous remark the conversation which seemed to him to be getting too animated: "I reckon upon your victories," exclaimed Metternich, "and I shall have need of them, for it will take more than one to bring your adversaries to reason;

but do not deceive yourselves, on the morrow of a victory you will find us as resolute as to-day."

Napoleon had at length compelled Austria to declare herself; and the position taken up by the latter in consequence of this premature explosion of her designs was not favorable to our policy. In spite of the protestations of firmness on the part of Metternich, the opening of the campaign and the first successes of Napoleon influenced his decisions, and facilitated the pleadings of the mediator in favor of France. Austria found herself henceforth relieved, in part, from the necessity for reticence. Her military preparations were completed. The Poles were called upon to lay down their arms, greatly to the wrath of the Emperor Napoleon. "I do not wish to be served by men dishonored!" he cried. Prince Poniatowski received orders to throw himself into the grand duchy, "as a partisan, in order to make a diversion, and draw multitudes of people to him." From the 17th of April Napoleon was at Mayence.

He had set out from Paris on the 15th, after having solemnly confided the regency to the Empress Marie-Louise, with the assistance and counsel of the Arch-chancellor Cambacérès. The latter was growing old; he felt worn out, and dreaded the responsibility; the emperor exacted from his devotion the acceptance of the task confided to him. Napoleon spurned the idea of confiding the care of the empire to one of his brothers. The composition of the Council of Regency was regulated by a *sénatus consulte.* Napoleon calculated on the attachment of the Emperor Francis for his daughter, and on the satisfaction he would experience at the tokens of confidence lavished on her by her husband. It was with evident emotion that he separated from her, and from his son. Meanwhile he was full of confidence as to victory. "I shall fight two battles," said he, on quitting St. Cloud, "one upon the Elbe, the other upon the Oder; I shall raise the blockade of my fortresses; and on reaching the Niemen I shall stay my course, for I do not wish for endless war. The peace I shall dictate will cost neither more nor less than the independence of Poland, and the security of Europe."

"We have played King of France long enough," said Henri IV., when the Spaniards were besieging Amiens; "let us now try King of Navarre." The Emperor Napoleon resolved in the same manner to leave behind him all imperial pomp. "It is my intention," he gave orders to the marshal of the palace, "to arrange my equipages on an entirely different scale than during the last campaign. I wish to have fewer people about me, fewer cooks, fewer plates and dishes, no great dressing-case—and all this as much for the sake of example as for the diminishing of encumbrances. In camp and on march, the tables, even my own, shall be served with a soup, a boiled and a roast joint, and vegetables, with no dessert; in the great cities one may do as one pleases. I wish to take no pages with me, they are of no use; perhaps I may take such of the huntsmen as are twenty-four years of age, who, being accustomed to fatigue, may be of use. Diminish in the same way the number of canteens; instead of four beds, only have two; instead of four tents, let there be only two, and furniture in proportion. We must be lightly equipped," said Napoleon, "for we shall have many enemies to fight against; and in order to achieve success, we shall have to march quickly."

On the 26th of April he quitted Mayence. Prince Eugène, with 60,000 men, was waiting for him at the confluence of the Elbe and Saal. Marshal Ney had pushed forward upon Weimar with 48,000 men. Marmont was still organizing his forces at Hanau, and was ultimately to take up his position, with 30,000 or 32,000 men, along the Elbe. The guard did not include more than 15,000 or 16,000 men. Davout was ordered to take and occupy Hamburg. General Bertrand was forming an army of reserve in Italy. About 200,000 men were marching with cries of "Vive l'Empereur!" acclamations that were always wrung from the soldiers by the presence of Napoleon, whatever might be the spite and anger towards him which many of them nursed in secret. Already they were defiling the whole length of the Saal, which Prince Eugène ascended, whilst the Emperor advanced in the opposite direction. The allies had not foreseen this manœuvre: their forces were not yet complete. Many of the German princes, after hesitating a long time, decided at last upon furnishing their contingent to the French army. Austria remained neutral; the Swedes had not yet arrived; the allied powers could not reckon up more than 110,000 or 112,000 men under their flags. The Prussians were as numerous as they were eager.

On the 1st of May, Napoleon commenced the march forward, and Prince Eugène joined him. Marshal Ney repulsed the enemy at Weissenfels, happy and proud at the conduct of the young troops which he commanded, and who were now under fire for the first time. "These boys are heroes," wrote he to the emperor; "I shall achieve with them whatever you wish for." Next day, upon the same piece of ground, whilst debouching into the plain of Lutzen, an engagement of the vanguard cost Marshal Bessières his life. He fell, shot in the breast. "Death is very near us!" said the emperor, as he saw carried away in his cloak the commander of the cavalry of his guard, the faithful companion of his campaigns, who had wished upon this very day to follow him more closely. The charges of the enemy's cavalry were repulsed, and the night was passed at Lutzen. Napoleon visited the monument erected by the grateful remembrance of his people to King Gustavus Adolphus, who had died on this plain more than 180 years before. "I will have a tomb erected here for the Duke of Istria," said the emperor. He had already directed the army to move towards Leipzig.

On May 2nd, at two o'clock in the morning, Napoleon quitted Lutzen, placing the corps of Marshal Ney in a group of villages which was to serve as the pivot of his operations. General Maison, who had gone on in advance, attacked Leipzig with a vigor which was soon crowned with success. As the emperor debouched before the place, he saw it taken by his troops. At the same time the cannonade announced that the allies were attacking the villages occupied by Ney. The marshal was personally accompanying the emperor. "We were going to outflank them: they are trying the same manœuvre. There is no harm done; they will find us everywhere ready." Modifying his plan of battle in a moment, and sending clear and precise orders to all his generals, he himself hastened towards the midst of the combat. In spite of the division of the command, and the recent death of old Kutuzoff, who had at last succumbed to his fatigues, the allies had wisely arranged their plans; and they profited on the plain of Lutzen by all the advantages that were assured to them by the splendid cavalry which they had at their disposal. Since the Russian campaign, in spite of the energetic efforts of the Emperor Napoleon, our armies had been deprived of this precious resource; Murat and his cavalry had disappeared.

The five villages were fiercely attacked; the passionate ardor of Blücher and the Prussians forced our young divisions to fall back. Two successive attacks had dislodged the regiments which occupied Gross-Gorschen, Klein-Gorschen, and Rahna. The French were entrenched in the villages of Kaja and Starsiedel; Marshal Marmont was coming up with his corps. Ney,

advancing from Leipzig at a furious gallop, rallied upon his
route several divisions, whom he immediately led to the assault of the abandoned villages.   They fought with their
bayonets with equal vigor on both sides.   Blücher wished at
any cost to free his country; Ney was resolute to defend the
greatness of France.   Fortune had not yet abandoned the
latter; the young soldiers advanced fearlessly under fire, and
drove back the Prussians as far as Gross-Gorschen.   The
Emperor Napoleon had just arrived on the field of battle.

Blucher dashed forward afresh; wounded in the arm, he did
not the less urge forward the attack.   The villages were retaken; Kaja itself was threatened.   On this occasion Napoleon
did not keep himself aloof from the combat, as at the battle of
the Moskowa; he himself brought back the trembling conscripts against the enemy.   "Young men," said he to them,
"I have reckoned upon you to save the empire; and you flee!"
At the same time Count Lobau drove back the Prussian guard
from the positions of Kaja.   The combat and the carnage
spread out over the plain for the space of two leagues.
Blücher sent requests to the Czar and King Frederick William
to combine in a grand effort upon the centre.   The want of
unity in the command rendered the orders feeble and confused.
Meanwhile the forces of Wittgenstein and of York were advancing to the aid of Blücher.   The divisions of Marshal Ney,
exhausted by a desperate struggle, gave way before this new
assault.   Kaja was once more outflanked by the enemy, who
pushed forward beyond it to engage the guard.   The reserve
corps at this moment arrived on the theatre of combat.   Already the columns of attack were directed against Kaja and
Starsiedel; the artillery was raking in flank the lines of the
hostile infantry.   The allies fell back in their turn.   Blücher
was still pleading for a final effort; but the sovereigns dreaded
to engage their reserves.   Ammunition was beginning to fail.
Prudence carried the day, and the Prussian and Russian corps
commenced the retreat.   A charge of Blücher against the corps
of Marmont carried for a moment disorder into our ranks on
the side of Starsiedel.   Meanwhile the enemy disappeared,
little by little, without the possibility of pursuing them for
want of cavalry.   The French army rested on the field of.
battle, in the midst of the dead and the dying.   "We are
beaten, it may be," said Narbonne, when the first news of the
battle was inaccurately reported at Vienna.   "We shall see
to-morrow what route is taken by the conquered and the con-

querors." The movements of the two armies soon justified the
foresight of the former war minister of King Louis XVI. The
allied sovereigns retired beyond the Elbe; the Emperor Napoleon advanced upon Dresden, where the Russians did not wait
for him. The emperor received the keys of the town, sharply
reprimanding the Saxons, who had been unfaithful as allies,
and declaring that his clemency to them was only due to the
affection, virtues, and loyalty of their king. That honorable
prince, still more terrified than his subjects, had already taken
measures to obey the emperor's peremptory commands. He
again took the road to Dresden, accompanied by his court and
troops. On the 12th May, Napoleon came to meet him, pre-
tending ignorance of the old king's negotiations with the court
of Vienna, and the shortcomings of his loyalty. Overwhelmed
with honors and confidence, the King of Saxony was, without
a struggle, brought again under Napoleon's authority; the
latter regaining possession of the Saxon army, while solemnly
restoring his states to the sovereign who had so recently been
a fugitive. Babua had just arrived, entrusted with a letter
from the Emperor Francis, and pacific propositions from
Austria.

From his conversation with the King of Saxony, as well as
by intercepted despatches and Narbonne's reports, Napoleon
was enabled to understand the diplomacy of Austria, her
treatment of her enemies, and the fixed resolve of the Emperor
Francis, as well as his minister, to make peace if possible, but
in any case not to allow themselves to be drawn into a war in
the train of France. He was therefore in his secret mind, annoyed and suspicious, with a new inclination towards direct
relations with Russia, and disposed to grant concessions to the
Czar and to England which he refused to Austria. Nevertheless, he felt it necessary that that power should take the first
step towards a congress which should allow him to treat with
the allies. After giving way to his anger, which Babua allowed to pass without reply, the emperor seemed to calm down.
He listened to the propositions of Austria, which were still the
same, and had reference to the German territories. The title of
Protector of the Rhenish Confederation, and the question of
the Hanse towns, alone interested Napoleon personally. He
insisted upon those two points without violence, and showed
himself ready to admit the Spanish insurgents to the congress.
Whilst thus officially agreeing to the congress, and the armistice rendered necessary by the congress, Napoleon wrote to

his father-in-law:—"I am deeply touched by what your Majesty tells me in your letter regarding the interest you have in me. I deserve it from you by the sincerity of the sentiments which I have for you. If your Majesty takes some interest in my happiness, I trust you will be careful of my honor. I am determined to die, if need be, at the head of the men of generous feeling in France, rather than become the laughing-stock of the English, and allow my enemies to triumph. May your Majesty think of the future, and not destroy the fruits of three years' friendship, or revive by-gone plots which should precipitate Europe into convulsions, and wars with interminable issues, or sacrifice to wretched considerations the happiness of our generation, of your life, and the true interest of your subjects, and (why should I not mention it?) of a member of your family, sincerely attached to you! May your Majesty be ever assured of my attachment!"

Whilst the Emperor Napoleon was thus speaking and writing, he commanded Caulaincourt to present himself to the advanced posts of the allied sovereigns, in order to institute direct negotiations with them regarding the armistice. The following were his formal instructions:—

"The main point is to declare one's self. You will let me know, from head-quarters, what has been said. By knowing the Emperor Alexander's views we shall at last come to an understanding. My intention, moreover, is to make him a golden bridge, to save him from Metternich's intrigues. If I must make sacrifices, I prefer to do so for the advantage of the Emperor Alexander, who is an honorable foe, and the King of Prussia, in whom Russia takes an interest, than for that of Austria, who has been a false ally, and who, under the title of mediator, wishes to arrogate the right of disposing of everything, after having done what suited herself. By treating now, all the honor of the peace will belong to the Emperor Alexander alone; whereas by making use of the mediation of Austria, the latter power, whatever be the result of peace or war, should seem to have weighed in the balance the fate of all Europe."

The allied sovereigns refused to negotiate directly, and Caulaincourt was politely referred to Stadion, who had been appointed to treat the question of a congress in the name of the mediating power. "A direct mission to the Russian head-quarters would cut the world in two," Napoleon had said. It was this rupture of European interests which the allied powers were resolved to avoid.

Meanwhile every preparation was made for a second and terrible battle. Leaving Dresden on the 18th May, Napoleon reached Bautzen on the 19th. Prince Eugène had set out for Italy in order to organize a new army intended to alarm Austria. To these forces 20,000 Neapolitan troops were to be added. Napoleon had sent for Murat, who though daring and invincible on the battle-field, had proved himself a timid and commonplace sovereign, more occupied with preserving his throne than in maintaining towards the emperor the fidelity which he owed him. Napoleon was well aware of his disposition. It was by his victories that he counted upon rallying round him all his trembling allies.

The armies of the allies were grouped round the small town Bautzen, which lies at the base of the Bohemian mountains covered with gloomy pine forests. The river Spree, in front of the place, was strongly defended. The emperor at once understood the necessity of a double battle, which should probably occupy two days. Engagements had already taken place at several points, and on the 20th, about noon, a battle began on the banks of the Spree. Marshal Oudinot on the right and Marmont on the left crossed the river, driving back by main force those who defended the position indicated by Napoleon. In the centre, Marshal Macdonald had taken the stone bridge leading to Bautzen, and carried the town at the point of the bayonet after the artillery had burst open the gates. General Bertrand crossed the nearest branches of the Spree, at the foot of the heights occupied by Blücher, but his movements had been delayed; the position was strong, and well defended. He encamped on the left bank, guarding the passage across, and waiting for next day's attack. The emperor entered Bautzen, and encamped under the walls of the town.

The allied armies held nearly all the heights, excepting Tronberg, which had been carried on the previous evening by Marshal Oudinot. They were also protected by strong redoubts and the marshes formed by the river. The attack was therefore certain to be difficult and dangerous. Napoleon determined to divide it; Marshal Ney being ordered to cross the Spree at Klix, two leagues from Bautzen, in spite of the resistance there presented by General Barclay de Tolly, and then pass behind the mamelons occupied by Blücher, in order to take him in rear. The emperor intended to wait for Ney's approach, which was to be announced by discharges of artillery,

before attacking the centre of the enemy's position. At daybreak on the 21st May, the cannon began to roar along the
whole line. Muffling, an officer on the Russian staff, had alone
perceived the danger which threatened Klix. He urged the
Emperor Alexander to fortify this point; but he was not
listened to. A keen engagement soon began between Marshal
Ney and Barclay de Tolly. The village Preititz, held by the
Russians, was twice taken and retaken. If Ney, in the isolation of his movements, had not hesitated to advance to intercept from the enemy the road to Hochkirch, Blücher's retreat
would have become a disaster. Threatened in rear, keenly attacked in front by Marmont and Bertrand, the Prussian general, in spite of his heroic obstinacy, found himself compelled
to withdraw. He had time to evacuate the mamelons by one
of the sides, whilst Ney was climbing the other; Marshals
Marmont and Mortier having at the same time crossed the
stream which covered the Russian positions. Oudinot, at first
driven back from Tronberg by Miloradowitch, again assumed
the offensive. The enemy were everywhere keenly pursued.
The emperor at once sent Oudinot to march upon Berlin,
against General Bulow, while he himself advanced upon Breslau in pursuit of the allies, marching at the head of his army,
and commanding the attacks of the advanced guard. It was
thus that in the Reichenbach valley he had a cavalry engagement, which enabled him to ascertain both the warlike enthusiasm of his enemies, who were daily becoming more formidable, and the relative inferiority of his horse soldiers, who were
lately formed, indifferently mounted, and less experienced in
war than his former troops. The ground, however, was free,
and the emperor, dismounting, was giving orders to have his
tent pitched, when he was told that General Kirgener was
killed, General Bruyère having already succumbed in a cavalry charge. "Fortune has certainly a spite against us to-
day," exclaimed the emperor, and at the same moment some
one called out that Duroc was dead. "Impossible!" said Napoleon, turning round quickly. "I have just been talking to
him!" The marshal, however, was then being carried off the
field, struck in the stomach by a bullet which had glanced
against a tree: he was already dying, and in great agony. Of
a serious and sorrowful disposition, he had said to Caulaincourt a few minutes previously, "You see the emperor, my
dear fellow, he is to-day gaining victories. After our misfortunes in Russia, it is now time to take advantage of the lesson;

but he is always the same, insatiable and indefatigable. That must all end badly!" On coming near his old friend, Napoleon, full of grief and emotion, said, "This is not the end, Duroc. There is another life, where we shall meet again; perhaps soon," he added, as he yielded to the dying man's earnest request that he would leave him. His eyes were full of tears, and he appeared for a moment to rise above merely temporal consolations; but he allowed no religious ceremonies at the obsequies which he ordered in Paris to be celebrated in honor of the two friends of whom death had deprived him within a few days. Villemain and Victorien Fabre were appointed to pronounce a funeral oration over Marshals Bessières and Duroc. "I will have no priests," wrote Napoleon to Cambacérès.

A partial engagement, following upon a surprise, placed Ney and General Maison in danger at Haguenau, whilst at Sprottau a very large park of artillery fell into General Sebastiani's hands. On the 27th the whole of the army had reached the Oder, and the French garrison, which had been blockaded for five months in Glogau, was set at liberty. The emperor had now reached Liegnitz, and was threatening Breslau.

The position of the allies was become critical. They had begun the campaign with the disadvantage of a great numerical inferiority, which became still greater by the battles of Lutzen, Bautzen, and the other smaller engagements which had taken place. Barclay de Tolly affirmed that he must withdraw into Poland to reform his army; and the entrenched camp of Bunzelwitz, with which they expected to be able to stop Napoleon, had been recently dismantled by the French. The armistice, therefore, became an indispensable condition of the very existence of the coalition. Nesselrode set out for Vienna with instructions to persuade Austria in favor of this. In case Metternich should still hesitate, the Emperor Alexander was to receive Caulaincourt, and enter upon direct negotiations with France. General Kleist, in the name of the Prussians, and Count Schouwaloff, in the name of the Russians, went on the 29th May to the French advanced guard. The emperor had eight days previously announced that he was ready to treat about an armistice. In spite of the recent defeats of their armies, the commissioners remained proud, deeply impressed with the justice of their cause, and fastidious as to the terms of the convention. Napoleon at first found himself bound by his promises, whatever advantage he might have gained by actively pursuing the war and destroying the allied forces before they could be reinforced. He also wished to supplement his resources, send for the 250,000 men, which were still wanting, strengthen his cavalry, and after the hot weather resume the series of his triumphs for the purpose of imposing peace upon his enemies without the mediation of Austria, which had now become hateful to him. With this object, he agreed to an armistice which was unnecessary to him, and in principle to the congress which he did not really wish for, and laid down theoretically the bases of a peace which he was determined not to ratify. So much insincerity and falsehood were certain to prove fatal to him; and Blücher and the Prussian patriots were seriously in error as to their country's interest when they violently insisted upon immediately continuing hostilities.

The armistice was at last concluded, on the 4th June. Napoleon had definitely rejected Austria's last conciliatory propositions, transmitted by Bubna, which put off till the general peace the consideration of the Hanse towns and the Rhenish Confederation. He agreed to neutralize the territory around Breslau, and let the position of the Hanse towns be fixed as should have been decided by the fate of war on the 8th June at midnight. Marshal Davout was upon the point of entering Hamburg, a fact which told in our favor. Including the day of declaration, the armistice was to extend to the 26th July.

Instigated by his pride, the Emperor Napoleon practically refused Austria's mediation, which he had accepted in principle, and thus surrendered to his adversaries all the advantages which had been gained at so great cost since the beginning of the campaign. His actual secret intentions were opposed to the peace which he pretended to wish for, and he considered the rest asked from him, by France as well as Europe, to be dishonorable. Yet he was sure of preserving, as the price of his long years of warfare, Belgium, the Rhenish provinces, Holland, Piedmont, Tuscany, the Roman States. No one objected to the vassal kings of France retaining Westphalia, Lombardy, and Naples. The possession and redistribution of the Spanish territory still remained an open question. The sacrifices demanded from us in exchange for the peace were, the cession of the grand duchy of Warsaw, and its partition in favor of Russia and Austria, the restitution of the free towns of Hamburg, Bremen, and Lubeck, the restoration of Illyria to Austria, and the abolition of the Rhenish Confederation. Such was the cost, in 1813, of the general peace.

The Emperor Napoleon preferred to assemble the congress,

in order to gain the time necessary for his military preparations. No information of it was yet given in France, and he
took measures to conceal the proposals which had been made
to him. The anxiety shown by several of his great functionaries with reference to the peace excited his displeasure. On
the 13th June he thus wrote to General Savary, Duke of
Rovigo:—"I am dissatisfied with the tone of your communications; you constantly annoy me about the need for peace. I
know better than you the situation of my empire; and that
tendency given to your correspondence produces no favorable
impression in me. I wish for peace, and I am more interested
in it than anybody; your remarks on the subject are therefore
useless. But I shall not make a peace which would be dishonorable, or would in six months bring back a more determined war. Make no reply to this: these matters are no business of yours; do not interfere in them."

The desire for peace in opposition to Napoleon's intention,
and which he in vain sought to evade, was universal. On the
day after the signing of the armistice at Pleiswitz, Bubna returned to Dresden, instructed to announce that the allied
powers accepted Austria's mediation, and to ascertain what
conditions of peace Napoleon intended submitting to the congress. The Austrian envoy waited, and when at last the emperor deigned to reply to his urgent application, it was by
chicanery, discussing technicalities of his mission, and the
part Austria had taken in the negotiation. The days of the
armistice were passing away; Metternich resolved to handle
this important question himself. In order to provoke Napoleon's jealousy, he set out at first for Oppontschna, where the
allied sovereigns were. They had just concluded a treaty
with England as to subsidies. The Austrian minister with
some difficulty succeeded in making the allies accept the
bases of the peace as he wished, and as he had several times
proposed to Napoleon. "The emperor will never grant what
you ask," declared the Russian and Prussian diplomatists.
"Should he not consent, the emperor my master will be free
to join the alliance," replied Metternich. He at once set out
for Dresden, and, as he expected, Napoleon had already sent
to summon him for an interview.

I borrow from Thiers the account of the interview of the
Emperor Francis's minister with the angry and suspicious
conqueror: by means of an account written by Metternich
himself, he has modified the official reports of the imperial

diplomacy. The truth was already obvious under the reti-
cences of Bassano and Baron Fain, but in the sad recollections
of the distinguished diplomatist it assumes an incisive force.
"Ah! there you are, M. de Metternich!" exclaimed Napoleon,
as he saw him enter. "You are very late." Then, recount-
ing his grievances against Austria, he said, "I have thrice
restored his throne to the Emperor Francis; I have even committed the fault of marrying his daughter: nothing could
bring him to a better way of thinking. Last year, reckoning
upon him, I concluded a treaty of alliance, by which I guaranteed to him his states, and he guaranteed to me mine. Had
he told me that that treaty did not suit him, I should not have
insisted upon it, nor should I have even engaged in the Russian
campaign. But he signed it; and after a single campaign, which
the elements rendered unfortunate, you now see him wavering,
interposing between my enemies and me—to negotiate the
terms of peace, he tells me; but in reality to stop me in my
victories, and rescue from my hands enemies whom I was
about to destroy. Under the pretext of mediation you have
been arming; and then when your armaments are completed,
or nearly so, you pretend to dictate to me conditions which
are those of my enemies themselves. Explain yourself: do
you wish to have a war with me? The Russians and Prussians, emboldened by the misfortunes of last winter, dared
to come to meet me; and I have beaten them—thoroughly
beaten them, although they have told you the contrary. Do
you therefore wish also to have your turn? Very well, let it
be so; you will have it. I make an appointment with you in
Vienna for October."

Metternich listened, hurt by this disdainful vanity, without
wishing to appear so. He dwelt upon the necessity for peace,
indispensable for France as well as Europe. The emperor
stopped him after each proposition. "Oh, yes! I understand
you!" he exclaimed at last. "I know your secret; I know
what you all really wish! You Austrians, you wish for the
whole of Italy; your friends the Russians wish for Poland, the
Prussians for Saxony, the English for Holland and Belgium.
If I give way to-day, to-morrow you will ask me for those
objects of your desires. But in that case, prepare yourselves
to raise millions of men, to pour out the blood of several generations, and then come to treat at the foot of the heights of
Montmartre."

The emperor walked up and down in his private room, ex

cited by his own words. Metternich tried to calm him. "All admire the courage of France," said he, "and the ardor which she devotes to your service. But, sire, France herself has need of rest. I have just passed through your army: your soldiers are children. You have raised anticipated levies; and as soon as the present generation, who are scarcely formed into armies, are destroyed by the war now waging, whom will you call out? Will you again anticipate?"

Napoleon became pale. No one knew better than himself the value of the objection raised by Metternich. He went up to his visitor, letting his hat fall, which the Austrian minister did not pick up. "You are not a soldier, sir," he exclaimed; "you have not, like me, a soldier's soul; you have not lived in camps; you have not learned to despise the life of another man, and your own, when need be. What care I for 200,000 men?"

Metternich turned to him, full of emotion in spite of his impassibility as a German and diplomatist. "Let us open the doors, sire! open them!" he exclaimed. "And if the doors are not sufficient, open the windows! that the whole of Europe may hear you. The cause which I have been defending before you will lose nothing by it!"

Napoleon calmed down, feeling that he was at fault. But his unconquerable pride still refused to think for a moment of any concession whatever to those sovereigns whose armies he had conquered, whose capitals he had occupied, and whose empires he had dismembered. "Take no part in this quarrel," said he to Metternich; "you run too many risks; you have too little to gain from it: remain neutral. You wish for Illyria; I cede it to you. The peace which you wish to gain for Europe, I shall give to it with certainty and justice. But what you propose to me, in the name of a mediation, is an imposed peace: they wish to lay down the law to me—to me, who have just gained two brilliant victories. If you wish for war, you shall have it. Good-bye, till we meet in Vienna!"

Metternich left. The conversation had been a long one, and the courtiers were waiting very anxiously. "Well," asked Marshal Berthier, "are you satisfied with the emperor?" "Yes, I am satisfied," replied the Austrian minister, "for from to-day my conscience is at rest. I declare to you, marshal, solemnly, that your master is out of his mind."

It was Napoleon's custom to show a speedy reaction from his fits of passion, and remove the effects by kindness. When

Metternich left Dresden he had arranged with Bassano to pro- long the armistice till the 10th August, as the emperor had long wished to do; the question of a conference in common, or of the exclusive interference of mediation, being left unde- cided. Napoleon showed himself accommodating upon every formal point. The negotiator had gained nothing, except a profound conviction that in his real heart the emperor wished for war, always war, so long as the imposition of peace did not lie entirely with him. Nevertheless, the plenipotentiaries were summoned to meet at Prague on the 12th July, and the Aus- trian court had already moved to the suburbs of that town.

The Emperor Napoleon, on his part, concluded from his in- terview with Metternich, that war with Austria must result from the attempts to negotiate. He therefore chose his line of operations along the Elbe, and employed himself in fortifying it in every part with that watchful foresight which had so often secured his success. The ramparts of Dresden had been restored, and the military supplies were collected there in great abundance. Works had been ordered at Torgau and Wittemberg, provisions collected at Magdeburg, and barracks built at Werden. Marshal Davout took up his head-quarters at Hamburg, imposing enormous contributions from the wealthy merchants, who had recently risen against France, and had for a short time taken refuge in Altona. They asked leave to return. " If, on the day after your arrival," wrote the emperor to Davout, "you had got a few of them shot, it would have been well; it is now too late, and pecuniary pun- ishments are better." The war contributions of the Ham- burgers served to fortify and provision their town. Davout refused to listen to their complaints, and Napoleon would not receive them. The fortress of Gluckstadt was entrusted to the keeping of the Danes, who had been compelled, by the necessities of the coalition, to form a closer union with us. Before the expiration of the armistice the emperor counted upon having under his flags 400,000 men in active service; he kept 80,000 men in Italy, and 20,000 in Bavaria, without count- ing the garrisons still kept in the strongholds. The cavalry were being daily improved.

Meantime, however, the news arriving from Spain depressed and irritated Napoleon during his constant exercise in the suburbs of Dresden and as far as Magdeburg and Torgau. The winter had passed without any serious hostilities; but Well- ington, in spite of some opposition from the Cortes of Cadiz, had been named generalissimo of the Spanish army, as he was already of the Portuguese army, and had been preparing, instructing, and forming his auxiliaries, in the hope of crushing the French power in the Peninsula. On the emperor's peremptory order, King Joseph had at last followed Marshal Jourdan's advice, abandoning Madrid, and falling back upon Valladolid; the army of Portugal, commanded by General Reille, marched from Salamanca to Burgos; General Clausel, with the army of the north, was appointed to destroy the bands of guerillas, who interrupted communication in every direction; Count Erlon, with the army of the centre, covered Valladolid and Madrid; while the army of Andalusia, under the orders of General Gazan, occupied the Douro and Tormès. Marshal Suchet still wisely governed Aragon. The best officers and soldiers in Spain had been ordered by the emperor to join the campaign in Saxony. Marshal Soult's departure had lessened the difficulties of the command, without rendering it more prudent or energetic; Jourdan, now old and worn out, saw the faults, without being able to avoid them. Wellington began the campaign in May, with 48,000 English and 25,000 Spanish, fairly disciplined; and having at once crossed the Ezla, he advanced towards Salamanca and Tormès. The French forces were scattered, holding extended positions, which rendered their concentration difficult, when, on the 24th May, they heard of the approach of the enemy.

Napoleon's real intention was to make use of Spain some day as a means of concluding peace with England, by restoring Ferdinand to the possession of his hereditary states, except the provinces north of the Ebro, which were to be made into French departments. With this object, therefore, he had ordered the capital to be abandoned, and all our forces to be collected in the north. Wellington seemed to have guessed this purpose, and the first movements of the campaign of 1813 appeared only intended to drive us slowly back towards the Pyrenees. General Reille fell back before the enemy, covering the line of retreat from Valladolid to Burgos. King Joseph and his court had already gained the latter town, but stayed only a short time, being annoyed by the scarcity of food and the advance of the English. On leaving Burgos, orders were given to blow up the fortress, which had recently stopped Wellington himself. After some hesitation, Joseph resolved to march towards Vittoria. All detached troops were recalled; and the arrival of General Clausel was specially hoped for—an able soldier, at the head of a considerable army. On the evening of the 19th June, after several skirmishes, in which the army of Portugal was successful, 54,000 French troops, in good condition had collected near Vittoria. General Clausel had not arrived being informed only after considerable delay, of his danger, as well as of the place of meeting, by peasants who were false to us or stopped by the enemy. The enormous convoys which accompanied our troops marched towards Bayonne. Jourdan who alone was capable of directing the military operations, was ill of fever; their positions were bad, and the inferiority in number great. On the 21st June, Wellington fell upon General Gazan and the army of Andalusia, at the moment when that general was ordered to occupy the heights of Zuazo. The Spanish had already taken possession of the Sierra Andia, and the disconnected attempts of the French to dislodge them were at first unsuccessful. In spite of Reille's heroic resistance, the English at the same time forced a passage over the Zadorra, the bridges not having been destroyed. In vain had Marshal Jourdan and King Joseph placed a battery of guns at Zuazo; the artillery was not supported. The English everywhere succeeded in taking our positions; and orders for retreat were given, which, with some of the forces, became a rout. All who had been left in Vittoria took to flight. The horses' traces were cut, to abandon their guns and baggage-wagons; and even the king's carriages and papers were lost. Joseph found himself obliged to take refuge in the valleys of the Pyrenees, covering the last limits of our frontiers, at St. Jean-Pied-du-Port, and Bastan on the Bidassoa. General Clausel, arriving too late to prevent the disaster of Vittoria, had fallen back upon Saragossa, in order to protect Marshal Suchet's rear. Spain was henceforward lost to us; and Soult's last efforts to rally the army, and still check the English, only served to delay the invasion of France.

Badly informed by his war minister, and absorbed in the incessant cares of a decisive campaign, Napoleon did not at all weigh the difficulties and impossibilities of the position which he had imposed upon his brother; he did not trace to their real causes his failures in Spain; nor did he take into account the new ardor with which the Russians had been inspired by the misfortunes of his Russian campaign. He let his anger fall upon King Joseph, at once replacing him in the command by the Duke of Dalmatia; and to overwhelm him with disgrace, sent him to his castle of Montefontaine, without allowing him time to visit Paris and see his family—without even granting him the right to receive any one. Perpetually haunted by the incurable distrust of despotic power, he had now come to fear the intrigues of even his brothers, and could not rest unless he felt them bending under his hand or crushed beneath the weight of his displeasure.

Meantime the time was passing away during the constantly increasing agitation of men's minds. The news of the English victory at Vittoria came to revive the hopes of the allied plenipotentiaries, now about to set out for Prague, without inspiring Napoleon with any wisdom. He had appointed Narbonne and Caulaincourt as his representatives at the congress; but under pretext of some disagreement as to the final date of the armistice, the second, and principal, of the envoys had not set out. Even Narbonne was hampered by his instructions. "I give you more nominal power than real influence," were the words of the Duke of Bassano to him; "your hands will be tied, but your legs and mouth left free to walk about and dine." The only thing thought of by Napoleon was gaining time, to complete his military preparations, and then fall like a thunderstorm upon his enemies with much superior forces. Amongst those intended to be crushed the principal was Austria, still entrusted with a mission of conciliation.

Scarcely had Narbonne arrived at Prague before being convinced that Austria would certainly soon join the coalition if Napoleon continued to mock her and the general desire for peace felt by Europe. The minister of the Emperor Francis complained of the delay caused in the meeting of the congress. "Let the Emperor Napoleon not deceive himself," said he; "the limit of the 10th August having arrived, not another word concerning peace will be spoken, and war will be declared. We shall not be neutral; let him not flatter himself as to that. After having used all imaginable means to bring him to reasonable conditions—which did not admit of being changed, since they constitute the only situation Europe can endure— nothing remains for us, if he refuses to agree to them, but to become belligerents ourselves. Should we remain neutral, which is what he really desires, the allies would be beaten; but after their turn, ours would come—and we should well deserve it. At the present moment, whatever you may be told, we are free. I give you my word, and that of my sovereign, that we have entered into engagements with nobody. But I give you my word also, that at midnight of the 10th August we

shall have done so with everybody except you, and that on the
morning of the 17th you will have 300,000 Austrians besides to
cope with. The emperor my master has not taken this resolution lightly, for he is a father and loves his daughter; but we
prefer everything, even the chance of defeat, to dishonor and
slavery. Let no one, therefore, after the event tell us that we
have deceived you. Till midnight of the 10th August everything is possible, even at the last hour; the 10th of August
once passed, not a day, not a moment; war! war! with everybody—even with us." "What?" asked Narbonne, "not even
if negotiations were begun?" "No," replied Metternich, "unless all the bases of peace are accepted, and nothing remains
but the arrangement of details."

The Austrian minister thus anticipated the new expedient
devised by Napoleon for gaining time without forming any
serious engagement. A great effort was at this moment being
made by those about him to induce him to embrace the overtures of peace still presented to his haughty will. For all
those who had guessed, or who knew the conditions offered,
the conclusion of the peace had become an object most passionately desired. His servants who were most compromised and
least scrupulous, as well as the most honorable and faithful—
Fouché, Savary, Cambacérès, Caulaincourt—incessantly repeated to him all the reasons which made rest necessary to
France and glorious to himself. Angry, and ill at ease, he shut
the mouths of soldiers who took the liberty to criticise his
operations, and bluntly told his most intimate councillors to
hold their tongues. He sent Fouché to Illyria, where General
Junot had recently lost his reason: and at last ordered Caulaincourt to set out for Prague, while at the same time purposely delaying his journey. Before setting out on the 26th
July, Napoleon's plenipotentiary, a man of honor and candor,
conscientiously felt it his duty to write as follows to his master, who had just started for Mayence:—

"Sire,—I wish to ease my mind, before leaving Dresden,
that I may carry to Prague nothing but a sense of the duties
which your Majesty has imposed upon me. It is two o'clock,
and the only instructions conveyed to me by the Duke of Bassano are the replies of Neumarkt, and your Majesty's orders
prevented me receiving them sooner. They are so different
from the arrangements to which you seemed to agree when
persuading me to accept this mission, that I should not hesitate
again to refuse the honor of being your plenipotentiary if, after

so much time lost, every hour were not counted at Prague, while your Majesty is in Mayence, and I am still in Dresden. Whatever, therefore, may be my repugnance to negotiations so illusory, I resign myself entirely to duty, and obey. But, sire, permit your faithful servant's reflections to find a place here. The political horizon is still so gloomy, everything looks so serious, that I cannot resist the desire of beseeching your Majesty to form, as I trust you will do, a salutary resolution before the fatal limit of time. May you be convinced that time is pressing—that the irritation of the Germans is extreme— and that by this exasperation of men's minds, still more than by the fear of cabinets, events are irresistibly hurried with in- creasing speed. Austria is already too much compromised to retreat, if the peace of the continent does not reassure her. Your Majesty well knows that it is not the cause of that power which I have pleaded with you; it is certainly not her deser- tion of us in our reverses that I beg of you to recompense; it is not even her 50,000 bayonets which I wish to remove, although that consideration is somewhat important; but it is the rising of Germany, which the former ascendancy of that power might cause, that I entreat your Majesty, at any cost, to avoid."

The patriotic rising of Germany, which Caulaincourt justly dreaded, was already formidable, and everywhere contagious; but Napoleon's haughty obstinacy was more dangerous than the warlike excitement of his enemies. I forbear giving in de- tail the petty tricks, the systematic delays, the insolent acts or childish cunning, which the emperor up to the last moment made use of to render the peace negotiations impossible or illu- sory. On the 6th August secret proposals, entrusted to Cau- laincourt alone, were addressed to Austria, with no other object but to hinder that power from entering upon the campaign. Metternich replied by stating the indispensable conditions of peace, which had from the beginning been laid down with an invariable discretion and moderation. Caulaincourt accom- panied that communication with the following requests:— "Sire, this peace may cost something to your self-conceit, but nothing to your glory, for it will cost nothing to the real great- ness of France. I earnestly beg of you to grant this peace to France, to her sufferings, to her noble devotion to you, to the imperious circumstances in which you are placed. Take no notice of that fever of irritation against you which has taken possession of the whole of Europe, and which even the most decisive victories would excite still more instead of calming. I ask it of you not for the empty honor of signing it, but because I am certain that you can do nothing more advantageous to our country or more worthy of yourself."

Napoleon did not reply till the 11th, making some fresh proposals, which were really inadmissible, though they seemed to contain some concession. It was too late, Austria having signed her adhesion to the European coalition. Metternich transmitted the emperor's overtures to the allied powers, with the declaration, "We are no longer mediators." The Emperor Alexander had, in his turn, been seized by the war-fever; and there were now nearly 600,000 men ready to take the field in the name of the allied powers, who rejected Napoleon's late and insulting advances. The latter dared not publish in France the conditions of the peace rejected by him. Even Cambacérès was persistently deceived. Napoleon had just taken leave of the Empress Marie-Louise, who visited him at Mayence, with many tears and alarms. He sent her back to France before the breaking up of the armistice, arranging for her a journey into Normandy, in order to divert her attention at the time when her father and husband were to meet on the battle-field. The lot was now cast, and the last struggle was beginning which proved fatal to Napoleon, as well as to France, in spite of the heroic efforts of the nation, and the incomparable genius of its sovereign.

On this occasion Napoleon again deceived himself by despising the resources and determination of his enemies. The armistice and its prolongation were of more use to the allies than they could be to him. On the 17th August, 1813, he counted about 380,000 men under his flag, and his reserves were not equal to those of the allied army. Three armies were advancing against him—that of Bohemia, commanded by Prince Schwartzenberg; that of Silesia, under the orders of Blücher, and that of the north, entrusted to the Prince Royal of Sweden.

Bernadotte had joined the allied sovereigns at their headquarters in Trachenberg, full of pretension, and unreservedly claiming to play the part of generalissimo. The Germans had a strong antipathy to this intruder, the armies feeling but small confidence in him. In their real hearts, Blücher's officers regarded the French general who had become a Swedish prince with feelings analogous to that expressed by General Dufresse, commander of the French garrison at Stettin, when some shots were fired from the ramparts at Bernadotte, as he rode under the walls. The armistice still existing, the Swedes complained, on which the commandant said, "Oh, it's nothing; the guard saw a deserter pass, and fired upon him."

Bernadotte was not the only one of the military chiefs of our great wars who took that oportunity to fight against us. Having become a foreigner by a distinguished adoption, the Swedish prince had undertaken towards his new country, duties which he accomplished without reference to the country to which he owed his life and glory. General Moreau, who had just arrived in Sweden (20th July, 1813), and at once went to the head-quarters of the enemy, had contracted no obligations towards our enemies, and was not, like Bernadotte, followed by 25,000 brave and well-armed men. Buoyed up by his chimerical hopes, Moreau made use of his military authority, his consummate experience, his long knowledge of the theatre of war, as well as of soldiers, and of Napoleon himself, to serve a deep-seated hatred and personal rancor, justified by the past —the lamentable passions of a generous mind, which had been embittered by misfortune and injustice. Moreau was received at Trachenberg with special attention. He was accompanied by General Jomini, of Swedish origin, so skilled in the art of war that his opinion even with Napoleon had often been of great weight. Badly recompensed, badly treated by Berthier, with whom he had often disagreed, dissatisfied with the situation of the French army, and invited by the Emperor Alexander, who knew his merit, Jomini had recently joined the 'service of our enemies. "The Czar thinks that the French can only be beaten by French generals," muttered Blücher, angrily. The advice of Jomini and Moreau had, in fact, modified the plan of campaign of the allies. At first it was proposed to march upon Leipsic; now, on the contrary, the troops were advancing towards Dresden, the defence of which had been entrusted to Marshal Gouvion St. Cyr.

Napoleon had already marched to Bohemia, and thence to Silesia, where Blücher attacked Ney, almost without waiting for the expiration of the armistice. After several well-fought engagements, the Prussians were obliged to fall back upon Jauer. Macdonald was appointed to keep them behind the Bober, and had to intercept communications between Bohemia and Prussia, in order to stop the operations which might hamper Marshal Oudinot's movements upon Berlin. Napoleon's desire of again occupying that capital by a bold stroke had decided him in extending much too far the lines of his troops. Henceforward, it was upon Dresden that his principal efforts were to be directed.

Napoleon's scheme was to take up position on the camp at Pirna, after crossing the Elbe at Kœnigstein, intending to descend thence on the enemy's rear, and push him towards Dresden, so that he might be caught between his armies, the Elbe, and Marshal St. Cyr. The terror which seized Dresden, and the king and court of Saxony, at the approach of the allied armies, prevented the emperor from abiding by his first intentions. General Vandamme, with 40,000 men, was ordered to march by Kœnigstein and Pirna, while Napoleon himself advanced upon Dresden with the main army. He arrived there on the morning of the 26th August, and was welcomed with cheers by the population and soldiers. Marshal St. Cyr, after gallantly defending his advanced positions, had fallen back under the walls of the town. His arrangements already made were approved of by the emperor. The enemy still hesitated about making the attack, when Napoleon's arrival quickly decided the question. The battle began at three o'clock, just as the clocks of Dresden were striking the hour. The fighting was keen, and nearly all the redoubts were attacked at the same time; one of the works was already carried, and the defence at other points was becoming difficult, when the arrival of the guard changed the face of affairs. The French began the offensive, leaving the redoubts to march on the enemy. Murat was again at the head of the cavalry. The enemy were obliged to withdraw. Our success had cost us little, and the joyous confidence of victory animated the troops. "I shall see them again, to-morrow," said Napoleon, reviving by his courage the depressed heart of the King of Saxony. All the orders for the military operations had been given by the emperor before he took rest or food. On the 27th, the fighting began at daybreak, under a downpour of rain, which quite neutralized the first operations on both sides. Barclay de Tolly refused to effect a concentrated movement which had been recommended, against Marshal Ney's forces. "The fields are too much soaked," said he, "and the canals intersecting the plain overflow in all directions." A movement, which Napoleon had the night before ordered Murat and Victor to perform, threw the Austrian army into the valley of Plauen, and they were obliged to lay down their arms. The left wing of the allies was destroyed. In the centre, Napoleon, himself directing the artillery against the Austrians posted on the heights, sent forward several guns towards Racknitz, where the Emperor Alexander was. General Moreau was beside him, and said, "It is rather warm here;" when, after the Czar advised him to withdraw, a ball struck Moreau on the legs, and overthrew him and his horse together. "That Bonaparte is always lucky!" he exclaimed as he fell. He was carried dying into a hut, and his dog, bearing a collar with his name, brought by the soldiers to his master's bedside. The report of the illustrious general's death spread in both armies. General Vandamme had left Kœnigstein, and driven the Prince of Wurtemburg into the camp of Pirna. The battle of Dresden was lost by the allied sovereigns; they retired, leaving us masters of the battle-field, and fell back upon Bohemia by different roads. They had undergone considerable loses.

Napoleon, however, was not deceived by the brilliant victory, but wished immediately to follow up his advantage. Advancing to Pirna, he despatched General Vandamme in pursuit of the Russians. Several checks, undergone by Oudinot in his movement towards Berlin, and by Macdonald in opposing Blücher, brought the emperor back to Dresden; the main army pursued the allied columns in all directions. On the morning of the 29th, Vandamme defeated the Russian rear-guard, and the Emperor Alexander halted opposite Kulm, being resolved to fight him. The time was now passed when Napoleon's victories inspired his opponents with permanent fear. After a terrible struggle, lasting the whole day, the French remained in possession of Kulm, which they had carried even in the morning, without being able to dislodge the Russians from Priesten. General Vandamme asked for assistance, and on the 30th still waited in vain. The emperor's return to Dresden, the movements which he had ordered, and those which he was preparing, and the pursuit of the enemy's columns, all removed the forces which might have arrived in time. The allies at first limited themselves to restraining Vandamme; and whilst he still expected the assistance of Marshals Mortier and Gouvion St. Cyr, some Prussian forces, under General Kleist, who were about to retreat, fell upon the rear of Vandamme's army. His soldiers had fixed their bayonets on their muskets, determined to force a way through; and the French general himself had now no resource but a last desperate effort. He went up the Peterswald highway, leaving his artillery, which had been doing good execution upon the Russians, when the Emperor Alexander's entire army rushed upon him, and in the confusion of men and horses, the French divisions, crushed by the enemy, at last wavered, and a large number of soldiers took to flight. Generals Vandamme and Haxo, wounded and taken prisoners, were no longer present to rally their troops; the army was decimated; and the allied sovereigns, so soon smiled upon by fortune after their defeat before Dresden, again took courage and confidence. Henceforward, our very victories were without advantage or result.

The skilful combinations of the Emperor Napoleon had, moreover, failed in nearly every quarter under the hands of his most able lieutenants. Marshal Oudinot, defeated at Gross Beeren by General Tauenzien, had been forced back to Wittemberg by Bernadotte. Macdonald, thrown back upon the Katzbach by Blücher, was now at Bautzen, so vigorously pressed that Napoleon himself was obliged to go to his assistance. Blücher did not wait for him; but scarcely had the emperor returned to Dresden before Marshal Ney, who had been detached to assist Oudinot and recommence the movement upon Berlin, was in his turn beaten at Dennewitz, by the combined army of the Swedes, Russians, and Prussians. The Saxon regiments having disbanded, a large number deserted, accompanied by several Bavarian battalions. The marshal could not succeed in re-forming his army till they reached the gates of Torgau. For the first time his mind was overwhelmed with discouragement, and like Macdonald and Oudinot, he entreated the emperor to be relieved from the command. "It is my duty," he wrote from Wurtzen, on 10th September, "to declare to your Majesty that, with the present organization of the fourth, seventh, and twelfth army-corps, no good results can be expected from them. They are united by duty, but not in reality. Each of the generals-in-chief does almost what he thinks suitable to his own preservation; and things are at such a pass that I have great difficulty in getting a position. Both generals and officers are demoralized; I should prefer being a grenadier. I do not require, I believe, to speak of my devotion. I am ready to shed every drop of my blood, but I wish it to be done usefully. As things at present are, the emperor's presence alone can restore general confidence, because the wills of all yield to his genius, and all petty vanity disappears before the majesty of the throne. Your Majesty ought to be informed that the foreign troops of all nationalities show a very bad disposition, and that it is doubtful if the cavalry which I have with me be not more hurtful than useful."

Thus, under the blows of misfortune, was destroyed that bundle, painfully composed, of so many inconsistent and discordant elements, and till then obstinately kept together by the grasp of an all-powerful hand. Having had his combinations baffled or badly executed, and being ignorant of the plans of the enemy, who were now retreating after having a second time appeared in the suburbs of Dresden, Napoleon halted at Pirna, where he joined Marshal St. Cyr. The latter wished to pursue the allies, in order to intercept their advance to the Geyserberg, and the emperor agreed to this movement, which was in fact begun; but on the 11th September, being uneasy about the increasing difficulties of the march, anxious about the position of the Austrian forces, which he had received no information about, and afraid of his lieutenants being again worsted, Napoleon suddenly resolved to fall back upon Dresden. His intention was to form cantonments there during the winter; he had again grouped all his troops on the line of the Elbe, and was increasing his military supplies. The perpetual and repeated attacks of the enemy, the wide distribution of our forces, and the defeats undergone by several armies, had seriously diminished our resources, and the numerical disproportion between our troops and those of the allies became constantly greater. The minister of war had already been instructed, by a letter in cypher from the Duke of Bassano, to put the Rhenish fortresses in a state of defence. "Our army is still large, and in good condition," said the minister, who constantly shared all his master's secrets, "but the generals and officers, wearied with the war, have no longer that action which formerly led them to great exploits; the theatre is too extended. The emperor is victorious whenever he can be on the spot; but he cannot be everywhere, and the generals who command in his absence seldom answer to his expectations. You are aware of what happened to General Vandamme; the Duke of Tarento met with some reverses in Silesia; and the Prince of the Moskwa has just been beaten in marching upon Berlin. I present you with this picture in order that you may know all, and take steps accordingly."

The war, nevertheless, was still prolonged, gradually exhausting the strength of all; and the allies at last resolved to strike a decisive blow. They had long avoided the Emperor Napoleon, attacking his lieutenants, and incessantly harassing his armies; but being now assured of their crushing superiority in numbers, and urged on by the ardor of Blücher's staff, the sovereigns resolved to penetrate into Bohemia, and advance by different roads upon Leipsic, after again threatening Dresden. Their whole effort was, for a short time, to deceive Napoleon; with the purpose of concentrating the allied forces before he could attack the armies apart. Blücher was appointed to push on first in advance, to compel Bernadotte to cross the Elbe at Roslau. The Germans impatiently blamed the backwardness of the prince royal of Sweden. "He dare not attack the French," said they.

Napoleon, also, as well as the allies, wished for a battle. Having some idea of the plans of the enemy, he guessed their combinations, but counted upon delays which, as it happened, they did not make. His first thought was to abandon the Elbe and Dresden, and by marching with all his forces towards Leipsic, separate the three allied armies from each other. He made preparations for this purpose, and allowed the old King of Saxony to accompany his armies. Marshal St. Cyr was already rejoicing at the thoughts of leaving Dresden, when the emperor, on reaching Dresden, became hopeful of beating Bernadotte and Blücher in rapidity of march, and thus fighting the armies of the north and of Silesia, before they could effect their junction with the army of Bohemia. For this purpose, it was necessary to keep Dresden, in order to recross the Elbe there, and the evacuation of the town was deferred. This unfortunate measure deprived us of 30,000 men, and Marshal St. Cyr, and was, moreover, useless, as the rapid concentration of the enemies round Leipsic soon compelled Napoleon to resume his march towards that place.

I have no intention of narrating, in all their technical details, the successive battles then about to be fought under the walls of Leipsic, to decide the fate of France and Europe. The feeling of the lowest soldiers, as well as of the emperor himself, was, that the hour of final struggle was at hand. "Boys!" said General Maison, on the morning of the 16th, when joining battle, "this is France's last battle, and we must be all dead before night." The same gloomy ardor reigned throughout all the ranks. Everywhere men hastened to fight, without illusion, with the courage of wounded lions. "You are long in coming, my old Augereau," cried Napoleon to the marshal, as he reached the head-quarters; "you have kept us waiting; you are no longer the Augereau of Castiglione!" "I shall always be the Augereau of Castiglione," replied the old soldier of the republic, "when your Majesty gives me back the soldiers of

the army of Italy." Those were dead; their sons also were
dead; their grandchildren had not had time to grow, and had
already been mowed down on the field of battle. Napoleon had
just prepared the decrees for a new levy, calling upon 280,000
more men to join his flag, 120,000 being from previous contin-
gents, and 160,000 from the conscription of 1815. On reaching
Leipsic, on the 15th October, the French army could not
amount to more than 190,000 men, whereas the united forces of
the allies reckoned 300,000. Napoleon himself felt the load that
lay upon his shoulders. "What an intricate problem is all
this!" said he. "No one but myself can get me well through
it, and even I shall find it no easy task."

The exterior difficulties and complications constantly increased around the emperor, opposing or threatening his military operations. The kingdom of Westphalia, composed of
heterogeneous elements, and provinces differing in origin and
interests, had just crumbled to pieces before a charge of Czer-
nichef's Cossacks. Arriving, without opposition, at the gates
of Cassel, they found King Jerome almost deprived of troops.
The defence was but for an instant, the population being everywhere hostile to him; the dethroned monarch was obliged to
withdraw to Coblentz, and his States no longer existed. News
of another danger was brought. The King of Bavaria had
asked for reinforcements, having long been displeased to
see his army, under the orders of General Wrede, exposed
on the Inn to the attacks of the Austrians. Marshal Augereau's departure for Leipsic having rendered assistance hopeless, the prince yielded to his personal desires and fears, as
well as to the enthusiastic wishes of his people. On the 8th
October, Bavaria adhered to the coalition by a treaty secretly
signed at Munich. Behind us every way of escape was being
closed. Before us opened the battle-field of Leipsic.

Napoleon carefully inspected the ground on the 15th, trying
to form an idea of the position of the enemies, and their plan of
battle. The army of Bohemia, under Prince Schwartzenberg,
threatened our positions at Mark-Kleeburg, Wachau, and Lie-
bert-Wolkwitz. Blücher with his forces on the Halle road,
several leagues from Leipsic, was eager to reach the battle-
field. Bernadotte was still some distance off on the lower
Saale, two of his divisions being on the march along the right
bank of the Elbe. Two days' marching would bring the allies
a reinforcement of 110,000 men. Of the troops at the disposal
of the French, those of General Regnier only had not yet

reached Leipsic, and they did not amount to more than 15,-
000 men, mostly foreigners. The emperor could not delay
giving battle, which therefore began on the 16th, at nine o'clock
in the morning.

The fighting was continued the whole day with the same
keen determination. When, in the evening, by the last rays
of twilight, Napoleon rode over the field of the dead, he saw
that his soldiers had fallen in their ranks, as men of honor;
but the enemy had shown equal courage. Incessantly taken,
and retaken, by the opposing tides of combatants, the positions
were defended, attacked, and turned, without any decisive
result. Napoleon several times put forth a great effort to reach
a definite success, which he felt necessary, but a skilful movement of the enemy constantly hampered his plan. At the
sheep-farm of Avenhayn, at the village of Gulden-Gossa, at the
wood of the University, dead bodies were heaped up in vain.
The cannon in the distance were heard resounding, in reply to
the thunder of the main battle-field. At Lindenau, General
Margaron had difficulty in holding his own against Giulay. At
Mockern, Marshal Mazaron had been stopped in his march towards Leipsic by the arrival of Blücher, who was hastening to
the combat. Alone he had to struggle with the army of Silesia,
and when at last compelled to fall back upon the Partha, the
Marshal had lost 6000 men. Nothing now prevented the junction of Blücher and Schwartzenberg.

Though 20,000 Frenchmen lay strewed over the ground
at Wachau, we had not lost our positions, or retreated a step.
The situation, however, was not less terrible and threatening,
in presence of the enormous masses which were advancing to
surround us on every side. Napoleon felt this. On the 17th,
he for a short time thought of retreating. That was to confess
his defeat, and risk the loss of the excellent troops still shut up
in the strongholds at Dresden, Hamburg, Dantzic, Glogau, and
Stettin. The emperor sent for Merveldt, the Austrian general,
who had been taken prisoner on the evening of the 15th, in a
skirmish at Dölitz. "Did they know I was here when they
made the attack?" he asked. "Yes, sire." "You wished then,
this time, to give me battle?" "Yes, sire." Then, after some
remarks as to the respective numbers of the two armies, "Will
you attack me to-morrow?" "Yes, sire." "This struggle is
becoming very serious; should we not put a stop to it?" continued the emperor; "will there be no thought of peace?"
"May God grant it!" exclaimed the Austrian; "that is all we

are fighting for. If your Majesty had agreed to it at Prague!"
"Let England give me back my colonies, and I will give her
back Hanover." "She will want more than that." "I will
restore the Hanse towns, if need be." It was now too late;
Merveldt spoke of Holland. He at the same time pointed out
the determination of the allies with regard to the independence of Italy. The kingdom of Westphalia no longer existed.
With reference to an armistice, the emperor said, "I know
that you maintain it is part of my military policy, yet we
might in that way avoid much bloodshed. During the negotiations I should retire as far as the Saale." "The allies would
never agree to an armistice on these terms," objected Merveldt:
"they reckon to go to the Rhine this autumn." "To the
Rhine!" exclaimed Napoleon. " Before I retire as far as the
Rhine I must lose a battle, and till now I have yet lost none.
Set out, nevertheless. You know my opinion of your merit; I
restore you to liberty on parole. You may repeat what I have
told you."

Merveldt's report went to strengthen the allied sovereigns in
their intention of following up their advantages to the end.
The emperor, however, had resolved to beat a retreat in a lei-
surely and dignified manner, through Leipsic, as if merely to
modify the position of his troops. At two o'clock in the morning the whole army was to effect a concentric movement upon
Leipsic, so that when the circle was completed round the town
they might reach by the Lindenau bridge the small town
divided from Leipsic by the Elster; beyond that extended the
plain of Lutzen, which General Bertrand was ordered to clear
of the few troops of the enemy occupying it. General Rogniat
was to throw bridges over the Saale. They neglected, however, to build several over the Elster.

After having everywhere given his orders personally, the
emperor was returning to his bivouac at Probstheyda on the
18th, at daybreak, when he saw three columns of the enemy
advancing upon his new line of battle. The allies, like Napoleon, had allowed the 17th to pass without a battle, because
they waited for the arrival of Bernadotte, whom Blücher had
compelled to cross the Partha, and advance before Prince
Schwartzenberg. On every side of the battle-field, the French
army, who had fallen back within their new positions, now
found themselves simultaneously attacked. The Austrians
charged Probstheyda; Poniatowski and Augereau defended
themselves at Connewitz. Marshal Ney and Marmont, at-

tacked by Blücher and Bernadotte, had seen General Reynier suddenly deserted by the Saxon forces, who passed over to the enemy, and turned their guns against Durutte's division, with whom they had served for several years. Napoleon hastened up with the cavalry and artillery of the guard, to close the breach opened in our lines by this defection. The news of it quickly spreading in both armies, stimulated still more the hopes of one side, and the heroic despair of the other. Prince Schwartzenberg had now given up the attempt to carry Probst-heyda, and limited himself to bombarding our works. The batteries were still vomiting flames at nightfall, yet the French had not modified their positions; the rows of dead men alone showed at what price our lines had been defended, and how much our forces had been weakened.

Henceforward resistance became impossible, with 40,000 soldiers dead or wounded in our ranks, and the retreat began immediatel*y*. The emperor had entered Leipsic to issue his orders. The wounded had been abandoned on the battle-field, but some of the victims of the engagements on the 16th were carried off. The ambulance-wagons, and those for baggage and artillery, already blocked up the bridge leading to Linde-nau, which was very long and narrow, and soon covered with a crowded throng of soldiers, prisoners, and camp-followers, who were frequently trodden under foot by columns advancing in good order. The guns commenced their roar at sunrise, as the rear-guard were still fighting in the suburbs. The passion-ate anger of our troops lent them new strength against the enemies who ventured to pursue them. It was at the point of the bayonet that several regiments forced their way towards Lindenau.

These last defenders of the national honor were soon to pay dearly for their devotion. The bridge had been mined on the Leipsic side, where it crosses the main branch of the Elster, and orders were given to set fire to the train when the French troops were replaced at the bridge-head by the enemy. This frightful duty was entrusted to a simple corporal of the sappers. In the confusion of battle, while the remains of the seventh, fifth, and eleventh corps were still fighting on the ramparts of the town, some of Blücher's soldiers, mixed with ours, were seen through the streets of the suburb Halle. "Set fire to it! set fire to it!" immediately shouted those who were already in safety, terrified at the thought of pursuit. The corporal, shar-ing in the alarm, obeyed, and the bridge was blown up, cover-

ing both banks with its ruins, and condemning to death or captivity 20,000 Frenchmen, who were thus deprived of all communication with the army.   A cry of despair arose, and while
the last ranks of our soldiers still rushed upon the enemy,
many of the others threw themselves into the river, where the
majority speedily perished.   In that number was Prince Poniatowski, who had been raised on the previous evening to the
dignity of marshal.   Macdonald succeeded in gaining the opposite bank.   The Generals Reynier and Lauriston fell into the
hands of the enemy.   The Emperor Alexander gave the King
of Saxony to understand that he must consider himself a
prisoner of war.   A few hours previously, Napoleon had bidden
adieu to the unhappy sovereign, whom he was drawing on to
his ruin.   The defection of the Saxons on the field of battle was
destined to save neither their king nor their country.

The battle of nations was finished, and the lot of arms had
decided against us.   Napoleon now hastened to reach again
those limits of the Rhine which he had recently scorned as too
confined, fortunate in being able to pass freely over the Saale,
thanks to the energy of Bertrand and Mortier, and hurrying to
be before the enemy, who were advancing to bar their passage.
The Austro-Bavarian army came to encamp on the Mein,
whilst the emperor rested at Erfurt, their object being to intercept his march to Mayence.   The remains of the army, re-
formed by Napoleon's personal vigilance, at last crossed the
passes of Thuringia; but disease, desertion, and disorder daily
weakened our resources.   Of 100,000 men who left Leipsic,
50,000 at most endured the fatigue and hardships of the march.
Napoleon had less than 20,000 men under him when he attacked
the Bavarians at Hanau, on the 30th October, and brilliantly
forced his way through them.   "Poor Wrede!" said the emperor, disdainfully, as he cast a glance over his adversary's
positions.   "I made him a count, but I could not make him a
general!"   The Bavarians were crushed, and the French army
entered triumphantly into Mayence, though reduced to the
number of the smallest of the army-corps which had so recently
passed through that town, one after another, marching to new
conquests and new victories.   The Rhine was not defended,
and the garrisons which ought to have been protecting it were
scattered from the Oder to the Vistula, delivered up beforehand, in spite of their heroism, to the vengeance of the allies.
After making his final arrangements for distributing in the
Rhenish strongholds the troops left him, the emperor set out

from Mayence on the 7th November, and on the 9th reached Paris, still proud in spite of his profound dejection. His last words at Mayence were a challenge to the German princes who had deserted him. "The King of Bavaria and I will meet again," said he. "He was a little prince whom I made great; and now he is a great prince, whom I shall make little."

CHAPTER XV.

THE FALL (1813—1814).

IMMEDIATELY after the battle of Dresden, during the depression of defeat, the allied powers renewed and gave reasons for their alliance, being more than ever resolved to strengthen it in their misfortune; and after the battle of Leipsic, after gaining a brilliant victory which the conquered could not dispute, the allies wished to declare to all the world their mutual engagements and their reasons for continuing the alliance. "The allied sovereigns declare," said they, " that they do not make war upon France; that they desire that she may be strong and happy, that her commerce may revive, and the arts again flourish; that her territory may remain more extensive than it ever was under her kings—because the French influence, great and powerful, is in Europe one of the fundamental bases of the social system—because the tranquillity of a great people depends upon their happiness—because a brave nation does not sink lower on account of having in its turn undergone reverses. It is upon the emperor alone that they make war; or rather, upon that excess of influence which he has too long brought to bear upon nations foreign to his own, to the misfortune of France and Europe."

We have in 1870 heard analogous declarations, and been able to estimate their value. In 1813 the allied sovereigns were sincere, as was proved by their conduct in 1814, and France understood their declarations to be earnest. She was at once annoyed, exhausted, and tired; tired of her past glories now vanishing before the present reverses, exhausted by the supernatural efforts she had for so many years been exerting, and annoyed at seeing a peace which she felt to be honorable and practicable scorned by the unconquerable pride of her master,

immediately after the victories of Lutzen and Bautzen. All
the oppressions which had gradually more and more weighed
down all classes of society, the increasing burdens caused by
requisitions, the hardships under which commerce groaned on
account of the ports being closed, and above all the constant
mowing down of men, and almost boys, in all the battle-fields
of Europe, with families destroyed, and hopes ruined, such
were the evils accumulated upon France by fifteen years of
military despotism, succeeding to ten years of revolution. The
imperial police were no longer sufficient to smother the complaints and murmurs. No one now believed in the declarations
of the official journals; and tragical rumors exaggerated even
the facts of our disasters. The cry of the mothers rose to the
very heavens.

It was certainly not in favor of the various parties, long
crushed under a powerful hand, that those elements of disturbance and fermentation were in agitation. The republicans,
still numerous, remained silent, or dreamt of an enthusiastic
stirring up of the country analogous to that of 1792, which
would drive back the enemy far from our threatened frontiers;
the constitutionals seemed to be forgot; the royalists criticised
in the drawing-rooms, and ironical smiles again were seen on
women's lips. Several intriguers were coming and going,
though no attempt of importance, nor any effective influence,
had yet resulted from the secret party-meetings. The most
alarmed of all those whom Napoleon would see or hear on his
arrival in France, in November, 1813, were amongst his most
confidential servants. Those most resolved to injure him in
the future had recently been of service to him, and he had
assisted in raising them to the brilliant social and moral position which they occupied. In Illyria, Fouché, Duke of Otranto,
a terrorist and spy, revolutionary and venal; in Paris, Talleyrand, Prince of Benevento and Vice-Grand-Elector—both suspected by Napoleon, and both removed from any active share
in his government—were both meditating schemes of vengeance, still only vague, and subordinated to their personal interest. Talleyrand could reckon upon able and devoted friends
—the Abbé Louis, formerly clerk to the "Parliament" of Paris;
the Duke of Dalberg, who had been, like himself, made a councillor of state by the emperor, and who still nursed some grievances against the imperial power. These men both kept up in
Talleyrand's mind the sense of injury. He, however, still hesitated, and the emperor had more than once thought of entrust-

ing important missions to him. They both felt themselves on
the brink of a gulf of unfathomable depth, the opposite side of
which still remained hid to even the most daring eyes.

This gulf was constantly becoming greater, and the situation
from hour to hour became more gloomy, as if the prestige of
victory, so long attached to our colors by the powerful hand
of Napoleon, had all at once escaped from his grasp. In Spain,
Marshal Soult had for a short time tried to force Wellington
back beyond Pampeluna and St. Sebastian, which he then held
in a state of siege; but both places succumbed, and the French
army after recrossing the frontiers found itself attacked and
stormed at St. Jean de Luz by the English. Wellington first
set foot on the soil of France on the 11th November. 1813.

In Germany the fate which Napoleon had foreseen threatened the various garrisons, which had been left to themselves,
isolated in a country which was daily becoming more hostile,
without mutual communication, without personal attachment
among the officers in command. The majority still held out,
though reduced by disease, gallantly resolving to defend themselves and sell their lives dearly. Dresden had just capitulated. Count Lobau had made an unsuccessful attempt to
force his way to Torgau, in order to secure a retreat for the
garrison; but the effort being too long delayed, and made with
insufficient resources, had not succeeded, and Marshal St. Cyr,
dissatisfied and depressed, agreed to an honorable capitulation.
The 30,000 soldiers shut up in Dresden were to return to France
upon laying down their arms, without any condition to prevent them again serving the country, so dear to them, which
they were about to see again. They were already on the
march, and leaving Dresden, when General Klenau, who had
treated with Marshal St. Cyr, suddenly announced that the
Emperor Alexander, having had no share in the negotiation,
refused to agree to the capitulation, and that the French
troops must return to Dresden or acknowledge themselves
prisoners of war. Most of the works of defence were destroyed, the provisions consumed, and many of the soldiers ill.
The alternative was deceptive, and in spite of his indignant
protestations, the marshal found himself compelled to submit
to the conqueror's unjust demands. Generals and soldiers
were reduced to captivity.

The Emperor Napoleon disliked Marshal St. Cyr, whose independence of character often rendered him ill-natured and
rude; but on this occasion he did justice emphatically to his

rare merit, in a manner as honorable to himself as to his illustrious lieutenant. "It is not for the 28,000 men of the garrison that the Emperor Alexander and Schwartzenberg have
done that," said he on being informed of the disloyal rupture
of the capitulation of Dresden; "it is in order to have Gouvion
St. Cyr: they are well aware that he is the first man of our
time for defence; I surpass him in attack."

It was for defence that the Emperor Napoleon was this time preparing, the greatly reduced remains of his army no longer supplied with sufficient forces to repel the invasion which he foresaw. The levy of 280,000 men announced in October had now
become too weak a resource against the enemy, and a "sénatus-consulte" ordered out 300,000 new combatants upon the
past conscriptions, which had already been so often subjected
to fresh calls. On this occasion the order extended back to the
year 1803. Since July, 30,000 supplementary conscripts had
been raised in the southern departments for the defence of the
Spanish frontiers. For the future the interior was to be garrisoned by the cohorts of the national guard.

The effort was something enormous, and to have carried out
Napoleon's plan was beyond the resources of the exhausted
country. The emperor knew this to a certain extent, and did
not reckon upon collecting under his colors all the soldiers
whom he demanded from the country. He had already
given orders to delay levying the contingent of 1815, and he
especially urged calling out the three last conscriptions. He
counted upon the winter months to complete his military
preparations. Count Daru had just been appointed minister
of war, which was an assurance that the utmost pains would
be bestowed, with skill and energy. General Drouot was
placed in command of the guard, now largely increased, and
was appointed to regulate their recruiting as well as their
equipment. Money was now wanting, because the resources
formerly supplied by imposing contributions upon the conquered countries had disappeared with victory. On the 17th
November, Napoleon thus wrote to his minister of finance:

"M. le Comte Mollien, in times of penury like the present,
the Treasury cannot be administered on the same principles or
in the same manner as in times of abundance, such as we have
had till now. All the orders of the war administration for
supplies, all those of the war minister for the expenses of
engineering, artillery and the re-arming of strongholds, are not
paid; hence most disastrous results to the defence of the State.

It is a misfortune that the public debt, the pensions and salaries of Holland, Rome, Piedmont, and even France, are behind-hand; but that misfortune is in no respect to be compared to what would result from the least delay in the payment of the orders of the war administration or the war minister. The public safety has no law; these orders ought to be paid before the salaries of civilians and the public dividends. In the present circumstances there has not been an inch of ground stirred anywhere, because the war orders remained everywhere unpaid. I have not more than 30,000,000 of silver in the treas-ury of the crown, and I give you ten of them, though with a strong feeling of repugnance, for I was keeping it against a rainy day, and if that money were used in civil expenses it would be a sacrifice of the last resource."

The Emperor Napoleon had at his disposal a resource more precious. The Spanish war had for five years absorbed, in men and money, a considerable part of the strength and life of France. The hopes which Napoleon had conceived as to the provinces to the north of the Ebro, vanished with his power. The time for annexation was past. Marshal Soult was still de-fending the southern frontiers, and Suchet still held Catalonia, having garrisoned the strongholds of Aragon: 80,000 men of excellent troops could be restored to the country in her neces-sity. The emperor resolved to negotiate, and sent Laforest to Ferdinand VII. at Valençay. The old king, Charles IV., and his wife, always accompained by the Prince de la Paix, had left Compiègne, to take up their abode at Marseilles, and after-wards at Rome. It was with their son, who alone was popular in Spain, and whose name had served as a rallying-cry in the National war, that the Emperor Napoleon, wearied and threat-ened, at last consented to negotiate.

An unjust and disloyal policy was legitimately punished by meeting at every step with distrust and treacherous complica-tions. No one in Spain amongst the chiefs of the insurrection could trust to the word or advances of the Emperor Napoleon. and none of them was inclined even to receive instructions com-ing from a captive prince, who might be inspired by his jailers. Caulaincourt had recently replaced the Duke of Bassano as foreign minister, the emperor being obliged to sacrifice the lat-ter to public opinion; and the new minister's advice was to set the King of Spain at liberty, after making a bargain with him as to the conditions of his restoration, so that he might plead with his subjects his own cause and that of France. Napoleon did not aaopt that idea, being mistrustful, not without reason, of the Spanish prince, who was more cunning and deceitful than ever in his isolation and captivity. At first Ferdinand refused to discuss matters with Laforest, declaring that he was ignorant of what was going on in the world and in Spain, and that he wished to remain at rest under the emperor's protection. A proposal was made to him that his states should be completely restored to him, on condition of the withdrawal of the English, the freedom of the prisoners, and the integrity of the Spanish colonies, none of which were to be ceded to Great Britain. A proposal of marrying Ferdinand to one of King Joseph's daughters had been considered; but Laforest, from diplomatic reticence, reserved that condition.

Joseph Bonaparte refused to take part in the negotiation, unless assured of some compensation in Italy. Napoleon exclaimed indignantly against this claim. "Joseph blames himself for having committed some military faults; he has no thought of such a thing. He is not a soldier; he could not commit them; he has not committed them! In fact, he has lost Spain, and will certainly not recover it. Let him consult the lowest of my generals, he will see if it is possible to claim a single village beyond the Pyrenees. But if I wished to make a treaty with Spain, I should not be even listened to! The first condition of any peace with Europe is the restoration, pure and simple, of Spain to the Bourbons—happy if at that price I can rid myself of the English, and bring back my armies of Spain to the Rhine! As to compensations in Italy, where are they to be found? Can I turn Murat out of his kingdom? I have difficulty in keeping him to his duties towards France and me. How should I be obeyed if I went to ask him to descend from his throne in favor of Joseph? As to the Roman States, I shall be compelled to give them up to the Pope, and I am resolved to do so. As to Tuscany which belongs to Elisa, Piedmont which belongs to France, or Lombardy where Eugène has so much difficulty in maintaining his position, how can I know what they will leave me? To keep France with its natural limits, I must gain many victories; but to gain anything beyond the Alps, I should have to gain many more. And if they leave me some territory in Italy, could I, on Joseph's account, take it away from Eugène, that son so devoted and brave, who has constantly risked his life for me and for France, and never incurred my displeasure? The

Spanish and I can very well dispense with King Joseph, and replace Ferdinand VII. on the throne of the Spains."

The Spaniards at the head of the insurrection were not eager to see their sovereign very soon, united as he was to the Emperor Napoleon by a treaty. They wished to avenge themselves; and the English had no wish to lose the fruit of their victories. Ferdinand had no liking for the liberal principles which ruled the insurgent leaders, and the Cortes disliked abdicating in his favor. Napoleon, however, sent to Valençay the Duke of San Carlos, formerly a special favorite of the Prince of the Asturias, and long imprisoned at Lons-le-Saulnier. Canon Esquoiquiz and José Palafox were anxious to regain their liberty and secure the independence of their country. On the 13th December, after long negotiations, the duke started for Madrid, bearing a treaty, signed on the 11th at Valençay, between the Emperor Napoleon and King Ferdinand VII. At the same time, and by another road, the illustrious defender of Saragossa was carrying into Spain a copy of the conventions. Henceforward, Napoleon was anxious to free himself from the burden which he had formerly been eager to lay upon his shoulders. The justice which reigns supreme over human actions rendered this renunciation difficult to him at the very time when the thrones which he had raised were crumbling to pieces round his own, or escaping from his control. Murat had already seemed to waver in his fidelity: the intrigues of Austria had influenced the mind of Queen Caroline, who had complete power over her husband. He aimed at becoming the head of an independent Italy, and asked Napoleon himself to furnish the means. Such was the advice given by Fouché, who had been sent to strengthen his fidelity. Only a few months more were to elapse before Murat, thinking he should save his throne by treachery, signed with Austria and England a treaty of alliance (6th, 11th January, 1814), which he was soon after to violate, in order to pay at last with his life for the vacillations of a mind which was always unstable and weak, unless when face to face with the dangers of the battle-field and under the constraint of military honor.

Time was pressing, and Napoleon began to think that he could not make use of the whole winter to complete his warlike preparations. Probably even the allied powers would not allow him time to recall by his negotiations the troops still occupying Spain and those which he wished to bring away from the German strongholds. Scarcely 40,000 men of the new

levies were yet brought together in the depots; from 50,000 to
60,000 weary soldiers still occupied the Rhenish frontiers; and
in Italy Prince Eugène had not collected 40,000. After the
battle of Leipsic the allies stopped, as if astonished at their
success, hesitating to pursue him and beard the lion even
in his den. About the middle of November the sovereigns,
who had met in Frankfort, had some intention of negotiating.

The Prussians were enthusiastic, from the ardor of vengeance, and the necessity of reconstituting their dismembered
country with some glory. The Russians were fully aware of
the difficulties of carrying out an enterprise against France to
the very end: they had been fighting incessantly for eighteen
months, and were anxious for rest. Their emperor was more
eager than his generals to pursue his advantages; he believed
himself the arbiter of Europe, and wished to efface the humiliations which Napoleon had recently subjected him to. When
stepping upon French territory, Lord Wellington addressed to
his troops that famous proclamation: "Let the officers and
soldiers of this army not forget, that if the nations are at war
with France, it is only because the ruler of France will not
allow them peace, and because he aims at subjecting them to
his yoke." The English Cabinet had sent as a plenipotentiary
to the allied sovereigns, Lord Aberdeen, still very young, but
already remarkable by his calm yet self-reliant disposition.
Favorable in their real hearts to that restoration of the house
of Bourbon which England had always considered the surest
guarantee of lasting peace in France, Lord Castlereagh and his
ambassador were not disposed to make it a condition. The
Emperor of Austria and his minister still hoped to obtain from
Napoleon the concessions necessary to restore peace: it was
their wisdom and influence that produced the harmony which
presided over the resolutions of the allied princes. It was Metternich who took the initiative at Frankfort in pacific overtures towards the emperor, entrusting with that duty St.
Aignan, the brother-in-law of Caulaincourt, who had recently
been French Minister at Weimar. Caulaincourt was asked to
gain information for negotiations on the base of the natural
limits of France—the Rhine, the Alps, and the Pyrenees. The
sovereigns did not aim at the humiliation of their illustrious
and now defeated enemy, but were resolved upon granting
nothing beyond what they had already stipulated. Nesselrode
and Lord Aberdeen spoke to the same effect. The chargé,

d'affaires set out for Paris bearing a summary of the conditions
of the peace.

It required a great effort to renounce the habits of illimitable
power, and learn, after fifteen years of indisputable authority,
to reckon with the various powers abroad and at home. While
accepting the idea of a negotiation, and specifying no place for
the future congress, the Emperor Napoleon did not condescend
in his first reply to touch upon the question of the bases of the
peace; and when at last, on the 2nd December, Caulaincourt
succeeded in obtaining his explicit agreement to the Frankfort
proposals, it was too late. England claimed a share in the advantages of the victory, and Aberdeen's instructions were
modified. Time had advanced, and events advanced with it.

Public opinion in France was advancing, together with time
and events, and the emperor acknowledged it with an angry
feeling, which he was unable to contain. A month after the
Legislative Body had been summoned, the session was at last
opened by the emperor, on the 19th December. The faces of
all were gloomy, and their hearts full of the anxiety which
weighed upon every household in France. The partisans of
the imperial régime exerted themselves in vain calming the
general uneasiness and imposing silence upon just complaints,
when Napoleon himself thus addressed his Parliament:—

"Senators, councillors of State, deputies of the Legislative
         Body,—

"Brilliant victories have shed lustre upon French arms during the present campaign, but unparalleled defections rendered
those victories useless, and everything turned against us.
France herself would be in danger without the energy and
union of the French.

"I was never seduced by prosperity, and adversity would
find me above her assaults.

"I have several times given peace to the nations when they
had lost everything. With part of my conquests I raised
thrones for kings who have deserted me. I conceived and
executed great schemes for the prosperity and happiness of the
world. A monarch and a father, I feel what peace adds to the
security of thrones and of families. Negotiations have been
begun with the allied powers. I have adhered to the preliminary bases proposed by them, and was therefore in hopes that
before the opening of this session the Congress would have assembled at Mannheim; but new delays, for which France is
not blamable, have deferred that event, which all are eagerly

awaiting. I have given orders that all the original documents of the Department of Foreign Affairs should be laid before you. You will receive information of them through a commission, and my councillors will acquaint you with my intentions respecting them. There is on my part no opposition to the restoration of peace. I know and share in all the sentiments of the French people. I say the French people, because there is none of them who desires peace at the cost of honor."

" When the emperor laid before the Senate and the Legislative Body several of the documents of his negotiations with the allied powers," says Guizot, in his *Memoirs*, " and wished for an expression of their sentiments, if he had had a real purpose of making peace, or of seriously convincing France that if peace were not made it was by no means on account of the obstinacy of his overbearing will, he would certainly have found in both houses, however enervated they might be, energetic and popular support. I frequently conversed on intimate terms with three of the five members of the Commission of the Legislative Body, Maine de Biran, Gallois, and Raynouard, and from them knew also the opinions of the remaining two, Lainé and Flaugergues. Biran was, like Royer-Collard and myself, a member of a small philosophical club, where we freely dis cussed everything, and kept us well informed of what was going on in the Commission and in the Legislative Body itself. Though originally a royalist, he was independent of all parties and intrigues, conscientious almost to a fault, sometimes even timid when his conscience did not absolutely impose courage upon him, with little liking for politics, and in any case ever averse to the adoption of an extreme resolution or any active initiative. Gallois, a man of the world and a student, a moderate liberal of the philosophical school of the eighteenth century, was more concerned about his library than public notoriety, and wished to perform worthily his duty to his country without disturbing the habitual serenity of his life. With more energy of manner and language, as a provençal and a poet, Raynouard was nevertheless disinclined to rash measures, and his complaints, which were said to be severe against the tyrannical abuses of the imperial administration, would not have prevented him being contented with those moderate reparations which in the meantime save honor, and give hope for the future. Flaugergues, an honest republican, who put on mourning for the death of Louis XVI., unyielding in disposition and character, was capable of energetic resolution, but he could not communicate it to others. He had but small influence upon his colleagues, though he spoke a great deal. Lainé, on the contrary, had a warm and sympathetic heart under a downcast manner, and a nobleness of mind without much originality or power. He spoke with great point and force when his feelings were moved. Formerly a republican, and afterwards simply a disinterested partisan of the liberal ideas and sentiments, he was at once appointed leader of the commission, and agreed without hesitation to be its mouthpiece. But, unlike his colleagues, he had no premeditated hostility or secret engagement against the emperor. They all wished only to convey to him the earnest desire of France for a really pacific foreign policy, and the respect for the people's rights at home with legal exercise of power.

" With such men, animated with such views, it was easy to come to an arrangement; but Napoleon would not even grant them a hearing." He had beforehand chafed the remains of self-respect which were reawaking amongst the deputies by ignoring their right to present a list of candidates for the presidentship. The Duke of Massa (Regnier) formerly one of the high judges, minister of justice, and who had just been replaced in the cabinet by young Count Molé, was named President of the Legislative Body. To explain this transformation, which was announced by a *sénatus-consulte*, Molé had recourse to singular arguments. "It might happen," said he, "that the candidates presented by the Legislative Body, however honorable or distinguished, have never been personally known to the emperor, or that they themselves were unacquainted with the forms and ceremonial of the palace. Whereas, on the contrary, by the emperor choosing the president directly, the Legislative Body will be sure of finding in him a useful intermediary, a guide and support."

Lainé's report was keenly discussed by the commissioners of the government who were present at the meetings of the five deputies. Massa was also there; and on his charging Raynouard with making unconstitutional claims, the author of *Les Templiers* turned quickly to him and said, "I see nothing here that is unconstitutional, but your presence and functions."

The Archchancellor Cambacérès obtained several modifications in the original form of the report, yet when the document was submitted to the emperor, he burst into a violent rage. He pretended to see in the terms used by the Commission of

the Legislative Body a return to the claims and passions of the
revolutionary assemblies; and in spite of all that could be
urged by several of his councillors, more particularly Cambacérès and Rovigo, he determined to suppress the report and adjourn the Legislative Body. The decree appeared in the *Moniteur* of the 1st January, 1814, and when the deputies appeared
at the Tuileries to pay their respects on the occasion of the new
year, the emperor abruptly stopped them, and getting into a
passion, exclaimed, with the most violent gestures and language, such as he sometimes gave way to: "Deputies of the
Legislative Body, you can do much good, and you have done
much harm. I summoned you to assist me, and you have
come to say and do what is necessary to help the foreigner.
Eleven twelfths of you are good, the rest are factious, and you
have been their dupes. Your commission has been inspired by
the spirit of the Girondins. M. Lainé, who drew up your report, is a worthless man. He is sold to England, with whom
he has communication by means of Desèze, the barrister: I
shall keep my eye upon him. Two battles lost in Champagne
would have done less harm than his report. M. Raynouard
said that Marshal Masséna pillaged a citizen's country-house;
M. Raynouard is a liar . . . How can you blame me for my
misfortunes? You say that adversity has given me good advice. Is it by reproaches that you propose to restore the glory
of the throne? I am one of those men who can face death, but
not disgrace. Besides, what is the throne? Four pieces of
wood covered with a piece of velvet: everything depends upon
him whose seat it is. The throne is in the desire of the nation,
whom I represent; I cannot be attacked without attacking it.
Four times have I been called by the nation; I had the votes of
5,000,000 of citizens. I have a title, and you have none. You
are only deputies of the departments. Is this a time for re-
monstrance when 200,000 Cossacks are crossing our frontiers?
Your theorists ask for guarantees of defence against power; at
this moment France only asks for those against the enemy.
You speak of abuses and vexations, which I am as well aware
of as you; they are due to the circumstances and misfortunes
of the times. When before Europe in arms, why speak of our
domestic quarrels? One's dirty linen should be washed at
home. You surely wish to imitate the Constituent Assembly,
and begin another revolution? I am beyond reach of your de-
clamations. In three months we shall have peace, or I shall
be dead. Our enemies have never conquered us, nor will they

conquer us. They will be driven away more speedily than they came."

Even when his passionate outbursts were genuine and painful, the Emperor Napoleon always considered what effect they might produce, and tried to make use of it. When communicating to the commission the documents of the negotiation, he forbade the Duke of Vicentia to place amongst them that which laid down the conditions on which the allied powers were ready to treat, not wishing to agree to any basis of peace. The Duke of Rovigo undertook to carry to its utmost extremity the indiscretion of his anger. "Your words are very imprudent," he said to the members of the commission, "when there is a Bourbon in the saddle."

"Thus in his great extremity, under the blow of the most startling manifestations, human and divine, the despot at bay made a display of absolute power; the conquered conqueror showed that the negotiations for peace were, so far as he was concerned, only a means of waiting till the chances of war should again turn in his favor, and the tottering head of the new dynasty proclaimed himself that the old dynasty was there, ready to take his place."*

The Senate was more deferential than the Legislative Body, and Fontanes in his speech expressed the wish of the nation under the form of a panegyric. "Sire," said he, "obtain peace by a final effort worthy of yourself and of Frenchmen; and may your hand, so many times victorious, lay its sword aside after securing the repose of the world." It was the senators whom the emperor appointed to go to the departments to stir up patriotic zeal. His last interview with them was touching. Like King Louis XIV., on his death-bed holding in his arms the little prince who was about to become King Louis XV., he acknowledged the wrong which he had done to his people. "I have made too many wars. I formed immense projects, and wished to secure to France the empire of the world. I counted too much upon my good fortune, and must expiate that fault. I shall make peace, and shall do so according as the circumstances require; it will be mortifying to no one but me. It is I who have been deceived, and I ought to suffer, not France; she has freely shed her blood for me, and spared no sacrifice. Tell the French that I no longer claim their efforts for myself and my projects; I ask from

---

* Guizot's *Mémoires pour servir*, Etc., **vol. i.**

them only the means of thrusting back the enemy out of our territory. Alsace, Franche-Comté, Navarre, and Béarn are invaded; I wish to treat on the frontiers, and not in the bosom of our provinces laid waste by a horde of savages. I summon the Frenchmen of Paris, Brittany, Normandy, Champagne, Burgundy, and the other departments, to the assistance of their brothers. To rescue these from the enemy is the only point at issue; there is no longer any question about recovering the conquests which we formerly made."

Napoleon still spoke of peace, but he knew well that at that moment war alone was preparing for France as well as him, a war of fury and desperation. Up to the time of his return from the campaign of Saxony, after the defeat of Leipsic, he wished to beat down the conditions of peace, but his hesitation and falsehood, so much regretted by the allies who were willing to negotiate, supplied arms to those who were hostile. Count Stein, formerly leader of the national rising in Germany against Napoleon, and now governor of the German territories recovered from France, was openly opposed to any pacific overture; and with the Emperor Alexander, whose intimacy he already shared, Count Pozzo di Borgo displayed against the Emperor Napoleon an hereditary hatred, of that sort, both persistent and keen, which is frequently called a Corsican hatred. Sprung from a family always at feud with the Bonapartes, belonging traditionally to the aristocratic party, and defeated in Corsica by the French revolution represented by General Bonaparte, he had run over Europe inspired by his revenge—England, Austria, Russia, Sweden—stirring up enemies against us, provoking annoyance and difficulties, creating or exciting distrust and suspicion. Singularly suited for this task by his political genius, so supple and yet comprehensive, keenly determined to pursue it even to the day when the Emperor Napoleon's deposition was pronounced by the Senate, Count Pozzo di Borgo was soon after to whisper to a lady's ear, when sitting with the diplomatists, "I told you that I should kill him!" At the close of the year 1813, during the terrible crisis which threatened the power and throne of the Emperor Napoleon, he appeared amongst the allies as a skilful adviser, anxious to forewarn them against the perfidies of their adversary, and inspiring the most complete distrust. Henceforth England claimed Antwerp and Flushing. She had again conceived the idea of checking France with that strong barrier which had formerly been the subject of so many nego-

tiations at the time of the threatening conquests of Louis
XIV. ·She wished to establish a kingdom of the Netherlands,
which could protect the coast from the Texel to Antwerp.
The spontaneous insurrection by which Holland had just regained her national independence was of the most important
service to the plans of the English cabinet.

Holland had docilely submitted to the yoke imposed upon
her by revolutionary France, assisted by those parties of her
own citizens who were rending her bosom. She had afterwards seen her burden grow heavier and her chains tighten.
King Louis Bonaparte had reigned with difficulty, and the annexation to the French Empire was the cause of profound dissatisfaction, which was constantly kept alive by their commercial grievances and the crushing load of the conscription.
Partial risings took place, and were severely repressed. When
fortune seemed to desert the Emperor Napoleon, Holland was
worked upon by agents of the allied powers who promised to
support the national movement. The approaches by sea were
blocked by Admiral Missiessy with the fleet of the Scheldt,
and Admiral Verhuell with the fleet of the Texel. Bernadotte
had been appointed to support the Dutch patriots by entering
their territory on the land side, but had directed his forces
towards Denmark, in order to secure the possession of Norway, and was treating with Marshal Davout about the evacuation of Hamburg. The allied princes were annoyed at his
selfish delay, and the prince royal of Sweden was obliged to
detach part of his army against General Molitor, who had a
very small number of troops at his command. When the
general advanced upon Utrecht to guard the line from
Naarden to Gorkum the national insurrection immediately
burst forth at Amsterdam, with shouts of "Long live Orange!"
repeated a thousand times. The Amsterdam patricians, steadfast supporters of the old republic of the United Provinces,
understood that the people ought to rally round the honored
name of the house of Nassau, twice their liberator from the
most cruel oppression. They accepted the popular revolution,
and did not conceal from the Arch-Treasurer Lebrun their
resolution to support the cause of national independence.
Thereupon the French authorities, civil and military, found
themselves no longer able to resist the national movement;
General Molitor withdrew upon the Waal, and Prince Lebrun
took the road to France. All the Dutch towns imitated the
example of Amsterdam. The Prince of Orange did little

after his return. An army of 6000 English landed on the
coast, and the foundation of a kingdom of the Netherlands
became the most important article in Lord Aberdeen's new
instructions. Henceforth the allied powers no longer adhered
to the propositions of Frankfort, which Napoleon at last
agreed to accept as base of the negotiations. Following the
lead of England, the sovereigns now allowed France no other
limits than those of 1790.

Nevertheless, after long hesitation and some dissension
among themselves, which had placed the coalition itself in
danger, the allied armies violated the Swiss neutrality which
the Diet had taken care should be acknowledged even by
Napoleon. The emperor had in fact recalled his troops from
Ticino, declaring that his title of "Mediator of the Confederation" was only intended to recall the services rendered to
Switzerland by France. Some risings which took place in
Berne and several other towns in favor of a counter-revolution, suited the wishes of Prince Schwartzenberg and the purposes of the Austrians. On the 21st December, 1813, the
Austrians and Russians advanced by Berne and Geneva
towards Besançon and Dôle, while the Bavarians marched
upon Belfort. The Prussians with Blücher were between
Mayence and Coblentz, waiting for the moment to cross the
Rhine in their turn, when they at once marched towards the
fortress protecting that river. The allied army amounted to
about 200,000 men. The emperor had sent as quickly as possible his conscripts to Marshals Macdonald, Marmont, and Victor,
who had been appointed to defend the Rhenish frontiers. He
was at the same time organizing an army at Lyons for the
purpose of blocking the roads from Switzerland and Savoy.
Then entrusting old Marshal Kellermann, Duke of Valmy,
with the care of organizing an army of reserve before Paris,
he himself started for Chalons on the 25th January, 1814, after
tenderly bidding his wife farewell, though he did not know it
was the last, and leaving her invested with the cares of the
regency under the direction of the Arch-chancellor Cambacérès. When appointing the council, he openly expressed
his distrust of Talleyrand, whose presence in it he could not
dispense with. "I am well aware," said he, "that I have in
Paris other enemies besides those I am going to fight, and that
my absence will leave them the field open." He had, however, recalled to Paris King Joseph, and recommended the
empress and his son to his care. Murat had by this time

openly completed his defection. The government of the
Spanish Cortes had not replied to the communication of the
treaty concluded with King Ferdinand. Wellington and the
English still threatened the departments of the south, and the
army of Spain was therefore not available. Napoleon had
just sent the Pope to Savona, as a preparation for that restoration of the Roman States which he seemed now to be resolved
upon. He had sent Caulaincourt himself to the head-quarters
of the sovereigns, which was already at Lunéville, ordering
him to demand a reply to the pacific proposals formerly sent
from Frankfort by St. Aignan. "The emperor having adhered to the projected bases," wrote his plenipotentiary, "was
astonished to see negotiation growing languid."

Napoleon's most faithful servants were not deceived as to the
uselessness of the last efforts which he was still putting forth
to defend his tottering power. "We are about to undertake a
task not only difficult, but very useless," said the Duke of
Vicentia, as he left Paris; "do what we may, the era of the
Napoleons is drawing to a close, and that of the Bourbons is
recommencing." Napoleon himself fully realized the terrible
results of that invasion, which he wished to check with exhausted troops, in a country depopulated by war. One of his
ministers * asked him for instructions in case communications
should come to be intercepted between Paris blockaded by the
enemy and head-quarters. "My dear fellow," replied he, "if
the enemy reach the gates of Paris, there is no more empire."

"I have still before my eyes the appearance of Paris," says
Guizot, in his *Mémoires;* "for example, the Rue de Rivoli,
which was then only partly built. No workmen, no movement, materials in heaps unused, deserted scaffolding, erec-
tions abandoned from want of money, hands, and confidence,
new ruins. Everywhere the population seemed uneasy and
restlessly idle, like people who are in want both of work and
rest. On the highways, and in the towns and villages, there
was the same appearance of inaction and agitation, the same
visible impoverishment of the country, many more women and
children than men; young conscripts, sadly on the march to
join their corps; sick and wounded soldiers pouring back to
the interior; a nation mutilated and attenuated. Moreover, in
addition to this physical distress, there was great moral perplexity, the disturbance caused by contrary sentiments; the

* Vieil-Castel, *Histoire de la Restauration,* vol. i.

eager desire for peace, and violent hatred of the foreigner, with the alternatives of anger against Napoleon or sympathy for him; at one time cursed as the author of so many woes, at another celebrated as defender of the country and avenger of her wrongs. There was no enthusiasm in his defence, and but small confidence in his success, but no one made any attempt to oppose him. There were some hostile conversations, several preparatory announcements, some going and coming according to the results anticipated, but nothing more. The emperor acted in perfect liberty, and with all the energy to be expected from his isolation and the moral and physical exhaustion of the country. Never was such public apathy seen in the midst of so much national anxiety, or discontents refraining to such an extent from all action, or agents so eager to disavow their master while remaining so subservient to his purposes. It was a nation of harassed onlookers, who had lost all habit of taking any share themselves in their own lot, and knew not what determination they were to desire or to dread for the terrible drama in which their liberty and national existence were at stake."

The sudden changes in the drama became daily more urgent. Being surprised, with their forces insufficient or badly prepared, the Marshals Victor, Marmont, and Ney found themselves compelled to abandon their positions, and fall back to the river slopes of the Vosges. The departmental administrations withdrew before the enemy, and thus delivered up without resistance Alsace, Lorraine, and Franche-Comté. The population, troubled, disarmed, abandoned to their own resources and suggestions, were divided in their real sentiments by different and contradictory opinions. "Among the well-to-do and intelligent classes the desire for peace, disgust with the demands and speculations of imperial despotism, the certainty of its overthrow, and the near approach of another political rule, were evidently the ruling ideas. The people, on the other hand, only intermitted their weary depression to give themselves up to patriotic rage and revolutionary recollections. No moral union in the country, no common thought or feeling, in spite of a common experience and misfortune."* The old soldiers of Napoleon were still to show prodigies of courage in his name and under his orders; but the conscripts grumbled as they joined their regiments, and many deserted their colors.

* *Mémoires pour servir à l'Histoire de mon Temps.*

When Napoleon reached Chalons-sur-Marne, along with the shouts of "Long live the Emperor!" he heard ringing in his ears, "Down with joint taxes!" As usual, the popular anger first showed itself against the taxes.

"Does your Majesty bring reinforcements?" asked the marshals as they gathered round Napoleon. "No," replied he; and he passed in review the forces whom he had at hand, making an estimate of those who might soon join them. Victor and Marmont had each kept 10,000 men, and Ney reckoned 6000. General Gerard and Marshal Mortier together made up more than 20,000 soldiers, and General Lefebvre-Desnouttes brought from 6000 to 7000. Macdonald was returning from the Ardennes with 12,000 men, and Marshals Soult and Suchet had detached several divisions of the army of Spain, which were coming up with all speed by the Bordeaux road. Bodies of reserve were being prepared at Troyes and on the Seine. At first, in order to meet the attack of 220,000 allies, the soldiers about Napoleon did not amount to 60,000. There was a large supply of excellent artillery, and the emperor revived by his courage all who were disheartened. He occupied all the passages over the Marne, the Aube, and the Seine, fixing his head-quarters at St. Dizier, which he had just recovered from the enemy. Blücher had already set out to join Prince Schwartzenberg on the Upper Marne; and the allied sovereigns met at Langres where Lord Castlereagh had just arrived, the head of the English cabinet, having decided to direct personally the important negotiations which were in preparation. Châtillon-sur-Seine was designated as the seat of the future congress. Caulaincourt had hitherto only received evasive replies, and remained at the advanced posts of the enemy's army. "We are waiting for Lord Castlereagh," was the reply sent him by Metternich.

A favorite disciple of Pitt, and passionately engaged, since the beginning of his political career, in resisting France, whether revolutionary, republican, or absolutist, Lord Castlereagh brought to the congress an influence which was certain to become preponderating. His firmness and simplicity of mind, and resolution of character, well fitted him to play the great part which was reserved for England in the congress of nations. For a long time she had sustained, with her pecuniary resources, a principal share of the burden of the war. She alone had persistently remained hostile to Napoleon, and never became subject to his yoke. Her adhesion or opposition was to decide upon peace or war, and all the powers were disposed

to grant her great concessions. The foundation of the kingdom
of the Netherlands, with the possibility of a matrimonial union
which should bind the new state to the English monarchy, and
the reduction of France to the frontiers of 1790, were the points
fixed at the commencement of the negotiations by the head of
the English cabinet. He did not admit that the question of
maritime rights should even be discussed; and, as soon as his
conditions were accepted, he brought the whole weight of his
influence to bear on the side of moderation, and came to agreement with Austria as to those views and intentions which
were not affected by the question of a French dynasty.
Popular opinion in England was becoming more and more
favorable to the restoration of the house of Bourbon, that
being regarded as necessary to the peace. The diplomatists
assembled at Langres had not yet come to a decision on this
point, though they all foresaw that the question of maintaining
the imperial throne would not occasion dissension in the coalition. The Emperor Francis gave them to understand that he
should not claim the crown for his grandson, if his son-in-law
were overthrown. The idea of placing Bernadotte on the
throne had sometimes occurred to the mind of the Emperor
Alexander.

The plenipotentiaries had already been designated for all the
allied nations: Metternich and Stadion for Austria, Castlereagh and Aberdeen for England, Pozzo di Borgo and Rasou-
moffski for Russia, Wilhelm Humboldt for Prussia. Metternich and Schwartzenberg had proposed that the armies should
remain at Langres to wait for the result of the negotiations;
the two first divisions of the work of the coalition being accomplished—the advance to the Rhine and the invasion of
France—there remained only the march upon Paris to be decided upon. The Austrians were not eager to hasten it, and
thus ensure the triumph of Russia and the passionate vengeance of the Prussians. Blücher baffled those calculations by
the temerity of his operations. The plenipotentiaries had just
started for the Châtillon, and Metternich sent to inform
Caulaincourt, urging him to persuade his master to treat on
this occasion, whatever sacrifices might be imposed upon him.
All at once news was brought that Napoleon had come up to
Blücher when separated from part of his forces, and beaten
him before Brienne (29th January, 1814), after a keenly-contested battle. Prince Schwartzenberg immediately set out
from Langres for the purpose of supporting the Prussians.

On the 1st of February 170,000 allies were collected in the suburbs of Rothière, while the Emperor Napoleon, with 32,000 or 33,000 men, was supported on one side by the Aube, and on the other by the heights of Ajou. The battle recommenced with fury, and, in spite of the frightful disproportion of the forces, Napoleon held his positions till the evening, falling back during the night upon Troyes. He had been obliged to abandon part of his artillery—too important, considering the resources at his disposal, which were reduced by every engagement. The first rush of victorious ardor was already diminishing among the troops, and the population of Champagne made no effort to revive their courage. Napoleon was compelled to reckon upon the faults and crimes of his adversaries, of which he took care to inform Caulaincourt, who had just set out for Châtillon. "The enemy's troops behave everywhere in a shocking manner," he wrote, on the 2nd February; "all the population take refuge in the woods. No peasants can be found in the villages The enemy eat up everything, take all the horses, all the cattle, all the clothes, even to the peasants' rags. They beat everybody, both men and women, and commit crimes of every sort. This picture, which I have seen with my own eyes, must make you easily understand my great desire to extricate my people from this state of misery, and suffering so truly horrible. The enemy will also be obliged to reflect, for the Frenchman is not long-enduring, and is naturally brave; I expect to see them organize themselves into bands. You ought to make an energetic picture of these excesses. Towns of 2000 souls like Brienne have not a single inhabitant."

The proposal of an armistice, made by Caulaincourt, had been rejected by Metternich, without being even communicated to the congress, to the great indignation of the emperor. "The letter which Metternich has addressed to you is quite absurd," he wrote on the 4th and 5th February, to Caulaincourt; "but I see in it what I have long known, that he believes he leads Europe, while everybody is leading him. It is very natural that, at the moment when negotiations are being opened, several days should pass without anything being done, even without making an armistice on that account. To-day I stay at Troyes, expecting to receive news of the congress and conferences of the 3rd. It seems you have only commenced on the 4th. If they wish for peace, and this is not a feint to unanimously prolong the hostilities, they ought to finish promptly, and be able to come to their decisions in the early conferences;

for in fact there will be a general engagement in a few days, which will decide everything. I am now going to Nogent to meet 20,000 men of the army of Spain, who arrive to-morrow and the day after. After that there must be an engagement, to cover Paris. Therefore matters must be decided immediately. Since the allies have already fixed the bases, you ought to have them already. Accept them if they are acceptable; and in the contrary case we run the risk of a battle, and even of the loss of Paris, and all that may result therefrom. I have told Besnardière all that I think on the present state of France, and the necessity of delivering ourselves from these guests, who are burning and robbing the country. You ought already to know how to decide."

That was precisely what Caulaincourt did not yet know. The most absolute secrecy was kept over the terms which were to be offered to France. Our plenipotentiary was unable to learn anything even from Lord Aberdeen, the most moderate, and, so far as we are concerned, the best-disposed of all the diplomatists met at Châtillon. Urged on all sides by his eager councillors, by the fears of the empress, King Joseph, and Louis Bonaparte, the emperor had angrily consented to grant Caulaincourt full liberty of action. That permission did not last long, not having been sincere in Napoleon's mind. A few days afterwards, resuming his military operations, he ordered his minister not to make any haste. Hope was again springing up in that unconquerable soul; but the Duke of Vicentia was unable to share his illusions, as he now knew what were the terms of peace, which no one had dared to enunciate beforehand, and which were now put in place of the Frankfort proposals. To be reduced to her frontiers of 1790, deprived of the conquest both of the republic and the empire, isolated in Europe, and without a vote in the council of the powers about to decide the lot of the countries removed from her authority, and compelled to give an immediate reply to those insulting proposals—such was the abdication which the allied sovereigns claimed the right of imposing upon France, recently still flattered by the hope of keeping the Alps and the Rhine! Caulaincourt's despair was soon increased by being assured that, though he used, in their full extent, the powers which he still possessed, he should not obtain the immediate cessation of hostilities, which was the only possible chance still left of saving Paris. His anger and protestations being in vain, he communicated the sad details of the negotiation to the emperor.

The conferences were suspended at the formal request of the Emperor Alexander. Napoleon had left Troyes, and was again marching against Blücher, watching for the favorable moment when some fault would enable him to recover the upper hand. "There is a probability," he wrote, on the 2nd February, to the Duke of Feltre, "that Blücher's army may advance between the Marne and the Aube, towards Vitry and Chalons; according to circumstances, I shall endeavor to delay the movement of the column, which is now marching, as I am assured upon Paris by Sens, or to return and delay Blücher's march by manœuvring."

"The day was come when even glory no longer is a reparation for the faults which she still conceals. The campaign of 1814, an uninterrupted masterpiece of ability and heroism on the part both of the leader and the soldiers, nevertheless bore the imprint of the false thought and false situation of the emperor. He constantly wavered between the necessity of covering Paris, and his passion to reconquer Europe, wishing to save both his throne and his ambition, and changing his tactics at every moment, according as fatal danger or favorable opportunity seemed to be in the ascendant. God was avenging justice and reason, by condemning the genius who had so often defied them, to succumb in hesitation and doubt under the weight of his irreconcilable desires and impossible resolutions." *

Before falling upon his enemies like a thunderstorm at the head of the heroic soldiers whom he had collected around him, Napoleon took care to destroy the fatal clogs which had so long interfered with his policy. He gave orders to conduct the Pope to Rome, as he might be of service to him by hindering the King of Naples in his treason. He opened the gates of the castle of Valençay to Ferdinand VII., who promised to remain faithful to the treaty recently concluded, the conditions of which he alone could impose upon his people. He ordered Marshal Suchet to evacuate Catalonia, and forward his troops to Lyons; while Prince Eugène was to evacuate Italy, and march in the same direction. Thus 50,000 men of the old troops would threaten the enemy, and might turn them from their march upon Paris.

It was Paris, in fact, that Napoleon wished at any cost to protect, while keenly conscious of the danger with which he was threatened. He had given order that, in case of the approach of the enemy, the King of Rome and the empress should be conducted towards the Loire. Owing to the increasing alarm of the population of the capital, there was some hesitation in following this order, which would naturally throw Paris into terror. On the 8th February the emperor thus wrote from Nogent to his brother King Joseph:—

"I confess that your letter of the 7th was painful to me, because I see no consistency in your ideas, and you are weak enough to listen to the silly opinions of a heap of persons who do not reflect. Now I will speak to you frankly: if Talleyrand for some reason holds that opinion of leaving the empress in Paris if our forces evacuate it, it is an act of treason implying conspiracy. I repeat to you, have no trust in that man. For sixteen years I have had experience of him, and have even shown favor for him, but he is certainly the greatest enemy of our house, now that fortune has for some time abandoned it. Adhere to the advice which I have given you. I know more than those people. Should there occur a lost battle and news of my death, you will be informed of it before my ministers. Cause the empress and the King of Rome to leave for Rambouillet; order the Senate, the Council of State, and all the troops, to assemble on the Loire; and leave to Paris the prefect, or an imperial commissary, or a mayor. Never leave the empress and the King of Rome to fall into the hands of the enemy. Be certain that from that moment Austria would be disinterested, and would carry him off to Vienna in state; and under the pretext of seeing the empress happy, the French would be persuaded to adopt all that the English Regent and Russia might suggest. Thus all our party would find itself overthrown by that horrible league between the republicans and royalists which would have killed it, instead of having, as in the contrary case, an unknown result, on account of the national will and the large number who are interested in the revolution. Moreover, it is possible that on the enemy nearing Paris I may fight them; it is also possible that I may make peace in a few days. It is clear in any case, from your letter of the evening of the 7th, that you have no means for defence. To understand my advice to you, I find your judgment always at fault. Besides, even the interest of the country is inseparable from their persons, and since the world began I have never heard of a sovereign allowing himself to be taken in open towns. The wretched King of Saxony was wrong to let himself be taken at Leipsic: he lost his states, and was taken prisoner. In the very difficult circumstances of the present crisis one does his duty, and leaves the rest to chance. Now, if I live I ought to be obeyed and I have no doubt will be so; if I die, my son and the empress in regency ought, for the honor of the French people, not to allow themselves to be taken, but withdraw to the last village with their last soldiers. Recollect what was said by the wife of Philippe V. What in fact would they say of the empress? That she had abandoned her son's throne and ours. The allies, too, would prefer to make an end by conducting them prisoners to Vienna. I am surprised that you did not think of that. I see that fear is turning all the heads in Paris. As for my opinion, I should prefer that my son's throat be cut rather than ever see him brought up at Vienna as an Austrian prince; and my opinion of the empress is so good that I believe she is also of the same way of thinking, as far as a wife and mother can be so. I never saw Andromache on the stage without pitying the lot of Astyanax in surviving his house, and considering him happy in not surviving his father."

All the edifice which he had erected was now about to be overthrown, more completely than he anticipated, without that favor being reserved for him of being himself struck by the lightning. He had well estimated the misfortune of his son and the sad fate awaiting his Astyanax. The Empress Marie-Louise was not an Andromache.

Then began "the great week," as they termed the final effort of the Emperor Napoleon and France against the crushing mass of their enemies—against the woes and humiliations of invasion, which they had formerly inflicted upon all the peoples now allied against them. The allied sovereigns resolved to force back the emperor towards Paris, by outflanking him, now on one wing, now on the other, so that at last they might throw themselves all together upon his exhausted troops, and destroy him. Blücher had rallied the reinforcements recently arrived, those of York, Langeron, Kleist; and the army of Silesia now amounted to 60,000 men. He advanced according to arrangement with Schwartzenberg, who kept 130,000 men. The Prussians were to operate on the Marne, drive back Marshal Macdonald, who was covering Paris, and take Napoleon in rear in order to hem him in a net of enemies. As the two armies were separating to accomplish their movement, Schwartzenberg, with the view of defending his left flank against the troops which were said to be arriving from Lyons, gradually in-

creased the distance between him and Blücher. Napoleon perceived this, and rushing like a tiger upon his prey, reached
Sezanne, after crossing the marshes of St. Gond on the 10th
February, and fell upon the Russian troops under Olsouvieff,
then occupying the plateau of Champaubert. They were
small in number, and were completely destroyed, the general
and staff being taken prisoners. On the 11th, Napoleon advanced upon Montmirail, in pursuit of Sacken, who was marching along the left bank of the Marne to attack Marshal Macdonald. General York followed the right bank, intending to
cross the river to support Sacken, but the latter had already
been beaten between Épine-aux-Bois and Marchais. On the
12th, York in his turn was attacked at Château-Thierry by
Napoleon's cavalry. The infantry, grouped before the town,
were broken. The French soldiers and those of the allies
fought in the streets, and the inhabitants seconded the emperor's efforts, because they had been ill-treated by the Prussians. The latter had unfortunately destroyed the bridge
over the Marne, and pursuit was momentarily stopped; but
while Napoleon was renewing his communications, Blücher
returned towards Montmirail, and Marshal Marmont, to whom
that district had been entrusted, having too few forces to
oppose him, fell back upon Vauchamps. The emperor ran
thither, and on the 14th, after a keenly-fought engagement,
Blücher was driven back with great loss. By the four engagements with the Silesian army, Napoleon gained 18,000
prisoners, whom he at once sent to Paris, in order to raise the
depressed spirits of the populace. In that, however, he only
succeeded imperfectly, for while Blücher was beaten on the
Marne, Prince Schwartzenberg advanced up the Seine near
the capital. The emperor Alexander, excited against Napoleon by a haughty and vindictive passion, pressed forward
their military movements, and resisted any attempt to reopen
negotiations; he had told Blücher to wait for him before entering Paris. Austria and England, however insisted on the
necessity of conferences; Metternich showed Caulaincourt's
letter, written at Châtillon, to obtain at least a momentary
cessation of arms. It was on this base, supposing all the conditions imposed upon France were accepted, that the preliminaries of peace were drawn up. The severity of the terms
was a concession granted to the Emperor Alexander.

Napoleon had just reached Meaux and Guignes, after rejoining Marshals Victor and Oudinot on the Yères, when he

attacked (on the 17th February) Count Wittgenstein's van, and after beating it marched towards the bridges over the Seine at Nogent, Bray, and Montereau. Some delay in Victor's operations hindered this movement, to the emperor's great annoyance, and thus a keen engagement, which took place at Villeneuve on the 17th under General Gerard's orders, led to no result. It was only on the 18th that the bridge of Montereau could be taken from the Wirtemburgers who defended it. Count Colleredo had had time to withdraw his Austrians. Napoleon advanced upon the Seine against Schwartzenberg's main body, and our troops were already defiling by Montereau to march towards Nogent and Troyes, which were still held by the Emperor Francis.

At the moment he was mounting his horse at Nangis, after the battles of Mormant and Villeneuve, the emperor received an ill-timed request of an audience from Count Parr, Schwartzenberg's aide-de-camp. He had come with the proposal of a suspension of arms, and pleaded the importance of a renewal of conferences as likely at least to diminish the hostilities. Napoleon deferred his reply and pursued his journey towards Montereau, but from this procedure of the allies he derived new hopes and illusions. He wrote immediately to Caulaincourt:—" I gave you carte blanche in order to save Paris, and avoid a battle which was the last hope of the nation. The battle has taken place, and Providence has blessed our arms. I have made from 30,000 to 40,000 prisoners, taken 200 cannon, a large number of generals, and destroyed several armies, almost without striking a blow. Yesterday I made a commencement with the army of Prince Schwartzenberg, and I expect to destroy it before it recrosses our frontiers. Your attitude must remain the same: you should do your best to secure peace, but I wish you to sign nothing without my order, because I alone know my position. If the allies had received your proposals on the 9th, there should have been no battle, and I would not have risked my fortune at a moment when the slightest failure was the ruin of France; moreover, I should not have known the secret of their weakness. It is true I have the advantage of the chances which have turned in my favor. I wish for peace, but not one that would impose upon France more humiliating terms than those of Frankfort. My position is certainly more advantageous than at the time when the allies were at Frankfort: they could defy me; I had gained no advantage over them, and they were far from my territory.

To-day the case is very different. I have had enormous advantages over them, advantages to which a military career of twenty years and some celebrity presents nothing comparable. I am ready to cease hostilities, and allow the enemy to return home undisturbed, if they sign the preliminary bases on the proposals of Frankfort."

While thus detailing the favorable turns his luck had taken, and reckoning his chances, the great gamester seems to have forgot what cards the enemy held in his hand. In his bold illusions he transformed strength into weakness, and dwelt upon the invasion as an argument fatal to the allies. At Châtillon, Caulaincourt bitterly contemplated the reverse of the medal. He had received on the 17th the preliminary project, as severe as the protocol of the 9th, and still more unfeeling in its form, all the sacrifices demanded from France being enumerated at length. According to these terms, hostilities were to cease immediately: the only restitution promised to France was that of Martinique and Guadaloupe, on condition that Sweden should agree to restore that colony, which had been left her by England. Caulaincourt sent the plan to the emperor. The plenipotentiary, hopeless and powerless, had listened in silence to the proposals which were breaking his heart, but his master's rage burst forth, as usual, with a violence that shows itself in the following letter written on the 19th February to Caulaincourt:—

"I look upon you as under restraint, ignorant of my affairs, and influenced by imposters. As soon as I reach Troyes I shall send you the counter-project which you have to give. I thank heaven that I have that document, for there is not a Frenchman whose blood will not boil with indignation at the sight of it. I therefore wish to make my ultimatum myself. I should a hundred times prefer the loss of Paris to the dishonor and annihiliation of France. I am not pleased that you have not formally intimated that France, in order to be as strong as she was in 1789, must have her natural limits in compensation for the partition of Poland, the overthrow of the ecclesiastical system in Germany, and the great acquisitions made by England in Asia. Say that you are awaiting orders from your government, and that it is very natural they should keep you waiting, since your couriers are obliged to make a détour of seventy-two miles, and three of them have already not turned up. I have given orders to arrest the English couriers. I feel so deeply the infamous proposal

which you send me, that it seems a dishonor even to be supposed to be in the circumstances assumed in their proposal. I
shall let you know my intentions at Troyes, but I think I
should rather lose Paris than see such proposals made to the
French people. You are always talking of the Bourbons; I
should prefer seeing the Bourbons in France, on reasonable
terms, to accepting the infamous proposals which you send
me. I repeat to you my command to declare by protocol that
the natural limits only give France the same power which
Louis XVI. had."

While the army was advancing beyond Montereau, the Emperor Napoleon halted in the château of Surville, and took
time to glance over the affairs still under his management in
various parts of Europe, everywhere threatened by the
enemy. Prince Eugène had beaten the Austrians on the
Mincio, and from his delight at this victory the emperor unfortunately determined still to hold Italy in his hands, as a
pledge of his victories, and as something to fall back upon in
the negotiations still pending. Marshal Suchet was obliged to
evacuate Catalonia and withdraw upon Lyons. Soult still
kept Wellington and the English on the Adour, after being
compelled to abandon the line of the Bidassoa, and that of the
Nive. General Maison, with insufficient forces, was defending
our positions in Belgium. Carnot had offered his services to
the emperor, and now held Anvers with a garrison which was
decimated by bombardment. Augereau was at Lyons, exerting himself to organize the recruits and national guards, and
impatiently waiting for the troops from Spain, that he might
join in the campaign, and annoy the allies by taking Chalons
and Besançon. Napoleon thus bitterly reproached him for
delay :—

"The Minister of War has placed before me your letter written to him on the 16th, and it has deeply wounded me. What!
six hours after receiving the first troops arriving from Spain
you had not yet started the campaign! A rest of six hours
was sufficient for them. I gained the battle of Nangis with
the brigade of dragoons come from Spain, though they had
not unbridled since leaving Bayonne. You say the six battalions of the Nîmes division are in want of clothes and equipment and not yet drilled; what a poor excuse to give me,
Augereau! I destroyed 80,000 of the enemy with battalions
composed of conscripts, who had no cartridge-boxes and were
badly clothed! You say the national guards are in a pitiable

condition; I had 4000 of them who came from Angers and Brittany with round hats and wooden shoes, without cart- ridge-boxes, yet I got good work out of them. There is no money, you go on to say; and where do you expect to get money from? You can have none till we have forced our income from the enemy's hands. You are in want of harness; then take it wherever you can find it. You have no stores, you say: but it is quite ridiculous. I order you to set out within twelve hours after receiving this letter, in order to take the campaign. If you are still the Augereau of Castig- lione, retain the command; if your sixty years weigh upon you, resign it in favor of one of your general officers, accord- ing to seniority. You must have a nucleus of more than 6000 men from the best troops. I have not so many, yet I have destroyed three armies, made 40,000 prisoners, taken 200 can- non, and thrice saved the capital. The enemy flies from all quarters towards Troyes. Be there when the ball begins. There is no chance now of doing as in recent years, but we must to saddle, with the resolution of '93! When Frenchmen see your plume at the advanced posts, and see you the first to expose yourself to the musket-balls, you can do with them what you like!"

Napoleon nevertheless left Montereau with 70,000 men, having never since the campaign opened had so many troops at his disposal. He expected to cross the Seine at Méry, reach the neighborhood of Troyes before Schwartzenberg, and then offer him battle after having re-crossed the river. But Blücher had just appeared on the right bank, after speedily rallying all the remains of his forces, and an engagement took place on the 22nd, on the half-demolished bridge of Méry; the town was burnt, and our soldiers were obliged to withdraw. The Emperor took the main road to Troyes, expecting to meet the Austrians and join battle; but Prince Schwartzenberg prudently refrained, and between Chatres and Troyes, Napo- leon received a new proposal of armistice. Being thus con- vinced of the embarrassment of the allies, as well as the reviving superiority of his arms, he avoided replying to the messages of the Austrians and entered Troyes after the re- treating rear-guard of the allied princes had left. On the 21st, at Nugent-sur-Seine, he had written to the Emperor Francis, trying by indirect means to separate him from the coalition, by proving how important were the interests both of his States and his family. The offers of peace on both sides were of no effect. One of the Emperor's aides-de-camp, Count Flahaut, was sent to the enemy's outposts, and a preliminary conference was opened at the village of Lusigny. The single point to consider, said the foreign commissioners, was determining the line of demarkation between the armies while the negotiations lasted. The starting-point and intentions of the belligerents being absolutely contradictory, a rupture was inevitable. Meanwhile hostilities were not suspended, and on the 26th February, Napoleon again left Troyes to march against Blücher.

The Prussian general's ardor frequently chafed against his sovereign's prudence. He addressed himself to the Emperor Alexander, who took share personally in the struggle against Napoleon. On the day after the battles which so nearly annihilated the Silesian army, he asked for the troops of Bulow and Wintzingerode to be added to his own. These 50,000 men served under the Prince Royal of Sweden, who thought of nothing but his conquest of Norway, and the allied sovereigns were afraid lest Bernadotte should take offence, and therefore leave them. He had already shown his annoyance at the protection granted by Austria to Denmark, as well as at the refusal made to admit a Swedish plenipotentiary at the congress. The great powers had undertaken to treat for the small states. When the council of allied princes was met, Lord Castlereagh took upon him the responsibility of obtaining the consent of the Prince Royal of Sweden. The English subsidies were indispensable to Bernadotte, and the English prime minister had besides entirely at his disposal the army lately formed in Holland under the Prince of Orange, the number of which was about the same as the detached corps of the army of the North. Castlereagh placed under Bernadotte these troops in the English pay. At the same time, to avoid the disputes which often threatened the very existence of the coalition, the English plenipotentiary proposed to conclude a treaty between the four great powers, which should bind them solemnly to one another, at first till the conclusion of the existing war, and then for twenty years afterwards. So long as peace was not signed to the satisfaction of the coalition, each of the contracting parties was to furnish a contingent of 150,000 men. After the peace, each power was to maintain an army of 60,000 men for the service of those allies who might be attacked by France. England, moreover, undertook to furnish, during the whole duration of the war, a subsidy of fifty million francs each, yearly, to Russia, Austria, and Prussia. By this bold initiative Castlereagh secured both to his country and himself an indisputable preponderance in the congress, and in all the military or diplomatic resolutions which were taken by the allied powers. The treaty was signed on the 1st of March, at Chaumont, where the sovereigns then had their headquarters. The prolongation of the negotiations at Châtillon was at the same time resolved upon, but for a limited time, and the propositions addressed to Napoleon remained open for a fortnight longer.　If he refused to admit them, the powers were to break all negotiations with him, and thus declare him an outlaw to all Europe.

The formal summons to fulfil engagements was final and complete. Just after the signing of the treaty of Chaumont, Napoleon wrote to Caulaincourt to reiterate his resolution to accept no base of negotiations except the Frankfort proposals, "the minute presented by the plenipotentiaries of the allies not being a proposal, but a capitulation, which in several points is dishonorable to France." He at the same time ordered King Joseph to communicate to the council of the regency the terms offered by the allies, and the replies which he had addressed personally to the Emperor Francis, and officially to the congress of Caulaincourt. "I do not ask a formal opinion," he wrote, "but I am glad to know the various sentiments of individuals." To Cambacérès he wrote: "you will see from what King Joseph communicates how moderate these gentlemen are; just like their soldiers, who pillage, slaughter, and burn everything."

Meanwhile, Marshals Mortier and Marmont, who had been appointed to keep the Silesian army in check, while the emperor was pursuing Prince Schwartzenberg, had scarcely had time to throw themselves into Meaux, while Blücher, henceforth free in his movements, advanced towards the Marne. Napoleon at once conceived the idea of taking him in rear and crushing him between two of his army corps, before the reinforcements brought by Bulow and Wintzingerode could effect a junction. Leaving Marshals Oudinot and Macdonald to guard the Aube, he concealed his march from the enemy, and ordering from Paris some bridge apparatus, which he had for several days previously asked for in vain, he advanced as far as Ferté-sous-Jouarre. Blücher was not expecting him, and after vainly trying to force the line of Ourcq, which was held by the marshals, he fell back on the 3rd of March towards the

Aisne, hoping to join the auxiliary forces. His situation, however, was serious. The emperor was about to cross the Marne, and the bridge of Soissons, the only outlet by which he could cross the Aisne, was in our power, as well as the town. The emperor made haste in order to intercept from the enemy the Rheims road; and after crossing the Marne, he advanced towards Château-Thierry, and then Oulchy; Marmont and Mortier having occupied Fère-en-Tardenois. Blücher was cantoned in the direction of Soissons, when Napoleon halted, on the evening of the 3rd March, at the village of Bézu-St. Germain.

The emperor's soldiers were full of hope, and the 4th was waited for with impatience; but while the army marched to meet Blücher, thus entrapped, the news came of the surrender of Soissons. Moreau, who was in command of the garrison of the town, had lost courage before the threatening and imposing forces of Bulow and Wintzingerode, united round its weak walls, and capitulated without any attempt at resistance. Blücher therefore was now able to cross the Aisne, and effect a junction with his reinforcements. The indignation of Napoleon equalled the consternation of his troops. "The enemy were in the greatest embarrassment," he wrote on the 5th to the minister of war; "we were hoping to reap to-day the fruit of several days of fatigue, when the treason or idiocy of the commandant of Soissons delivered the place up to them. On the 3rd, at noon, he marched out with the honors of war, taking with him four cannon. Let the wretch be arrested, as well as the members of the council of defence; have them brought before a court-martial composed of generals, and in God's name! let the result be that they are shot within twenty-four hours on the Place de Grêve! It is time some examples were made. Let the sentence be printed, with the reasons set forth, posted on the walls and sent everywhere. I am now compelled to throw a trestle-bridge over the Aisne, and must thus lose thirty-six hours, and encounter difficulties of every sort."

General Nansouty, however, had with his cavalry carried the bridge of Berry-au-Bac, which was badly guarded by the Russians; and Napoleon being enabled to cross the Aisne, marched towards Laon. The enemy held all the plateau of Craonne, on the road to that town. The emperor's object then was to beat Blücher before he threw himself back upon Schwartzenberg. On the morning of the 6th, the town of Craonne was attacked and carried; and on the 7th, after a fight lasting till the evening, which cost us a large number of soldiers on account of the strong position of the enemy, and our inferiority at the time in artillery, the plateau was taken, and Blücher compelled to withdraw to the plains of Laon. The bloody victory, however, was useless unless we succeeded in intercepting the enemy's road to Paris; and Marmont was ordered to effect a diversion by bringing his troops out to the plain by the Rheims road, while the emperor led his soldiers by the pass between the Étouvelles heights at Chivy. On the morning of the 9th, Ney forced the passage. Blücher had entrenched himself in the town, and on the rocks defending it like a natural growth in the midst of the plain. He had determined to make a desperate resistance. His forces were twice as many as ours, yet the suburbs were twice taken and retaken. General Charpentier, with two divisions of the young guard, effected a flank movement in order to attack Laon in rear. Marshal Marmont did not arrive; night came before he could push beyond Athies, which he had taken from General York. He took up position there about evening, in a dangerous situation, without proper guard, and being surprised during the night, his conscripts were seized by a panic and ran away, the artillerymen leaving their guns. When the rout halted on the heights of Festieux, the diversion on which the emperor calculated had failed; he wished to attack Laon to carry it, but the Russians were already attacking the positions taken on the previous evening in our rear. All the emperor's attempts upon Laon were useless, so well was it defended by Blücher, and our troops being inferior in number, could not long protect the villages which they had taken. Napoleon decided to fall back upon Soissons, which the enemy had merely passed through. He was dejected, his plan having failed and his situation now rendered dangerous; and a victory gained on the Rheims road against a body of 15,000 men commanded by a French emigrant, Count St. Priest, was not sufficient to raise the dejected spirits of our soldiers. Oudinot and Gerard, after gallantly defending the passage of the Aube, had fallen back upon the Seine, which was still protected by Marshal Macdonald. Schwartzenberg again occupied Troyes, and threatened the Seine from Nogent to Montereau. The conferences of Lusigny had been abandoned.

The Châtillon congress was also soon to be closed. Caulaincourt had not produced the counter-project asked of him, Napoleon having forbidden it. "They cannot insist upon us offering ourselves the sacrifices which they openly propose to force from us," said he. "If they wish to give us a drubbing, the least they can do is not to compel us to give it to ourselves." Caulaincourt had, however, been informed that the last hopes of peace were certainly doomed if he did not consent to offer some proposals. He was made aware by Vitrolles, an agent of the princes, of the intriguing pursued by the royalists at the headquarters of the allies. On the 15th of March he resolved to detail in a memorandum the sacrifices to which France consented: to give up Westphalia, Holland, Illyria, and Spain; to restore the Pope to Rome, and Ferdinand VII. to Madrid. Napoleon claimed an appanage for the Princess Baciocchi and Prince Eugène. He gave up Malta to England, as well as most of her colonial conquests.

The foreign diplomatists were never for a moment deceived. In other words, the emperor was still obstinate in claiming for France her natural limits, the Rhine and the Alps, according to the proposals made at Frankfort. The plenipotentiaries did not enter upon a useless discussion, but declared that the negotiation was broken up. The reply of the sovereigns to the counter-project was to be sent to Caulaincourt on the 17th, and the congress dissolved on the 18th. Lord Aberdeen expressed his intense regret to Caulaincourt; and the latter informed the emperor of the result, at Rheims.

The diplomatic communications addressed to the council of the regency in Paris by no means excited the indignation which Napoleon anticipated. Pliant for fifteen years under his despotic laws, the emperor's highest servants showed no energy at the hour of resistance. They surrendered to him the liberty which he granted them, but a secret instinct, nevertheless, inclined them towards a peace of some sort. A messenger was despatched to the emperor to inquire if it should be his pleasure that the peace so much desired be asked from him by formal procedure. Napoleon's mind was more steadfast than that of his councillors: he despised their prudent weakness, and abused them indignantly in a letter to the Duke of Rovigo:—

"You tell me nothing of what is done in Paris. They are occupied only with clever shifts, the regency, and a thousand intrigues as silly as they are absurd. None of those people ever think that, like Alexander, I am cutting the Gordian knot. Let them be well assured I am the same man I was at Wagram and Austerlitz, that I will have no intrigue in the State, that there is no other authority whatever but mine, and that in an urgent crisis it is the regent that exclusively possesses my confidence. King Joseph is feeble, and allows himself to be led into intrigues which might be fatal to the State, and especially to himself and his plans, unless he promptly returns to the right course of conduct. Mark well, that if they had drawn up an address contrary to authority, I should have arrested the king, my ministers, and all who had signed it. They are spoiling the national guard, as well as Paris, through their weakness and ignorance of the country. I will have no tribune of the people. Let it not be forgotten that I am the great tribune. The people will then act always as is suitable to their true interests, which are the object of all my thoughts."

At almost the same moment (12th March), as if to prove to the very last day the unconquerable pride which sprang up more indignantly than ever when surrounded by adversity, the emperor wrote to King Joseph: "I am pained to see that you have spoken to my wife about the Bourbons, and the opposition which might be made by the Emperor of Austria. I beg of you to avoid such conversations. I have no wish to be protected by my wife. Such a notion would spoil her and compromise us. Let her live as she has lived; say nothing to her of what she should know before signing; and above all avoid any conversation which might lead her to think that I agree to be protected by her or her father. For four years the word Bourbon or Austria has never passed my lips. The Emperor of Austria can do nothing, because he is weak, and led by Metternich, who is in the pay of England—that is the secret of the whole. . . . You always write as if the peace depended upon me, yet I sent you the documents. If the Parisians wish to see the Cossacks, they will have cause to repent; still the truth should be told them."

The agitation in Paris constantly increased, not only on account of the rupture of the negotiations for peace, the successive checks to Napoleon's most skilful manœuvres, but of the new arrivals from the south of France. Soult, slowly driven by Wellington, had to leave Bayonne, blockaded by the enemy, and, after leaving the river at Oléron, fell back upon that at Pau, in the suburbs of Orthez, where he was attacked by the English on the morning of the 27th February, over a long line of defence. Generals Reille and Clausel kept their positions, but the marshal would not risk a second battle with the loss of the only French army which still remained complete. He abandoned the Bordeaux road, which he had been ordered to cover, and marched towards Toulouse, hoping to draw the enemy in pursuit. Wellington did, in fact, follow him, but after detaching General Hill for Bordeaux. The English were well informed as to the state of public opinion in the south of France, which has always been favorable to extreme parties, and was then somewhat influenced by royalist agents. The Duke of Angoulême, eldest son of Count d'Artois, had not been admitted to the English head-quarters; but when the gates of Bordeaux were opened without resistance to the English columns, the prince was at the same time summoned by the spontaneous action of the citizens. He hastened to respond, and the restoration of the Bourbons was proclaimed by the mayor, in the midst of shouts of joy from the merchants who had been ruined by the continental blockade. There was none who misunderstood the official protest of Wellington against the Bordeaux manifestation. The example was dangerous, and the popular excitement increased. The yoke began to weigh heavily on the shoulders of all as soon as ever the possibility of shaking it off appeared on the horizon. Nevertheless, the emperor had no fear of a popular excitement in Paris resembling that of Bordeaux; he was then planning a great movement towards the north, which should enable him to rally all his garrisons, and intercept the communications of the allies with Germany. It was, moreover, necessary to withdraw from the capital, now threatened from every quarter. Napoleon resolved to attempt another blow at Prince Schwartzenberg.

The latter had fallen back upon Troyes, summoning round him his scattered forces, which the Czar Alexander thought were threatened by Napoleon. This retreating movement confirmed the emperor in his intention of marching eastward in the meantime. He therefore went towards Arcis-sur-Aube, without waiting to encounter the Bohemian army. Several general officers had informed him of Schwartzenberg's concentrations, but he would not believe it. On the the 20th of March, between Troyes and Arcis, he found himself face to face with the enemy. The first charge of the Russian cavalry threatened the emperor's person, and a Polish battalion had scarcely time to form in square for his protection. A few minutes afterwards a shell fell at his feet, and severely wounded his horse. Ney defended the village of Grand-Farcy, and General Friant

HF (E)   Vol. 8

came up with the old guard. The soldiers, though only one against three, fought everywhere with prodigious valor, but all their efforts could only succeed in rendering the result doubtful. "Your Majesty has no doubt other resources, which we are not aware of?" asked General Sebastiani in the very midst of the fight. "Nothing more than is before your eyes," replied Napoleon. "Then, why does your Majesty not think of a general rising?" "Such ideas are purely chimerical, my dear Sebastiani, fine recollections of Spain and the French revolution! A general rising in a country where the revolution destroyed the nobles and priests, and where I myself have destroyed the revolution!"

The emperor had destroyed the life and strength of the revolution, and the national vigor by which the country was formerly defended; but he had not extinguished the revolutionary germs—so much the more full of life that the despotism had long diverted France from the real and earnest government of its affairs. He had exhausted the military ardor by constant misuse of it, and the wearied country called aloud for rest. That is what Caulaincourt tried to make him sensible of, when he again met him at St. Dizier, to which Napoleon had transferred his head-quarters after the indecisive and useless engagement at Arcis-sur-Aube, from a conviction that he could not at once risk a second battle without absolutely compromising his subsequent operations. "You did well to return," said the emperor; "if you had accepted the ultimatum of the allies, I should have disavowed you. They wish to ruin us, or weaken us till we are reduced to nothing. Death is preferable to that. We are old enough soldiers to have no fear of death. But you are going to see something worth while. The enemy are evidently following me. Schwartzenberg has not dared to advance upon Paris, because he knows that I threaten his communications. As soon as I have rallied the 30,000 or 40,000 men in the garrisons, I shall burst like a lightning-cloud upon whoever is nearest, Blücher or Schwartzenberg, no matter which, and crush him, leaving the peasants of Burgundy to finish. The coalition is as near its ruin as I am to mine."

The most faithful of Napoleon's servants could not be deceived by such language, whether sincere or pretended; and the allies had not allowed themselves to be so far drawn by military considerations as to despise political combinations. They knew well that the war could only finish at Paris; and did not anticipate much resistance before its walls. The general discontent, the weariness caused by the empire, and the crushing load which weighed down men of every class, were betrayed by too certain proofs for the Emperor Francis to be now deceived as to the stability of his daughter's throne. The thought of a general march upon Paris gradually rallied men of the greatest prudence. Intercepted letters from the empress, King Joseph, and the Duke of Rovigo confirmed the sovereigns in their convictions as to the moral and political state of the capital. The Emperor Alexander and the King of Prussia resolved to advance; the Emperor of Austria remained behind. He could not himself go to the gates of Paris arms in hand. Schwartzenberg and Blücher had effected the junction of their armies. Wintzingerode was appointed to watch Napoleon's movements with 10,000 horse. On the 25th March, the allied armies commenced their march to Paris.

Marmont and Mortier, left behind to defend the Aisne, had been obliged to abandon their positions in presence of superior forces. They at first fell back upon Fismes, with the view of rejoining the emperor by Château-Thierry; but being separated by the whole army of the enemy from the eastern road, they resolved to advance towards Paris to cover the capital, and meantime made an appointment together for Sommessons, with the object of retreating as far as Fère-Champenoise. The Generals Pacthod and Compans, at the head of detached corps, took the same direction. On the 25th, at mid-day, just after the two marshals had met, they were suddenly attacked by the allied army; and after bravely defending the position which they had taken on the road, between two hollows, found themselves obliged to retreat slowly, overwhelmed by the enemy's fire and whirlwinds of heavy hail. General Pacthod's corps, almost entirely composed of national guards, was surrounded by the enemy. Before these improvised soldiers would agree to surrender, the Emperor Alexander was obliged to send them one of his aides-de-camp to stop the fighting. The losses of our little army were irreparable. The marshals had difficulty in avoiding being taken by the enemy. On the 29th they arrived under the walls of Paris; several other corps rallied round them, 20,000 or 25,000 men of the regular troops, and 10,000 or 12,000 of the national guards. Such were the resources to be disposed of for the defence of the capital, then without fortifications. We have seen the ramparts of Paris prolong the resistance without, however, sufficing to save France when invaded, but the Council of the Regency and

Napoleon's lieutenants scarcely had ordinary walls; and the population of Paris were not disposed to attempt such efforts of heroism as they did in recent times. After a stormy and long-continued deliberation, the majority of the Council insisted upon requesting that the empress and King of Rome should remain in Paris. Talleyrand strongly pleaded for this. King Joseph produced the emperor's formal commands, such as that given on the day after the battle of Rheims:—"You must under no circumstances allow the empress and the King of Rome to fall into the hands of the enemy. Should they advance towards Paris with such forces that resistance is impossible, then the regent empress, my son, the great dignitaries, the ministers, the officers of the Senate and presidents of the Council of State, the grand officers of the crown and treasury, must leave, and go in the direction of the Loire. Do not leave my son; and remember that I should rather know he was at the bottom of the Seine than in the hands of the enemies of France. The fate of Astyanax as prisoner with the Greeks always seemed to me the most unhappy fate in history."

The Council gave way, and the empress, turning to her brother-in-law and her husband's most intimate servants, said, "Tell me what I must do, and I shall do it." Nobody dared to advise her to disobey Napoleon's wish, so clearly expressed. Going out on a last reconnoitring expedition, King Joseph and the Duke of Feltre found that Paris was surrounded by the armies of the enemy, against which they could only make a pretended resistance. The carriages were standing ready, with the crowd looking on, silent and gloomy, like people who are deserted by those who ought to protect them. The last extremity of pain and disgrace could not reach Paris so long as her sovereigns made it their residence. Several officers of the national guard obtained admission to the empress, and entreated her to stay. She wept, full of hesitation and alarm. The King of Rome asked what they wished to do, and refused to go into the carriage, clinging to the curtains of the palace which he was about to leave forever. The long train of imperial carriages took the road to Rambouillet, escorted by 200 soldiers of the old guard, whose sorrow was more bitter than that of the courtiers, full of consternation at the fall of grandeur. The all-powerful emperor was again become an adventurer.

Meanwhile Paris was full of disturbance. The preparations for the defence were confused, bandied from General Hullin, gov-

ernor of the city, to Marshal Moncey, who commanded the
national guard. These again had no muskets, and scarcely
half of them were armed. Several guns were placed on the
heights of Montmartre, St. Chaumont, and Charonne, but they
had not enough of harness for the artillery. No horses were
requisitioned from private persons, and nowhere were barricades thought of. A recollection of old times crossed M. Real's
mind, when he proposed to the Duke of Rovigo that they
should take up the paving-stones from the streets and throw
them down upon the enemy, at the same time firing at them
from the windows of the houses. "Why, that is a revolutionary mode of defence," exclaimed General Savary; "I shall
most certainly not do that. What would the emperor say?"

The resistance of Paris was to be confined to a battle before
the octroi-wall, between 29,000 soldiers and 170,000. The result
was known beforehand, and it was the remains of their honor
and ours which the two marshals defended. Mortier took his
station at the foot of the heights of Montmartre, his right resting on the Ourcq canal and his left on Clignancourt. Marmont
was to occupy the plateau of Romainville, and extend as far as
Prés-St.-Gervais. When he advanced towards the heights, the
advanced guard of Barclay de Tolly was already posted there,
but it was driven back, and the marshal's troops deployed
between Charonne and Vincennes: Montreuil and Bagnolet
were occupied. The enemy's armies, divided into three columns under the orders of Barclay, the Prince Royal of Wurtemberg, and Blücher, were to attack on the east, south, and
north; Romainville, the Barrière du Trône, and the heights of
Montmartre being the points threatened.

It was at the last post that King Joseph had fixed his head-
quarters. On the morning of the 30th there was already some
fighting in the east of Paris, and the plateau of Romainville
was several times taken and retaken. Blücher and the Prince
of Wurtemberg had not yet arrived. The generals, however,
were not deceived with false hopes; the soldiers said they were
determined to be killed to the last man, but Paris would certainly be compelled to surrender. This news, and the sight of
the enemy's columns on the horizon, filled up the measure of
King Joseph's alarm, being fully resolved not to fall into the
enemy's hands. He deliberated with the ministers who still
remained with him, and they all advised him to fly, urging
that the emperor had given that order beforehand. Joseph set
out, accompanied by the Duke of Feltre, and Paris was now

left without government, and its defenders without any political supervision. Only one order was sent to the marshals, in these terms:—"If M. le Marshal Duke of Ragusa and M. le Marshal Duke of Trevisa cannot hold their ground, they are hereby authorized to enter into pourparlers with the Prince of Schwartzenberg and the Emperor of Russia now before the walls.   "JOSEPH.

"Montmartre, 30th March, 1814, at a quarter past twelve, noon.—They will withdraw upon the Loire."

Thus abandoned to themselves, with no hope but that of a glorious death, the generals in command everywhere joined battle. Blücher, after approaching Montmartre with caution, because he thought this important point was strongly fortified, took possession of it without difficulty. The Prince of Wurtemberg carried the bridge of Charenton against the national guards and the pupils of the Alfort School. Some vigorous fighting took place at Pantin, Bagnolet, and Charonne. Romainville was on the point of being taken by the enemy, when Marshal Marmont made a charge, sword in hand, against the enemy's centre, but was driven back, and very nearly made prisoner. The defence was concentrated upon Belleville and Ménilmontant. Mortier still held Villette, and the fighting there was keenly contested. The pupils of the Polytechnic School had been vigorously attacked at the Barrière du Trône, but they succeeded in holding their ground, though many were killed by their guns. A rumor ran that the emperor had arrived, but it was without foundation; General Dejean alone had succeeded in passing the enemy's posts, announcing Napoleon's approach. It was sufficient, he said, to hold out two days, for the army to come and back the efforts of the brave defenders of Paris; the emperor was already advancing with his staff to the assistance of the capital, hastening across the country by relays of horses, and they must make an attempt to gain time. The emperor had written to the Emperor Francis, proposing to reopen the negotiations; and Schwartzenberg, as soon as he was informed of it, would most certainly grant a suspension of arms. Marshal Mortier, having heard this from General Dejean, immediately sent an orderly to the prince. Marmont had already twice sent messengers, but they had been killed before reaching the generals of the enemy, and his third emissary reached Prince Schwartzenberg at the same time as the officer bearing Mortier's request. "I have had no information of the renewal of negotiations," said the Austrian general, "and therefore cannot grant an armistice; but it depends upon the marshals to put a stop to this butchery, if they agree to deliver up Paris to me immediately." Several hours previously, when Marmont received the authorization to treat which was sent by Joseph, he replied that they were not yet come to that. Now, at mid-day, with his back against the octroi wall, driving back the enemy, some of whom were already advancing into the Rue du Temple, fighting himself like a soldier in the ranks, on foot, in the midst of his officers falling around him, the marshal had no resource left but capitulation. An aide-de-camp had reached the château of Bondy where the Emperor Alexander and the King of Prussia were. " It is not my intention to do the least harm to the town of Paris," said the Czar; " it is not upon the French nation that we are waging war, but upon Napoleon." " And not upon himself, but upon his ambition," added Frederick William. The suspension of arms was granted, and the only point at issue was the withdrawal of the army and the capitulation of Paris. The terms of agreement were drawn up at Villette between the marshals, Nesselrode and a few of the enemy's officers. The allies at first declared they would insist upon the defenders of Paris giving up their arms; they also insisted upon their withdrawal to Brittany. These two articles having been rejected, the marshals remained at liberty to direct the movements of their troops as they pleased. The convention, generally termed the " Capitulation of Paris," was confined to several articles exclusively military:—

" The corps of the Marshals the Dukes of Trevisa and Ragusa will evacuate the town of Paris on the 31st March, at seven o'clock, forenoon. They will take with them their regimental property and furniture. Hostilities cannot be resumed till two hours after the evacuation of the town, viz., on the 31st March, at nine o'clock, forenoon. All the military arsenals, workshops, establishments, and stores will be left in the same state as they were in before the present capitulation was discussed. The national or city guard is entirely distinct from the troops of the line, and will be preserved, disarmed, or disbanded according as the courts appointed by the allies may think proper. The municipal gendarmes corps will be treated exactly as the national guard. The wounded or marauders who remain in Paris after seven o'clock, will be prisoners of war. The town of Paris is committed to the generosity of the high allied powers."

Such was the convention signed on the 30th March, at six o'clock, afternoon, by the marshal's aides-de-camp, in a small public-house in Villette, in the midst of the disturbance and consternation which were reigning in the capital. Her last defenders were making their preparations to leave; Marshal Marmont, his face blackened with gunpowder, and his clothes torn by balls, was surrounded by his friends in his house in the Rue Paradis-Poissonnière. "And Paris?" they exclaimed, when he had announced the conditions of the armistice. "Paris is no business of mine; I am only leader of a corps, and my troops have done all that was humanly possible to do. I fall back upon Fontainebleau, where the emperor is. A capitulation will be made for Paris." It was at last decided that the two prefects of police and administration should wait upon the allied sovereigns, to obtain the treatment to which Paris was entitled. These were the only remains in Paris of the imperial government. Clear-sighted men could already distinguish the aurora of new influences. Talleyrand did not leave Paris along with the court.

Meanwhile the Emperor Napoleon had reached as far as Fromenteau, being himself in advance of the whole army. Retained for several days in the neighborhood of St. Dizier and Vassy, by the vain hope of fighting Schwartzenberg's army, which he thought was still following him, he was able to see, by a well-fought battle between St. Dizier and Vitry, that the only troops behind him were a cavalry-corps. One of the enemy's bulletins, also, which had fallen into his hands, informed him of the affair at Fère-Champenoise, from which he inferred the movement of the allied armies upon Paris. Napoleon hesitated, inclined to follow up his plan, so that he might attack the enemy when he should have collected some forces; but the troops were seized with excitement, and all asked to march to the assistance of Paris. The danger of the capital implied that of many families, and threatened the honor of France. The emperor was obliged to yield. Always rapid in his resolutions, he advanced by forced marches, being conscious, moreover, of the imminent danger, and suspecting, not without reason, that it was too late to save Paris. He hurried his journey as far as Villeneuve-l'Archevêque, where he threw himself into a carriage and flew towards Paris. At Fromenteau, about midnight, he was told that a body of cavalry were approaching. "Who is there?" he exclaimed. "General Belliard." Napoleon stepped out of the carriage and drew the general to the road side. "Where is the army?" he asked. "Sire, it is coming behind." "And the enemy?" "At the gates of Paris." "And who holds Paris?" "Nobody, it is evacuated." "What! evacuated? And my son, my wife, the government, where are they?" "On the Loire, sire." "On the Loire! who sent them there?" "Sire, it was said to be by your orders." "My orders did not imply that. Where is King Joseph, and Clarke, and Marmont, and Mortier?" "Sire, we did not see King Joseph or the Duke of Feltre; the marshals did all that it was possible for men to do. A defence was made in every part, and the national guards fought like soldiers. We had nothing, not even cannon! Ah! sire, had you been there, you and your troops!" "No doubt, if I had been there,—but I cannot be everywhere. Joseph lost Spain, and now he is losing me France! And Clarke, too; if I had believed that poor Rovigo, who always kept telling me that he was a coward and traitor! But we must go there at once! My carriage, Caulaincourt!" The officers threw themselves before the emperor, to stop him as he proceeded to walk along the road. "It is impossible, sire! It is too late! There is a capitulation! The infantry is behind us, and will presently reach us." Some of the detachments were already coming in sight. Napoleon let himself fall by the roadside, holding his head in his hands and hiding his face. The onlookers, with heartfelt sorrow, silently stood by him. On that solitary road, at the dead of night, the grand empire, founded and sustained for fifteen years by the incomparable genius and commanding will of one man alone, had now crumbled to pieces, even in the opinion of him who had raised it.

CHAPTER XVI.

THE FIRST RESTORATION (1814—1815).

THE Bourbons had long been forgot by Europe, even when showing some kindness personally to the princes of that illustrious race. England alone had occasionally supported them in their attempts, but the support was always insufficient and late. The French princes paid little attention to the noble effort made by the country gentlemen and peasants in Vendée; when they believed the dying spark could be revived they encouraged the Quiberon expedition, but without resolving to share in it themselves. The Count d'Artois had something to do with the conspiracy of Georges and Pichegru, and his personal friends were engaged in it. The emigrants were divided into two classes, the "observers" and the "conspirators," so termed during the last days of the monarchy according to their bias, one towards Monsieur, the other the Count d'Artois. The advisers differed in like proportion; so long as men of eager and rash disposition fostered the count's illusions, and encouraged him to believe that it was impossible to return to the past, Monsieur, or "the king," as the emigrants now called him, chose, amongst the most liberal and sensible of the royalists in Paris, some friends for the purpose of letting him know the state of public opinion, and managing his affairs. This "royal council" was composed of only four persons, chosen by Royer-Collard, one of them being the Abbé Montesquiou. On the 18th Brumaire, Clermont-Gallerande, who was also a member, received from Louis XVIII. instructions to lay before the first consul certain proposals of alliance. His credentials were conceived in the following terms:—"I give to the bearer of these presents all necessary power to treat in my name with General Bonaparte. I do not instruct him to propose either conditions or recompences to that general. The faithful interpreter of my sentiments will give him the assurance that all that he may ask for his friends will be granted immediately after my restoration. The safety of my people will be the guarantee of my faithfulness in fulfilling my promises."

At first no reply was sent to the prince's letter. When he made a second attempt, Bonaparte's refusal was as peremptory as was afterwards that of Louis XVIII. in 1803, to the proposal that he should renounce his claim to the throne. "I do not confound M. Bonaparte with those who have preceded him," replied the king to the President of the Diet of Warsaw, who had been entrusted with that commission by the first consul. "I owe him thanks for several acts of his administration, because the good done to my people will always make me grateful; but he is deceived if he thinks to persuade me to traffic with my rights: so far from that, he himself by his present procedure would strengthen them, if they could become matter of dispute. I know not what may be God's purposes regarding my race and myself, but I know what are the obligations he has laid upon me by the rank to which by His will I have been born. A Christian, I shall fulfil those obligations till my latest breath; the son of St. Louis, I should be able like him to act worthily even in chains; the successor of Francis I., I wish to be able at least to say as he did, ' All is lost, save honor.' " Royer-Collard in name of the secret Council wrote a long letter to Louis XVIII., approving and commenting on the prince's conduct; which letter was published afterwards, when a serious disagreement broke out between the restored Bourbons and their wisest and best servants.

As the princes of the house of Bourbon had protested against the crimes of the revolution, so they protested against the setting up of a throne which they were not called upon to occupy. "By taking the title of emperor," said Louis XVIII. in his protest of the 5th June, 1804, "and wishing to render it hereditary in his family, Bonaparte has just put the seal to his usurpation. The new act of a revolution in which everything from the first has been without legal effect, can certainly not weaken my rights; but accountable for my conduct to all the sovereigns, whose rights are not less assailed than mine by the principles which the Senate of Paris has dared to put forward, I should consider myself a traitor to the common cause by keeping silence on this occasion. I therefore declare, in presence of all the sovereigns, that far from acknowledging the imperial title which Bonaparte has just got bestowed upon himself by a body which has not even a legal existence, I protest against that title, and against all the subsequent acts to which it may give place."

The protest was of no use, as was well enough known by the prince who pronounced it. Several months later (2nd December, 1804), to satisfy the need for action felt by Count d'Artois and his friends, he published a declaration promising to uphold all the rights gained by the revolution. " My proclamation contains everything," he wrote to Mittau. "Is it the military question? The soldier's rank and employment are retained, promotion according to length of service—all are secured. Is it a question of a public man? He will be continued in office. Or one of the lower orders? The conscription, that tax of persons, the most burdensome of all, will be abolished. Or a new proprietor? I declare myself the protector of the rights and interests of all. Or, finally, those who are guilty? Prosecutions will be forbidden : a general amnesty is announced. Nevertheless everything, in France and without, since the beginning of the Revolution, turns in a vicious circle. Placed between two parties, I cry to both ' You are

wrong!' But my voice is not heard by the one, or listened to
by the other."

Dating from this formal declaration, which he considered
due to his family and the monarchical traditions, Louis XVIII.
aimed at nothing more than a quiet and dignified retreat.
This he long found at Mittau, remaining an entire stranger
to the intrigues in the midst of which the Count d'Artois was
actively employed. When the Emperor Alexander, conquered
and cajoled at the same time by Napoleon, gave the illustrious
exile to understand that his presence in Courland was troublesome, the prince asked for an asylum in England, the only
nation in Europe that still refused to acknowledge the all-
subsiding power of the Emperor of the French. It was a characteristic proof of this power that the English cabinet for a moment hesitated to receive Louis XVIII. He was at last allowed
to reside in England, and had lived there seven years when the
tottering state of Napoleon's throne again revived the hopes of
the few friends who remained true to his cause. England
openly showed her indifference for the royalist cause:—"The
only opinion I can form," wrote Wellington to Lord Bathurst,
"is that twenty years having elapsed since the princes of the
house of Bourbon left France, they are as much, and perhaps
more unknown there, than the princes of any other royal
family in Europe; that the allies should agree amongst themselves to propose to France a sovereign in place of Napoleon,
who must be got rid of before Europe can ever enjoy peace;
but that it matters little whether it be a prince of the house of
Bourbon or one of any other royal family." The English general wrote this at the time when the Duke d'Angoulême followed his army, without ever being able to obtain an intro-
duction. The Duke de Berry's stay in Jersey produced no
rising of the royalists in Vendée or Brittany. Count d'Artois,
after crossing the eastern frontier along with the allied armies,
had great difficulty in obtaining permission to pass through
Vesoul from the Austrian general in command of the place.
The Russians allowed him to enter Vesoul on condition that
he came alone, without cockade or decorations, took no political title, and occupied no public building. The allied sovereigns were on their guard against every manifestation which
might give a dynastic color to their political or military action.
They were not disposed to lend an ear to the urgent requests of
the royalists, nor to place much confidence in their declared
assurance as to the state of public opinion. "If they were to

give up treating with Bonaparte," said Vitrolles to the Emperor Alexander, "and march upon Paris, determined to allow public opinion full liberty, it would declare itself. I leave my head in your Majesty's hands, and am willing that it should fall at the block, if Paris—if public opinion, does not declare itself."

Vitrolles was bold, enterprising, and unscrupulous. His supple and subtle mind was well-suited for intrigue. He had risked his liberty, and even his life, by coming to Châtillon to sound the secret intentions of the powers with reference to the Emperor Napoleon. Two unfortunate gentlemen had displayed the white colors of the royalists at Troyes during the stay of the allies in that town, and when Napoleon regained possession of it one of them, named Gault, was shot. Vitrolles was sent to Châtillon to prove to Stadion, his former friend, the identity of the Duke of Dalberg. Around Talleyrand and his intimate friends there had already begun a movement in favor of the new posture of affairs, and he did not oppose it, though he refrained from taking an active share in it. The Emperor Napoleon's distrust, and unmistakable weakness of his fortune, had, however, determined the quondam bishop, afterwards vice-grand-chancellor under the imperial rule. The instinct of the race, his personal interest, and a sense of the wants of the country, all combined in Talleyrand's mind to separate him henceforth from the threatened dynasty. When King Joseph left Paris, a few hours after the capital was invested by the enemy, Prince Benevento proceeded to follow; but the guard stationed at the gates showing some resistance, he returned to Paris without insisting upon it. Before the departure of the marshals for Fontainebleau he had an interview with the Duke of Ragusa, and strove by arguments to weaken his military fidelity to a chief who was no longer accompanied by victory. As soon as the allied sovereigns took possession of Paris, they were careful to request Talleyrand to remain.

On the 30th March, 1814, was seen the first declaration of the allies in Paris, signed by Prince Schwartzenberg as generalissimo. It clearly announced their intention of no more treating with the Emperor Napoleon.

"Inhabitants of Paris," it said, "the allied armies are now before your walls. The object of their advance upon the capital of France is the hope of a sincere and lasting reconciliation with her. For twenty years Europe has been flooded with

blood and tears. The attempts to put a stop to so much wretchedness have been in vain, because there exists in the very
power of the government which oppresses you an insurmountable obstacle to peace. Who is the Frenchman that is not convinced of the truth of this? The allied sovereigns are sincerely
anxious to find a tutelary authority in France that can cement
the union of all nations and governments with her. It belongs
now to the city of Paris, in the present crisis, to hasten the
peace of the world. Let her declare herself, and immediately
the army now before her walls becomes the supporter of her
decisions. Parisians! you know the situation of your country,
the conduct of Bordeaux, the occupation of Lyons, the evils
brought upon France, and the real inclinations of your fellow-
citizens. You will in these examples see the limit of foreign
war and civil discord. Make haste to reply to the confidence
placed by Europe in your love for your country and in your
good sense." Preparations were already being made for the
entry next day into Paris of the allied sovereigns.

We have in our time heard words less sympathizing, and,
like our fathers, have known the anguish caused by the faults
and reverses of absolute power. The population of Paris remained calm and dejected. When, on the 31st, the allied sovereigns approached the rich quarters, they were hailed with
the joyful shouts of a band of royalists, who displayed the
white Bourbon flag, and welcomed with delight Napoleon's
conquerors. Women gave way to the same enthusiasm. By
the hope of peace their children were snatched from deadly
danger; several of them distributed white cockades. This display of different passions, which had long been silently repressed, was confined to a small number of houses and streets.
When the Emperor Alexander, who marched in front, and attracted the looks of all, reached the hotel in the Rue St. Florentin which Talleyrand had put at his disposal, a large crowd
gathered round the doors, full of curiosity and adulation. In-
doors, earnest negotiations had begun.

It is a characteristic of critical junctures that they bring to
the front those men who are destined to exercise preponderating and decisive influence upon human events. By his foresight and acuteness Talleyrand prepared beforehand the place
which he was to take in that formidable crisis of our destinies,
no one disputing it with him, and the allied sovereigns at once
acknowledged him as the natural and inevitable plenipotentiary
of France. Caulaincourt, who had been sent by Napoleon, was

received by the Czar at Bondy; but he obtained nothing but courteous expressions, and the sad conviction that his master was to be opposed. On his return to Paris for the purpose of renewing the attempt, he had secretly resolved to accept, if need were, the Châtillon terms of peace. He considered the contrary resolutions were emphatically expressed.

On March 31st, a proclamation from the allied princes was everywhere posted up.

"The armies of the allied powers have occupied the capital of France. The allied sovereigns respond to the prayer of the French nation. They declare:—

"That whilst material guarantees were necessarily included in the terms upon which peace could alone be concluded when it was a question of restraining the ambition of Bonaparte, yet these terms must be made more favorable when by an inclination towards good government France offers assurances of tranquillity.

"The allied sovereigns consequently proclaim that they will no longer treat with Napoleon Bonaparte, nor with any member of his family; that they respect the integrity of ancient France, as it existed under its legitimate kings; they may even do more than that, for they acknowledge the principle that for the welfare of Europe it is necessary for France to be great and strong.

"That they will recognize and guarantee the Constitution which the French Nation shall form for itself. Accordingly they invite the Senate to appoint a provisional government which may provide for the necessities of administration, and prepare such a constitution as may meet the views of the French people."

Such were the results of the conferences which had taken place in the morning between the allied sovereigns, Talleyrand, and the Duke of Dalberg. Upon one point only were the victorious allies thoroughly agreed—the downfall of the Emperor Napoleon, the author of all the evils that oppressed Europe, the insatiable conqueror whom no treaty of peace could bind. The regency of the Empress Marie-Louise, Prince Bernadotte, even the republic, all seemed to offer certain advantages. The preferences of the allies in favor of the house of Bourbon were as yet only feeble. Lord Castlereagh was not present to plead their cause; Talleyrand took charge of it. So far as he was concerned he had fully made up his mind. A member of the Constituent Assembly, a great nobleman and a bishop, he had been too close an eye witness of the terrible tragedies resulting from revolutionary fury and of the humiliations of the Directory to believe in the possibility of the re-establishment of the republican *régime.* His clear judgment rejected the idea of government by Marie-Louise in the name of an infant—the imperial dynasty with all its faults, and without its power, under the continual menace of a despot banished in vain. He did not tolerate for a moment the absurd idea of the elevation of Bernadotte to supreme power; the Bourbons alone could assure tranquillity to France. France could exact from them guarantees for its liberties. "The republic is an impossibility; the regency, or Bernadotte, means nothing but perpetual intrigue; the Bourbons alone represent a principle." Such was the sum of the thoughts of Talleyrand, strongly supported by the men of intellect who surrounded him, and who were soon admitted into the presence of the sovereigns.

"If we are to believe the enemies of the restoration, it was imposed upon France by hostile bayonets, and nobody in 1814, either in Europe or in France, cared much about it. Puerile blindness of party spirit! The more it can be proved that no general desire, no great force, internal or external, demanded and accomplished the restoration, the more do we bring into view its own innate force, and that supreme necessity by which the issue of events was determined. In the fearful crisis of 1814 the re-establishment of the house of Bourbon was the only natural and serious solution, the only one that was linked with principles as independent of mere force as of the caprices of human wishes. In accepting this solution anxiety might be felt for the new interests of the French people, but under the ægis of institutions mutually accepted, there was reason to hope for that of which France had the most pressing need, and which had been most wanting to it for five-and-twenty years— peace and liberty. Thanks to the two-fold hope, not only was the restoration accomplished without a struggle, but in spite of revolutionary memories it was promptly and easily accepted by France. And France was right, for the Restoration in fact gave it peace and liberty.

"Never had peace been more talked about in France than during the last twenty-five years. The Constituent Assembly proclaimed: No more conquests! The National Assembly proclaimed the union of peoples. The Emperor Napoleon concluded in fifteen years more treaties of peace than any other king. Never had war so often broken out; never had peace been so short-lived a lie. Treaties were only truces during which new combats were prepared for. It was the same with liberty as with peace; at first enthusiastically celebrated and promised, it soon gave place to civil discord, even amidst renewed celebrations and promises. Then in order to put an end to discord, liberty also was put an end to. Just as people became intoxicated with the word without caring to realize the thing, so also in order to escape from a fatal intoxication, both name and reality became almost equally proscribed and forgotten.

"Real peace and liberty returned with the restoration. For the Bourbons, war was not a necessity, neither were they passionately fond of it; they could reign without having recourse every day to some new display of force or some new excitement of the popular imagination. With them foreign governments might hope for, and in fact did hope for, a sincere and lasting peace. In the same way the liberty that France recovered in 1814, was not the triumph either of a philosophical school or of a political party; it gave no satisfaction to the lawless and unbridled appetites born of turbulent passions, extravagant theories, and imaginations at once ardent and unoccupied; it was truly that social liberty which consists in the practical and legal enjoyment of the rights essential to the active life of citizens, and to the moral dignity of the nation." *

The allied sovereigns dimly comprehended these higher reasons for the restoration of the Bourbons, whilst simply yielding to what appeared to them to be the unanimous wish of the chosen men who appeared before them to represent France immediately after the capitulation of Paris. The public declaration of their intentions was meant to facilitate the manœuvres of Talleyrand in the Senate. The conquerors having resolved not to treat with Napoleon, or with any member of his family, the Senate could not hesitate to declare itself in favor of the Bourbons. The Corps Législatif, which had been less submissive than the Senate to the imperious will of the master, had still stronger reasons for concurring without difficulty in his overthrow. In vain did Caulaincourt argue with Talleyrand in favor of a regency for Marie-Louise. "It is too late," said the Prince. "I have done all I could to save them by detaining them in Paris; but a letter from this man, who has lost everything, has ruined them in their turn, by leading

* Guizot: *Mémoires pour servir à l'histoire de mon temps,* vol. i.

them to decide on flight. Think of France, and also of your own children." The loyal servant of Napoleon, who had so long deplored the intoxications of unbridled ambition, henceforth sought in vain to reanimate the courage and fidelity of those whom he had formerly seen upon their knees before the master of all their destinies. The Senate had already appointed the members of the provisional government, carefully chosen by Talleyrand. He was assisted in this difficult task by the Duke of Dalberg, of German origin, and on friendly terms with all the foreign diplomatists; General Beurnonville, formerly war minister of the Convention; Jaucourt, a sincere Protestant, and a gentleman of good family, the descendant of a daughter of Duplessis-Mornay, and who had sat on the right in the Legislative Assembly; and lastly, the Abbé Montesquiou, one of the wisest friends of King Louis XVIII., and a constant member of his secret council at Paris, witty, amiable, and liberal minded. The Senate was ready to stretch its complaisance yet further. It set about proclaiming the dethronement of the Emperor Napoleon, but not without taking care to assure itself beforehand of some recompense for its services. The following were amongst the fundamental principles of the constitution determined upon by the senators: 1st. That the Senate and the Corps Législatif should be integral parts of the projected constitution, admitting such modifications as might be necessary in order to assure an unrestricted suffrage and freedom of opinion. 2nd. That the army, and all superannuated officers and soldiers, and the widows of such, should retain their various grades, honors, and pensions. 3rd. That there should be no repudiation of the public debt. 4th. That the sales of the national domains should be considered as irrevocable. 5th. That no Frenchman should be brought under examination as to any political opinions he might have given utterance to. 6th. That freedom of worship and of conscience should be maintained and proclaimed, as well as the liberty of the press, excepting only the legal repression of abuses of that liberty.

Great were the precautions taken as regards material interests; and the fundamental guarantees of liberty did not occupy a prominent position in these first foundations of the new social system as suggested by the personal motives and prejudices of the senators. Talleyrand and his wise associates were, however, specially careful not to let imprudent men rush forward, and events be precipitated, before the bases of a mutual accord could be arranged between the legitimate sovereign and the nation which recalled him. An untimely manifestation by a part of the Municipal Council of Paris, and the zeal of Vitrolles, who thought the way for the return of the princes was already open, were counterbalanced by the repugnance of the national guard to mount the white cockade, in spite of the friendly disposition manifested by General Des-solle, who had just been appointed its commander. Besides, the Emperor Alexander took pleasure in showing how com-pletely the French people were left at liberty to regulate their internal affairs in accordance with their own will and pleasure. Appeased by his victory, and the downfall of his enemy, he resumed the natural mildness of his character—he displayed in favor of the Parisians that desire to please which had formerly led him to show too much partiality towards the all-powerful conqueror. The Senate had just voted the dethronement of the imperial dynasty, when Talleyrand selected ninety out of the 400 senators, and officially presented them to the Emperor Alexander. The latter effusively praised them for their patri-otic zeal, and said he thought he could do nothing to give them greater pleasure than the restoration to liberty of all French prisoners detained in Russia. Lambrechts was ap-pointed to set forth the grounds for the act of dethronement. It was a duty which naturally devolved onone of those rare members of the Senate who had remained in opposition; they alone had not participated in the errors and the crimes with which every one was now reproaching the fallen *régime.* I will give the text of this Act of Accusation, which fell back like a chargeo f cowardice upon the greater number of those who had just voted for it.

" The conservative Senate—considering that in a constitu-tional monarchy the monarch only exists by virtue of the con-stitution, or the social pact; that Napoleon Bonaparte during a few years of firm and prudent government gave the French nation reason to expect in the future acts of wisdom and jus-tice, but that subsequently he destroyed the pact which united him to the French people, notably by levying imposts and es-tablishing taxes otherwise than by legal authority, contrary to the express tenor of the oath which he took on his accession to the throne; that he has sought to take away the rights of the people, even by adjourning without necessity the Corps Légis-latif, and causing to be suppressed as criminal a report of this Corps, whose very title and part in the national representation

he has contested; that he has carried on a series of wars in violation of the 50th article of the Act of the Constitutions of the
22nd Frimaire, in the year VIII., which ordains that a declaration of war be lawfully proposed, discussed, decreed, and promulgated; that he has unconstitutionally issued many decrees
bearing the penalty of death, seeking to have a war recognized
as national, when it was only carried on in the interests of his
unbounded ambition; that he has violated the constitutional
laws by his decrees relative to State prisons; that he has annihilated the responsibility of ministers, confused the authority, and destroyed the independence of the judicial bodies; considering that the freedom of the press, established and consecrated as one of the rights of the nation, has been constantly
subjected to the arbitrary censure of his police, and that at the
same time he has always made use of the press for flooding
France and Europe with facts of his own invention, false max-
ims, and doctrines favorable to despotism and to outrages
against foreign nations; considering that instead of reigning, in
accordance with his oath, solely for the interests, the welfare,
and the glory of the French people, Napoleon has brought the
misfortunes of the country to a climax, by refusing to make
peace on conditions which the nation's interests required him to
accept, and which did not compromise the honor of France—by
the bad use he has made of all the men and money entrusted to
his care—by the abandonment of the wounded without medical
care, attendance, or even the means of subsistence—by various
measures resulting in the ruin of the cities, in the depopulation
of the country districts, in famine and contagious maladies; ·
considering that for all these reasons the Imperial government
established by the sénatus-consultum of the 28th Floreal, in the
year XII. has ceased to exist, and that the manifest will of all
the French people calls for a new order of things, of which the
first result shall be the re-establishment of general peace, and
which shall be also the epoch of a solemn reconciliation
amongst all the States of the Great European family—the
Senate declares and decrees as follows:

"Napoleon Bonaparte is deposed from the throne, and the
hereditary rights established in his family are abolished. The
French people and the army are relieved from the oath of
fidelity towards Napoleon Bonaparte."

The cry that rose up from the inmost soul of France vanquished, wounded, and bleeding, was more eloquent, as it was
more simple, than the long exposition of the grounds of action

drawn up by Lambrechts; the decree of the Corps Législatif, tardily and unwillingly convoked by the Provisional Government, was more dignified in its cold brevity.

"The Corps Législatif, having seen the Act of the Senate of the 2nd instant, by which it pronounces the deposition of Bonaparte and his family, and declares the French people absolved from all civil and military duties towards him; having seen also the decree of the Provisional Government of the same date, by which the Corps Législatif is invited to participate in this important operation; considering that Napoleon Bonaparte has violated the constitutional pact—the Corps Législatif, concurring in [the Act of the Senate, recognizes and declares the deposition of Napoleon Bonaparte and the members of his family."

All the constituted bodies hastened to give in their adhesion to the declarations of the Senate and the Corps Législatif. The army alone still remained, to all appearance, faithfully gathered around the Emperor Napoleon, who remained at Fontainebleau, where he awaited the results of the mission of Caulaincourt, at the same time concentrating little by little the corps that had become scattered, or hindered from assembling. Upon the Duke of Vicenza devolved the sorrowful duty of announcing the fact of his deposition to the sovereign, to whom he had always extended the firmest and wisest counsels. The emperor had already collected his old guard in the great court of the chateau; he was on horseback, having just come from visiting the cantonments, and he advanced towards the ranks: "Officers, subalterns, and soldiers," said he, "the enemy has stolen upon us three marches. He has entered Paris. I have offered to the Emperor Alexander a peace involving great sacrifices—France with its ancient boundaries, renouncing our conquests, and relinquishing all that we have gained since the Revolution. Not only has he refused, he has done still more: through the perfidious suggestions of these emigrants, to whom I have granted life, and whom I have loaded with benefits, he has authorized them to carry the white cockade, and will soon desire to substitute it for our national cockade. In a few days I am going to attack Paris. I count upon you. Am I right? We are about to prove that the French nation knows how to be supreme in its own territory, and that if we have long been so abroad, we shall not be the less so at home. We will show that we are capable of defending our cockade, our independence, and the integrity of our territory."

The soldiers, with enthusiastic cries, responded to the words of the Emperor; they were still ready to follow him and to give him all that was left of their blood. The officers took a sounder view of the situation; the generals felt that the cause was lost, and that resistance would be impossible and murderous. Some amongst them were not quite clear of selfish motives. Many were influenced by the feeling that France was weary of fighting, and in evident need of peace. The first to feel and express this idea were the most illustrious and most heroic of the marshals. Whilst the soldiers were swearing that they would march upon Paris, with the emperor, to-morrow, Lefebvre, Oudinot, Ney, Macdonald (who had just arrived with his corps), entered the room of Napoleon, resolved upon forcing him to comprehend the truth. The emperor was very excited, already forming a plan for his last battle, reckoning up the forces still at his disposal, and the reinforcements that he might expect in a few days. "They are scattered in Paris," said he; "the people will rise in revolt and deliver them into my hands; they are lost. All who flee from Paris I shall hurl back into the Rhine, and we shall once more become masters of the situation. There is one last effort to be made to reconquer the world."

Napoleon appeared at first absorbed in his own thoughts; he presently addressed himself to the men who surrounded him— to those companions of his life who had so often gained battles for him, and whom he judged to be still animated with his own indomitable ardor. Their countenances remained frigid, and their words were embarrassed. They dwelt upon the horrors to be expected if the battle took place within the walls of the capital. "It is not I who have chosen the place," cried the emperor. "I grapple with the enemy wherever I meet him. It is my only chance—and your only chance also. How would you bring yourself to live under the Bourbons?" All protested emphatically against this idea. "The Regency could not last," replied the Emperor, "in a fortnight you would be making overtures to the Bourbons . . ." Here the marshals hesitated; their thoughts were revealed in their faces. The strong judgment of their master had forestalled their own. That which he deemed impossible they were themselves disposed to attempt; but in order to place the crown upon the head of the King of Rome, the abdication of Napoleon was necessary. No one as yet dared to pronounce this word.

Marshal Macdonald held in his hand a letter from General

Beurnonville, who had long been his friend. The emperor asked him what news he had received. "Very bad news," said the Marshal. "I am assured that there are 200,000 allies in Paris. If we give battle it will be a frightful affair; is it not time to bring all this to a close?" The emperor asked from whom the letter came. "Beurnonville, sire. I have nothing to hide from you; read it." The Duke de Bassano read the letter aloud. It conjured Macdonald to abandon the tyrant, and take part in restoring peace and liberty to France under the rule of the Bourbons. "Your Bourbons won't last long," said Napoleon; "instead of pacifying, they will make worse confusion everywhere. In a battle of four hours' length we could re-establish everything." "Possibly," said Macdonald, "by fighting in the midst of the ashes of Paris, and over the corpses of our children." All the marshals supported these words. "Besides," said they, "we cannot count upon the obedience of the soldiers." Napoleon saw that defection and opposition were getting too strong for him. With a gesture he dismissed his lieutenants, who left him to himself. "I shall weigh the matter, gentlemen," said he, "and apprise you of my resolutions."

Napoleon was not deceived by this bitter sign of his fall. "Poor fellows!" he said, "they have been persuaded that during the regency they may keep their honors and endowments. They don't see that all this is nothing but a dream, and that the Bourbons are played out. Ah! men! men! men! These owe me everything." Caulaincourt, always sincere, insisted on the idea of abdication in favor of the King of Rome, generally accepted, he said, and which might serve as the basis of negotiation. The emperor after reflecting a moment said, "In any case we shall gain time by it. Caulaincourt, I wish it success. Return to Paris; take with you two or three marshals; you will relieve me of them—that will be something gained. While you are negotiating, I shall finish my preparations, and, sword in hand, I will fall on Paris and make an end of the matter. Take Marmont with you—no, I want him at the Essonne; he will do well there with his corps. Take Ney; he is the bravest of men, but I have others who will do as well as he. Take care not to let him fall into the hands of the Emperor Alexander, or M. de Talleyrand; he is a child, watch over him." It was decided that Ney should be accompanied by Macdonald, who was not suspected of complacency towards the emperor, and whose military talents were appreciated everywhere. Napoleon re-

vised himself the act of his conditional abdication, and ordered
the marshals to enter. "I have reflected," he told them, "and
I have made up my mind to put the loyalty of the sovereigns
to the test. They consider me as the only obstacle to the peace
of the world. I am ready to abdicate in favor of my son, who
will be placed under the regency of the empress. What do
you think of it?" And he handed them the paper which he
had just been writing.

"The allied powers having proclaimed the Emperor Napoleon
as the only obstacle to the re-establishment of the peace of Europe, the Emperor Napoleon, faithful to his oath, declares that
he is ready to abdicate, to leave France, and even to die for the
good of his country, independent of the rights of his son, of
those of the regency of the empress, and of the laws of the empire. Written in our Palace of Fontainebleau, April 4th, 1814."

Those present applauded, and showed their admiration and
gratitude. The emperor looked at them sorrowfully, and said,
"And yet, if we would, we might beat them." Then taking up
the pen, he signed, and the marshals left. Caulaincourt only
knew Napoleon's second thoughts, and the hope which he was
still nourishing. The soldiers thought they were carrying
away the fate of the imperial dynasty. They had obtained the
authorization to add Marmont to their number, and stopped at
Essonne for him to join them.

Marching through France at the head of their corps, even at
Fontainebleau and in the presence of the emperor, Macdonald
and Ney had felt the influence of the general emotion; they
had felt the weariness and the irresistible need of rest
which seized the whole of France; they had spoken and acted
in the name of the country, of whose misfortunes they well
knew. The companion-in-arms they were going to visit, the
brilliant and weak Marmont, had been exposed to more subtle
and direct temptations. Talleyrand had enveloped him already
with his seductions and flatteries before he left Paris on account of the capitulation; his agents had followed him to
Essonne, insisting on the necessity of breaking definitively
with the emperor, who was drawing France into an abyss of
calamities. The Duke of Ragusa was able to restore peace to
his country by joining the temporary government charged to
negotiate with the allied powers. The fate of France depended on him; the honors which he would thus merit from
the restored dynasty would surpass all the benefits from the
Emperor Napoleon. The marshal had entertained his generals

with these ideas, and he had found them ready to accept them. All the instruments of the imperial ambition revolted at once against the incessant abuse of their devotedness. Marmont had entered into negotiations with the Prince of Schwartzenberg, who had established himself in the Chateau de Petit-Bourg; he had consented to turn his army towards Normandy, placing it at the disposal of the temporary government. Only one condition had been stipulated in writing in that agreement which tarnished his military honor—Marmont claimed for the master he was deserting, his life, his liberty, and an establishment worthy of his dignity. Thus a third of the troops which were at Napoleon's disposal for the realization of his hopes, were at a stroke placed beyond his reach.

The arrival of the marshals at Essonne, their importunities, their reproaches when they became acquainted with Marmont's meditated act, troubled the latter deeply. Vain and ambitious, he had allowed himself to be drawn into a line of action the culpability of which he acknowledged; he consented to accompany the negotiators to Paris, and even passed by Petit-Bourg in order to obtain a release from his promise from the Prince of Schwartzenberg. The generals who were implicated in the plot had to wait for new orders, or the return of the marshal, before being able to accomplish the projected move. The plenipotentiaries of the Emperor Napoleon arrived at Paris at ten o'clock in the morning of April 5th, and were immediately received by the Emperor Alexander.

There was great uneasiness among the members of the Provisional Government, and the same feeling animated all those who had already boldly broken with the imperial dynasty. The Czar's will was dominant over his allies, capricious, and subject to sudden impulses. General Dessolle, who was present at the interview, tried to mitigate the effect which the words of the marshals produced on the Emperor Alexander. Marshal Macdonald was the first to state Napoleon's proposals. Caulaincourt, always certain of the Czar's good intentions, did not interrupt his colleagues, who were eager to acquit themselves of the task for which they had solicited. Their reception was neither respectful nor flattering.

"Agree among yourselves," said the Emperor Alexander; "adopt the constitution you desire; choose the chief who is best adapted for such a constitution; and if it is from among yourselves, who by your services and glory have acquired so many titles, that the new chief of France has to be chosen, we

will consent most heartily, and receive him eagerly, provided
he does not threaten our peace nor our independence."

The marshals eagerly rejected this suggestion, which could
only apply to Bernadotte. They agreed also in their resolution
not to serve any longer the unbounded ambition of Napoleon;
but they claimed the right of the army to appoint his son his
successor, and to remain the support of a throne which he had
erected himself.

The Emperor Alexander appeared touched by their reasons,
so eloquently and ardently unfolded. General Dessolle tried
in vain to recall the steps already taken, and the interests of
all those who had committed themselves. The negotiators retired at last, full of hope. It was now day, and the *salons* of
the Emperor Alexander were already filling. Marshal Macdonald shocked by his rude fidelity all those who had too soon
abandoned the emperor's cause. He repulsed General Beurnonville, who held out his hand to him. "Away!" he said;
"your conduct has effaced a friendship of twenty years;" and
to General Dupont, who had just been made minister of war,
"They have been hard upon you, general, but you have certainly chosen a bad time to revenge yourself." The plenipotentiaries refused to confer with Prince Talleyrand. "We do
not acknowledge your Provisional Government," said Macdonald, "and therefore we have nothing to say to it." A
second interview with the Emperor Alexander was fixed for
the following day.

It was not at Paris, but at Essonne, where the grave question, which for the moment at least should settle the fate of
France, was to be decided. The emperor sent for Marshal
Marmont, and as he failed to appear, the general officer appointed to replace him. This office had been confided to General Souham, an old servant of the Republic, habitually discontented, and but little in favor of Napoleon, whom he had
served well however. Peremptorily called to Fontainebleau,
he thought that the secret convention concluded with the
Prince of Schwartzenberg was known, and that the lives of
the generals engaged in these negotiations were threatened.
He therefore assembled his comrades, and told them his suspicions. They were all surprised at the non-appearance of
Marshal Marmont, and resolved not to wait for him, but to
take without him the course in which they were all agreed.
Without informing the troops of the object of their march,
notwithstanding the objections of Colonel Fabvier, Marmont's

NAPOLEON RETURNING TO FRANCE

France, vol. eight.

aide-de-camp, the generals of the 6th corps gave orders to leave the quarters of Essonne, and to advance upon Versailles on the 5th at four o'clock in the morning. Marshal Marmont received this news while with Marshal Ney, in company with his colleagues. "I am lost!" he cried; "I am dishonored!" He gave vent to his irresolution and weakness in wailings and lamentations. The marshals were bewildered when they had to return to the Emperor Alexander. The allied sovereigns and their representatives were awaiting them; none of them knew of the move of the 6th corps. The plenipotentiaries of Napoleon renewed their importunities; the Czar, less hostile than his allies to the regency of the Empress Marie-Louise, seemed to hesitate, when an aide-de-camp entered, and announced quietly the great event of Essonne. "The whole corps?" inquired the Czar. "Yes, the whole corps."

The die was cast. The Czar, after a moment of deliberation with the allied princes and their ministers, informed the negotiators that they must give up the maintenance of the imperial dynasty. The army itself being divided, the emperor had no longer at his disposal any power with which it was possible to treat. Then, leaving the military men under the impression that they were receiving the most courteous treatment, he drew Caulaincourt aside for a moment, renewed to him his assurances concerning Napoleon, insisting on the offer of the island of Elba, which he had already formally offered, and promised a principality in Italy to Marie-Louise and the King of Rome. "Make haste!" he said, "for every hour the situation of your master is losing what the Bourbons are gaining; you will very soon find it out of your power to treat at all."

Marshal Marmont had not dared to show himself at the hotel in the Rue St. Florentin; he had just returned from a hurried visit to Versailles, where a mutiny had occurred among the soldiers, who had discovered the defection of which they were the unconscious instruments. The Provisional Government had flattered and urged Marmont; he appeared in the midst of his troops, explaining to them the danger which threatened them from the side of the enemy, beseeching them to return to obedience, and to trust him. "They knew him," he said; "they knew very well that he would not lead them aside from the path of honor." The soldiers were appeased; the allied armies were already advancing to cut off the road to Fontainebleau. Marshal Marmont returned to Paris, laden with praise and thanks from the royalists—henceforth dishonored before that tribunal of public opinion which rarely takes into consideration the difficulties of the situation, and loves to visit on one man the faults and misfortunes of all.

In time the negotiators had returned to Fontainbleau: Marshal Ney ardently resolved to obtain from the emperor an abdication pure and simple, which he had imprudently promised to Talleyrand. Caulaincourt and Macdonald explained in sadness to Napoleon the insurmountable obstacles they had to deal with. The emperor was aware of the revolt of the 6th corps, and spoke bitterly of Marmont. "I have treated him as my own child," he said, "and the wretch has ruined me. The others blame him, but they are sorry not to have been before him. One hundred and fifty thousand men are left to me; but if I had them all at hand, I could only carry the war beyond the Loire, draw the enemy into the heart of France, and increase our misfortunes. No, there is an end of it. But to leave France in this state! I wanted her to be so great; and how small she has become! And to think that in a few hours' time I might have been able to raise her up. Oh, Caulaincourt, what joy! I have, however, no more taste for reigning; your hearts are tired of me, and eager to give themselves to others. I frighten them, and the Bourbons must be allowed to come. God knows what will be the result! To-day they are going to reconcile France with Europe; but into what state will they bring her to-morrow? They will bring on an internal war. They will not even know how to take care of Talleyrand. Never mind, I must surrender; the struggle it would be necessary to engage in would entail horrible calamities. You will see how content they will be to act like Marmont without dishonoring themselves."

Caulaincourt insisted on the material conditions of the agreement. The emperor seemed to disdain them, without losing sight of the interests of his family. He wanted to secure Tuscany for his son; but the Emperor Alexander, when he was sounded on the subject, replied that Austria would not consent. "What!" cried Napoleon, "not even Tuscany in exchange for the French Empire?" He also made a pretence of stipulating advantages for the army; his faithful negotiator delicately hinted that he no longer reigned, and that the great national interests were no more at his disposal. He brought him back to the cession of the island of Elba, which had seemed to satisfy him. "Attend you to that matter," replied the emperor; "think of my family, Caulaincourt: such de tails are hateful to me. Let them allow me an old soldier's pension; I want no more!"

The last official act of the Duke of Vicentia, and his last service to his fallen master, was to carry to Paris the formal deed of abdication, expressed in almost the same terms as when he had reserved the throne for his son, and the regency for his wife. He loftily and unreservedly relinquished that power which by transcendant genius he had raised so high— which by his faults and overmastering ambition he had undermined and destroyed. Joy burst forth on every side, scarcely restrained by shame, or any feeling of remorse. In Paris the demonstrations of delight of all parties, monarchical, republican, or constitutional, exceeded the bounds both of reason and propriety; the most cringing of Napoleon's worshippers showed the most eagerness in insulting him. Those who had shown self-respect enough to resist his despotism, now forgot their dignity in giving full sway to their gratified hatred. Chateaubriand published an abusive pamphlet, which he had prepared during the last days of the empire. Napoleon's statue, which some royalists had in vain attempted to throw down from the top of the Vendôme column on the day the allies entered Paris, had been carefully unscrewed, and now rested in a warehouse. "I frequently told you that statues were of no use," said Napoleon, on hearing of this insult. He tried, when too late, to recall his abdication. "Since I am the only difficulty, there is no need at all for a treaty," said he; "a simple arrangement for exchange of prisoners is enough to secure my liberty." The sovereigns allied against him wished to have other guarantees, though even these were soon to prove insufficient to secure them repose.

The treaty was concluded, securing to the Emperor Napoleon entire sovereignty of the island of Elba, with an income of 2,000,000. The same sum was to be every year divided between his brothers and sisters. Parma and Placentia became the dowry of the empress and the little king of Rome. The Empress Josephine kept an income of 1,000,000. With the "extraordinary treasure," formerly increased by war-contributions from conquered nations, the emperor had at his command a capital of 2,000,000 to recompense his servants. Napoleon's agents defended his interests in so haughty and offensive a manner, that but for the Emperor Alexander's determination to be generous they would have had no support. Napoleon accepted everything, not without irritation and

painful recollections of the past. "If they had shown courage
for two hours longer, I might still have saved France," he
repeated.

For twenty-five years the men who had successively ruled
the destinies of France promised her, one after another, to
save her. They had dragged her through the massacres of the
Terror, the degradations of the Directory, and the pomp of
the Empire, from battle-field to battle-field; in the midst of
glory and bloodshed she had driven back, and then conquered,
Europe; and after holding in her hands the history of the
world, she was now vanquished and exhausted, calling aloud
for rest at any price, and for order and liberty. The Emperor
Napoleon was conquered like her, and more than her, and he
conceived the idea of escaping from those humiliations and
griefs which nations can endure with courage, being certain of
their existence at least. On the night of the 11th he tried to
poison himself. Long previously, during the extreme dangers
of the Russian campaign, he had had this remedy prepared
against the captivity which he dreaded, and kept it ever since.
The poison acted feebly and imperfectly, and Napoleon did
not succeed in procuring death. He felt ashamed of his momentary cowardice. "God does not allow it," said he, referring the result, as he always did at important junctures of his
life, to that Supreme Will which he often believed was in
alliance with his own. He signed the treaty on the 11th
April, while waiting at Fontainebleau for the completion of
the formalities necessary to put him in possession of the island
of Elba, and now every day deserted by some of those who
recently served him on their knees. When Marshal Berthier
set out for Paris, he promised to return. "I shall see no
more of him," said Napoleon to Caulaincourt. Berthier did
not come back.

I have no wish to dwell upon the painful details. Only a
few faithful friends, the Duke of Vicentia, the Duke of Bassano, Generals Drouot and Bertrand, still remained with
Napoleon when, on the morning of the 20th April, he for the
last time assembled before him the regiments of the old guard.
He was visibly affected, and his voice faltered. "Soldiers,"
said he, "my old companions in arms, I now bid you farewell. For twenty years I have constantly found you on the
road to honor and glory. In these recent days, as well as in
those of our prosperity, you never ceased to be models of
valor and fidelity. With men such as you our cause was not

lost; but the war was interminable, and would have been a
civil war, rendering France only more unhappy. I have
therefore sacrificed all our interests to those of the country.
I go away; you, my friends, continue to serve France. Its
happiness was my sole thought, and will always be the object
of my desires. Be not sorry for my fate; if I have consented
to survive myself it is in order to assist your glory. I wish to
write the great deeds we have done together! Farewell, my
children! I wish to press you all to my heart; at least, let
me embrace your general and your flag!"

He, at the same time, clasped in his arms the brave General
Petit, who was bathed in tears, and held the eagle of the old
guard. Many voices, choking with emotion, replied to the
voice of the emperor. He cast a parting look over the faithful companions of his battles and fatigues, who had heroically
devoted themselves, without personal ambition or secret motive, and then rushed into his carriage and drove off, abandoning the throne and power which he had so misused, and taking
with him that incomparably brilliant renown which only he
alone could have tarnished, and was again to tarnish.

General Drouot agreed to command the small corps of the
old guard which was to accompany Napoleon to the island of
Elba. General Bertrand's personal devotion kept him close to
his master. The commissioner of the allied powers accompanied the great captive to his place of exile. "You will answer to me for him with your head," said the Emperor Alexander to Count Schouvaloff. During the last days of the journey, when Napoleon had to cross the southern departments,
which were violently excited by old royalist passions against
the man who was to them the representative of revolution,
oppression, and war, all in one, the protection of the foreign
commissioners was almost indispensable to Napoleon's personal safety. When giving up Lyons, Marshal Augereau had
issued against him an abusive proclamation. The emperor
was for a short time compelled to put on the uniform of an
Austrian officer, in order the more easily to conceal himself in
the ranks of his own escort. This last stage of bitter disgrace
only lasted for a moment, and as they approached the sea the
people appeared more kind or indifferent. The deposed emperor embarked on the 28th April, in the gulf St. Raphael, on
board the English frigate the *Undaunted*, and on the 3rd May
cast anchor in the harbor of Porto-Farrajo, with shouts of joy
from the Elban population, who were proud of the sovereign

whom the chances of fortune had just thrown upon their shores. His wife and son were at the same time leaving Rambouillet, where the Emperor Francis had come to fetch his daughter. She took the road for Vienna, after sending assurances to her illustrious spouse of her constant attachment, and the wish she felt to visit him soon with her son. The princes of the imperial house were now scattered, and Napoleon remained alone.

"Since I have taken any share in the government of men," writes Guizot in his *Mémoires*, "I learned to do justice to the Emperor Napoleon, a genius of incomparable activity and power, to be admired for his horror of disorder, his profound instincts of government, and his energy, rapidity, and success, as a reconstructor of the social system: a genius, however, without bounds or restraint, that would receive neither from God nor men any limit to his desires or will, and therefore remained revolutionary when opposing the revolution; of superior intelligence with regard to the general conditions of society, but with only an imperfect, or shall I say coarse? understanding of the moral wants of human nature, and at one time doing them justice with sublime good sense, at another misunderstanding and outraging them without impious haughtiness. Who could have believed that the same man who made the Concordat and reopened the churches in France, should take away the Pope from Rome, and keep him prisoner in Fontainebleau? Amongst great men of the same rank, Napoleon was the most necessary to his time, for no one ever with such promptitude and success brought order out of anarchy; but he was also the most chimerical in the view of the future, for after obtaining possession of France and Europe, he found himself driven by Europe from France itself; and his name will remain greater than his works, the most brilliant of which, his conquests, immediately and entirely disappeared with himself. While paying homage to his greatness, I am not sorry that my appreciation of him was only in his last days, or after his removal. Under the empire, in my opinion, there was too much arrogance of power, and too much disdain of right and justice, too much revolution, and too little liberty."

What were henceforth to be the guarantees for liberty, and therefore for all the interests which liberty was herself to guarantee? By what institutions should the control and influence of the country in its government be exercised? That was the great problem discussed at Paris while the Emperor

Napoleon saw gradually disappear around him the last traces of his fallen greatness. The Senate had got rid of the prudent direction of Talleyrand, and eagerly, though with difficulty, pursued a two-fold purpose, that of preserving its influence and wealth under the new régime, while at the same time maintaining in the new Constitution the revolutionary principles and theories. Those who drew up the project mostly belonged to the minority in the Senate, derived from the Republic. They were keenly opposed to the Abbé Montesquiou, who passionately defended the royal prerogatives. The executive power and the nomination of the High Chamber were conceded to the sovereign, but his elevation to the throne was exclusively attributed to the spontaneous motion and free will of the nation. Louis Stanislaus Xavier, of France, brother of the last king, was only to be proclaimed king of the French after having officially accepted the Constitution and promised to respect it. An additional article secured to the senators then in office, that their salaries were to be in perpetuity, and not shared by their future colleagues. On the 6th April the Senate enthusiastically voted for the new Constitution, and it was at once ratified by the Legislative Body.

" The senators of 1814 have been much and justly blamed for the self-conceit with which, when overthrowing the empire, they attributed to themselves not only the integrity, but the perpetuity, of the material advantages which, owing to the empire, they had enjoyed. It was in fact a cynical fault, and one of those which are most prejudicial to the powers and the minds of a people, for they offend both honorable sentiments and envious passions. The Senate committed another, which was less glaring, and more conformable to national prejudices, but still more serious, both as a political blunder and from its consequences. At the moment of proclaiming the return of the ancient royal house, they made a display of their claim to choose the king, thus misunderstanding the monarchical right whose empire they were accepting, and practicing the republican right even when restoring the monarchy. This was a startling contradiction between their principles and actions, a childish boast with respect to the great action to which homage was being paid, and a deplorable confusion both of rights and ideas. It was obviously from necessity, not from choice, and on account of his hereditary title, not as the elect of the day, that Louis XVIII. was recalled to the throne of France. There was no truth, dignity, nor prudence, but in this procedure

alone: to openly acknowledge the monarchical right of the
house of Bourbon, and ask of it to acknowledge openly in its
turn the national rights as proclaimed by the state of the country and the spirit of the times. This mutual avowal and respect for mutual rights constitutes the very essence of free
government. It is by a steady adherence to that, moreover,
that monarchy and liberty develop together; and it is by
frankly returning to it that kings and peoples have put a stop
to those civil wars called revolutions. Instead of that the
Senate, being at the time obstinate and timid, while wishing
to place the restored monarchy under the flag of republican
election, merely summoned up the despotic principle to oppose
the revolutionay principle, and excited the rivalry of the
absolute right of the people and the absolute right of the
king." *

For several days the representative of the absolute principles of the royalty, in his own mind as well as in public opinion,
Count D'Artois (soon afterwards termed "Monsieur") had been
making preparations to return to Paris, through his able agent
Vitrolles; and on the 12th April he made his entry as the
king's lieutenant-general, a title soon after confirmed by a vote
of the Senate. It was with great difficulty that the prince was
induced to accept this condition of his new power, and the Emperor Alexander had to interpose to persuade Vitrolles that it
was absolutely necessary for the house of Bourbon to enter
into the sentiments and ideas of new generations. The Count
D'Artois insisted on keeping the white cockade, but consented
to wear the uniform of the national guard. The kind and
courteous manner which had always characterized the youngest
brother of Louis XVI. again appeared in the affecting words
used by the prince as he entered, after so many years, into the
capital of his ancestors: "Why should I be tired?" said he;
'it is the first happy day I have had for thirty years." It was
observed, however, that no engagement was entered into, and
that no indication of the future intentions of the government
escaped from the lips of the lieutenant-general of Louis XVIII.
The *Moniteur* undertook to fill up the omission by attributing
to the prince the following short speech, which was composed
by Count Beugnot after the event:—"Gentlemen of the Provisional Government, I thank you for all you have done for
our country. My emotion prevents me from expressing all that

* Guizot's *Mémories*, etc., vol. i.

I feel. No more divisions; peace and France; I return to her. Nothing is changed, unless it be that there is now one Frenchman more."

The prince's speech to the Senate was more explicit and authentic. It was composed by Fouché, who had recently returned from Illyria, and took an active part in the negotiations of the Provisional Government with Monsieur's councillors, though at the same time without yet presenting himself before the latter. "I have received information of the constitutional act calling the king, my august brother, to the throne of France," said the count. "I have not received from him power to accept the Constitution, but I know his sentiments and principles, and have no fear of being disavowed when I give the assurance in his name that he will accept its bases. The king, by declaring that he would maintain the present form of government, has acknowledged that the monarchy must be counterbalanced by a representative government divided into two chambers, viz., the Senate and the Chamber of the Deputies of Departments; that taxation will be according to the free consent of the representatives of the nation, political and individual liberty secured, the liberty of the press respected, with the restrictions necessary for the public order and tranquillity, and the liberty of religious worship guaranteed; that property will be inviolable and sacred, ministers responsible, and liable to prosecution by the representatives of the nation; that the judges be appointed for life, tne judicial power independent, none being separable from the courts to which it naturally belongs; that the national debt will be guaranteed, military pensions, grades, and honors preserved, as well as the old and new nobility, and the legion of honor maintained, the king deciding who shall receive the decoration; that every Frenchman will be admissible to civil and military service, that no person will be prejudiced by his opinions or votes, and that the sale of national property will be irrevocable. These, gentlemen, seem to me to be the bases essential and necessary to consecrate all rights, define all duties, secure all existences, and guarantee our future."

The Senate expressed itself satisfied. The Legislative Body, showing more cordiality, was received with marked favor. The crowds in the streets showed good-will, as well as curiosity and astonishment. The involuntary eagerness of Marshal Jourdan—who had suppressed the use of the tri-color amongst his soldiers from a conviction that the Duke of Ragusa had

done the same—quietly disposed of the difficult question of the
national colors, and by an order of the Provisional Government
the whole army resumed the white cockade of Bourbon.

Meantime the congress of sovereigns had just been completed
by the arrival of the Emperor of Austria and the Prince Royal
of Sweden, neither very popular, though in different ways and
for different reasons. Count d'Artois took in hand the management of affairs, and added to the members of the Provisional
Government Marshals Moncey and Oudinot, and General Des-
solle. The names of heads of departments were not changed,
though the prince's confidants, with Vitrolles at their head, retained full influence with him. There were already frequent
disputes about nominations, and even the financial resources;
Baron Louis, appointed minister of finance, had some difficulty
in securing the addition to the Treasury of the 5,000,000 which
had been uncivilly taken from the carriages of the Empress
Marie-Louise, at Orleans. A continuance of the taxes decreed
by the Emperor Napoleon without consent of the Legislative
Body was decided upon, and an issue of Treasury bonds
ordered, the financial difficulties being enormous, as well as the
burdens left by the empire. The resolution and ability of the
new minister, however, now began to inspire confidence. The
only tax suppressed was the war-decime, added to the indirect
contributions.

A diplomatic convention preceded (23rd April) the definitive
treaty which was to determine the position of monarchical
France in Europe. It secured the evacuation of the territory as
fixed in the month of January, 1792, and decided what places
still held by French troops beyond those limits were to be
restored. All the conquests of the revolution and empire were
thus taken from us under the head of preliminaries, and without "affecting the arrangements for the peace." In the very
midst of the enthusiasm excited among certain classes of society by the fall of Napoleon and the restoration of the monarchy,
there was felt generally a painful sense of depression. So
much blood shed to no purpose, so much wealth spent without
result, constituted fatal charges against the fallen régime,
which cast their shadow upon the disarmed princes who had
been unable to defend us against our victorious enemies.

Meantime, King Louis XVIII. had embarked at Dover.
When at Hartwell he recently gave a cold reception to La-
rochefoucauld-Liancourt, whom he disliked personally, and
whom Talleyrand had stupidly chosen to inform him of what

was taking place in Paris. The restored monarch was speedily inundated with advice from his brother and friends. The Emperor Alexander had taken care to send Pozzo di Borgo to wait upon him. Some unfortunate words addressed to the Prince Regent as he was leaving England displeased the royalist liberals in France as well as the Emperor Alexander. "It is to the advice of your Royal Highness," said Louis XVIII., "to this illustrious country and the confidence of its inhabitants, that I shall always attribute, under divine Providence, the restoration of our house to the throne of its ancestors." The people, however, everywhere hailed the king's progress with shouts of joy, and on the 29th April he reached Compiègne. Politicians alone were anxious to know under what title the monarch intended resuming his authority. The corporate bodies and chief officers of the army hastened to overwhelm him with their homage, though it sometimes lacked dignity. Marshal Berthier assured Louis XVIII. that his armies would be happy to be called upon to second his generous efforts by their devotion and fidelity. The king received their eager civilities with much kindness and dignity. Leaning on the arms of the marshals who were beside him, he said, "Come closer, and stand round me; you have always been good Frenchmen. I hope France will no longer require your swords; but if we ever are compelled, which God forbid, to draw them, as gouty as I am I should march with you." The embarrassment which some naturally felt in no degree lessened their vanity. The deputation of the Legislative Body was received with marked distinction. The Senate was not represented.

Talleyrand undertook to lay before the monarch the new Constitution. "We shall have a constitution," he had assured the anxious senators, "but our king is a man of culture and education, and you must be ready to defend your work." His first interview with Louis XVIII. convinced him that he had a difficult and useless task before him. He had just rendered most eminent services to the House of Bourbon, supporting their cause with distinction, and preparing beforehand the way for the triumphant return of the monarch who now kept him waiting in his ante-chamber. On his entering, Louis XVIII. at once reminded him of their former discussions, before the opening of the Constituent Assembly. "If results showed that you were right," he added, "you would say to me, 'Let us sit down and talk!' and as I have triumphed I say to you, 'Sit down and let us talk together.'" The conversa-

tion led to no result. The king avoided any positive engagement as to the terms of the Constitution which he had evidently resolved to substitute for that projected by the Senate.

The Emperor Alexander, in his turn, set out for Compiègne.
Since his overthrow of Napoleon and rejection of the imperial
dynasty, the Czar openly supported Talleyrand and the liberals,
even beyond the actual and natural sphere of his influence, and
believed that by the enormous leverage of the services he had
rendered Louis XVIII., he should impose upon him the acceptance pure and simple of the Constitution drawn by the Senate.
He insisted strongly, reminding the king, who had scarcely yet
again stepped on his native ground, that his return was due to
foreign arms. "Less is asked from your Majesty than from
Henry IV.," said he, "yet he conquered his kingdom himself."

Louis XVIII. acknowledged the necessity for a constitutional government. He had never liked the violent proposals
of the emigrants, but kept carefully aloof from them; yet he
was profoundly impressed with the greatness of his race and
the rights which it conferred upon him. To the claims of the
Senate, the urgent pleading of Talleyrand, the intervention of
the Czar, he still proved inflexible. He rejected a scheme for
a royal declaration, which was drawn up by Talleyrand; and
instructed his private councillors, Blacas, Maisonfort, and
Vitrolles, to prepare his preliminary programme of a Constitution. The impassioned eagerness and enthusiasm which were
visibly increasing every day around him, confirmed him in the
belief that he was free to act as he chose. "What would you
have me to do?" said the Czar to Lafayette. "My wish was
that instead of them giving a Constitution, the Bourbons
should receive one from the nation. I went to Compiègne in
the hope of getting from the king a renunciation of his nineteen years of reign, and other claims of that sort; but the
deputation of the Legislative Body had been there before me
to acknowledge it unconditionally. Against the king and the
Legislative Body I was powerless."

It was after advancing to the Chateau St. Ouen, near Paris,
that Louis XVIII. at last issued the royal declaration which
afterwards became the "Charter." No copy had been communicated to Talleyrand, when on the 3rd May, before the
king had left his room, it was posted everywhere:—

"Louis, by the grace of God, King of France and Navarre,
to all who shall see these presents.

"Recalled by the love of our people to the throne of our fathers, enlightened by the misfortunes of the nation which we are destined to govern, our first thought is to invite that mutual confidence so necessary to our power and their happiness.

"After giving our careful attention to the plan of a Constitution proposed by the Senate at its sitting of the 6th ultimo, we acknowledge that its bases are good, but that many of its articles, bearing the marks of the precipitation with which they were drawn up, cannot in their present form become fundamental laws of the State.

"Resolved to adopt a liberal Constitution, and wishing that it may be wisely constructed, while unable to accept one which necessarily implies correction, we convoke on the 10th of the month of June, of this year, the Senate and Legislative Body, promising to lay before them the result of our labors with a commission chosen from both these chambers, and to give as basis of that Constitution the following guarantees:—

"The representative government will be maintained as it at present exists, consisting of two bodies, the Senate and the Chamber of Deputies of the Departments.

"Taxation will be by free consent.

"Public and personal liberty secured.

"The liberty of the press respected, with the precautions necessary for public tranquillity.

"The liberty of religious worship guaranteed.

"Property will be inviolable and sacred; the sale of what belonged to the nation irrevocable.

"Responsible ministers can be prosecuted by one of the Legislative Chambers and judged by the other.

"Judges will be appointed for life, and the judicial power independent.

"The public debt will be guaranteed; and military pensions, grades, and honors preserved, as well as the old and new orders of nobility.

"The legion of honor shall be maintained, the decorations being at our disposal.

"Every Frenchman will be eligible for civil and military service.

"Finally, no person will have need to be anxious on account of his opinions or his votes."

As a matter of fact, King Louis XVIII., while maintaining the principle of his sovereign and free will, accepted all the guarantees of liberty claimed by the Senate; granting, moreover, what was claimed by public opinion, which had no very clear notions as to constitutional rights, and was for the most part unfavorable to the Senate, despising them for their former complaisance and recent defection. The partisans of absolute power, the very men who afterwards ranked as the moderates of their party, with Villèle at their head, pleaded various arguments against this contrivance of English importation, foreign to French history, ideas, and manners, and which would cost more to establish, said they, than our former organization would cost to repair.

For all parties it is difficult to learn the lesson that a return to the past is impossible. The royalists of 1814 could not go back to absolute power. "Henceforth with us it can only belong to the revolution and its descendants, they alone can assure the masses of their interests by refusing them the guarantees of liberty. With the house of Bourbon and its partisans France has need of being free, and she only accepts their government when herself sharing in it. The Charter was already written in the experience and mind of the country; it was the natural result of the thoughts of Louis XVIII. returning from England as well as of the deliberations of the Senate when throwing off the yoke of the empire. It was the product of the necessity and reason of the times. Power and liberty found in it something to employ themselves upon, or defend themselves with success. The workmen were more likely to be scarce than tools or work." *

The Senate accepted, though rather ungraciously, the royal declaration, and waited upon the king at St. Ouen, under the presidency of Talleyrand, who in his speech took care to dwell upon the liberal guarantees. The public satisfaction was general when Louis XVIII. made his entry into Paris, on the 3rd May, 1814, at eleven o'clock forenoon.

Beside the king, in the open carriage drawn by eight white horses, was seated one who attracted the looks of all by a natural and touching sympathy—the Duchess of Angoulême, formerly the royal princess, who when a child left the Temple, after the cruel death of all her family, and had never since left her uncle's protection. Her face showed that many tears had been shed by those fair eyes, as had long previously been said by Madame de Sévigné of Marie d'Este, wife of James II.

---

* Guizot's *Mémoires*, etc.

Shouts of joy resounded round the royal procession, which proceeded at once towards Notre Dame. Only the grenadiers of the old guard, lining the street, showed in their looks some indications of a past that was still threatening. Motionless and stern from their unbending discipline, they seemed cut out of marble, each like a terrible image of restrained anger. "If at that moment they had been summoned to take revenge," says Chateaubriand in his *Memoirs*, "it would have been necessary to exterminate them to the last man or they would have eaten everything." On entering the palace of the Tuileries, which she last left on the 10th August, 1792, the Duchess of Augoulême fainted.

Meantime neither the allied sovereigns nor their soldiers had appeared in the procession of the king now returned to his country and capital. Next day they defiled before him, as if to honor him and say farewell. The negotiations were already being arranged for the definitive treaty of peace, which was to restore the French frontiers to the limits of 1792, and restore our colonies, except the Isle of France, St. Lucia, and Tobago. Part of St. Domingo formerly belonging to Spain was again restored. Some rectifications of territory added about 500,000 souls to the various eastern departments. The Great European questions as to the new formation of states lately conquered or dismembered by Napoleon, were mostly referred to the congress which was soon to be opened in Vienna. The kindness of the Emperor Alexander, with the justice and prudence of Castlereagh, alone made those conditions acceptable. Public opinion in England, and the passion for revenge of the Germans, demanded excessive severity. On the 2nd and 3rd June the allied sovereigns left Paris, the highways being all already crowded with the columns of their soldiers; and on the day when the King opened the Chambers (4th June, 1814), the foreign troops had evacuated the capital and immediate suburbs.

The charter had been discussed by a commission chosen in the Senate and Legislative Body, including Barbé-Marbois, Barthélemy, Boissy d'Anglas, Chabaud-Latour, Fontanes, and Lainé. The king's commissioners were Ferrand, Count Beugnot, and the Abbé Montesquiou, who had recently been appointed home minister, and had immediately chosen as secretary-general, M. Guizot, still quite young, and recommended to him by Royer-Collard. This choice seemed to moderate men an omen of good. Talleyrand, of course, became

foreign minister; and Blacas, the king's friend and private
secretary since the death of the Duke of Avary, became
minister of the royal household.

"I believe it was quite possible," says Guizot in his memoirs,
"for a king of energy and steady purpose to employ three
such men at once, whatever difference and inconsistency there
might be amongst them. None of them aspired to govern the
State, and each in his sphere could be of service. Talleyrand's
principal object was to treat with Europe alone; Montesquiou
had no desire to rule at court; and Blacas, calculating, prudent, and faithful, could be a useful favorite in opposition to
the claims and intrigues of the princes and courtiers. But
Louis XVIII. was not qualified to govern his ministers; as a
king he had great negative talents, but nothing active or efficacious. Of an imposing presence, judicious, shrewd, and self-
possessed, he could restrain, stop, or baffle, but was unable to
direct, inspire, or convey impulse while holding the reins. He
had few ideas and no passion, and steady application to work
scarcely suited him any better than movement. He supported
well his rank, rights, and power; he guarded himself from
faults; but, if only his dignity and prudence were unassailed,
he was led anywhere or did anything, having too little mental
and physical energy to govern men and make them assist in
accomplishing his purposes."

The Constitutional Charter, promulgated on the 4th June,
1814, was generally in faithful agreement with the spirit and
principles of the declaration of St. Ouen. Its preamble was
drawn up by Beugnot, but so hurriedly that he had not time
to show it to the king, who was then engaged with the speech
he was about to make. The new peers of France were invited
to the sitting, and fifty-five of the senators were excluded from
the list, twenty-seven as foreigners, and twenty-eight as regicides or revolutionists. Forty great lords of the old régime,
and nearly all the marshals of the empire, were added to the
remaining senators. The Legislative Body was termed the
Chamber of Deputies, and was to sit for its regular time.
From the very diversity of its sources, the Chamber of Peers
was necessarily doomed to be divided and powerless. The
Chamber of Deputies, however, generally in favor of the
Restoration, recovered with the regular exercise of its power, a
confidence and energy never seen under the empire, and it was
its hands that were to exercise a real and preponderating action
in a government which was confused and badly assorted,

worked upon from within by different tendencies and inspirations. Nevertheless, the king's speech at the opening of the Chambers, had the good fortune to satisfy nearly all parties. The king himself was greatly delighted at his success.

A statement of the condition of the kingdom, mainly drawn up by Montesquiou, and published soon after the opening of the session, was deficient in grandeur and display compared with the pictures—often false, but always bearing the stamp of indisputable power—which Napoleon used to flaunt in the eyes of the nations. It left no doubt as to the liberal and earnest intentions of King Louis XVIII., and had the merit of making known the state of affairs, and the necessity for remedying the evil of every kind under which France was laboring. Baron Louis undertook to lay out in fuller detail the state of the finances; the statement of his method, which was of extreme simplicity, depended upon two things—constitutional order in the State, and the credit of the Government; reckoning, with these two conditions, upon public prosperity and public honesty, he was afraid neither at debts to be paid nor expenses to be made.* The empire left debts exceeding 800,000,000; yet the whole of the ministry bravely supported the baron, and his budget was passed.

At one time new burdens seemed about to be laid on the State. When proposing to the Chambers that emigrants should be re-possessed of their properties which had not been sold, Ferrand, the Postmaster-General, who held the rank of a minister, and had been appointed to state arguments in favor, excited a violent discussion in the Chamber. He threw out hopes of still larger restorations in the future, which were impossible in the financial circumstances, and added a eulogium upon emigration, which caused universal censure. Thanks to the minister's imprudence, the proposal as to the unsold property was very nearly lost. The law as to the press was also keenly attacked. "In its first and fundamental idea," says Guizot, "this project was sensible and sincere. Its object was to consecrate by law the liberty of the press, as the general and permanent right of the nation, while at the same time imposing on it, immediately after a revolution of long despotism or at the commencement of a free government, several limited and temporary restrictions. The two persons who mainly drew up the scheme, Royer-Collard† and myself, had

---

* Guizot's *Mémoires*, etc.   † Then " Director of the Press."

this double end in view—nothing more and nothing less. But that good sense may prevail, there must be frankness and daring. The attitude of the government was embarrassed; and in presenting the scheme, the real meaning or true intention of it was not pointed out. An amendment was necessary in the Chamber of Peers to give to the measure that political and temporary character which it should have borne at first, and which showed its real origin as well as its proper limits. The moderate liberals themselves became alarmed and violently resisted any return to censure. Thus, through not being presented under its proper designation, the measure caused more discredit to the government than any security its success could have gained."

The reorganization of the army and its necessary reduction, the payment of arrears of pay, and placing a multitude of officers on the reserve list, also caused threatening difficulties, which were complicated by the restoration of the old military household of the king, for the purpose of supplying employment and food to that part of the emigrant and ruined nobility towards whom the restored monarch was conscious of great obligations. Titles of honor granted in the army to princes of the royal family also produced discontent, since it caused those generals to whom Napoleon had formerly granted them to be deprived. The legion of honor, however, was continued, the only modification being that the head of Henry IV. was substituted for that of Napoleon, on the cross. Talleyrand proposed to place on it that of Louis XVIII. himself, but the king refused. The attentions paid to the national guard were not successful in rallying them freely. At the first muster of the body-guards, they expected to supplant the absent national guards. Even amongst the military chiefs, dissatisfaction soon displaced their first enthusiasm. Masséna had been excluded from the Senate as a foreigner. Davout had by his long resistance at Hamburg offended the allied sovereigns, and on the king refusing to receive him, he at once became the idol of the army, and in spite of his military severity, which he never relaxed, he was incessantly surrounded by the half-pay officers who thronged Paris, and even by those who were under orders to join their regiments, thus incurring the censure of the Minister of War. The marshal retired to his property of Savigny.

In presence of the general dissatisfaction fermenting in the army and amongst the public, the king asked General Dupont to resign, and appointed Marshal Soult to be Minister of War. The last of Napoleon's lieutenants, he had had the honor of gaining a battle, and for a moment driving back the English, before Toulouse (12th April, 1814). At first he had been unjustly treated on this account, because he fought during a suspension of arms, of which he was ignorant, and had even been excluded from the Chamber of Peers; but his great display of ardor as a royalist had effaced this fault, and Blacas went himself to announce his promotion. The "direction" of the police was at the same time taken from Beugnot, whose temperate and cautious reports were at variance with the secret police of the Count d'Artois and his friends. He was appointed minister of marine in place of Malonet, who had just died. Monsieur wished to appoint to the police the Duke of Otranto, who had gained favor with the most fanatical royalists; but the king refused, choosing Andre, who had been a member of the Constituent Assembly, an honorable and moderate man, yet popular among the emigrants, to whom he had frequently been of service. Talleyrand had just set out for Vienna, appointing Jancourt as interim foreign minister. The insufficiency of the cabinet became daily more obvious, and prejudices became daily more general and serious.

"Scarcely had France entered upon her new régime when distrust took possession of her, and became daily worse. This régime was liberty, with its doubts, struggles, and dangers; no one was accustomed to liberty, and it satisfied no one. By the Restoration, the men of old France had promised themselves victory; from the Charter, new France expected security. Neither the one nor the other finding satisfaction, they on the contrary found themselves face to face with their mutual claims and passions. A wretched disappointment for the royalists, to see the king victorious without being so themselves; a stern experience for the men of the Revolution, to have to defend themselves—they who had so longed ruled. Both were astonished and annoyed at the situation, as to a wrong done to their dignity and rights. In their irritation they both gave themselves up to all kinds of chimerical plans and proposals, to any passionate longings or alarms.

"That was only the natural and inevitable result of the very novel state suddenly introduced into France by the Charter put into practice. During the Revolution men fought, under the empire they kept silence; the Restoration brought liberty into the midst of peace. In the general inexperience and susceptibility, the movement and bustle of liberty, it was the civil war ready to begin again." *

To be sufficient for such a crisis, to maintain both peace and liberty, no government would have been too strong or too able. In their timidity and inexperience, the councillors of King Louis XVIII. were constantly committing faults, which they tried in vain to correct. The philosophical spirit, sprung from the eighteenth century and the revolution, was on its guard against the attacks which it feared from the liberty of thought. An order of Count Beugnot as to the observation of Sundays and holidays, intended to quiet the consciences of Count d'Artois and the Duchess of Angoulême, gave offence to the liberals, and was not carried out. A request was made to the Pope to abolish the Concordat; and Pius VII. himself, on being restored to Rome, claimed the restitution of Avignon and the Comtat-Venaissin. Much popular excitement was caused at the funeral of the actress Mdlle. Raucourt, because the Church, in accordance with its former rules, refused to read the service over her body. This common fear and distrust found dangerous interpreters in the newspapers. The *Censeur*, a liberal organ, keenly attacked the faults of the government and the procedure of the partisans of absolute power, while declaring its devotion to the house of Bourbon; but its heavy and solemn style rendered it already harmless. The pungent jokes of the *Nain Jaune* against the "throne and altar party" struck more dangerous blows at the new State, and served the cause of the exiled Napoleon. Pamphlets were circulated in great number; and Carnot having conceived the strange idea of addressing to the king a defence of regicide, his brochure was soon published. It gave expression to the public disappointment and regret: "We did not reckon up the sacrifices to recover the son of Louis IX. and Henri IV., but the return of the lilies has not produced the effect which was expected." Chateaubriand replied with much talent and moderation to Carnot's accusations and sophisms.

The government of the king strove in vain to calm the increasing fermentation. The princes made journeys into the provinces, with but little success. The army gave many indications of annoyance and discontent: General Vandamme was reported to have been insulted. General Exelmans had written to Murat to offer his sword in defence of Naples, and

---

* Guizot's *Mémoires*, etc.

the letter falling into the hands of the police, he was put on half-pay, and received orders to report himself at Bar. He maintained that, being no longer on active service, the minister of war had no right to fix his residence, and remained in concealment. His wife being near confinement when a forced search was made in her house, she addressed to the Chamber a protest, which was referred to the government. The Chamber passed to the order of the day when the general's petition came before them, and by a royal order he was sent before the court at Lille, where he was unanimously acquitted, and received an ovation from the officers of the garrison.

The reorganization of the magistracy also supplied grounds for serious charges. The reduced "Court of Cassation" saw several of its members discharged; and a bill as to the respective duties of the magistrates was so much changed by amendment, that the government gave up the idea of bringing it before the Peers. A plan for reconstituting the University also met with much opposition. Fontanes, recently "Grand Master" of the Imperial University, a post which he occupied with distinction, found himself obliged to retire, with a pension of 30,000 francs (1200*l.*), and the grade of grand officer of the legion of honor. Every day the spirit of opposition and distrust was more developed in the country as well as the Chambers. Moderate and honorable, the king's government "held no formidable designs whatever against the new interests and rights of the country; but it was without initiative or vigor, isolated in its own country as if foreign, divided and hampered within, weak with its enemies, weak with its friends, its only object being security, and rest, and daily called upon to treat with a restless and daring people, who were passing suddenly from the severe shocks of revolution and war to the difficult labors of liberty." *

The Chambers were prorogued on the 30th December. On the 21st January, an expiatory ceremony, which was natural and legitimate on the occasion of removing the remains of Louis XVI. and Marie Antoinette, awoke painful memories and passions, still only half-extinguished. Anxiety and anger were mixed in the minds of those who had formerly been compromised in the crimes of the French Revolution. There was heard everywhere that wind the forerunner of the tempest which Napoleon with clear-sighted malevolence saw, when he

---

* Guizot's *Mémoires*, etc.

said, "The Bourbons will put France at peace with Europe, but how will they put her at peace with herself?"

While the horizon, recently serene, was thus becoming gloomy at home, Talleyrand's steadfast mind and consummate skill was securing for us at the Congress of Vienna a position which on account of our recent misfortunes was more honorable than influential. The plenipotentiary of France had from the first taken his position as representative of legitimacy, that divine right which had just replaced the head of the house of Bourbon on the throne of his ancestors; and it was by the assistance of this principle that he maintained the national dignity in face of the arbitrary claims of the four great allied powers, England, Austria, Prussia, and Russia, whose ambition was to regulate as they pleased the affairs of the world, without admitting sovereigns of a lower order to the discussion. Nearly all the monarchs of Europe were assembled at Vienna, or had sent their most eminent statesmen. The Porte alone was not represented in this great congress of nations. The Pope had sent a legate.

Two great questions were laid before the congress, that of Poland and that of Saxony. The Emperor Alexander had formerly shown himself disposed to reconstitute, himself and under his sovereignty, an independent kingdom of Poland, but the difficulties and opposition which he encountered in Russia removed the desire. He continued, however, well disposed towards the Poles; but the national instinct of Russia aimed at nothing short of claiming possession of the whole of Poland, just as public opinion in Prussia loudly insisted upon the annexation of Saxony. Austria was naturally opposed to this double ambition, though Metternich's prudence moderated the expression of his anxiety. England attached no great importance to the fate of Saxony, but kept anxious watch upon the excessive aggrandizement of Russia, and therefore found it necessary to look to the French plenipotentiary for the assistance which Castlereagh's haughty bluntness was loath to request. Talleyrand had instructions to protect the interests of the King of Saxony, who was allied to the royal family of France, and whose misfortunes moreover were due to his long-continued attachment to the French cause. Another important part of his duty was to obtain the overthrow of Murat, and the restoration of the Bourbons to the throne of Naples, as well as an indemnity for the Parma branch, who had been dispossessed by the appanage granted to Marie Louise and the King of Rome.

Talleyrand's personal intentions went still further. With a painful sense of the disadvantages caused by the isolation of France, he resolved to use every effort to break the coalition recently formed to fight against us, and the various contradictory interests discussed at the congress supplied him with both opportunity and means. Castlereagh failed in his wish of separating Russia from Prussia, and joined with France in a treaty, to which Austria at once adhered. On the 3rd January, 1815, Talleyrand signed a diplomatic and military alliance with these two powers. The secondary states speedily sent in their adhesion. France had regained her rank among the great states, and her plenipotentiary's joy and pride broke forth in his correspondence. "The coalition is broken," he wrote Louis XVIII. "Fifty years' negotiations would not have been worth so much to France as the federative system which we have secured for her."

Thus all parties were bound together upon the great questions of diplomacy, while exteriorly their affairs seemed to make no progress. "If the congress does not go on, it dances," said the old Prince of Ligne, when attending one of the innumerable evening parties where the sovereigns and ministers daily met together. Negotiations still proceeded, however; and the new alliance had a decisive influence upon the resolutions of the congress. In March, 1815, the question of Poland, much reduced by the abandonment to Prussia of the Grand Duchy of Posen, was nearly disposed of. The Emperor Alexander kept Warsaw as the centre of his new state; and Prussia had reduced her claims upon Saxony, which was to recover her independence and her sovereign at the cost of one third of her territory. The kingdom of the Netherlands was formed, consisting of Belgium and Holland, and receiving Luxemburg and Limburg in exchange for the Rhenish provinces, now ceded to Prussia. Hanover became a kingdom, with some increase of territory. Denmark lost Norway, and in exchange for Swedish Pomerania—which had been promised her, but excited Prussia's cupidity—received the Duchy of Lauenburg, though not without a struggle. The territory of Genoa was granted to Piedmont, as an additional guarantee against France. The negotiations seemed generally rather unfavorable to the French project against Murat, some engagements having been

entered into with him; but Castlereagh had need of Talleyrand
to obtain from the congress a unanimous adhesion to the noble
crusade undertaken by England against the slave-trade.   The
Duke of Wellington had just arrived at the congress in order
to take the place of the English prime minister, who was recalled to London by the opening of Parliament: he was well-
disposed towards the Bourbons, and disliked Murat's presence
in Italy as being an element of disorder.   He was also disposed
to second Talleyrand in wishing to see Napoleon removed from
the French coasts to a further distance than Elba.   Metternich
had no objection to transport him to the Azores, but the Czar's
generosity and loyalty were obstinately opposed to this.   He
rightly considered himself the author of the treaty of the 11th
April, and peremptorily insisted on its strict fulfilment.   He
even made a claim upon the French government for the payment of the sums stipulated in Napoleon's favor.   The latter
had received no money.   The Empress Marie-Louise refused
to leave the Duchy of Parma, which they wished to restore to
the Queen of Etruria, and the Emperor Alexander supported her.
When they still kept urging him, he at last lost temper and
said, "Why, they may some day, very possibly, let loose the
monster who is so much dreaded by Austria and many
others!"

The "monster" was meanwhile fully informed of all that
took place at the Congress of Vienna.   The great negotiations
were completed, and the sovereigns preparing to separate, entrusting their plenipotentiaries with the duty of drawing up
the articles, when all at once the news came that the Emperor
Napoleon had left Elba and landed at the Gulf Juan.   Their
surprise was exceeded by their alarm.   The final operations of
the congress were immediately prorogued.   It was no longer a
time for treating, but for fighting.   The bonds of coalition
were drawn tighter by the common danger.   They waited for
news from France, all the foreigners believing instinctively
that Napoleon would march upon Paris.   Talleyrand alone
attempted vainly to persuade himself and others that the emperor was directing his march towards Italy.

For several months there had been a general persuasion,
secret or declared, that a new shock was in preparation, and
that the new government, which was scarcely founded, was to
be shaken in its insufficient authority.   There were numerous
plots of various kinds.   "They plotted openly," says the Duke
of Rovigo in his *Memoirs*, "even at the corners of the streets;

and everybody, except perhaps the ministers, knew what was
going on." Generals, such as Davout, Savary, Maret, and
Lavalette, who remained faithful to Bonaparte, and displeased
with their treatment at the hands of the Restoration, or who
had naturally no share in the royal favors on account of having
so long served Napoleon, plotted simply and purely for Napoleon's return from Elba and his restoration to the throne.
Other generals, who were formerly attached to the emperor,
and shared in the illustrious memories of his victories—Lefebvre-Desnouettes, Drouet d'Erlon, Lallemand—were preparing
a military movement in the forces under their command, to
compel King Louis XVIII. to accept the conditions of a more
liberal government. In case of refusal, these conspirators intended to conduct the monarch and his family to the frontier,
and proclaim the regency of the Duke of Orleans, whose opinions were considered, on good grounds, to be favorable to the
constitutional party. It was also upon the Duke of Orleans
that the hopes of those liberals were fixed who determined to
attempt the work of legal reform by means of the Chambers,
though some had dreams of a republic. Fouché had a share in
all these plots with more or less ardor and display; his connection with Elba was unimportant and unfrequent.

It was against the government of the Bourbons, and the tendencies with which it was charged, that public opinion was
excited. The majority of the conspirators had no wish for
Napoleon's return, yet he was hovering over the situation like
a threatening phantom, and all men felt secretly convinced
that he had not ended his life. Some pitied him, some dreaded
him, some hated him, but nobody had yet forgotten him.

CHAPTER XVII.

THE HUNDRED DAYS (26TH FEBRUARY TO 15TH JULY, 1815).

"THE question has been much discussed as to who were the
conspirators that on the 20th March, 1815, overthrew the Bourbons and brought back Napoleon. This is a minor point and
is only interesting as an historical curiosity. The silliness of
those who organize plots is boundless, and when results seem
to prove that they were in the right, they take credit to them-

selves for what is due to causes much greater and more complicated than their machinations. It was Napoleon alone who
in 1815 overthrew the Bourbons, by evoking in person the fanatical devotion of the army and the revolutionary instincts of
the people. However tottering the recently restored monarchy
might be, it required this great man and his great strength to
lay it low. France was stupefied, and allowed the event to be
accomplished without either resistance or confidence. Napoleon's own opinion of the matter was formed with admirable
good sense: ' They have allowed me to come,' said he to Count
Mollien, ' just as they allowed me to go.' "*

The Emperor Napoleon never finally abandoned confidence
in his cause, though it had seemed absolutely ruined on the
6th April, 1814, when he signed his abdication at Fontainebleau.
On leaving France to shut himself up in the island of Elba, he
always cherished the hope of returning. When apparently
occupied with securing his position in his narrow kingdom, he
took care to form a small body of troops, 1100 men strong, most
of whom belonged to his old guard. With over 3,000,000 francs
which he had brought with him, he was able to buy four small
vessels. He carefully read the newspapers, and received some
private news from France, which kept him informed of the
state of increasing agitation in the army and the nation. From
Vienna he was informed that the allied sovereigns proposed to
remove him from the coasts which he still menaced by his
presence, and at the same time learned that the negotiations
were finished and the congress about to break up. This double
news caused him some alarm, because he had long feared lest
he should be removed to such a distance as would render his
proposed enterprise impracticable. The faces of his companions told him how utterly weary they were of waiting. "When
do we set out for France?" they sometimes asked. Several soldiers had already left the island, tired of the first sorrows of
exile. Napoleon's plans were already becoming less vague,
and he had secretly begun to prepare to leave, when a young
man, Fleury de Chaboulon, formerly an "auditor" in the Council of State, landed (22nd February) at Porto-Ferrajo. He
came from France, and being supplied with a pass-word from
the Duke of Bassano, received at once the emperor's attention.
His instructions were to inform the illustrious exile of the
actual state of affairs in France, and the discontent in the

---

* Guizot's *Mémoires*, etc., vol. i.

army. He had himself requested the mission, and now delivered his message with enthusiasm. "Then, they still remember me?" said the emperor two or three times; "the soldiers
have not forgot me?" Then, looking keenly at the young man,
he said, "What are your instructions for me? What do they
advise me to do?" No one had dared to take the responsibility
of an opinion, as Fleury declared to the emperor, who on dis-
missing him had him conveyed to Naples, lest the secret of
which he had had a glimpse should prove too much for the
young emissary of his friends. The emperor's mother alone
knew of her son's determination, having taken up her abode
with him to console him in his exile. Though generally firm,
even to impassibility, she was for a moment alarmed at the
terrible chances of another tragical enterprise. Then summoning up her strength, she said, "Go! and may God protect you,
as He has so many times protected you! You cannot remain
here."

On the 26th February the soldiers of the little army were still
engaged in some works at the harbor when they received orders
to go on board. Several days previously Colonel Campbell,
who had orders from England to keep a secret watch upon
Napoleon, had gone to Leghorn on duty. A merchantman
which was seized in the harbor, and two small transport vessels freighted for Rio, constituted the little fleet. All other
preparations being completed, no notice was given to the soldiers, but they all knew the object of the voyage. The Princess Borghese, who came frequently to Elba to see her brother,
was present with her mother at the embarkation. For two
days an embargo had been laid on all vessels, and no news of
his departure was possible. The Emperor Napoleon put to sea.

The wind being uncertain, the sailors were doubtful as to
what course to take. Some ships-of-war were seen out at sea,
but Napoleon was resolved not to go back. On meeting a brig
of the French navy he ordered his soldiers to lie down on the
decks of the small vessels. The Elba flag floated in the breeze
—white, strewed with bees. The captain of the brig recognized
the commander of the small imperial fleet, and they hailed
each other. "Whither bound?" asked Captain Andrieux of
the royal marine. "Genoa." "We are for Leghorn: how is
the emperor?" "Very well." The vessels resumed their
course; and a favorable wind starting up, the small vessels
cast anchor on the morning of the 1st of March in Gulf Juan,
the soldiers landing with shouts of "Long live the Emperor!"

The population of Cannes showed neither opposition nor enthusiasm. A sudden attack made upon Antibes had not succeeded, but several artillerymen escaped from the town and joined the small army. They procured horses and provisions. The emperor ordered a table and chair to be brought, and sat down in a wood of olive-trees to examine his maps. He resolved to follow the road to Dauphiné because it was rough and hilly, and therefore more suitable for his purpose. Another reason was, that the garrisons on that route were weak, and more easily gained over than large forces commanded by superior officers. It was upon the "nation of camps" that Napoleon calculated to exercise the prestige of his presence, the leaders of the army having for the most part escaped from his influence. By following the road along the coast he would have to meet Masséna, who was in command at Marseilles; and besides, the mountain road led to Grenoble, a bustling town not well-disposed to the Bourbons, which he might stir up for his cause. At eleven o'clock in the evening the bivouac on the coast was raised, and the little army was drawn up in marching order, having resumed the eagles and tricolor almost as soon as they planted foot on French soil. After the emperor had ordered them to close their ranks, the handful of faithful and devoted men who had accompanied him heard him read with a loud voice the proclamation, which he thus addressed to the whole of the French army:—

"Soldiers!

"You have not been conquered! Two men from our ranks betrayed our laurels, their prince, their benefactor. Those whom for twenty-five years we have seen overrun Europe to stir up enemies against us, or who passed their lives fighting against us in the ranks of foreign armies, and cursing our beautiful France—how will they presume to command and chain up our eagles, they who never dared look upon them? Shall we suffer them to inherit the fruit of our glorious labors, to take possession of our honors and property, to slander our glory? Should their reign last, all would be lost, even the memory of those immortal days. With eagerness do they change their natures! They are trying to poison that which is the admiration of the world; and if there still remain any defenders of our glory, it is amongst those very enemies with whom we fought on the battle-field.

"Soldiers! In my exile I heard your voices, and am come

through all obstacles and dangers. Your general, summoned
to the throne by the prayer of the people, and raised upon
your shields, is now restored to you; come and join him. Tear
down those colors which were proscribed by the nation, and
which for twenty-five years all the enemies of France have
rallied round. Display the tricolor which you carried in our
great battles. We ought to forget that we were the rulers of
the nations, but we ought not to permit any one to mix himself in our affairs. Who would pretend to be, who could be,
our master? Get back those eagles which you had at Ulm,
Austerlitz, Jena, Eylau, Friedland, Tudela, Eckmühl, Essling,
Wagram, Smolensk, Moskowa, Lützen, Würtchen, and Montmirail! Do you think that that handful of Frenchmen, to-day
so arrogant, could bear the sight of them? They would return
whence they came, and there, if they wish, they would reign,
as they pretend to have done for nineteen years. The veterans
of the armies of the Sambre and Meuse, of the Rhine, Italy,
Egypt, the West, and the grand army, are humiliated; their
honorable scars are mocked at; their successes would be
crimes; these brave men would be rebels if, as the enemies of
the people pretend, their lawful sovereign were in the midst of
foes. Honors, rewards, their affection, are for those who
fought for them, against the fatherland and against us.
Come, soldiers! stand by the banners of your chief! His
existence is only yours; his rights are only yours and the
people's; his interests, his honor, and his glory are only your
interests, your honor, and your glory. Victory will march
at the double; the eagle, with the colors of the nation, will fly
from steeple to steeple, even to the towers of Notre Dame! and
then will you be able to boast of your deeds, then will you be
the liberators of your country!"

A second proclamation, conceived in the same spirit, but
more explicit as to the "treason" of Marmont and D'Augereau,
was addressed to the French nation. A number of copies of
these two incentives to civil war had been prepared during the
voyage, and were immediately printed. Napoleon spoke to
the nation and the army; the moment had now come for
action. From Grasse, where he arrived at daybreak, he
directed his steps towards Sisteron, crossing the snow. The
population remained curious and indifferent. On his way over
the mountain, the emperor stopped for a few moments in a
cottage to warm himself. " Have you any news from Paris,"

he asked the mistress of the place: "do you know what the
king is doing?" The old woman shook her head. "The king!
the emperor, you mean; he's always down there. People don't
know much in these parts." On these heights, life always
flows smoothly in the same channel of ignorance. Five-and-
twenty years before this, some mountaineers of the High Alps
first learned of the French Revolution by going down to the
plain to buy salt. They had got a good bargain, and it was
while inquiring the cause of this diminution in price that they
were informed in the same breath of the abolition of the tax,
and of the events which turned France and the world upside
down. On the 4th of March Napoleon arrived at Sisteron, and
on the 5th at Gap. The country people began to be roused into
enthusiasm, and the peasants' carts were placed at the disposal
of the worn-out soldiery. The news of the landing, sent by express from Draguignan, began to spread, but the officers still
remained shut up in the mountain recesses, with much ado to
restrain their soldiers. Nowhere did Napoleon find any obstacle to hinder his rapid march. General Mouton-Duvernet,
who had arrived at Grenoble post-haste from Valencia, placed
himself in the emperor's way with the view of disputing the
mountain passes with him; but he had already overcome these
difficulties, and the general fell back upon Grenoble, where
great excitement prevailed. The lower orders were, like the
peasantry, favorably disposed towards Napoleon, even though
they had not, like these, acquired any large quantity of the
national property. The bourgeoisie was divided; the royalists
talked big. Generals Marchand and Mouton-Duvernet, and
the *savant* Fourier, prefect of the Isère, ordered a general concentration of troops, the regiments stationed at Vienne and
Chambéry being called out. Labédoyère, the colonel of one
of the latter, was young, of good family, and distinguished
bravery; and his influence with the troops was reckoned on to
keep them to their duty. A detachment of engineers was told
off to destroy the bridge over the Bonne at Ponthaut. The inhabitants opposed this, and the soldiers had no heart in their
work. They had been reinforced by a battalion of the 5th of
the line, and a small body of Polish Lancers attached to Napoleon, had just arrived to protect his passage over the river,
when the men began to mingle and to converse amicably with
each other. Lessard, the commander of the battalion, fell
back with his corps upon the mountain passes; and, almost at
the same moment, General Cambronne appeared upon the

scene with the grenadiers of the island of Elba, who at once proceeded to take possession of the abandoned bridge. The emperor himself advanced with the bulk of his following. Several scouts had already appeared, announcing the arrival of Napoleon, and calling upon the soldiers of the 5th not to fire. The lieutenant-colonel ordered them to retire. "They won't fire," said some citizens or half-pay officers who had made haste to get near Napoleon, and who knew the temper of the men. The emperor approached the soldiers in person.

"What do you wish me to do?" said the brave Lessard to one of General Marchand's aides-de-camp, who happened to be near him; "see how they tremble like aspens at the bare thought of seeing him." He had ordered the retreat, but Napoleon appeared at the same moment. "Soldiers of the 5th," he cried, "do you recognize me?" "Yes, yes!" exclaimed every voice. "What man among you would fire upon his emperor?" A unanimous shout of "Long live the emperor!" was the immediate response. The lieutenant-colonel, alone and dismayed, saw all his soldiers throwing themselves at the feet of Napoleon, when the latter advanced towards him. "Who made you lieutenant-colonel?" "You, sire." "And captain?" "You, sire." "And you wished to fire upon me?" "Yes, sire, because it was my duty." So saying, he tendered the emperor his sword. The latter took it, and pressed his hand. "We shall meet again at Grenoble," he said: then, turning to Generals Drouot and Bertrand, "There, that's all right; to-night we shall be in Grenoble, and in ten days in Paris."

In truth, all was over. The irresistible prestige of Napoleon's presence had had its effect on the first body of troops which he had encountered, and would, by its swift contagion, gain over all those who had not yet beheld him, but who were rushing to meet him. Colonel de Labédoyère called out his regiment, raised the eagle of the 7th on leaving General Marchand's house, and left the town, marching at the head of his soldiers to join the emperor. They embraced, and Napoleon thanked the young chief for his ardent devotion. "We are tired of seeing France humiliated," said Labédoyère; "but, sire, everything is much changed, a new reign must be inaugurated." "I know it, and am resolved upon it," was the emperor's reply.

He repeated this to every one who visited him at Grenoble during the next few days. At the news of his coming the au-

thorities retired; General Marchand went over into the department of Mont-Blanc, in the hope of assembling some elements of resistance about him. The prefect, dreading, on his
own account, the charm of the presence of Napoleon, whom he
had accompanied in Egypt, and continued to cherish a great
liking for him, had directed his steps towards Lyons, not without apologizing for his departure. The town gates were closed,
but the peasants on the one side, and the townspeople on the
other, succeeded by their efforts in breaking them open, and
soon the little troop of soldiers from the island of Elba was
saluted by the frantic cheers of the populace, as well as the
soldiers. The massing of the troops ordered for the defence of
Grenoble against Napoleon would immediately furnish him
with a small army, and with enormous resources, both in
artillery and ammunition. Such guns as had come from the
island of Elba the emperor had left on board his ships. "It
is not with cannot-shots that I am going to make this campaign," he had said. The same enthusiasm spread like wild-
fire through every regiment. Seven thousand men, ready to
perish in his cause, set out on the 8th for Lyons. The soldiers
had all mounted their old cockades with the tricolor, which
they had carefully kept. "To-morrow I will be at your head,"
Napoleon told them. The news of the landing of Napoleon in
the bay of Juan, on the 1st of March, did not reach Paris till
the 5th. At first, it was kept a close secret, and only troubled
for a moment the king, Louis XVIII., naturally calm, and a
little dull of comprehension, by age and infirmities. The first
thought was to place the princes at the head of the armies
which were charged with the task of opposing the invader.
The Comte d'Artois offered to repair to Lyons, and took with
him the Duke of Orleans, much against his will; the Duc
d'Angoulême was at Bordeaux; the Duc de Berry remained
near the king, while Marshal Ney advanced on Besançon;
Marshal Macdonald was to join the Duc d'Angoulême at Nîmes.
These two commanders had negotiated the abdication of Napoleon, and their fidelity was reckoned on accordingly. Marshal
Ney displayed the greatest zeal. He is reported to have said,
in his soldier-like, passionate manner, "Fear nothing, sire; I
will bring him to you in an iron cage." The public was confirmed in its fears by the convocation of the two chambers.
An ordinance was promulgated, enjoining all citizens to pursue
Napoleon, and to seize him alive or dead, in order to deliver
him over to a military commission. The ministers, particularly

Blacas and the Abbé de Montesquiou, were troubled at these
grave events, without putting any great faith in them; Marshal Soult knew better the redoubtable spirit which was about
to enter the lists, and he meanwhile made a show of necessary
zeal. The public was divided; among sensible men, sadness
and uneasiness reigned supreme over all other sentiments.
War appeared to all to be inevitable abroad; it was threatening at home; the remembrance even of past oppression and
suffering was not yet effaced. Meanwhile the towns were
animated by various interests, and almost everywhere in the
country districts the return of Napoleon was eagerly welcomed, for those who had acquired national property had
learnt mistakenly to tremble for the security of their possessions. The country regarded with apathy the recommence-
ment of that terrible struggle, of which it was the stake, and
in which it had not yet learnt to take any important part.
The army was agitated by the keenest passions. The feeling
of duty, or, in some cases, personal animosity, caused several
of the leading military men to incline rather to resistance,
while the great body of the officers and men yielded to the
powerful charm which compelled them to follow in the foot-
steps of their emperor. The Comte d'Artois had been coldly
received at Lyons, and all the efforts of Marshal Macdonald
were unavailable in extracting from the troops a single shout
of "Long live the king!" Napoleon was already approaching
the city gates, and the princes took their departure in the sad
conviction that the soldiers were going to break forth into
cheers at the sight of their old general. Macdonald, once
more attempting to gain over the army, awaited the arrival of
Napoleon's advance-guard, and placed himself at the head of
the leading battalions. Meanwhile, the hussars preceding the
emperor, uttered shouts of triumph, to which the marshal's
soldiers were not long in responding. These latter now hastened to overthrow the barricades erected on the bridges and
ran to meet their comrades, making, like them, the air resound
with the cry of "Long live the emperor!" Macdonald spurred
his horse to the gallop, accompanied only by his aides-de-camp.
Some of his troopers insisted on pursuing him, in the hope of
bringing him back to the emperor, and effecting a reconciliation, but the marshal made good his escape from their somewhat obtrusive zeal. Napoleon was already established at the
archiepiscopal palace as the guest of his uncle, Cardinal Fesch.
His language was evidently affected by his triumphal progress;

it was less modest upon the necessities of the new government, less exclusively preoccupied with the wants and views of the people. Yet Napoleon knew what the force was upon which he depended for aid, and also that the hidden groundwork of revolutionary instincts was still favorable towards him. He announced his intention of immediately convoking the electoral bodies in Assembly. The coronation of the empress and the King of Rome would then be celebrated, and the nation itself would preside over the carrying out of such changes in the constitution of the empire as might be desirable. This convocation was announced by decree from Lyons, and other measures followed, restoring to office procurators and magistrates who had been dismissed by the Restoration Government. Thus Napoleon, at the first blow, and by an act of daring, regained the power of a master for the moment absent from the throne. He nominated, as prefect of Lyons, Fourier, who had fled from Grenoble to avoid him, and the illustrious *savant* accepted the post.

Vengeance occupied the first place in Napoleon's thoughts on his return to France. All the émigrés who had not obtained, prior to 1814, the regular erasure of their names from the revolutionary list, were to be forthwith expelled, while those who had purchased commissions in the army were degraded. The white cockade and all orders before or subsequent to the Legion of Honor were abolished; the decrees of the assembly which had reference to the old nobility and titles were re-established; and the goods of the Bourbon princes were confiscated, as also were those of Talleyrand, Dalberg, and Vitrolles; and the same measure was put in force against the Mayor of Bordeaux and Marshals Marmont and Augereau. These latter were to be tried impartially. Grand Marshal Bertrand, now the emperor's major-general, raised objections to such severities, which he thought neither generous nor well-timed. "You will listen to nothing," said the emperor, angrily, and postponed the decree in the meantime. A fortnight after his arrival in Paris, he ordered Bertrand to countersign it. "Sire," responded his faithful servant, "a minister who countersigns an act of the sovereign is morally responsible for it. Your Majesty has declared by your proclamations that you will grant a general amnesty; these I countersigned with all my heart, but I will not countersign the decree which revokes them." The decree appeared without the countersign.

Meanwhile the emperor was hastening his march, for he felt

around him the pressure of a paramount necessity. The south was agitated, passionately excited by royalist tendencies and the recollection of long-slighted interests. At Marseilles, the populace dreaded the return of the continental blockade which caused its ruin, and a column of volunteers was advancing upon Grenoble. Marshal Masséna did not oppose this; he remained sad and motionless in his military command, restraining with much ado the fury of the populace and resolved simply to do his duty. Marshal Ney was advancing to meet the emperor.

He had faithfully accomplished his task at Besançon, cheering the sinking courage of the royalists, making up the deficiency in military preparations, and strongly convinced that Napoleon cherished a personal grudge against him for what he had dared to say and do at Fontainebleau at the time of the abdication. Generals de Bourmont and Lecourbe were charged with the command of the two divisions of his brigade. The one was an old royalist and former chief of Vendeans; the other, an old republican of the army of the Rhine who had been disgraced by the emperor. They advanced with the marshal to Lons-le-Saulnier.

The attitude of the troops began to grow doubtful. Napoleon had arrived at Mâcon amid the mad enthusiasm of the populace, both town and country along the route bursting forth into transports of rejoicing. The Burgundians, formerly animated by the most fervent revolutionary sentiments, bore themselves with corresponding delight before the great leader, born of the revolution, which he had subdued without forsaking, and which required his support in the future. The popular enthusiasm spreading, the marshal perceived around him its earliest effects. Flying into a passion, he fronted his royalist staff, who appeared somewhat restless. "Let them go," said he; "let them go; if they tremble, leave me alone; I shall know how to seize a gun from the hand of a dragoon and fire the first shot." A speech in which he had addressed his officers had left them cold and discontented; and the news received every day of the triumphant demonstrations of the people in the emperor's presence, increased his anxiety. With anger he heard of the evacuation of Lyons, but already Mâcon had driven out the royalist authorities, and Dijon was proceeding to proclaim the restoration of the empire. In the department of Ain, the prefect had been pursued by the insurgent inhabitants of Bourg. Everywhere people told with what dreadful facility the con-

flagration gained. A letter from Marshal Bertrand was conveyed to his old friend Marshal Ney on the night of the 13th.
Perhaps a letter from the emperor accompanied that of the
major-general. The officers entrusted with it commented upon
these words in the letter, used by Bertrand for the purpose of
gaining over his comrades in arms to the emperor's cause:—
"All the requisite measures are taken and success is inevitable." Marshal Ney believed he saw the vast network of
Bonapartist conspiracies embracing all France, the blow already struck at Paris, an understanding established in Europe
with the Emperor of Austria and the coalition powers: Napoleon, it was said, accepted the treaties and had no further desire for war. All the rumors floating in the air, eagerly caught
and magnified by the people, acted on the mobile spirit of the
illustrious soldier, himself drawn on to his destiny by the al-
lurement which moved the masses, alike military or rustic.
Believing himself duped by the government of the king, he
now suddenly saw in exaggerated proportions all the petty
injuries inflicted on his *amour-propre*, all the transient dis-
satisfactions which he had experienced since the restoration of
the Bourbons. "My dear," he wrote to his wife, "thou shalt
cry no more to get away from the Tuileries." He conferred
with his generals of division, and they both sadly perceived
the uselessness of resistance. "Thou hadst better not have
meddled in the affair at all," said Lecourbe, "and left me
alone in peace." The marshal caused the troops to be assembled. Some stir had already manifested itself in the barracks.
Ney advanced in front of the lines. "Officers, sub-officers,
and soldiers," he exclaimed, "the cause of the Bourbons is
lost forever. The legitimate dynasty which the French nation
has adopted is going to remount the throne. To the Emperor
Napoleon, our sovereign, belongs alone the right to reign over
our beautiful country! Whether the Bourbon nobility choose
to return to exile or consent to live among us, what matters it
to us? The times are gone when the people were governed by
suppressing their rights. Liberty triumphs in the end, and Napoleon, our august emperor, comes to confirm it. Soldiers, I
have often led you to victory; now I would escort you to join
this immortal legion which the Emperor Napoleon conducts to
Paris, and which in a few days shall reach the capital, where
our hope and our happiness shall forever be realized. Long
live the emperor!"

A cheer, loud and unbroken, burst from the lips of all in response to the marshal's cry; swords leapt from their scabbards, shakos waved on the points of bayonets, the soldiers rushed upon their general to kiss his hands and his garments. The marshal yielded to the enthusiasm of the men, whom he had freed by a single word from a restraint that was insupportable. The officers of his staff alone maintained an ominous silence. One of them, an old émigré, broke his sword, saying, "You should have warned us, monsieur le marshal, before making us be present at such a spectacle." Without exception the inferior officers participated in the feelings of the soldiers.

From Lyons, and as if he had never ceased to reign, Napoleon ordered the march of the army corps. On the eve of making his submission, Ney was troubled at the thought of again seeing Napoleon. "Tell him that I love him still, and to-morrow shall embrace him," said the emperor to Marshal Bertrand, when Ney joined him at Auxerre. Next day the marshal wished to attempt some explanations; "There is no need," said Napoleon. "I have always held you to be the bravest of the brave." "You have done well," replied Ney, "to count on me for the defence of the fatherland; it is for France that I have shed my blood, and for her I am ready to shed it to the last drop! I love you, sire, but the fatherland before all!" "It is for the sake of the fatherland that I have returned," interrupted the emperor. "I know her to be unhappy, and I shall render her all the aid that she expects of me." Four divisions were united at Auxerre, and they took the way for Fontainebleau. Everywhere the public gave themselves up to transports of irresistible excitement. To send troops against Napoleon was only to send him reinforcements.

The agitation was growing in Paris; and the precautions of the police, the indignant protestations of the constituted authorities, and the false news circulated by the royalist journals, were no longer able to conceal the rapid progress of a conflagration unexpected and terrible. The royalists, startled and exasperated, attacked all those who did not share in their indignation, or whom they could suspect of even a thought of defection. They were goaded into measures that were conflicting and badly conceived, promising to the army favors which they had but recently refused, re-calling to activity officers and non-commissioned officers who had been placed on half-pay, invoking the support of the national guard, replacing the minister of war, Marshal Soult, by the Duc de Feltre, and André, the minister of police, by Bourrienne. Fouché had declined the offer of the latter office. "It is weakness that has ruined us," said the newly appointed officers, who were resolved to employ force at the moment when power had escaped from their hands.

Meantime, Lainé, president of the Chamber of Deputies, and Montesquiou, minister of the interior, had formed a better understanding of the instincts of the country and the profound causes of discontent which delivered the nation over to a military sway. Lainé, held in esteem by all, and an eloquent and conscientious man, sought to rally around the throne the clear-headed and honest men who formed the constitutional opposition party. Lafayette and Benjamin Constant seconded his efforts; they promised liberal measures, they emphasized the dangers which liberty ran at the hands of the Emperor Napoleon, they attempted at the same time to obtain from the king a change of the ministry, and particularly the removal of Blacas, who was distrusted by all the constitutional party. But these efforts were fruitless; the friends of the Comte d'Artois, and even the confidants of Louis XVIII., were opposed to the concessions. The Bonapartist movement set on foot recently in the department of the Nord, by Generals Lallemand and Lefebvre-Desnouettes, had miscarried; from this they conceived the hope that the movement for the defence would here be able to find an effectual basis, and they prepared an army outside of Paris, which was to be commanded by the Duc de Berry, with Marshal Macdonald for major-general. The Duc de Orleans and Marshal Oudinot were charged with the task of concentrating the army corps. The king and the princes returned to the Chamber for the purpose of renewing their alliance with the people. The king had written his own speech; on his entering he was received with loud cheers.

"Gentlemen," said he, "in this moment of crisis, when the public enemy has entered a part of my kingdom, and when he menaces the liberty of all the rest, I come into your midst to draw closer the bonds, which, in uniting you to me, constitute the power of the State. I come, in addressing you, to explain to all France my sentiments and views. I have reformed my country, and have reconciled it with all the foreign powers,— powers which undoubtedly will be faithful to the treaties by which we have restored peace. I have labored for the good of my people; I have received—I receive every day—the most touching marks of their love. Could I, at sixty years of age, more fitly end my career than by dying in their defence?

" I fear then nothing for myself, but I fear for France. He who comes among us to light the torch of civil war, brings also the plague of foreign war; he comes to place our country once more under his iron yoke; he comes, in fine, to destroy this constitutional charter which I have given you,—this charter, my best title in the eyes of posterity—this charter which all the French cherish, and which I here swear to maintain. Let us then rally round it! May it be our sacred standard! The descendants of Henri IV. shall be the first to range themselves beneath it, and they will be followed by all good Frenchmen. Let the concurrence of both Chambers give all necessary support to the authority, and this truly national war shall prove by its happy result what a great people are capable of, united by the love of their king and the fundamental law of the kingdom."

It was too late to rally by conciliatory words the forces imprudently sundered; too late to incite an honest and courageous effort on behalf of constitutional liberty. The enthusiasm, popular and military, had brought back Napoleon with an irresistible impulse. Already he had reached Fontainebleau (19 March), re-entering with triumph the palace which, almost broken-hearted, he had quitted some months before. The next march he resolved to direct to the Tuileries. The more sanguine supporters of the government wished to advance towards the west, there, relying on the one side on Bordeaux, and on the other on Vendée, to raise up all this region, supremely royalist, against the usurper. Others, with the Duke of Orleans and Marshal Macdonald at their head, proposed to retire into a place in the Nord, Lille or Dunkirk, with a faithful following, in order to await on French soil the great duel which would infallibly take place between the Emperor Napoleon and Europe. The personal desire of the king, old and easily fatigued, was to abide in Paris as long as possible, and when flight was unavoidable, to pass immediately to England, the only asylum that was really safe. The émigrés in a body bitterly opposed the idea of again quitting France. Departure from Paris, meantime, became necessary, for the enemy was already at the gates, and the city was almost surrounded by the army. The king resolved to set out secretly, fearing a popular outburst and a pursuit. The retreat on Lille was decided, and Marshal Macdonald was charged with its protection. On the night of the 19th, at eleven o'clock, all the members of the royal family then in Paris set out stealthily to drive to St. Denis. The last

efforts of Lainé, by which, during the day, he attempted to reconcile the constitutional party, were useless; Lafayette had
vainly proposed to put himself at the head of the national
guard. At the same moment Madame de Staël, like the king,
prepared to quit Paris. Her drawing-room had been the centre
of the liberal movement: she fled before the return of the despot, who had for a long time pursued her with his hatred.
" Well, he is back again!" she had exclaimed a little while before to La Valette; " it is no illusion. My God! liberty is now
lost! Poor France! after so much suffering, and despite vows
so ardent and unanimous! Since he prevails, I go away from
this country! Ah! if the Bourbons had the power of will—if
they had listened to us! But no matter; I love them, I sorrow
for them. They are honest men, and they alone were able to
give us liberty."

So fled royalists and liberty, abandoning the game without
any resistance to the powerful genius who now advanced—
little caring for engagements contracted, and for the dangers
which menaced the country from within, or the terrible calamities of war ready to unloose themselves on us anew. One
hope still remained to France, overcome in these first movements by stupor and disquietude; liberty had not raised her
head in vain, she had reasserted her proper place, and her
power over the minds of men. It was in the name of liberty
henceforth that all parties fought, and even despotism was
obliged to raise her flag. Napoleon invoked the Revolution,
and the Bourbons invoked the Charter; times indeed were
changed. Already the emperor promised some liberal concessions. The whisper of an intention to resist all oppression
passed ere long throughout the whole of France.

On the 20th March, 1815, Napoleon once more entered Paris,
having been warned at daybreak of the departure of the royal
family. " Never was the personal grandeur of a man displayed
with more tremendous *éclat;* never had act more audacious, or
better calculated in its audacity, struck the imagination of the
people. And outward force failed not the man who found so
much of it in himself, and in himself alone. The army clung
to him with a blind devotion. Among the masses of the people
the revolutionary spirit and the warlike instincts, the hatred
of the old régime and the national pride, were stirred up by
his appearance, and rushed forth at his service. He re-mount-
ed, with an eager retinue, a throne forsaken at his approach.
But alongside of all this show of strength, brilliant and strik-

ing, there revealed itself, almost simultaneously, an element of
remarkable weakness. The man who came to traverse France
in triumph, carrying all before him by his personality, whether
friends or enemies, re-entered Paris by night, as Louis XVIII.
had left it, his carriage surrounded by cavaliers, and encountering in his passage only a handful of gloomy-looking people.
Enthusiasm had accompanied him on his route; at his destina-
tion he found coldness, doubt, liberal mistrust, prudent ab-
stentions, France profoundly disturbed, and Europe irrevocably hostile.

"The journey in the vicinity of Paris had enlightened Napoleon as to the state of feeling in the metropolis. Alighting
at the foot of the staircase in the Tuileries, he remarked to
Count Molé, who attended him, 'Well! I have played a fine
prank!'" *

The king and the royal family had meantime proceeded on
their way, and further than their best and wisest friends might
have desired. Once arrived at St. Denis, Louis XVIII. had
directed his course towards Abbeville, always inclined to draw
nearer to England. His household troops followed in great disorder; Marshal Macdonald alone preserved discipline in the
corps. The marshal rejoined the monarch at Abbeville, and
conjured him to proceed to Lille, where the Duke of Orleans
had already arrived, with Marshal Mortier. The gates of the
town were so jealously guarded, that Macdonald had some
difficulty in reaching the prince, who was able, he said, to assure to the king the possession of the place for a very short
time, on condition that he was not accompanied by his household troops. The soldiers in the garrison at Lille were not ill-
disposed, but they were persuaded that the émigrés wished to
deliver France over to the English. The royal party then ran
the risk of being received with bullets, and on the other hand,
the town was incapable of defence without considerable forces.
The advice of the Duke of Orleans was that the king should
shut himself up in Dunkirk, a small and very strong place, that
could be reached from England by sea, and which consequently
offered great guarantees for safety. The marshal supported
this advice, as also did Blacas, who accompanied the king on
his arrival at Lille. A visit made to the barracks confirmed
experienced soldiers in this view, and all were of opinion that
the king should fix his departure for the morrow.

---

* *Mémoires pour servir à l'histoire de mon temps.*

The will of Louis XVIII., although seldom exhibited, was absolutely unchangeable. He was anxious for repose, of which he could not be certain except in England. The twenty-five leagues, he declared, which separated Dunkirk from Lille presented serious dangers, and he preferred to pass at once into Belgium, where he would be free to return afterwards to Dunkirk. The arguments of the Duke of Orleans, and Marshals Macdonald and Mortier, being exhausted before the resolve of the king, the two military chiefs stated that they would escort his Majesty to the frontier, but that they were resolved on no account to emigrate, their intention being to retire into the country. The Duke of Orleans, who had shared the counsel of the marshals, did not believe it safe, in his quality of prince of the blood, to remain in France. Meanwhile, he himself proposed to leave the king at the Belgian frontier, the rallying-point of hostile troops, and to return to England, to the little house at Twickenham, on the banks of the Thames, which he had long inhabited under the empire, and which was his own property. Only Marshal Berthier, captain of a company of the body guards, felt impelled to accompany Louis XVIII., as he had formerly accompanied Napoleon. The household troops were disbanded, and only 300 men, under the orders of Marshal Marmont, left French soil to join the king, who, with the Comte d'Artois and the Duc de Berry, directed his course towards Ghent. The Duke and Duchess of Angoulême were still in the south of France; the Duke of Bourbon was in Vendée, and lost no time in embarking at Nantes. The military leaders who had attempted to oppose some resistance in the north and east, Marshal Victor in Champagne, and Marshal Oudinot in Lorraine, had abandoned their commands, finding that they could not control their troops. In Alsace, Marshal Suchet had hoisted the tricolor; while at Orleans, Marshal Gouvion St. Cyr had peremptorily ordered his corps to resume the white cockade, and put General Pajol in prison for exciting the troops in favor of the emperor. But meantime the movement had become too violent even for the energetic will of Marshal Gouvion St. Cyr; a regiment of cuirassiers revolted, and released General Pajol, putting to flight the royalist authorities, and Marshal Gouvion St. Cyr himself. The south alone was seriously agitated by rancorous political and religious passions. At Paris, the Emperor Napoleon had recovered the reins of government without obstacle.

The formation of his ministry was his first care. In sur-

rounding himself with devoted men, it was still important
that he should avoid names stained by associations of arbitrary
power; the Duke of Rovigo being inadmissible for the police,
the gendarmerie was entrusted to him, with instructions to
watch Fouché, who was said to have an understanding with the
Bourbons. The emperor shrugged his shoulders, having some
knowledge of the complicated and contradictory intrigues of
the Duke of Otranto; still he put him at the head of the police.
Decrès resumed his post as minister of the navy, Count Mollien
of finance, the Duke of Vicentia of foreign affairs, and Marshal
Davout of war, though not without some resistance on his part.
"I had always the misfortune to meet with little sympathy in
the army, being blamed for severity," said the marshal.
"That is precisely what I want," replied the emperor. "The
discipline is loose, and I must have a man of inflexible honor
and courage, with sufficient talent and resolution to meet with
me the whole of Europe face to face." Carnot was appointed
home minister, his former renown as a republican standing him
in good stead: his brilliant defence of Angers drew upon him
the public attention. The command of Paris, as well as of all
the movable troops, was entrusted to Count Lobau. Thus the
highest military authority was placed in the heart of France,
under the direction of men of the greatest ability and energy.
Replaced upon the throne by an insurrection of the army,
Napoleon had no intention of leaving the power at their mercy.
While reconstituting the empire, he resolved to reconstitute
the army.

Forces were already in preparation to guard the frontiers;
and on the 21st, 25,000 men assembled on the Place Carrousel.
The emperor was hailed on his arrival with loud and enthusiastic shouts. "Soldiers," said he, "I came with 600 men into
France, because I depended upon the love of the nation and the
memory of my veteran soldiers. I have not been deceived in
my expectation; and for that, soldiers, I thank you. The glory
of what we have just accomplished belongs to the people and to
you; mine merely consists in having known and appreciated
you. Soldiers, the throne of the Bourbons was illegitimate,
because it was raised by foreign hands, and had been proscribed
by the will of the nation, expressed in all our national assemblies; and also because the only interests it guaranteed were
those of a small number of arrogant men, whose claims are
opposed to our rights. Soldiers, the imperial throne can alone
guarantee the rights of the people, and especially the foremost

of our interests, that of our glory. Soldiers, we are going to
march to drive from our territory those princes, the foreigners'
auxiliaries. The nation will not only assist us with its wishes,
but will even follow our impulse. The French people and I
both depend upon you. We have no wish to meddle in the
affairs of foreign nations, but woe to him who meddles in ours!"

It was an unfortunate and irreparable fault of the Emperor
Napoleon on this occasion to throw upon Europe the blood-
stained burden of his own unbridled ambition, on account of
which the affairs of France had become those of the whole
world by the primitive right of self-defence. Though he had
long had an accurate knowledge of the various dispositions of
the allied sovereigns, he was now anxious to test the intention
of the Emperor Francis. The Austrian ambassador, like those
of the other powers, had asked for his passports as soon as the
ministry was constituted; and by a general order and arrangement, the couriers despatched by Napoleon to all the courts, to
announce the emperor's restoration to the throne of France,
had been everywhere arrested. Flahault, Napoleon's aide-de-
camp, who had previously been well received at Vienna, was
now unable to proceed beyond Stuttgart, and the despatches of
which he was the bearer were taken from him and sent on to
Vienna. On Fouché's recommendation the emperor gave secret
instructions to Montrond, a man of the world, a wit, but fond
of intrigue, and of doubtful character. He was intimate with
Talleyrand, and was supposed to have considerable influence
over that diplomatist, the most important of all to be gained
over. Montrond had been in the army, and when made
prisoner showed his rare courage even in his transactions
with the English who detained him on board a man-of-war.
Admiral Keith, commander of the squadron, was hot-tempered
and violent, and happening one day to fall into a passion before Montrond, he told him that Frenchmen were all rascals
without any exception; to which the prisoner immediately replied, "Englishmen are all well bred, my lord, with only one
exception." It was this daring and skilful man who succeeded
in reaching as far as Vienna, with instructions to carry off the
Empress Marie-Louise on certain conditions, if she seemed
willing to bring back her son to Paris. Fouché had added some
instructions to those of the emperor. Montrond was to speak
of the regency of the empress.

The course to be followed by the allies was irrevocably taken,
as Napoleon was well aware, at the very time when he was

still trying to negotiate through Montrond at Vienna, as well as by Queen Hortense's mediation with the Emperor Alexander. The Czar had intimate relations with her, and secured for her children the duchy of St. Leu. On the 13th March, at the very moment when the emperor was leaving Lyons to advance upon Paris, the representatives of the sovereigns assembled at Vienna signed a declaration, drawn up by Talleyrand, which was soon after published all over Europe:—

"Napoleon Bonaparte," said the manifesto, "by breaking the convention which assigned him a residence in the island of Elba, has destroyed the only legal title on which his political existence depended. By his reappearance in France, with projects of disturbance and revolution, he has voluntarily deprived himself of the protection of the laws, and has proved to the eyes of the whole world that peace or truce with him is impossible. The powers therefore declare, that Napoleon Bonaparte has placed himself without the pale of civil and social relations; and that, as an enemy and disturber of the peace of the world he has delivered himself up to public vengeance. They at the same time declare that they will employ every means and combine all their efforts in order to defend Europe from any attempt which should threaten again to plunge the nations in revolutionary disorder and wretchedness."

On the 25th March "the attempt" was consummated at Paris; the king and royal family were in flight. The allied powers renewed with each other the treaty of Chaumont, and began to devote their whole energies against the enemy of the general peace. They had not in every point fulfilled their engagements concluded with him on the 11th April, but he on his side had so notoriously violated them, that the shortcomings of the other contracting parties were entirely overlooked. The Emperor Alexander, who had been accused by his allies of being weak and fickle on account of his kindness to Napoleon, announced openly that he would spend against him his last soldier and last penny. Metternich and Wellington, with Talleyrand's concurrence, used their influence against the unhappy King of Saxony, to compel him to agree to his own spoliation. The final arrangements were completed, and the allied sovereigns took the title-deeds of their new States. The Duke of Wellington boldly undertook in the name of England to fulfil all the engagements comprised in the treaty of the 25th March. This procedure excited some stormy discussion in the English Parliament, but the opposition was more apparent and theoretical than earnest and practical. In their real hearts, with greater moderation and respect for the national liberty, the English wished for Napoleon's overthrow and the restoration of the Bourbons, as much as the Austrians, Prussians, and Russians. The habitual prudence of the Emperor Francis and his minister, as well as a consciousness of what was due to family considerations, modified at Vienna the national eagerness of Prussia, the wounded susceptibility of the Czar, and the hereditary hate of Pozzo di Borgo. The latter gave vent to his passion in his letters to Castlereagh. "We left Louis XVIII. face to face with all the elements of revolution," he wrote; "and when burdened with the results of our imprudence and his own, Bonaparte came upon the scene, the army overthrew the throne which they ought to have supported, the people were amazed and stupefied. They will applaud still more the contrary piece when, as I trust, we shall put it on the stage. But, if we wish for repose, we must put the king in a position to be able to disband the army and form a new one—to purge France of fifty first-class criminals, whose existence is incompatible with peace. The French ought to undertake the execution, and the allies ought to provide them with the opportunity of keeping their word."

In presence of such passions as these, in so violent a state of excitement, Montrond's mission had no chance of success. Talleyrand repulsed it with friendly but firm candor. After some short emotion on the first report of her husband's return to France, the Empress Marie-Louise still adhered as before to the resolutions and choice which had been made at Napoleon's abdication. She declared she would never return to the emperor, and preferred for her son the duchy of Parma to the throne of France. The little King of Rome, separated from his mother, had already been installed in the imperial palace at Vienna, and treated as an archduke of Austria. On the 13th April, the *Moniteur* published in Paris the declaration of the powers, which had previously been treated as an apocryphal document. A report by Caulaincourt proved the inutility of the efforts made with the allied powers to maintain peace. "The emperor did not expect any important result from such a procedure, and was but little surprised at not finding from family ties, and sentiments, some assistance against political interests and engagements. Without anger against any one, and probably also without blaming himself, he understood and accepted the position now forced upon him by his past life; it was that of an unrestrained gambler, completely ruined though still standing, who is playing a desperate game against all his rivals together, with no chance left but one of those unforeseen strokes of luck which the most consummate skill cannot bring about, but which is sometimes granted by fortune to her favorites."*

While Napoleon was thus accepting the challenge of Europe, and preparing to meet it, his affairs in France seemed to superficial observers to proceed still more and more triumphantly. The Duke of Bourbon's attempt at an insurrection in Vendée had temporarily failed. Vitrolles fixed his headquarters at Toulouse, to organize the attempts at resistance in the south. The Duchess of Angoulême was at Bordeaux, where the troops had recently sworn fidelity to her. She reckoned upon the royalist sympathies of the population; but General Clausel was advancing to take possession of the town in the emperor's name. He had brought no armed force with him, but rallied several battalions on his way, and at his approach the Blaye garrison displayed the tricolor. On reaching the bridge of Cubzac, which had been destroyed, the general held a conference with Martignac, the commander of the royal volunteers at Bordeaux, and soon after destined to a more illustrious career. The moderation of Napoleon's delegate did not conceal his confidence, and the increase of dissension in Bordeaux speedily proved it well-founded. The princess was soon informed by her most faithful friends of the hesitation shown in the regiments, and the personal danger she might incur. Disregarding all danger, she wished to ascertain personally the sentiments of the troops. The left bank of the Dordogne, recently held by the royalist outpost, was already abandoned, and the right bank also soon after. The duchess wished an attack to be made on the detachments seen near the river, with tricolor cockade and flag. "Madame," replied General Decaen, "we should certainly be taken between two fires, that of Clausel's troops and that of the garrison."

The duchess went herself to the barracks, and walked up to the soldiers, who were drawn up in the court. "Gentlemen," said she, "you are aware of the events now taking place; a stranger has just taken possession of the throne of your lawful king! Bordeaux is threatened by a handful of rebels; the national guard are resolved to defend the town, are you willing

* Guizot's *Mémoires*, etc. vol. i.

HF (H)   Vol. 8

to assist them? I wish you to answer me frankly, yes or no. I await your reply."

Nobody spoke; and the ranks remained silent as death. The princess again spoke: "Have you then forgotten already the oath you so short a time ago renewed in our presence? If there be still among you some men remaining faithful to the king's cause, let them show themselves." A small group of officers immediately gathered before her; and the duchess, as she looked at them said, "You are a very small number; no matter, one knows at least on whom to depend." Some voices in the ranks called out, "We shall obey our chiefs in all orders given for the service of the country, but we do not wish a civil war, and will never fight against our brothers." The princess received a similar reply fro m all the regiments which she visited with such fearless courage. At the Château Trompette, which was held by the Angoulême regiment, she asked them, "Do you no longer acknowledge me? Do you not call me your princess?" Then raising her eyes to heaven, as if at the same time declaring her resolution and throwing the disgrace of it back upon those who rendered it necessary, she exclaimed, "Good God! how hard it is, after twenty years of misfortune and exile, to leave one's country again! Yet I never ceased to pray for France, and always do it still, for I am a Frenchwomen; but you! you are no longer French! Go!"

Murmurs of complaint were heard, and the soldiers were themselves on the point of provoking that civil war which they so justly feared. The Duchess of Angoulême withdrew, assuring the people of Bordeaux that all she asked from their loyalty was calm, and temporary submission. Several quarrels having taken place in the suburbs, General Clausel fired some cannon on the right bank of the river. "It is to Madame the Duchess of Angoulême that you owe your safety," he said next day, on taking possession of Bordeaux. "I never dared fire upon the princess while she was writing the fairest page in her history." It was only on the 19th April that the Duchess of Angoulême reached the coast of England at Plymouth.

Meanwhile the Duke of Angoulême, after leaving Montpellier and Nismes, had carried Pont St. Esprit on the 28th March. On the 29th he marched to Montélimar, and on the 2nd April forced the bridge over the Drôme, which was defended by troops sent from Valence by General Debelle; and next day he took possession of Valence. At the same time, Vitrolles and his partisans were arrested at Toulouse by an

insurrection of the troops. At Nismes, General Gilly was at
the head of two regiments who revolted; they had been left in
the town by the Duke of Angoulême, and were encouraged by
the Protestant population to resume the tricolor. Pont St.
Esprit was retaken from the royalist volunteers, who had
charge of it. A column marching towards Grenoble, under
the orders of General Gardanne, also refused to obey, taking
their officers along with them. General Grouchy arrived from
Lyons, accompanied by a large number of militia-men, who
had volunteered their services, and the Duke of Angoulême,
seeing that he was in danger of being hemmed in, evacuated
Valence, only to find the Avignon road intercepted by Gilly.
The prince was surrounded, and compelled to capitulate; he
sent Damas to wait upon General Gilley, who showed the
greatest readiness to come to terms, granting to the duke full
freedom, on condition that the regular troops should enter the
imperial service, and the volunteers be disbanded. The capitulation was submitted to Grouchy for ratification, who thought
it necessary to refer it to the emperor. Napoleon's first
thoughts were in accordance with his orders to the generals
ordered to resist the princes, "Push them out." But, on hearing of the dissatisfaction among the troops, and the excitement of the revolutionary populations, which was shown by
great severity against the royalists, the emperor was, for a
moment tempted to retain the Duke of Angoulême; the previous despatch, however, had been forwarded hurriedly by
Bassano, and the prince, who had been well-treated during his
retention at Pont St. Esprit, was conducted to Cette, whence
he sailed, on the 16th April, for Barcelona. Marshal Masséna
had decided to declare himself in favor of the empire, and on
threatening Marseilles from Toulon, to which he had retired,
the municipality did not dare resist, and thus the restoration
of the empire was proclaimed throughout all the south of
France. The civil war was smothered; and on the 16th April
the emperor assembled the national guard of Paris, and announced this happy result. His real object was to show them
the entire nation submissive to his laws, in order to draw them
into the same way.

"Soldiers of the national guard," said he, "this very morning the Lyons telegraph has informed me that the tricolor-flag
floats at Antibes and Marseilles. A salute of a hundred guns,
fired on our frontiers, will let the foreigners know that our
civil dissensions are at an end. I say foreigners, because as

yet we have no experience of enemies; should they assemble their troops we shall also assemble ours. Our armies are all composed of brave men, who have gained distinction in a hundred battles, and who will present to the foreigner a barrier of iron, whilst numerous battalions of grenadiers and chasseurs of the national guard are defending our frontiers. Soldiers of the national guard, you have been compelled to display colors which were rejected by France, but the national colors were in your hearts. You swear ever to take them as a signal to rally round, and to defend this imperial throne, the only and natural guarantee of your rights! You swear never to suffer strangers, over whom we have several times shown ourselves masters, to interfere with our government! You swear finally to sacrifice everything to the honor and independence of France!"

The emperor spoke to the national guard of what then principally filled his mind, that impending struggle with the foreigner which had become the supreme question between him and France, and was presently to decide the actual possession of the throne. He had a deep sense, however, of other difficulties and dangers which were less obvious and glaring than the armies of the enemy, foreboding a threatening future, and already beginning to destroy that union of sentiment and purpose so indispensable to a people who must defend their national independence. Since his return from Elba, Napoleon made constant efforts to become or appear liberal. He abolished censure of the press, and restored to it perfect liberty. "After what has been written about me for a year," said he, "they cannot say more against me; whereas there are still many charges to lay on my adversaries." He prepared the "Act Supplementary to the Constitutions of the Empire," for the purpose of absolutely modifying their character; and, in spite of Madame de Staël's departure, it was to her friend, Benjamin Constant, that he applied to draw up that important document, the latter assenting, either because he was gained over, or from submission. Napoleon accepted in principle the constitutional monarchy, round which all liberals had rallied, while admitting beforehand the opposition he was likely to meet with from the Assemblies. "With reference to projects, I have now none but that of gaining a battle, regaining our independence, and avenging the misfortune of having seen 200,000 strangers in our capital! and that done, peace! When the only question left is the administration of

France, I shall certainly feel no humiliation in hearing the representatives oppose me with objections, or even refusals; after ruling and conquering the world, there is nothing so unpleasant in being contradicted at home that I cannot bring myself to submit. In any case my son will do so, and I shall try to prepare him by my lessons and example. But let me be allowed to conquer, only once to conquer, those sovereigns formerly so humble, to-day so arrogant: that is what I ask from God and the nation!"

"For intelligent men," says Guizot in his *Mémoires*, "it was a strange sight, and in two respects somewhat ridiculous: Napoleon and the liberal leaders engaged in a close struggle, not as enemies, but in order to persuade, gain over, or overmaster each other. There was no need for very close inspection to see that on neither side was their conference or its discussions considered trustworthy. The one, as well as the other, knew well that the real struggle was not between them, and that the question on which their fate depended would be decided by other means than their conferences. If Napoleon had conquered Europe, it is very certain he would not have long remained a rival of Lafayette and disciple of Benjamin Constant; and as soon as he was beaten at Waterloo, Lafayette and his friends applied themselves to the task of overthrowing him. From necessity, or of set purpose, men's real intentions and passions are sometimes concealed in the innermost thoughts, but they promptly rise to the surface as soon as they think there is a chance of reappearing with success. For the most part, Napoleon resigned himself with infinite suppleness, cunning, and intellectual resource, to the comedy which the liberals and he played together; at one time defending quietly, but obstinately, his old policy and present views; at another gracefully abandoning them, without denying them, and as if from courteous respect to opinions which he did not hold. Occasionally, however, whether purposely, or from want of patience, he violently became himself again, and the despot, who was both son and subduer of the Revolution, reappeared in his whole entirety. When asked to insert in the Supplementary Act the abolition of confiscation, as proclaimed by the Charter of Louis XVIII., he angrily exclaimed, 'I am being forced on a path that is not mine, weakened, and fettered! France wishes for me, but is not allowed to have me. Such an idea was excellent; it is execrable! France asks what had become of the emperor's arm, that arm which she is now in want of to subdue Europe. Why should I be told about kindness, abstract justice, natural laws? The first law is necessity; the highest justice is the public safety! Every day has its own difficulty, every circumstance its law, every man his own natural character. Mine is to be not an angel! When peace is secured we shall see.'

"On another occasion, when engaged with the same Supplementary Act with reference to the institution of the hereditary peerage, he gave full swing to the abundant fertility of his ideas, and considered the question from all sides, throwing in a multitude of opposing arguments and opinions, without drawing any conclusion. 'Peerage is out of harmony with the natural state of men's minds; it will offend the pride of the army, and raise against me a thousand individual claims. Where do you imagine I can find the aristocratic elements which a peerage demands? Yet a constitution without an aristocracy is only a balloon lost in the atmosphere. A ship is directed because there are two counterbalancing forces, and the helm finds a fulcrum; but a balloon is the sport of a single force, there being no fulcrum; the wind carries it away, and it is impossible to guide it.' When the question of principles was decided upon, and the Chamber of Hereditary Peers was about to be appointed, he was strongly inclined to call to it many names of the old monarchy. After mature reflection he gave up the idea—not without regret, we are told by Benjamin Constant, and declaring, 'We must nevertheless come back to that some time, but recollections are too recent: let us defer the matter till the fighting is over, and I can easily have them if I am the winner.' He would have liked to adjourn in the same way all questions, and do nothing till his return as winner. But liberty had returned to France along with the Restoration, and he himself had just awoke the Revolution afresh. He was face to face with those two powers, compelled to endure them, and was now attempting to make use of them until he should be able to conquer them."*

From an undefined but powerful sense of the eternal struggle which exists between them and liberty, the revolutionary masses were disposed to serve the Emperor Napoleon. In the faubourgs of Paris, the population organized a confederation, and resolved to go to the emperor and ask leaders and arms. He agreed to their wishes, giving them a name, "Confed-

---

* Guizot's *Mémoires*, etc., vol. i.

erates," which had no sinister associations, and their cohorts defiled one after another across the Place du Carrousel. "I remember," says Guizot, "meeting in the gardens of the Tuileries a group of about a hundred of the confederates, of rather disreputable appearance. They gathered under the windows of the palace, shouting ' Long live the emperor!' and trying to persuade him to show himself. After keeping them waiting a long time a window at last opened, and he appeared and waved his hand to them; but almost at the same instant the window closed, and I plainly saw Napoleon shrug his shoulders as he retired, much annoyed no doubt at having to take part in demonstrations the character and importance of which were disagreeable to him." A similar movement took place in several provinces, that in the west taking the form of reprisals for the hostilities of the Vendeans and "Chouans." The civil war again broke out.

Meantime the Supplementary Act had been completed, and was published on the 22nd April. The liberals asked for an entirely new constitution, which should confer upon Napoleon the imperial crown by the will of the nation, on condition that that condition was fulfilled. Napoleon when proclaiming it did not thus understand the sovereignty of the people. "You deprive me of my past," he said to his experts; "I wish to keep it. What would you make of my eleven years' reign? The new constitution must be a continuation of the old, and it will be the sanction of several years of glory and success." It was on the emperor's part a proof both of his skill and pride to maintain, both by the preamble and the very name of Supplementary Act, the old empire which he was re-forming. With the exception of the confiscation, which Napoleon did not consent to abolish, the additional act contained in principle all the liberties necessary, and justified the following declaration of the preamble:—"The emperor wishes to give to the representative system its full extension, while combining in the highest degree political liberty with the power necessary to secure respect abroad for the independence of the French people and the dignity of the throne."

It had nevertheless the bad fortune to be unfavorably received by all parties, except the constitutionals, who, owing to Constant's assistance, thought they had some interest in it, and moreover found in the new constitution several of their dearest theories. The revolutionists were violently opposed to this act, conceded by favor of the monarch, and the royalists

ridiculed it as a parody of the Charter. All were certain that
the imperious will of the master would soon be manifested behind the studied moderation of language, regardless of the guarantees granted at the moment. " Your constitution is better
than it is said to be," was said to Constant by Lafayette, who
was then much courted by partisans of the liberal empire; "but
you must get people to believe that; and to bring that about, it
must be at once put in force." The promulgation of the Additional Act took place on the 1st June at the Champ de Mai,
with a great display of the old imperial pomp—a useless and
painful reminiscence of the times when the glory of victory
made amends for demonstrations which were frequently
puerile. The Chambers were immediately convoked, and on
the 7th June the emperor himself gave the oath to the new
members. "Gentlemen of the Chamber of Peers, gentlemen
of the Chamber of Representatives," said he, "three months
ago circumstances and the confidence of the people reinvested
me with an unlimited power. To-day the most urgent desire
of my heart is fulfilled; I am about to begin the constitutional
monarchy. Men are powerless to guarantee the future; institutions alone secure the destinies of nations. The monarchy is
necessary in France to guarantee the liberty, independence,
and rights of the people. I aspire to see France enjoy all the
liberty possible,—I say possible, because anarchy always
brings back absolute government. A formidable coalition of
kings have a spiteful hatred against our independence, and
their armies are arriving on our frontiers. . . . It is possible
that the first duty of a prince will soon call me at the head
of the children of the nation in order to fight for our country:
we will do our duty, the army and I. As for you, peers and
representatives, show the nation an example of confidence,
energy, and patriotism; and, like the senate of the great
people of antiquity, be determined to die rather than survive
the dishonor and degradation of France. The holy cause of
our country will triumph!"

The war had already begun, and the Emperor Napoleon prepared to set out under sorrowful and painful auspices. With
few friends about him in his palace, often reduced to the
society of Queen Hortense and Lavalette, who had become a
favorite with him, he left to his brothers Joseph and Lucien a
certain amount of political action. They undertook of their
own accord to flatter and gain favor with the Chambers.
Joseph was partly responsible for the disaster which had fallen

upon one member of the imperial family. Before leaving
Switzerland, where he had recently taken refuge, he wrote to
Murat, urging him to join the emperor and join his forces to
his. "Reassure the Austrians, in order to separate them from
the coalition," said he. "Talk and act as your heart dictate;
march to the Alps, but do not cross them." Murat, through
the intervention of the Princess Borghese, had already been
reconciled to Napoleon, but the latter carefully advised him
not to begin hostilities. But the excitable and fickle-minded
King of Naples became inflamed with a return of warlike
ardor, and having collected 50,000 men crossed Italy, causing
much confusion. The Pope withdrew to Genoa as well as the
King of Sardinia, and the Grand-Duke of Tuscany set out for
Leghorn. Murat then, without consulting the emperor, or
making any reference to France, proclaimed himself King of
Italy, promising Italian unity as the result of that new authority. After several days' stay at Bologna, hesitating and
uncertain about his march, he saw his troops, who were still
more undecided, gradually disperse; and when he joined
battle with the Austrians at Tolentino and Macerata, he was
completely beaten. Returning to Naples in disguise, the
unhappy king said to his wife, who had disapproved of the
enterprise, "Madame, don't be astonished to see me still alive;
I did everything I could to die." All chance of victory or
revolution being lost, Murat set sail for Provence. Queen
Caroline came to terms with the Austrians and English, and
the house of Bourbon again ascended the throne of Naples.
The dethroned king having asked leave from Napoleon to join
him, received orders to remain in the department of Var. His
wife and children were conducted to Trieste, in spite of the
engagements entered into by the Austrians. Queen Caroline
merely claimed the right of personal freedom.

Thus fell to pieces the last of the thrones raised in Europe by
Napoleon for members of his family, a few days before the
commencement of the great struggle which was to decide his
fate as well as that of France, so imprudently identified with
his destinies. The military preparations, as well as was
possible within so short a time, were at last completed: and on
12th June the Emperor Napoleon left Paris, anxious about the
state of affairs in the interior, the excited and confused state
of men's minds, and that test of a new form of government
which was about to be tried in painful and difficult circumstances. He had information of all the intrigues carried on

about him or abroad, by some of his own servants even, under Fouché's direction. "You will not succeed in governing the Chambers," he said to his ministers on the eve of his departure. "If I don't soon gain a battle they will eat you all up, however big you may be. Fouché thinks that assemblies are ruled by gaining over several old members, by finding their price, and flattering several young enthusiasts; but he is wrong. That is intrigue, and intrigue does not go far. In England, though those means are not absolutely neglected, they have others, much greater and more important. Pitt used to govern the Chambers by a movement of the eyebrow, and Castlereagh still does the same. Ah! if I had the same tools to work with, I should not fear the Chambers. But have I nothing similar? At present, we must get out of the difficulty as we best can. If I am victorious, we shall easily compel everybody to confine himself to his prerogatives; if I am conquered, God only knows what will become of you and myself!" Even when signing the act constituting the Council of Government, he still repeated "Ah! it is indispensable for you that I should gain a battle!"

The whole of Europe was waiting for that battle—that day which was to decide the fate of all. For more than a month the belligerents had paraded their forces, and Napoleon made unparalleled efforts to fill up the gaps caused by the reductions of the Restoration. He had found 180,000 men under arms, and by calling out soldiers on leave and retired veterans, brought up the efficient forces to 288,000. He still awaited the levy of 1815, the mobilized national guards—resources of no use on entering a campaign. The line, therefore, who alone were really fit for service, had to supply the wants of the interior, as well as face the dangers on the frontiers. Only 180,000 fighting-men marched under the emperor's orders. The nucleus of the army was still composed of old troops accustomed to the hardships of war; even then and in the midst of those insufficient forces, a certain number of recruits marched for the first time against the enemy. France had not had an opportunity of resting after the efforts which had lasted for twenty-five years. "The moment is at hand to conquer or perish," said Napoleon to his soldiers on the 14th June, when reaching his head-quarters at Avesnes.

The forces of the allies had long been prepared. Wellington, resting on Brussels as the basis of his operations, counted about 100,000 men under his orders. Blücher, cantoned around Liège with 120,000 soldiers, excited their ardor by his insatiable passion. The Russians, Austrians, and secondary powers of Germany, formed on the east an army of 300,000 combatants, which was still further from the theatre of war, and could not enter upon the campaign before the middle of July. The emperor was informed of this situation of the enemy, and drew out his whole plan of operations accordingly. He resolved to take the offensive immediately, in order not to have upon his hands at once the armies of the north and east. He proposed therefore to throw himself between the Prussians and the English, and then beat them, successively and separately, with an army of about the same strength as those of Blücher and Wellington taken separately. It was with this object that he ordered a concentration of troops on the northern frontiers, Beaumont being chosen as centre. On the evening of the 14th all the corps had come up, with only thick forests between them and the enemy, from whom they concealed our movements. The ardor of the soldiers was extreme. "The excitement of the troops," wrote General Foy on that date in his military journal, "is not that of patriotism, or enthusiasm, but an actual madness to fight for the emperor and against his enemies; no one thinks there is any question about the triumph of France."

Napoleon had fully decided to march immediately upon the enemy. The Duke of Wellington had labored to moderate Blücher's impetuosity by showing him the necessity of combining his operations with those of the eastern army, in order to invade the French territory on all points at once. His main object was to protect the new kingdom of the Netherlands, as that of the Prussians to defend the Rhenish provinces. The Duke of Wellington's brilliant staff had a constant succession of balls and entertainments at Brussels, where the great English general remained in case of an attack by the sea-coast. On the night of the 14th, Charleroi, being insufficiently defended by the Prussians, was carried by Generals Pajol and Rogniat; and other corps having crossed the Sambre at Marchiennes, the enemy fell back on Quatre-Bras and Fleurus. The emperor thus found himself placed between the two armies of the enemy, and advanced towards Namur, the road to which was barred by General Ziethen. Resolving to prevent the movements of the English, which could only be effected by the Quatre-Bras road, Napoleon at once took measures to take this important post from the Prussians. Marshal Ney had just arrived unexpectedly; there being some embarrassment in their relations, the emperor had sent him on a mission to the frontier without any further orders. When Ney took part in the Champ de Mai ceremony, Napoleon dryly saluted him with, "Ah! there you are; I thought you had gone abroad!"

He had now need of the marshal in the great engagement which was about to take place, and immediately entrusted him with the command of the left wing, enjoining him to husband his forces carefully, without, however, neglecting the effort necessary to occupy Quatre-Bras. "Do you know this post?" asked the emperor. "I certainly ought to know," replied Ney; "I served in a campaign here in my youth, and remember that it is the point where all the roads meet." "Exactly so," continued Napoleon; "take possession of it; the English might by means of it join the Prussians."

The emperor at the same time himself advanced towards Gilly, to carry the Prussian position near the river Soleilmont.

During his long military career, Marshal Ney held the character of being brave even to extreme rashness. On the 15th June, 1815, in presence of the perilous position of the army and France, he showed hesitation and fear, and, believing that he was threatened by superior forces, did not dare to advance as far as Quatre-Bras; but leaving a division at Frasnes, at about a league from the post he was to occupy, returned to Charleroi for new orders. Our forces were thus scattered, and the emperor ordered a concentration in the plain of Fleurus on the morning of the 16th, Marshal Ney's corps being still ordered to occupy Quatre-Bras. The orders were somewhat late. General Gerard's corps were much grieved at the departure of General Bourmont, who had formerly, after being leader of the Norman "Chouans," served the emperor and then King Louis XVIII. Wishing to continue his career, he had again entered the service during the Hundred Days till he was influenced by fresh insurrections in Vendée, and withdrew to Ghent. "The Blues are always blue, and the Whites always white," said Napoleon on hearing this news.

At noon he arrived with the army near the village and stream of Ligny. The Prussian masses deployed before us to defend the highway leading from Namur to Brussels. There were three villages on its banks, St. Amand-le-Hameau, St. Amand-la-Haye, and St. Amand the Greater. The generals suspected that the English were near, but Napoleon said they could not have yet arrived, that at the very most the advanced guard might have attacked Ney at Quatre-Bras. He was now waiting for the signal of attack which was to have been given by his illustrious lieutenant's cannon; he had ordered him to fall on the Prussians' rear, after occupying the point where the roads met. When no cannon-shot was heard, Napoleon at last ordered the attack at half-past two, carrying immediately St. Amand the Greater and St. Amand-la-Haye. There was a keenly-contested struggle in the village of Ligny. After taking most of the houses, our soldiers could not pass beyond the village, because the Prussians' reserves were ranged out in an amphitheatre on the heights as far as the Windmill of Bry. The emperor had already twice sent an order to Ney to hurry his march, in order to execute the backward movement which he had already indicated. Forbin-Janson carried the following letter from the major-general; "Marshal, the engagement of which I gave you notice is very important; the emperor commands me to say that you are to manœuvre immediately so as to surround the enemy's right and fall sharp on his rear. The Prussian army is lost if you act with vigor; the fate of France is in your hands."

The greatest of all misfortunes for an illustrious warrior is to find himself in a critical juncture inferior to the resolution demanded by necessity. Ney had this misfortune on the day of Quatre-Bras, whatever personal heroism he may have displayed. After receiving late information of the movements of the French, the Duke of Wellington, after giving his army orders to march, secretly left Brussels in the midst of a grand ball given by the Duchess of Richmond, and hurried to Quatre-Bras with Count Perponcher and several officers of his staff. On being informed of his arrival, Ney, who was already in hesitation when face to face with the small army of the Prince of Saxe-Weimar, believed that he was about to be attacked by the whole English army. General Reille was seized with the same apprehension, and had not advanced with his corps beyond Gosselies. Count Erlon, who was placed in rear, was ordered to make two contradictory movements. The emperor had commanded him to march on the mill of Bry, and after he had taken that direction, Ney insisted on his coming to his assistance. He was impatiently expected at Ligny when he turned to go back, and thus deprived the gallant defenders of the village of the support necessary to complete their victory. After losing most valuable time in marching and counter-marching, Erlon arrived at Quatre-Bras too late to assist Marshal Ney.

Blood flowed in torrents in the plain of Fleurus, and the battle assumed quite a new character of ferocity. The movement upon the Prussian rear not being executed, the emperor ordered a fresh manœuvre which at last compelled the enemy to evacuate the positions which had been so many times taken and retaken during the day. The Prussians retired, leaving a large number of dead on the blood-stained field. The high road from Namur to Brussels remained in our hands, but the enemy were allowed to retreat unmolested. No news had arrived from Quatre-Bras when the emperor returned to Fleurus at about eleven o'clock in the evening, leaving his troops to bivouac on the plain, exhausted as they were with marching and fighting. The battle was gained most creditably, but Napoleon waited for the report of Marshal Ney's operations.

It was three o'clock before Ney made up his mind to attack the 20,000 men of the English army who had just arrived at the important post which he was directed to occupy. After allowing them time to take up their position before him, he charged all along the line: and attacked by a trouble to which he was entirely unaccustomed on the battle-field, he persistently tried to break the English lines, hurling upon them charge after charge of cavalry with complete success at several points; but he was finally repulsed by the unyielding obstinacy of the enemy. At six o'clock Wellington received a reinforcement of 10,000 men; and a last attempt by Valmy's cuirassiers having failed upon Quatre-Bras, the marshal determined to remain on the defensive, and held his ground about Frasnes with heroic courage. Advancing on foot in the midst of his soldiers, Ney felt bitterly the uselessness of his efforts. As the bullets whistled round him like hail, the illustrious soldier muttered sadly, " Would to heaven they were all in my body!"

The English, however, had been detained at Quatre-Bras the whole day, and were thus unable to bring assistance to the Prussians. Napoleon took this into account, and made due allowance for it, when the marshal informed him of the results of the battle. He at once sent him orders to advance towards Brussels, the direction which he intended to take himself. He hoped to fight the English in front of the forest of Soignies, without leaving them time to rally the Prussians. Marshal Grouchy with the right wing, was at the same time ordered to watch the Prussians, pursue them and keep them apart from the English, whilst the emperor with his centre and left wing, still amounting to 70,000 men both together, should advance against the Duke of Wellington.

On the 17th the whole day was occupied with the various movements necessary to come up to the enemy. A violent storm hindered the march, soaking the fields and rendering the transport of artillery extremely difficult. After staying some time at Quatre-Bras, the Duke of Wellington had fallen back upon the position on the height of St. Jean. He despatched an aide-de-camp to Marshal Blücher, to know if he could reckon upon being supported by one of his corps. "At one o'clock I shall be on the ground," replied the old hero, who on the previous evening had been trod under the horses' feet during the battle of Ligny; "if the French don't make an attack on the 18th, we shall certainly attack them on the 19th." In spite of their heavy losses, all the Prussian corps had rallied round Wavre, at four hours' distance from the English.

The emperor's last verbal instructions to Grouchy were "above everything push the Prussians forward vigorously and keep up constant communication with me by your left." During the whole day, on the 17th, the marshal, being led astray by indications which he had misunderstood, sought in vain for the Prussians, thinking they had marched towards the Rhine. In the evening the emperor sent him new instructions; "Pursue the Prussians with only one detachment, if they are on the road to the Rhine; do the same if they are marching upon Brussels. If they are posted in front of the forest of Soignies, keep them together and occupy them, while you detach a division to take the left wing of the English in rear." This order was as precise as it was prudent and masterly, and the fate of the day depended on its execution. Marshal Grouchy declared till the day of his death that he never received it. By an unfortunate neglect the message was not sent more than once, and over the confined area where the destinies of the world were then being decided there were numerous small detachments of the enemy. From Grouchy's personal report which arrived during the night, Napoleon felt somewhat confident that Grouchy had himself anticipated the manœuvre. His only fear now was lest the English should escape him by plunging into the forest of Soignies, and the two hostile armies effect a junction behind that thick curtain of verdure. At night, when out on a difficult reconnoitering expedition, under rain and cannon-shot, on suddenly coming in sight of the fires of the English behind Mont St. Jean, he exclaimed with heroic

joy, "Ah! I have them, those English! We have nine
chances out of ten against them!" "I know them well, sire,"
replied Major-General Soult; "there are no troops to match
them for the defensive; they will die on the spot, without stirring an inch." "I know all that," said the emperor, "but I
shall manœuvre." He went to bed at his bivouac at the village
of Rossomme; he slept, and the Duke of Wellington also re-
posed. The rain still continued falling. When Napoleon rose
before daybreak, the clouds seemed to be going off, and General Drouot assured him that in five or six hours the ground
would be firm enough to bear the weight of the artillery.
"That will give Grouchy time to arrive," said the emperor.
It was Blücher who gained by the attack being delayed.

I have no intention of entering upon a minutely detailed account of that keenly contested battle, so often described by
eye-witnesses with contradictory statements and conclusions.
The battle-fields extended over a space of nearly a league, from
the old château of Hougoumont on the right to La Haie-Sainte
on the left. It was crossed by the highway from Brussels to
Charleroi. Wellington occupied the small village of Waterloo,
at some distance from the road passing in front of the farm of
Mont St. Jean. The French army was grouped round the village of Belle-Alliance and the hamlet of Rossomme. The English positions were partly protected by the slope of the height,
the summit of which was provided with formidable artillery.
They had held their posts for some time; were well rested and
fed, and quite prepared to endure the fight, as in the fatal days
of the ancient struggles between the two nations at Crecy or
Agincourt. The French came to the battle without having
taken time to renew their strength by several hours of rest;
the ardor which animated them was sufficient for every effort.
The English general had taken the precaution to post a body of
reserve on the road from Mons to Brussels, and had written to
King Louis XVIII. to withdraw to Antwerp in case the French
should march upon Ghent. The long trains of ambulance
wagons which had gone to the capital with the wounded had
meantime caused much excitement and alarm there, and the
English, who were very numerous, were making preparations
to leave it. Brussels was awaiting in terror the triumphant
arrival of the Emperor Napoleon.

The fighting, however, was not begun before eleven o'clock,
when Jerome Bonaparte's corps attacked the hedges, walls,
and defences of the château of Hougoumont. The English

were dislodged from it, and the building set on fire, with a body of foot guards still in possession of the main court.

It was round La Haie-Sainte, however, that the fighting raged with greatest fury. A charge of English cavalry had forced through Ney's battalions, carrying off his batteries, cutting the horses' traces, and sabring the cannoniers and artillerymen. On Napoleon sending reinforcements the fighting again began. Wellington, motionless under a tree, listened to the bullets and balls which crashed through the branches over his head: "Well directed," said he; "they did not aim so well as that in Spain." Marshal Ney was now master of La Haie-Sainte, and wished to push forward on the Brussels road, but already the practised eye and foreseeing genius of Napoleon anticipated the approach of the Prussians. No news had been received from Grouchy, and it was necessary to stop the new enemies who were advancing. Count Lobau was entrusted with this duty, and took up a position parallel to the Charleroi highway. At three o'clock the Prussians were on the ground, having easily crossed the thick woods which had been left undefended on account of Grouchy's arrival being expected. They immediately joined in the fighting; and, before going himself to this part of the battle-field, the emperor, who had no more infantry at his disposal, sent General Milhaud's cuirassiers to Ney, with instructions to wait for his orders before charging the English centre. On his way, Milhaud said to Lefebvre-Desnouettes, who was in command of the light cavalry of the guard, "I am going to charge; support me." Without waiting for other orders, the general put his corps in movement, and a terrible mass of men and horses advanced to the front. Ney, full of joy, and the hope of a great triumph in his eyes, exclaimed, "I undertake, entirely alone, to put an end to the English army!" And without waiting a moment in his unrestrainable impatience, he ordered the attack, at the moment when the Duke of Wellington had just reformed his lines which were shaken by serious losses: the batteries had been abandoned. A first charge of our cavalry having failed at this point, the second charge forced the ranks of the English brigade and drove them back violently upon the second line of infantry; the confusion became general. Scarcely had the corps of Lefebvre-Desnouettes arrived, when Ney hurled them into the furnace of battle, where each soldier, "being only witness of his own feats of prowess, could not tell how the fate of the day inclined." One after another the corps of the English cavalry came to measure strength with our cuirassiers, fighting with a keen determination as unconquerable as the courage of their general. Ney, with his hat and clothes torn by bullets, mounting one horse as soon as another fell under him, always as inaccessible to fear as to death, rushed forward in the van of his soldiers; asking from the emperor the cuirassiers and grenadiers of the guards which he had not yet given. Napoleon beheld at a distance this terrible combat, begun without his orders. "It is too soon," said he; "too soon by an hour!" He ordered, however, the movement asked by Ney, who himself led the reinforcements to the attack, with shouts of "Long live the Emperor!" Once again the English lines were broken, but they re-formed again after each charge, frequently hemming in some of our cavalry in their fatal circle. Wellington had on his side sent forward all that remained of his cavalry. Thus, one after another, all the corps were engaged in this ever-renewing struggle. Ney, more ardent and indefatigable than when the fighting began, in a transport of heroism and despair, asked for the infantry of the guard in order to triumph at last over the English resistance. "If we don't die here under the English bullets," said he to General d'Erlon, "there is nothing left for you and me but to fall miserably under those of the emigrants!" The emperor had shrugged his shoulders and said, "Infantry! where does he think I can get any? You see what I have on hand, and look at what I have still to cope with . . . . !" In fact, Bulow's corps of 20,000 against Lobau's, 10,000 soldiers were now being joined by the masses of Blücher's army, fresh for the fight, and the old Marshal himself had already arrived on the battle-field.

It was an essential part of Wellington's plan to wait for this assistance, every moment more and more necessary. General Picton had been killed at the head of the left wing, and when General Kemp, who replaced him in command, sent to ask the general-in-chief for reinforcements, Wellington replied, "Tell him that I have no reinforcements to send him. He and I and all the Englishmen here have only one thing to do, to die at our posts." "Hold firm, 95th," he said, a few minutes previously, under the attack of Milhaud's cuirassiers; "what will they say in England if we give way?" "Don't be afraid, sir," replied the soldiers, "we know our duty." "This is hot work," repeated the Duke twice, as he threw himself within one of the squares which had just been formed to meet a charge of the French cavalry, "but we shall stand it out!"

In every part of this battle-field, so obstinately contested, there was displayed the same enthusiasm, ardent or restrained, full of passion and determination to win the victory. The emperor himself rallied the young guard when giving way before the Prussians, and ordered two battalions of the old guard to support them. "My dear fellows," said he, "now is the critical moment; shooting is no longer of any use; you must close with the enemy, man to man, and throw them down at the point of the bayonet into the gully from which they have come to threaten the army, the empire, and France!" "Long live the Emperor!" shouted the grenadiers in reply, as they drove back the Prussians for a long distance, and crossed in their turn the gulf which lay between. In the distance approached Blücher's soldiers. Ney loudly called for the invincible veterans, who alone might decide the victory, and supported by General Friant, he at last hurled them forward upon the English centre. That was the decisive moment. General Hill, who had just joined Wellington, said, "You may be killed here, what orders do you leave me?" "To die on the spot to the last man, so that the Prussians may be all on the ground," replied the invincible leader of the English army.

Meanwhile Grouchy had not arrived, and the Prussians were all at hand. After Ney's heroic imprudence, and the absence of reinforcements which might turn the tide of battle, the emperor had only one more chance to try, that of crushing the centre of the English army. To meet the attack of the old guard, Mortland's regiment, who had been lying on the ground on the plateau by Wellington's order, suddenly rose and fired their muskets when almost touching their opponents. General Friant was wounded, and some squadrons of English cavalry, now relieved by the approach of the Prussians, charged in their turn. Our heavy cavalry were destroyed, and only 400 chasseurs of the guard remained at the disposal of the emperor. They rushed against the hostile tide which was ever advancing, but were everywhere out-numbered. The cuirassiers who held Mont St. Jean found themselves compelled to fall back to avoid the danger of being separated from the main body, and D'Erlon's corps were dispersed at the same time. Wellington had taken the offensive. Night being come, the soldiers could no longer distinguish the emperor, from whom alone they now derived confidence. The terrible suspicion of treachery pervading their minds, the ranks were becoming conscious of defeat. There was no longer any reserve in the rear, the Prussians had forced our lines at Plancenois, and were all on the battle-field. The guard alone still resisted, forming in squares which kept constantly contracting as death made larger and larger gaps in their ranks. One cry was in the mouths of all, the expression of the single thought in all their hearts, whoever may have first chosen the words: "The guard dies, and never surrenders!" "Let none of us surrender!" was still repeated by the soldiers when there were not more than 150. The English fired with grape-shot upon this fortress of unconquerable hearts and arms. The wounded and dying took refuge behind the lines that were still standing. A final charge with the bayonet, urged by heroic despair and passion, signalized the last effort of the old guard. The emperor watched them from a distance, in the midst of the rushing and raging tide of battle. "All is lost; they are mixed together!" said he, when he saw the hairy hats of his grenadiers confounded with the English horses and soldiers. The confusion and rout were becoming general. Marshal Ney, after rallying the remains of the Durutte division, said to them, "Come, my friends, and see how a marshal of France dies!" and led them again to face the enemy, while the commander of the Rullière battalion detached the eagle from their standard and concealed it under his jacket. After a fifth horse had been killed under him, he headed the charge on foot, but without finding the death which he sought, and without receiving a single wound. A square of the 1st regiment of grenadiers surrounded the emperor with their ranks, and drew him to a distance from the battle-field. Not a word was spoken. On the Charleroi road, which was a crowded scene of frightful disorder, men flying and pursuing, foot soldiers and horse soldiers wounded and dying, all hurried on or fell in a confused mass. Wellington's aides-de-camp tried to draw him out of the danger in which he stood of being shot by both friends and foes. "What does it matter?" said the English general, as impassible in victory as during the fight, "let them fire as they like, the battle is gained!"

The Emperor Napoleon alone said a few words to the soldiers who were protecting him. His brother Jerome and the major-general marched by his side. No one knew what had become of several of the generals: some were killed, and a large number wounded, and more than 20,000 French soldiers remained on the battle-field. The Prussians had given no quarter. The English showed humanity to the wounded. "Leave it all to me," said Blücher to Wellington, when the two leaders of the allied army met between Belle-Alliance and Plancenois. "I undertake the pursuit." A large number of the flying soldiers fell into the hands of his cavalry. Fortunately fatigue obliged them to halt at the small river Dyle. The Belgians everywhere received the escaping army with kindness.

The emperor advanced to Charleroi, whence he set out for Laon, ordering Jerome and Soult to lead the remains of the army towards that town. By a despatch sent in search of Marshal Grouchy, he was informed of the disaster, and ordered to retreat upon Namur. The orderly who carried the message met the marshal and his corps between Wavre and Limal. The previous evening they had made an ineffectual attack on Wavre, and General Gerard was severely wounded; yet though certain of death, he tried, with General Vandamme's concurrence, to persuade their chief to march to the noise of cannon at Waterloo, which thundered in the distance. Nothing now remained for him but to obey the emperor's instructions, as he ran the risk of being surprised by the victorious enemy, and thus adding a new misfortune to the deplorable position of affairs. He commenced the march towards Laon with his corps, saying repeatedly to his lieutenants, "When you see my orders, gentlemen, you will admit that I could not act differently from what I have done."

It was the end, and everybody knew it; none better than the Emperor Napoleon. He had risked on one cast of the die his fortune and his empire, but fate had betrayed him. He vainly made a final effort to enumerate the resources still at his disposition. When he reached Paris, on the evening of the 20th, urged by his councillors to return to his capital, and sorry to leave the army, he for a moment gave vent to his bitter disappointment before Caulaincourt. "The army fought magnificently," said he; "they were seized by a panic terror, and all was lost: Ney acted like a madman; he made me massacre my cavalry. I am quite knocked up, and must have two hours' rest before I do anything. I am choking!" While a bath was being prepared he said, "I shall at once assemble the two chambers in special session; I have no longer an army or a single musket; my only resource is the country. I hope the representatives will second me when they feel the responsibility which rests upon their heads."

The Duke of Vicentia made no reply. He had in vain tried to enlighten the emperor as to the state of public opinion in

Paris and the Chambers.   The rumor of the disaster had spread
over the capital, in spite of the lying message read by Regnault
de St. Jean in the tribune of the representatives.   For three
days every battle had been represented as a brilliant victory,
and on the 21st the minister of state announced that a great
battle had been fought four leagues from Brussels; that the
English army, after fighting the whole day, had been obliged
to yield up the field, when some traitors by spreading alarm
caused a state of disorder which the presence of his Majesty
could not rectify; that some serious disasters were the result,
but that his Majesty having come to Paris to confer with his
ministers as to the means of restoring the material of the army,
also intended to consult the Chambers as to what legislative
measures present circumstances demanded.

No one considered the result of such false statements, not
even those who suggested them.   The emperor was aware of
the distrust with which several leading representatives were
animated against him.   On the day after the elections they
chose Lanjuinais to be president, as a living proof of their independence, and Napoleon felt greatly annoyed.   During his
absence, men's minds became more and more uneasy.   The
reports of Carnot, Caulaincourt and especially that of Fouché
on the home and foreign affairs of France, had aggravated the
alarm, without throwing the representatives into the emperor's arms.   When discussing the reply to the speech from
the throne, Lepelletier, an old " terrorist," proposed that the
title " saviour of the country" should be conferred upon the
emperor.   " But wait till he has saved it!" exclaimed Dupin,
then quite young.

Every hour the chance of safety seemed more doubtful.   On
the 21st of March, at the opening of the session, La Fayette
mounted the tribune and said, " Gentlemen, when for the first
time during many years I raise a voice which the older friends
of liberty will still recognize, I feel that I am called to speak
to you of the dangers of our country, which you alone at
present have the power to save.   Sinister rumors have spread
. . . . , and they are unhappily confirmed.   The moment has
now come for us to rally round our old tricolor flag of '89, the
flag of liberty, equality, and public order, and it is this only
which we have to defend against foreign pretensions and external aggression.   Permit, then, a veteran of this sacred
cause, who has never known party-spirit, to submit to you a
few preliminary resolutions the necessity of which I trust you

will appreciate:—The chamber of representatives declares the national independence to be in danger; it declares its sittings permanent; it invites the ministers to throw themselves forthwith upon its confidence."

The proposition was carried unanimously.

Whilst the ministers were being thus appealed to in the chambers, they were assembled in Council with the emperor. Marshal Davout had found him in his bath, his body worn out with fatigue and his mind weighed down by misfortune, but he had recovered his strength, announced his intention of claiming from the country the dictatorial power which was necessary to him at this supreme crisis. The ministers looked at each other, confounded in the presence of the illusions which still existed in the mind of their master. "The emperor is wrong to count upon the chambers," said the Duc Decrès, "they are resolved upon a separation from him." Regnault de Saint Jean d'Angély expressed himself in the same sense. "Speak frankly," said Napoleon, "it is my abdication which they desire." "Yes, sire," replied the Minister of State, "and if your Majesty does not tender it, the chamber will perhaps dare to demand it."

Lucien Bonaparte now rose, always faithful in the time of trouble to that brother whose imperial yoke he had but lately shaken off.

Since the chamber does not appear disposed to join the emperor in order to save France," he said, "the emperor must save her by himself. Let him declare himself dictator, put the country in a state of siege, and call all patriots and good Frenchmen to its defence." "I do not fear the deputies," cried Napoleon, "whatever they may do; the people and the army I have still. One word from me, and they would be annihilated." At the same moment the proposal of La Fayette arrived from the chamber. Napoleon was troubled. "I was wrong not to dismiss all these people before my departure," he said, "they will ruin France. Regnault has not deceived me; I will abdicate if I must." Meanwhile, after long uncertainty and several vain attempts at reconciliation, the emperor decided upon sending Lucien as bearer of his message to the chamber. He entered in the uniform of the national guard, accompanied by Carnot, Caulaincourt, Fouché, and Davout, and said, "Gentlemen, being appointed commissioner extraordinary from his Majesty to the representatives of the people, I come to propose to them certain means of sav-

ing the country." He at the same time announced that a committee had been charged with renewing and carrying out negotiations with the foreign powers with the view of putting an
end to the war. " But," added the emperor's message, "it is
necessary that there should be the most complete harmony.
I count upon the patriotism of the chambers and on their personal attachment to me."

Jay ascended the tribune. Moderate and honest by nature,
he was that day the instrument of Fouché's intrigues. In a
few simple but effective words, he asked the ministers if they
believed peace to be possible as long as the Emperor Napoleon
remained on the throne. Seeing their silence and embarrassment, he rose to eloquence, and described the deplorable condition of France, and concluded with a proposal that the chamber should demand the emperor's abdication. In vain did
Lucien courageously attempt to defend his brother and reproach France for her inconstancy. La Fayette rose, and
vividly expressed the general sentiment. "Prince, you are
calumniating the nation. It is not for having abandoned Napoleon that posterity will be able to reproach France, but, alas,
for having followed him too far. She has followed him in the
fields of Italy, in the scorching Egyptian sands, in the burning
fields of Spain, in the vast plains of Germany, and the icy
wastes of Russia. Six hundred thousand Frenchmen sleep by
the banks of the Ebro and the Tagus; can you tell us how
many have fallen on the banks of the Danube, the Elbe, the
Nieman and the Moskowa? Alas! had she been less constant,
France would have saved two millions of her children; she
would have saved your brother, your family, us all, from the
abyss into which we are to-day being dragged, without knowing if we will be able to extricate ourselves from it."

The real gravity of the situation burst upon the chambers.
It burst upon the Élysée Palace in spite of the emperor's agitation and changes of thought. He had received news from the
army; about 50,000 men had already rallied at Laon, and some
reinforcements could be counted upon; with the depots, some
hundred thousand men could be formed. The military party
was not absolutely lost, and the impassioned obstinacy of the
great gambler was unwilling to abandon it. Two commissions
had been appointed by the chambers, charged with deliberat-
ing with the ministers upon salutary measures. The home
policy was discussed, but at every motion, at every proposal,
the idea of the abdication cropped up in the propositions and

speeches. The representatives expected to hear it proclaimed on the morning of the 22nd of March. When they assembled in the hall at nine o'clock, they received a communication from General Grenier to the effect that several negotiators had been sent to the allies' camp charged with treating in the name of the chambers. The germ of the abdication was contained in this declaration, but the impatience of the representatives was not satisfied with this. It was said that the emperor still hesitated, and Fouché's creatures industriously disseminated the fear of seeing him all at once again vigorously take possession of power by a direct appeal to the people and the army. Forfeiture began to be talked of: a vote was even proposed. General Salignac, who had been disgraced under the empire, craved an hour of respite for his old chief, in order to give him time to take his resolution before voluntarily laying down the proudest sceptre in the world. "If I asked you to give him till to-morrow, or till this evening," he said, "I could understand your objections, but one hour!" "One hour! one hour! Let him have one hour!" was the cry from every bench. The news was immediately carried to Napoleon.

For a moment his pride revolted at the summons, and at the respite allowed him. "I will not abdicate for a hare-brained lot of Jacobins and adventurers!" he cried, "I ought to have denounced them to the people and turned them out; but lost time can be made up!" Then, recovering himself, and perceiving the vanity of his hopes and the uselessness of his anger, "Write to these gentlemen, that they need not disturb themselves," said he to Fouché, who took care to follow the progress of his own intrigues, "they are going to get all they want." Fouché wrote to Manuel. The emperor dictated his second abdication to Lucien Bonaparte. "Frenchmen, in commencing the war to sustain the national independence, I counted upon united efforts, united wishes, and on the concurrence of the national authorities. I had reasons for hoping for success, and I braved the declarations of all the powers against me. Circumstances appearing to be changed, I offer myself as a sacrifice to the hatred of the enemies of France. May they be sincere in their declarations that they have only cherished it against my person! My political life is over, and I proclaim my son Emperor of the French, under the title of Napoleon the Second. The present ministers will form provisionally the council of government. The interest which I take in my son

compels me to invite the chambers to organize a regency by
law without delay. Unite yourselves in the interests of the
public safety, and that you may remain an independent nation."

The emperor did not attempt to deceive himself as to the
meaning of the step which he took in abdicating. "My son!"
he repeated two or three times, "my son! what a chimera!
No, no. It is not in favor of my son that I am abdicating, but
in that of the Bourbons. They at least are not prisoners at
Vienna!"

After some waverings, which for a moment seemed to be favorable to the preferment of Napoleon the Second, the chambers
ignoring that part of the emperor's message, resolved upon the
nomination of an executive committee charged provisionally
with carrying on the government. Three of its members were
to be elected by the Chamber of Representatives and two by
the Chamber of Peers. Fouché, Carnot, and General Grenier
were immediately chosen by the representatives, and a deputation was appointed to thank the emperor for his self-sacrifice.
"I hope my abdication will be for the good of France," he replied to Lanjuinais, "but I do not expect it to be." Then, as
if to satisfy his conscience, he commended his son to his care.
"It is in his favor that I am abdicating," he said.

He repeated this to the delegates from the Chamber of Peers.
A sad and violent scene had taken place in their assembly.
Marshal Ney had arrived, still greatly distressed by the disasters of Waterloo, and declaring that all was lost and that noth
ing was left but to treat with the enemy. General Drouot had
prevailed upon him not to contradict these assertions, and the
imperial message had completed the work of sowing dissension
among the peers. Lucien Bonaparte had insisted upon the
proclamation of Napoleon II., some other members had protested against this, and Labédoyère had flown into a passion.
"There are some people here who, lately at the feet of Napoleon fortunate, wish to abandon Napoleon unfortunate. If his
son is not recognized, his abdication is annulled, and he ought
to take it back. The traitors will perhaps put the finishing
touch to their intrigues with the foreigner. I see some now on
the benches who have already done so."—A tumult of shouts
had interrupted the imprudent orator, and the chamber had
appointed as members of the Executive Commission, Caulaincourt and Quinette, formerly members of the convention.

In vain did certain revolutionaries and old servants of the
empire still adhere to the notion of a regency which they could

nominate under the name of Napoleon II. Public opinion, bold and steadfast in its good sense, went dead for the re-establish-ment of the Bourbons, the emperor once out of the way. Manuel, a young advocate of Aix, known to Fouché, who availed himself of his services without employing him, cleverly dissuaded the Chamber of Representatives from a vote in favor of Napoleon II., which might have the effect of interfering with its liberty of action. "What party have we to fear?" he said. "Is it the republican party? There is no reason to sup-pose, that that party longer exists, whether in heads devoid of or in those matured by experience. Is it the Orleans party? That party, doubtless, by the protection which it offers to the principles and to the men of the revolution, would seem to offer more chances than any other for the liberty and happi-ness of the people; but we know that it has not many opinions on its side. Finally, is it the royalist party? Every one opposes it in the chamber, and we are generally agreed upon the prom-ises of the future which it holds out to France. Nevertheless, it cannot be concealed that, especially among men who cannot rise above the level of their own selfish interests, there are nu-merous followers who are devoted to it, some from remem-brance, sentiment, or custom, others by love of peace, welfare, and quiet enjoyment."

Manuel concluded by moving an order of the day on the simple ground that, Napoleon II. being Emperor of the French in his own right, his proclamation was not necessary. The Chamber adopted his idea, and contented itself by appointing Generals La Fayette and Sebastiani, Pontécoulant, Argenson and Laforest, to go to the head-quarters of the allies, to an-nounce officially the abdication of Napoleon, and to treat for peace. Almost deserted at the Elysée, the emperor had retired to Malmaison, where Queen Hortense had been living since the death of her mother (May 29, 1814). The acts drawn up by the executive commission bore this significant title suggested by Fouché: "In the name of the French people."

Ever since the departure of the king, in the midst of that confusion of parties and opinions, there had existed on the part of the constitutional royalists, an ardent and sincere desire to let the fugitive monarch know the truth about the state of France, and to convey to him useful suggestions as to the course he should pursue. "It was not only necessary to insist upon the necessity for his persevering in the constitutional system, and in the open acceptation of French society, such as

modern times had made it, it was necessary to enter into personal questions; to tell the king the presence of Blacas near
him was essentially prejudicial to his cause; to demand the
banishment of the favorite; to call forth some act, some public
words which would serve to explain frankly the intentions of
the king before again possessing himself of the government of
his estates; to persuade him, in fine, to trust implicitly in the
counsels of M. de Talleyrand, with whom, moreover, at this
time, hardly any of the men who gave this advice had the
slightest relation, and for whom even the majority of them had
little liking." *

M. Guizot accepted this difficult mission, and has often been
blamed for its unfortunate conclusion. He found at Ghent his
friends, Jaucourt, Louis, Beugnot, Lally-Tollendal, and Mounier, sad and broken-spirited, bravely struggling against the
passions and designs, odious or ridiculous, of party-spirit. He
saw the king, calm in the midst of the storm which was raging
around him. "What troubles us, sire, is that, believing in
the re-establishment of the Monarchy, people have no confidence
in its lasting." "Why? when the great maker of revolution is
removed, the Monarchy will last. It is clear of course, that if
Bonaparte returns to the island of Elba, it will be begun afresh;
but when he is finished, revolutions will be finished too."
"There are other things to be feared besides Bonaparte, sire.
People fear the weakness of the royal government; its vacilla-
tion between old and new ideas and interests; the disunion, or
at least the disagreement, of its ministers." Guizot mentioned
Blacas. "I will stick to everything I have promised in the
Charter," replied Louis XVIII., "what does it matter to France
what friends I keep in my palace, so long as no act emanates
from it which does not meet her views?" The battle of Waterloo had precipitated events and rendered prompt decisions inevitable. The king set out for Mons; there he got rid of Blacas,
appointed ambassador at Naples; at the same time, and while
refusing his resignation, Louis XVIII. had coldly received
Talleyrand. This conduct was neither prudent nor clever.
Europe wished to see with whom she was going to treat, and
Talleyrand had made a great name in Vienna for success and
ability. On the advice of the Count d'Artois, the king directed
his steps towards Cateau-Cambrésis, the head-quarters of the
English army. Pressed by Pozzo di Borgo to put an end to

* Guizot's *Mémoires pour servir*, etc., vol. i.

these difficulties, the Duke of Wellington wrote to Talleyrand at Mons. "I greatly regret," he said, "that you did not accompany the king here. It is I who have eagerly persuaded him to enter France at the same time as we do. Had I been able to tell you the motives which have directed me in this circumstance, I do not doubt that you would have given the king the same advice. I hope you will come and hear them." Talleyrand immediately joined the king at Cambrai. A liberal proclamation, drawn up by Beugnot, and containing the indications of a sound policy, was signed without difficulty by Louis XVIII. Monsieur had protested violently, and he obtained with trouble a few unimportant modifications. The armies of the allied powers were already on the march towards Paris. A proclamation of the Duke of Wellington, dated June 24th, announced to the French people that he entered their country not as an enemy (except of that enemy of the human race, with whom he could have neither peace nor truce), but in order to aid them in shaking off the iron yoke which had oppressed them. Marshal Blücher, intoxicated with the vengeance which he had exercised, and with that which he was preparing, loudly announced his intention of seizing and punishing Napoleon if he could get him into his clutches, without waiting for what the allied powers should determine upon with regard to him. "It will not accord with the part we have played during these late events to debase ourselves to the trade of the executioner," the Duke of Wellington said to him. At Paris, Fouché had let Vitrolles out of prison, and charged him with making his advances to Louis XVIII. "Perhaps we shall not go quite straight, but we shall finish by arriving at him," the Duke of Otranto had said. "Have no fear for your head, it will be put on the same hook as mine, which is, it is true, in some very tolerable danger. All the madmen in the army have sworn to make me out a bad lot. We are working here in the king's service; perhaps meanwhile we shall have to go by way of Napoleon II. and the Duc d'Orleans."

"In the deplorable condition into which the enterprise of an heroic and chimerical egotism had thrown France, there was clearly only one course to follow, namely, to recognize Louis XVIII., to take action upon his liberal ideas, and to act in concert with him in order to treat with the foreigners. This was a duty in the interests of peace, and a course calculated to afford the best chances of diminishing the evils of invasion, for Louis XVIII. alone was able to repel them with some authority.

To accept without hesitation or delay the second restoration, and to place the king between France and Europe, was the course clearly pointed out by patriotism and common sense. But not only was this not done, but everything was done, or was allowed to be done, which was necessary to make the restoration appear the work of foreign efforts only, and to make France, after her military defeat, undergo a political and diplomatic one. The chamber of the hundred days lacked intelligence and resolution. It did not lend itself either to imperial despotism or to revolutionary violence, it did not become the instrument of any of the extreme parties, it applied itself honestly to the task of holding back France on the brink of the abyss into which they would have liked to push her; but its policy was entirely negative, it beat about timidly outside the harbor, instead of resolutely entering, shutting its eyes when it reached the bar, and submitting, not through confidence, but through weakness, to the infatuation and obstinacy of the old or new enemies of the king. It was to these hesitations, to these fruitless gropings of the only public power then in existence, that Fouché owed his importance and his ephemeral success. When honest men fail to understand and carry out the designs of providence, dishonest people undertake the task. On the spur of necessity, and in the midst of general impotence, there always gather together certain corrupt spirits, bold and sagacious in discovering what is likely to happen, and what contingencies may arise; and they make themselves the instruments of a triumph which does not actually belong to them, but by which they succeed in giving themselves airs in order to appropriate for themselves its fruits. Such a man was the Duke of Otranto in the hundred days. A revolutionary turned grand seigneur, and wishing to ingratiate himself under this double character with the old French royalty, he displayed in the pursuit of his object all the *savoir-faire* and audacity of a gamester, endowed with more foresight and wisdom than his fellows."* Through the endless labyrinth of these complicated and shameless intrigues Fouché marched, always with the definite view to the restoration of the Bourbons, but he required time in order to serve his personal interests under the Restoration; he was not anxious for the conclusion.

Others were more urgent, perhaps because they were honest and sincere. Marshal Davout had been badly treated by the

---

* Guizot, *Mémoires pour servir à l'histoire de mon temps*

court in 1814; he had at that time dipped into the military plots, and had actively and ardently served the Emperor Napoleon during the hundred days. After the battle of Waterloo, he saw France conquered, and ready to be once more torn by civil war; he took his resolution courageously, and received favorably the advances which Marshal Oudinot had been charged to make to him by Vitrolles. With the consent of Fouché a grand council was convoked, to which were nominated the presidents, vice-presidents, and secretaries of the two chambers. The marshal demonstrated from military reports that the army was henceforth unfit to oppose the allied forces; then, as all present remained silent, he repeated: "In the light of the tidings that have reached me from the departments, as well as from the corps posted on the Moselle, and the Rhine, I regard France as lost, if she does not hasten to treat with Louis XVIII." He immediately added some conditions. The king, he thought, ought to enter Paris without a foreign guard, accepting the national colors, guaranteeing the personal security of every one, and the conservation of all property and appointments, and, finally, maintaining the Legion of Honor as the principal order of the State.

The marshal thus cut the knot of the situation with a firm hand, accustomed to serve France resolutely; the hesitations and dislikes of the old conventionals, obstructed and delayed the decision. They were encouraged in their opposition by the report that certain commissioners had just been received, empowered to treat with the allies. Before advancing towards Haguenau, where the allied sovereigns were at the time, they had seen the Duke of Wellington and Blücher at Laon, and they had gathered some impressions rather than obtained any categorical declarations. They transmitted to the feeble executive power which governed France provisionally, their opinion that the allied princes were not absolutely opposed to the ascension of Napoleon II., and that they did not insist upon the restoration of the Bourbons. This assurance circulated in the chambers by the members of the grand council whose wishes it flattered, increased the excitement and uncertainty. Meanwhile the hostile armies approached Paris. The commissioners of the chambers had not been allowed to come near the sovereigns in Alsace; they had taken the way back to Paris, not without difficulty. Negotiators were chosen afresh, and were charged to treat for an armistice with the victorious generals. The intrigues of Fouché brought them within reach of the Duke of Wellington, who was always steady, sensible, and favorable to the restoration, pure and simple, of the house of Bourbon to the throne. He communicated to the commissioners of the executive the declaration signed at Cambrai by King Louis XVIII., counselling them to hold by the Charter of 1814, without claiming to impose on the king any humiliating conditions. A homogeneous and strongly constituted ministry was alone necessary to assure good government. Louis XVIII. had promised to confide the direction of it to Tallyrand. The Duke of Wellington did not conceal from the negotiators that the advice of the Austrians and of the majority of the allied princes was, that they should not grant an armistice, and that they should not consent to treat before occupying Paris. Already Marshal Blücher had caused the environs of the capital to be devastated by his cavalry. He had blown up several of the bridges on the Seine, and had posted his troops on the left bank.

The possible defence of Paris remained the last hope of the determined adversaries of the Restoration. More than 60,000 men were united under the hand, or were within the reach of Marshal Davout. "If he would only engage in a battle," said he, "I am ready to fight, and I hope to win." "Are you able to answer for the victory?" slyly asked Fouché. "Yes," replied the marshal; "if I am not killed in the first two hours." Carnot and Marshal Soult held the defence to be impossible, even after the gain of a battle.

It was necessary to be prepared for the most painful alternative; with hearts full of patriotic anger and sadness, the executive commission resolved to send plenipotentiaries to Marshal Blücher, who had drawn nearer to Paris than the Duke of Wellington, in order to obtain the renewal of the armistice negotiations. They believed themselves certain of a favorable reception. Marshal Davout, at the head of the troops, had great difficulty in restraining their eagerness to fight. He repressed at the same time his own indignation in the presence of the menacing enemy. The three negotiators, Bignon, interim minister of foreign affairs, General Guilleminot, and Bondy, perfect of the Seine, arrived, at his headquarters at Montrouge. They came to demand his signature to the projects of negotiation. The excitement was as great among the officers as among the soldiers. "Better to die fighting than to capitulate to the allies," reiterated the generals grouped around their illustrious leader. But France could not perish like her heroic defenders. After a brief and final reconnaissance, Marshal Davout signed, as all the members of the executive commission had done. " I have sent a flag of truce," he said to Bignon, "you can set out."

It was a clever thought of Fouché to direct the plenipotentiaries to the head-quarters of Blücher, who, always violently opposed to the French, was jealous of the Duke of Wellington, and therefore felt flattered by the appearance of the negotiators in his camp. The English general, however, was not slow in arriving. Each had taken a side, inflexible on the important points regarding which the commissioners were empowered to treat primarily. Discussion was impossible, and the instructions of the sovereigns were as summary as the decisions of their generals. The plenipotentiaries had proposed several plans, and they were reduced to accept conditions more unfavorable than they could have foreseen. The French army should evacuate Paris and the environs within three days, and retire beyond the Loire, carrying with it its arms, artillery, and baggage. The officers of the federates were assimilated to the regular troops. The allies, once in possession of Paris, should reinstate the national guard in the interior service. The commanders of the allied armies undertook to respect and to uphold the actual authorities as long as they were in force. Public property should be respected, except that which had relation to war. In virtue of this exception we should soon lose all the treasures accumulated in our museums by victory, and which the allies had spared in 1814. Article 12 stipulated that the persons and property of private individuals should be respected; "The inhabitants and generally the individuals within the capital shall continue to enjoy their rights and liberties, without being disturbed or affected in anything relative to the duties which occupy them or have occupied them, to their conduct and to their political opinions." The enemy's generals raised no objection to this article. In his declaration of Cambrai, King Louis XVIII. had announced the intention of making some exceptions to his general clemency.

The capitulation was signed in the evening of the 3rd of July, and at four in the following morning the plenipotentiaries returned to Paris, nearly heart broken with grief, but assured in their conscience that they obtained all that it was possible to obtain from the immovable resolution of the victors. Saint Ouen, Saint Denis, Clichy, and Neuilly had to be evacuated on the same day; Montmartre on the 5th, the day following; and on the 6th all the other barriers of the capital were to be handed over to the enemy. The movement of evacuation began immediately, at every moment interrupted by the passionate emotion of the army. Marshal Davout, at the head of his corps, seconded by the honest efforts of General Drouot, succeeded in re-establishing order in the exasperated multitude, ready to refuse obedience to the chiefs, whom it accused of having dishonored it. Meanwhile the indignation was directed especially against Fouché. The soldiers of Waterloo were still too devoted to the emperor to shift to his shoulders the grievous weight of the misfortunes of the Fatherland.

The army had slowly taken the road for the Loire, everywhere directed by Marshal Davout. Imposing even in his misfortune, he threatened the Austrians, who were preparing to cross the boundary agreed upon on the upper Loire, and held in check at the same time his enemies and his soldiers. He had laid down his functions as minister of war in order to fulfil this mournful mission, and would have no other title than that of "general-in-chief of the army of the Loire." Thanks to the generous advances of a rich banker, Laffitte, whose name was destined soon to become known, he had been able partly to discharge the arrears of pay due to the soldiers.

The capitulation of Paris had been facilitated by the removal of the Emperor Napoleon from the environs. It was one of the principal points in the instructions of the allied sovereigns that the person of Napoleon was to be delivered up to them. French honor shrank from this unworthy concession. Almost alone at Malmaison, Napoleon wavered between the desire of taking refuge in America and the idea of throwing himself on the mercy of Russia or England. He had finished by requesting that two frigates in the roads at Rochefort should be prepared to take him to America. "Since the society of men is denied to me," he had said, "I will take refuge in the bosom of nature, and there I shall live in the solitude which harmonizes with my last thoughts." Meanwhile he was troubled by the rumors which reached him concerning the chimerical projects of his friends as well as by the danger which threatened him from the hatred of the allies. At the last moment he proposed to the executive commission to place him again for a few hours at the head of the troops. "The resources of the enemy are exhausted," said he to General Beker, who was charged at the time with guarding and protecting him, "We can throw ourselves between them; and under my orders the army will fight with the courage of despair. I shall conquer not for myself but for France, and I pledge the word of a soldier to restore on the spot the authority to the Provisional Government. I shall not keep it for a single hour after victory."

Vain projects of an ardent and solitary imagination, driven to the last limits of an existence given up to the most unheard of adventures! The proposal was immediately rejected by Fouché, who hastened the departure of Napoleon, which had been already decided upon. On the evening of the 29th of June, the emperor left Malmaison on the way to Rochefort, accompanied by General Bertrand, the Duc de Rovigo, and General Gourgaud. All his relations were to join him in America. At the moment of his departure, Queen Hortense constrained the emperor to accept the diamond necklace which she wore. He took the road for Rambouillet, still repeating, while he was leaving for ever that capital to which the noble generosity of King Louis Philippe was one day to bring back his ashes, "The Provisional Government does not know the spirit of France, it is too anxious to get me away from Paris; if it had accepted my last proposition the appearance of matters would have changed."

Meanwhile, King Louis XVIII. was approaching Paris. At Roye, where he had stopped, the emissaries of Fouché had begun their final attack in order to assure for their chief the price of his services. Monsieur went into it with ardor. "That is a new passion and one which does not come to you through Divine inspiration," said the king, laughing. He made some resistance. "In spite of what he had said to me at Ghent with regard to the regicides," says Guizot, in his *Mémoires*, "I doubt whether he made any strong resistance. His dignity was not always sustained by strong conviction or by energetic feeling, and it could sometimes give way before necessity. He had as guarantee of the necessity in this circumstance the two authorities best calculated to influence his decision and to protect his honor, namely, the Duke of Wellington and the Comte d'Artois. Both pressed him to accept Fouché as his minister—Wellington, in order to assure for the king an easy return, and also in order that he himself, and England along with him, should remain the chief authors of the Restoration, while putting a quick stop to the war before Paris, where he was afraid of seeing himself compromised in the odious rage of the Prussians; the Comte d'Artois, by impatient activity, always ready to promise and to agree, engaged beforehand by Vitrolles in the snares which Fouché had planted everywhere for the royalists. Louis XVIII. yielded; he promised to nominate Fouché as minister of police, and on the 6th of July, at the Castle of Arnouville, the king signed the ordinance with a visible effort. Some hours later, Fouché, the regicide, one of the most hateful among the hateful tribunes of the "Terror," was received into the king's cabinet. This was an uncalled-for degradation, which by a little patience the royal dignity might have avoided. Fouché was not in possession of the keys of Paris, and France, by the necessities of the situation, was inevitably urged towards the Bourbons. Fouché was not to enjoy a long triumph, but his momentary triumph brought disgrace and weakness to the restored monarchy.

Fouché's excuse throughout his intrigues, and his determination, as boldly displayed before the chambers, was to impose liberal conditions on the monarch. The pretext of patriotism produced no result. In an interview which took place at Neuilly between the Duke of Wellington, Talleyrand, Pozzo di Borgo, and Golz, on one side, and the Duke of Otranto on the other, the latter found himself compelled to accept the king's voluntary promises thus summed up by Talleyrand:—"The whole of the old Charter, including the abolition of confiscation, the non-renewal of the law of last year as to the liberty of the press; the immediate election of a new chamber by the electoral colleges, the unity of the ministry, the reciprocal initiative in laws, by message from the Crown, and on the proposal of the chambers; an hereditary right to the Chamber of Peers."

It was, in fact, almost a return to the situation of the preceding year. Although Talleyrand accompanied that declaration with the most liberal assurances, they were not sufficient to satisfy the chambers, who were generally influenced by a strong antagonism against the House of Bourbon, and had for several days been discussing a proposal of a Constitution, which, in many points, indicated democratic and revolutionary distrust. It was, nevertheless, necessary to decide on a plan. "The English are now arriving!" repeated sensible men, tired of hearing useless theories pompously detailed in the midst of the dangers now threatening the country. "Though the English are on the spot," replied Dupin, "I shall insist on expressing my opinion, and shall enounce it." The Chamber of Representatives proudly voted a declaration of rights, to which they remained invariably attached. The Chamber of Peers refused to adhere to them. All the gates of Paris were already in the hands of the allies.

The day was now come to determine so much fatal indecision, which had become childish or hypocritical. The executive commission sat in the Tuileries, on the 7th of July, whilst the columns of the allies, poured, without disorder, through the streets and boulevards of the capital, and took possession in succession of all the public buildings, strongholds, and the Champ de Mars. There were cannon placed everywhere; the crowds gathered in the streets silently and gloomily. A Prussian officer entered into the Council-hall, and said, "I have orders to take possession of the palace." On Fouché protesting, the officer repeated his orders. The new Minister of Police of King Louis XVIII. took a sheet of paper and wrote to the presidents of the new Chambers: "Monsieur le President, till the present we were led to believe that the allied sovereigns had not come to an agreement in choosing a prince to reign over them. Our plenipotentiaries have given us the same assurances on their return. Nevertheless, the ministers and generals of the allied powers declared yesterday at the conference held with the president of the commission, that all the sovereigns had undertaken to replace Louis XVIII. on the throne, and that he must make his entry into the capital to-night or to-morrow. The foreign troops have just taken possession of the Tuileries, where the Government is sitting. Under the present circumstances, we can do nothing for our country, but express our best wishes, and since our deliberations are no longer free, we feel it to be our duty to separate."

In reality, and by the very force of circumstances, the allied sovereigns showed their intention to replace King Louis XVIII. upon the throne of France, and Fouché put in their mouths words which they had not really spoken. He showed equal audacity next day, in inserting the following paragraph in the *Moniteur:*—"The Commission of the Government has informed the king through its mouthpiece, the president, that it is just dissolved, and the peers and deputies appointed under the late Government have received information to that effect. The chambers are dissolved. The king will enter Paris to-morrow, at eleven o'clock. His Majesty will stop at the Tuileries."

The executive commission had entrusted Fouché with no

message to the king, and the representatives were violently excited against the sort of orders they had received. On presenting themselves next day at the doors of the Palais Bourbon, they found them closed by order of the Prefect of Police, and fifty-three of them signed a protest, and lodged it with Lanjuinais. On the following day, the 8th of July, King Louis XVIII. entered Paris, welcomed with real sincerity by the populace, but without the display of enthusiastic delight which signalized his previous arrival. Marshal Masséna, on the previous evening, had again attempted, in the name of the colonels of the national guard, to obtain permission from the king to retain the tricolor; and Oudinot assisted him, but Louis XVIII. obstinately refused, in spite of the advice of the Duke of Wellington. "What a people!" said the illustrious leader of the English army; "it is easier to make them accept a regicide than a reasonable idea!"

On the same day as Louis XVIII. entered Paris, General Beker, who had arrived at Rochefort on the 3rd of July with the Emperor Napoleon, received from the executive commission, who were still acting, the order to hasten the exile's embarkation. The latter had been hitherto delaying; the English cruisers, it was reported, threatened his safety and were ready to attack the frigates. The emperor wished a safe-conduct to be asked from Wellington. At Rochefort various plans for escape were proposed; and before leaving Paris he had refused La Fayette's offer to get him conveyed to America by a merchant-vessel belonging to that nation. The regiment of marines garrisoned on the island of Aix showed great enthusiasm for Napoleon, who amused himself in reviewing them. General Beker insisted on the necessity for departure; the Prefect of Marine was authorized to embark the emperor in a man-of-war's boat, if the state of weather or presence of the enemy prevented the use of frigates; but, should he prefer to go on board an English vessel or to England itself, an ambassador was to be put at his disposition. Only two English frigates closed the entrance to the harbor.

It was to Captain Maitland, who was in command of the "Bellerophon," that Napoleon sent Rovigo and Las Cases on the night of the 9th July. Their orders were to inquire about the safe-conducts which had been asked, and at the same time sound the English officer as to the manner in which he should think it his duty to treat the emperor if either taken when out at sea, or if he should present himself on board! With refer-

ence to the first point, the captain's answer was very simple.
He knew nothing as to the request for safe-conducts; in their
absence, he should, of course, stop any war-ship attempting to
force the blockade, and should also stop any neutral vessel
attempting to escape. He had received no instructions with
regard to the person of the emperor, but was disposed to believe that England would always show him the respect due to
the high position he had held.

After some hesitation and several new proposals for out-
witting the vigilance of the English cruisers, Napoleon decided
to fall back upon his original intention. Now at bay, and reduced to the necessity of risking an absolutely desperate attempt to save himself, he wished to make before the world a
final display as striking as it was painful. On the 14th of July,
he wrote as follows to the Prince Regent of England:—

"Your Royal Highness,—After being aimed at, both by the
factions which divide my country, and by the enmity of the great
powers of Europe, I have finished my political career, and now
come, like Themistocles, to sit down by the hearth of the English people. I place myself under the protection of their laws,
which I claim from your Royal Highness as the most powerful, the most steadfast, and the most generous of my enemies."

No law of the English constitution could extend its protection to the mortal enemy of England and Europe, after he had
just given a new proof that oaths were powerless in chaining
him down to enforced repose. Napoleon was secretly conscious of this, but he wished to risk this last chance of the
hostile nation being imprudently generous. He delivered himself up to the risk of appearing betrayed. "Don't accompany
me on board," he said to General Beker, when setting out to
embark on the "Bellerophon;" "I don't know what the English intend doing with me; and should they not respond to my
confidence, it might be said that you have sold me to England."

The emperor went on board the English frigate on the 15th.
General Gourgaud was not permitted to go to London with
Napoleon's letter to the Prince Regent. On the 24th, the
"Bellerophon" brought into Plymouth harbor its illustrious
passenger, who was speedily besieged by the insatiable British
curiosity, all Captain Maitland's endeavors to keep off visitors
being insufficient.

Meanwhile, the question was being discussed in London
what place would be sufficiently sure for the transportation of

the dangerous enemy who had at last, after so long and keenly-contested struggles, fallen into the hands of the English people. It had been decided to treat him as a prisoner of war, and that he should be deprived of his sovereign title and asked to give up his sword. Thus a vengeance legitimate enough to bear the name of justice was meanly gratified. Several members of the English cabinet proposed to deliver up the outlaw to the King of France; but at last the decision was that he should be conducted to St. Helena, a rock lost amid the Atlantic, between Africa and America, the most solitary of all prisons. Only three of his old servants were to be allowed to accompany him in his exile, and he was to be deprived of all personal resources.

When Lord Keith, the admiral in command at Plymouth, appeared before Napoleon with orders to announce the fate in store for him, the emperor listened unmoved, as if he had anticipated the whole. He discussed several points, and asked some questions as to the details, while retaining a quiet and natural dignity that imposed respect on the most hostile of his enemies. Throughout all England there were violent outcries against him, and the journals resounded with shouts of hatred and vengeance. When Lord Keith went towards Napoleon to demand his sword, the latter only replied by a look, at the same time placing his hand on the hilt. The admiral did not insist upon it.

It was on the 8th of August, 1815, that the Emperor Napoleon left the English coasts to cross the seas towards his prison. He was still in the prime of life, and having long enjoyed robust health, seemed still to have many years before him. Six years exhausted his physical strength and sometimes his moral courage. The weight of his captivity was to be unnecessarily increased by paltry annoyances and severity; and he resented them with a bitterness which the isolation and weariness alone might excuse. When, at last, he expired, on the 5th of May, 1821, Europe, astonished that " ce mortel était mort," felt itself delivered from a secret and perpetual apprehension. The French people preserved in their hearts a remembrance of which they were thirty years later to prove the persistence. Though exhausted, crushed, vanquished, and reduced, France always remained dazzled and giddy by the whirlwind of glory in the midst of which he had kept her for more than fifteen years. The rest of a long peace was now at last to heal her wounds, without exciting her gratitude for those who healed her, or effacing from her eyes the sight of the "deepest print ever left by mortal foot on the blood-stained dust of the world."

The genius and renown of Napoleon have nothing to fear from the light of history; justice is being done him and will continue to be done every new generation. Illustrious in the foremost rank amongst the greatest conquerors of enslaved humanity, whether subduing, ruling, or organizing, equally great by military genius, and by the supreme instinct of national government, he was constantly carried away by selfish passions and desires, whatever their importance or unimportance might be, and took no cognizance of the eternal laws of duty and justice. Corrupt, he corrupted others; despotic, he subdued minds and debased consciences; all-powerful, he constantly made a bad use of his power. His glorious and blood-stained traces remained soiled not only by faults but by crimes. The startling dream with which he dazzled France had disappeared; the memory still remains, weakened, but always fatal to our unhappy country, in her days of weariness and dejection. It is necessary that she should know what the glory and triumph of the first Empire cost her: nor must she forget the degradation and tears which were a second time to be brought upon her by the same name.

CHAPTER XVIII.

PARLIAMENTARY GOVERNMENT.   THE RESTORATION UNDER KING
LOUIS XVIII. (1815—1824).

THE Restoration of 1815 remained burdened with a bitter and heavy heritage, which it afterwards rendered more grievous by its own faults. The first months which elapsed after the definitive return of Louis XVIII. to France were disturbed by painful political antagonism, and by much imprudent severity displayed in the name of justice. We now, however, enter upon a new era, till then unexampled in our history, during which France, at peace in spite of its internal agitation, constantly tended towards that government of the country by the country which remains and shall remain the object of the most noble hopes. The sentence, "Happy the nation who has no history!" has often been ridiculed. It is indeed false in its first application, since every free people has a history daily recommencing with animation, ardor, and effect; but it is true in this point that the inner history of free peoples is especially engraven on men's memories by striking and simple traits. Its incidents from day to day are not striking enough to excite the attention of all: it is by practical results and the general result of its powerful influence on the destinies of the country that effects of the Parliamentary régime must be judged.

In July, 1815, King Louis XVIII. had scarcely entered the Tuileries before he had to form a "homogeneous" ministry, united in the same thought and from their common object. Talleyrand had already been appointed the leader by the king, in accordance with the express wish of England and Austria; and Fouché, by dint of intriguing and perfidious cunning, obtained a place which was granted with great repugnance by Louis XVIII. The ministry of the interior had been in vain offered to Pozzo di Borgo. Pasquier remained interim Home Minister, being at the same time Minister of Justice. He summoned Guizot from the Ministry of Justice to be Secretary-General, without much personal favor towards him, but from a strong conviction of his merit. From its very origin, and in spite of the conscientious efforts both of the king and his best councillors, the new power as constituted immediately after the fall of Napoleon was weak and was to remain so.

"Talleyrand performed a great feat in Vienna. By the treaty of alliance concluded on the 3rd of January, 1815, between France, England, and Austria, he put an end to the coalition formed against us in 1813, and cut Europe into two to the advantage of France. But the events of the 20th March overthrew his work, and the European coalition was again formed against Napoleon and France, which made itself or allowed itself to be made the instrument of Napoleon. There was now no chance of breaking this formidable alliance. The same feeling of disquietude and distrust with reference to us, the same purpose of firm and lasting union animated the sovereigns and peoples. In this close intimacy again formed against us, the Emperor Alexander was specially indignant against the house of Bourbon and Talleyrand, who had shown a wish to deprive him of his allies. The second restoration, moreover, was not, like the first, his work or personal glory. The honor now belonged mainly to England and the Duke of Wellington. From motives of self-love as well as policy, the

Emperor Alexander went to Paris, which he reached on the
10th of July, 1815, with coldness and ill-temper towards the
king and his councillors.

" France and her king were nevertheless in pressing want of
the Emperor's good services. They were now face to face
with the passionate rancor and ambition of Germany. Her
diplomatists drew up the map of our territory* deprived of the
provinces which they wished to take from us. Her generals
mined in order to blow up the monuments which recalled their
defeats in the midst of their victories. Louis XVIII. resisted
with dignity such foreign coarseness: he threatened to have
his chair placed on the ' Bridge of Jena,' and asked Wellington
openly if he thought that the English government would consent to receive him if he were to ask again for refuge." Wellington cooled down Blücher's passion as well as he could, and
tried to remonstrate with him. But neither the dignity of the
king nor the friendly intervention of England sufficed against
the German passions and claims. The Emperor Alexander
alone could restrain them. Talleyrand tried to ingratiate himself by personal intentions. When forming his cabinet he had
the Duke of Richelieu,† who was still absent, appointed minister of the king's household; and the ministry of the interior
was reserved for Pozzo di Borgo, who had of his own accord
exchanged the official service of Russia, to take part in the
government of France. Talleyrand had implicit faith in the
power of temptations, but this time they failed. Richelieu refused, probably by arrangement with the king himself; and
Pozzo did not obtain, or perhaps dared not ask from his master, permission to become again French. Of a keen and restless disposition, daring but suspicious, he felt his situation uncertain, and could not conceal his perplexities from penetrating
looks. The Emperor Alexander maintained his cold reserve,
leaving Talleyrand powerless and embarrassed in that arena of
negotiations, generally the theatre of his success.

" Fouché's weakness was different, and due to different
causes. Not that the foreign sovereigns and their ministers
were better disposed to him than to Talleyrand, his entry into
the king's council having caused great scandal to monarchical
Europe, Wellington alone still continuing to defend him; but

---

*After the treaty of peace, the Emperor Alexander presented Richelieu with this
map.
 †Richelieu had become the emperor's intimate friend during the emigration, and
was made Governor of the Crimea.

none of the strangers made an attack upon him or felt interested in his fall. It was within that the tempest arose against him. With a strange mixture of presumption and frivolity, he was confident of being able to deliver up the revolution to the king, and the king to the revolution, trusting to his skill and audacity to pass and repass from one camp to another, and govern the one by the other by betraying them in turn. It is our weakness and misfortune that in great crises the conquered become dumb. The chamber of 1815 could not yet be seen except in the distance; and the Duke of Otranto already shook, as if struck by lightning, at the side of the tottering Talleyrand." *

The military discipline, the profound and touching confidence inspired by their distinguished chiefs and all the sentiments of genuine patriotism, produced the submission of the army of the Loire, and maintained order in the ranks. The armed resistance which took place on various points of the frontiers was speedily disappearing. A few fortresses on the north and east still held out. The small town Huningue was defended till the 26th of August; and when at last General Barbanègre capitulated, and his garrison defiled on the ramparts, there were not more than about fifty men. The Archduke John, who commanded the blockading army, thought they formed only the advanced guard, and congratulated Barbanègre on his illustrious defence. The excessive severity displayed by the armies of occupation caused an expiation of the patriotic rage of the provincial populations; the violence and exactions of the Prussians, then more excusable than in recent times, frequently provoked the peasantry to secret and stern reprisals. As Secretary-General of Justice, Guizot one day saw a peasant of Burgundy brought into his private room, on charge of having killed several Prussians. The peasant having boldly denied it, Guizot wished to examine him alone. "I shall tell you by yourself," said the wine-grower, "I put seventeen of them into my well." I am very certain his confidence did not lead him into trouble.

On the 13th of July the electoral colleges were summoned by royal order to meet on the 14th of August for the new elections. The age of eligibility was reduced from forty years to twenty-five, and that of the electorate from thirty to twenty-one; while the number of deputies was extended from 250 to 402. It was decided that the peerage should be hereditary.

---

* Guizot's *Mémoires*, etc., vol. i.

The censure of printed works of less than twenty pages was abolished. A large privy council composed of prominent members of various parties assisted, on important occasions, in the deliberations of the government. These important reforms were not imposed upon the restored monarchy by any real necessity or strong expression of public opinion, but the cabinet wished to show itself in favor of a large extension of free institutions. They had moreover to conceal from people or cause them to forget the severity then exercised against individuals, under the violent pressure of the ultra-royalist journals, as well as upon the advice almost amounting to a command of the foreign sovereigns.

"It is only by making a striking example of Napoleon's accomplices that we can hope to make the monarchy last any time," wrote Lord Liverpool to Castlereagh. "Severity in their case would dispose public opinion in this country to be less stern with regard to France." The unchaining of reactionary passions in the interior was still more significant. During the hundred days the king, in his Cambray proclamation, had already announced the intention of making some exceptions to the general amnesty. On the 24th of July, 1815, two lists were published, one of which bore the names of nineteen persons to be tried by court-martial; Marshals Ney, Grouchy, Bertrand; Generals Lallemand, d'Erlon, Lefebvre-Desnouettes, Clauzel, Drouot, Cambronne; besides Labédoyère, Lavalette, and Rovigo. No title was granted to the most distinguished favorites of the fallen power. On the second list were inscribed the names of thirty-eight accused persons who were to leave Paris for certain towns indicated by the minister of police, until the chambers should have decided upon their fate. Marshal Soult and Bassano were in this number. It was with great difficulty that the ministers succeeded in erasing other names which had been originally indicated by Fouché, and which amounted to 110: the Duke of Vicentia, General Sebastiani, and Benjamin Constant were among these more fortunate exceptions. Twenty-nine peers were excluded by name from the upper chamber. Marshal Davout protested against the exceptional measures directed against those of his friends who like him had served the emperor during the hundred days. "It is my name that ought to be substituted for that of several of them," said he, "since they only obeyed the orders I had given them as Minister of War. It is obvious that to all the calamities weighing upon our unhappy country are to be added those of vengeance and proscription." He at the same time gave in his resignation as commander-in-chief of the army of the Loire; and was replaced by Marshal Macdonald, who began to disband the troops with great success. The order to that effect appeared on the 12th of August.

It was by a constant exercise of self-control and resolute patience that the king, the ministers, and the whole of the French government succeeded in enduring the hateful violence of the Germans, and the intentional severity of the other allies. On entering Paris, the Prussians imposed on the capital a war contribution of a hundred millions, an exorbitant demand which was further aggravated by exactions incessantly renewed. The museums had already begun to be despoiled, a severe measure due to the mad attempt of the hundred days. When opening the session of 1814, King Louis XVIII. was able to congratulate himself because those masterpieces of art thenceforward belonged to us by rights more secure and sacred than those of victory. In 1815 the English cabinet, with the exception of Castlereagh, was more eager in supporting the demands of the nations who had formerly been robbed by Napoleon. The directors of the museums alone protested: the king might probably have succeeded in retaining the works of art granted to France by treaties, but Talleyrand's advice was to make no resistance. "Let the Prussians disgrace themselves," said he, when the statues and paintings were being gradually sent back to the towns they had formerly adorned. The foreign troops were more than once obliged to protect the wagons loaded with them, against the strong indignation of the population of Paris.

Throughout the whole country, according to the various temperaments of the provinces, there reigned a violent and contradictory agitation. The cantonment of the allied armies in the centres of occupation kept up indignation without imposing order. The English army occupied the north; the Prussians, all the country between the Seine and the coast; the Austrians, Burgundy and the centre of France, and afterwards Provence and part of Languedoc; the Russians, Champagne and Lorraine; the men of Baden, Alsace. Only some western states still remained partially unoccupied; they were still in arms on account of the royalist risings during the hundred days. The calm and resolute attitude of the leaders imposed respect upon Blücher himself, who wrote as follows to General de Grisolles in command at Morbihan: "Sir, your request that I should send the troops under my orders into the cantonments occupied by the royal army in Brittany is so reasonable that I agree to it with much pleasure." There was no bloodshed in the west, but bands of men overran the country parts, demanding arbitrary contributions and ill-treating the inhabitants. The whole of the south was on fire.

It was a bitter inheritance of the keenly-fought struggles and long religious persecution that the population of the south of France were left divided into parties in violent or secret hostility, who had for more than a century been perpetually tossed between the alternatives of triumph and oppression. The Protestants, who had long bent under a painful yoke which years had scarcely alleviated, found themselves delivered by the dawn of the French Revolution, which they hailed with transport. Amongst them a certain number of the constitutionals had paid, on the scaffold of "The Terror," for their generous self-illusions in 1789. The mass of the Protestant population remained attached to the principles of the revolution. They had been well treated under the empire, and had been of service to it. The attempt of the hundred days found them generally favorable, and some acts of violence were committed against the royalists who in several places supported the brave efforts of the Duc d'Angoulême. Even where religious passions had no great influence, political passions were violently excited among those populations who were equally hot-headed in their opposition. Napoleon's final fall was the signal for a shameful letting loose of vengeance which had recently been accumulated. In their violence the populace, in various towns, selected startling victims. Marshal Brune was murdered at Avignon on the 2nd of August. An old soldier of the revolution, without favor under the empire, he had been appointed during the hundred days to a command in the Var. He retired immediately upon the restoration, after taking the Bourbon colors from the regiment, and was furnished with a passport from the king's government when he arrived on the morning of the 2nd of August, at the Hôtel de Poste in Avignon. Being quickly recognized and denounced, he was violently attacked by the maddened populace. In vain did the prefect and mayor, supported by several national guards, try to rescue him from the senseless mob. The carriage was stopped, the hotel surrounded and besieged; the marshal traced to his room and shot in the head. It was at once given out that he had killed himself to escape his execu-

tioners. The murderers broke up the coffin in which their
victim's body was concealed from them, dragged it to the
Rhone, and hurled it into its waters. The corpse was washed
ashore on the bank, but it was not till two years afterwards
that the marshal's widow succeeded in finding her husband's
remains.

At Toulouse similar scenes characterized the murder of General Ramel. Honorable and brave, he in vain exerted himself,
as commander of the department, in repressing the excessive
violence of the royalist population. He had dissolved the com-
panies of royal volunteers formed at Toulouse during the hundred days, and serving as the rallying-point of disorder. On
the 15th of August, when entering his hotel, the general was
attacked by an armed band. The sentinel before his door was
killed, and the general, severely wounded, succeeded with great
difficulty in entering his house. The crowd continued to increase, being at every moment encouraged and excited by
base and lying reports. The doors of the house and then the
chamber were forced open. The unfortunate general was
dragged from the bed whence he was rising to dress, and the
assassins threw themselves furiously upon him, but without at
once putting an end to his life. He expired at the end of thirty-
six hours in the most fearful agony. The authorities had
spread the report of his death in the hope of putting an end
to the violence of the populace. Marseilles and Carpentras
became the theatres of scenes of outrage. Information was
freely circulated against the partisans of the empire, but the
fury of the multitude did not await the vengeance of the law.
The efforts of the Duc d'Angoulême to organize the military
government of the five divisions of the south sufficed not to
check the most terrible disorder.

The prince soon found himself obliged to enter Gard in person, there to appease troubles more violent still, excited and
aggravated by religious animosities. Just after the fall of
Napoleon, various gangs of men had banded themselves together, drawn from the lowest classes, and driven on by the
shameful promoters of a cowardly revenge and an ignoble
greed. At their head marched some known leaders, Trestail-
lons, Quatretaillons, Truphémy,—names or surnames odious
still on account of the memories they excite among the Protestant population. Everywhere reigned the white terror; the
Protestants of Nîmes and Uzès were plunged in fear; the garrison had abandoned its artillery to the desperadoes who over

ran the streets, maltreating and insulting Protestant women; in retiring, a great number of the soldiers were killed, while the mob pillaged the barracks of the gendarmerie. In the country isolated houses were attacked and plundered. In the town, they forced the doors of numerous dwellings. The authorities, feeble or disarmed, remained powerless, lavishing proclamations in vain, without having recourse to effective repression. The contagion of the evil spread; for more than three months Nîmes and the environs remained a prey to this detestable rabble. When the Duc d'Angoulême arrived at Nîmes in the month of November, he ordered the reopening of the Protestant churches which had been closed under the pretext of shunning the disturbance. The day after his departure General Lagarde, protecting the entrance of the Protestants into the church, was seriously injured by the shot of a pistol fired quite close to him. A few moments afterwards, he said to Madame Guizot, "Keep near my horse, no harm will come to you." Some months later his assassin, although known to all, was to be acquitted by the jury, under the violent pressure of religious and political fanaticism, on the pretext that the general had himself excited the crowd and wounded inoffensive passers-by. Meantime the churches remained closed. Enraged by this horrible violence, the passions excited in all minds were for a long time to maintain in the departments of the south a sullen feeling of which the remembrance is not yet even effaced.

The disturbances of the elections had aggravated the popular violence at various points. The scrutinies were finished, the deputies arrived at Paris, but the whole extent of the new returns was not yet understood; enough, however, was known meanwhile to assure people that the chamber would be keenly royalist. The minister found himself deceived in his hopes; his leaders were not in a condition to face the struggle which was impending. A courtier and a diplomatist, not a man for government, and less for a liberal government than any other, M. de Talleyrand still suffered under the displeasure of the Emperor of Russia and the secret aversion of King Louis XVIII. Fouché was cleverly intriguing on his account and in his personal interest. A few days later both had to succumb, and their cabinet fell with them. Talleyrand was yet to render brilliant services to his country, but Fouché's career was ended. He accepted the petty and remote mission at Dresden, and left Paris under a disguise, which he only dropped at the frontier, in the dread of being seen in his native country, which he was never to look upon again.

"The cabinet of the Duc de Richelieu entered on its duties with the good-will of the king and even of the party which the elections had sent into power. It was a truly original and royalist ministry. Its leader, but recently returned to France, honored by Europe, loved by the Emperor Alexander, was for King Louis XVIII. what the king himself was for France, the pledge of a more durable peace. Decazes, young and amiable, distinguished from his first appearance in the magistracy, had pleased the king personally, and he was nominated minister of police. The new keeper of the seal, Barbé-Marbois, belonged to that generously liberal old France, which had accepted and sustained with an enlightened moderation the principles that were dear to new France."* Guizot filled as his colleague the office of secretary-general.

The Duc de Richelieu had a double mission. He had to negotiate peace with the allies and to direct the new chamber, as inexperienced as it was enthusiastic. The former task demanded at first all his efforts. He was more qualified for it than for the coming struggles in the political arena. Supported in his negotiations by the faithful friendship of the Emperor Alexander as well as by the fairness of Lord Castlereagh, he obtained several favorable modifications in the conditions of the treaty. The insane claims of Germany for the dismemberment of France had been long since abandoned. Reduced in theory to her frontiers of 1790, France kept the forts of Joux and L'Écluse and the fortresses of Condé, Givet, and Charlemont. The war indemnity was reduced from eight to seven hundred millions; the duration of the occupation of the fortresses of the east and of the north by the allies was fixed at five years instead of seven, but the districts of Belgium, Savoy, and Germany, which had been delivered to the French in 1814 by the treaty of Paris, were definitively taken away from them, and the fortifications of Hüningue were to be razed. When he at last signed, on the 20th of November, the vigorous conditions which he had disputed from point to point with the exigencies of the allied sovereigns, the Duc de Richelieu wrote to his sister, Madame de Montcalm: "All is over. I have put, more dead than alive, my name to this fatal treaty. I had sworn not to do it, and I had said so to

---

* M. Guizot, *Mémoires pour servir a l'histoire de mon temps.*

the king. The unhappy prince has beseeched me, melting in tears, not to abandon him. I have not hesitated; I have the assurance of believing that no one would have obtained so much. France, expiring beneath the weight of the calamities which overwhelm her, calls imperiously for a speedy deliverance."

Before the signature of the treaty, and when its principal conditions were in abeyance, the allied sovereigns successively left Paris (Sept. and Oct., 1815). They had once more renewed among themselves the engagements of Chaumont against that power of Napoleon, fallen from henceforth, and against the revolutionary spirit, which appeared to be conquered. They had at the same time concluded a new convention about which there has been much talk without clear understanding, and which has been confounded with the coalition recently formed against the French. Under the influence of the Emperor Alexander, himself inspired by a woman of great spirit, vain, and mystic (the Baroness de Krüdener), the sovereigns of Russia, Prussia, and Austria bound themselves by a treaty rather theoretical than practical, conceived in a vague spirit of religion, and prepared by the Czar. The three monarchs, convinced of the necessity of establishing mutual relations between the powers based on the sublime truths inculcated by the eternal religion of God the Saviour, had resolved to engage themselves in the ties of an insoluble fraternity as the delegates of Providence, charged with governing three branches of one and the same family, and hoping for a mutual reward for protecting religion, peace, and justice. They called upon their peoples, to grow stronger every day in the principles and the exercise of the duties which the Divine Saviour has taught to men, and they invited all the sovereigns to join themselves to them in order to tie the bonds of the holy alliance. In deference to the wishes of the Czar, almost all the allied princes adhered to this convention, as strange as it was sadly inefficacious. King Louis XVIII. did not refuse his consent. The Prince Regent of England alone took no part in it; the treaty was the personal work of the sovereigns, and was signed directly by them, while constitutional government as it was practised in England did not admit of the official intervention of princes in such negotiations. This abstention was much remarked upon when the text of the holy alliance was published, and curious spirits exercised themselves to discover in it a hidden meaning far from the thoughts either of the Emperor Alexander or of his devoted friend.

The work of external pacification was achieved, while that of the interior, still more necessary and important, appeared further than ever from attainment. The hundred days had done a still greater evil to France than the loss of the blood and the treasure which they had cost her; they rekindled the old quarrel which the empire had stifled and which the charter was intended to extinguish—the quarrel between old and new France, between the émigrés and the revolutionists. It was not only among political parties but among rival classes, that the struggle began in 1815 as it had burst forth in 1789. For the first time for five-and-twenty years the royalists saw themselves the stronger. While believing their triumph legitimate, they were a little surprised and intoxicated by it, and delivered themselves over to the enjoyment of power with a mixture of arrogance and ardor, as if they were little accustomed to conquer, and not very sure of the force which they hastened to display. Very different causes threw the chamber of 1815 into the violent reaction which has remained its historical characteristic. First and foremost were the passions of the royalist party, its good and bad feelings, its moral and personal sentiments, the intention of restoring to honor the respect for sacred things, old attachments, sworn faith, and the pleasure of oppressing its former conquerors. To the transports of passion was joined the calculation of interests. For the security of parties, for the fortune of persons, the new lords of France required to take possession of places and power; there the field was to be cultivated and the ground to be occupied, that they might gather the fruits of their victory. Then came the empire of ideas. After so many years of great occurrences and great strifes, the royalists had on all political and social questions systematic views to realize, historical traditions to perpetuate, and spiritual wants to satisfy. They were not working to destroy the charter and to restore the old régime, as has been often said of them; they hastened to put their hand to the work, eager to enjoy their victory, believing that the day was come at last to recover in their country both morally and materially, in thought as in deed, the ascendancy which they had lost for so long a time.

Their passions were represented by Bourdonnaye, while Villèle defended their interests, and Bonald their ideas. They were all three highly qualified for their parts, and conducted ably to its goal the party which was in power at the opening of the session in the chamber of 1815. Under their control this chamber had the merit of practising energetically the constitutional government, which in 1814 had hardly emerged from the torpor of the empire, but in this novel task it could guard neither equity nor propriety, nor moderation; it wished to dominate the king and France at the same time. It was proud and independent, sometimes liberal, often revolutionary in its proceedings towards the Crown, and at the same time violent and anti-revolutionary towards the country. This was too much to attempt; it was necessary to make a choice, and to be either monarchical or popular. The Chamber of 1815 was neither the one nor the other, the governing spirit, yet more necessary in a free government than under a despotism, was completely wanting in it.

Also there was seen promptly forming against it and in its very heart an opposition which became ere long at once popular and monarchical, for it simultaneously defended against the party in power the Crown which was thus rashly offended and the country which was deeply disturbed. And after some great struggles, sustained on both sides with sincere energy, this opposition, strong in royal favor and public sympathy, frequently overpowered the majority, and became the governing party. Serre, Royer-Collard, and Camille Jordan were from the first the eloquent leaders of the new party, pledged to the service of the restoration as against the reaction. Pasquier, Beugnot, Siméon, De Barante, and De Sainte-Aulaire supported them ardently. The struggle began just after the opening of the session. The king's speech had been sad and firm in its judicious moderation, and the almost unanimous election of M. Lainé as president, and the vote of the address had not raised any violent storms in the Chamber of Deputies. But the tendencies which were soon to manifest themselves so emphatically had made their appearance in the plan of the address of the Chamber of Peers. Chateaubriand had demanded that they should again place in the hands of the king the power of dispensing justice. Soon the thirst for revenge burst forth in the discussion of the laws proposed to the chambers by the government, some expressly temporary in their nature, as the law on the suspension of individual liberty and the establishment of courts martial, others permanent and belonging to the section of definite legislation, as those for the supression of seditious acts and for the amnesty. Everywhere the amendments proposed by the ultra-royalists, as they were soon called, tended greatly to aggravate the troubles; many exceptions to the amnesty were loudly called for. The moderate royalists eloquently defended the projects of the government. "It is not always the number of penalties which save an empire," said Royer-Collard, "the art of governing men is more difficult, and the glory of it is to be acquired at a higher price. We shall be punished enough, if we are wise and clever, never enough if we are not so." Serre repelled boldly the confiscations disguised under the name of indemnities to the state. "The revolutionaries have done so," said he, "they would do so again if they seized the power. It is precisely because they have acted thus that you should refrain from following their odious example, and that by the distorted sense of an expression which is untrue, by an artifice which would be altogether unworthy of the stage. Gentlemen, our treasure may be little, but it is pure!" The amendments were rejected; only the banishment of regicides remained inscribed in the project of law, without which no one might dare to plead in their favor. "There are divine laws which the human powers cannot prevent, but which they should know not to oppose when revealed by the course of events."*

The exceptions to the amnesty remained numerous enough and important enough. Many of the accused had already been arrested, others had succeeded in escaping; Lavalette was himself constituted a prisoner. Labédoyère had been recognized in a stage coach by an agent of police at the moment when he was bidding good-bye to his wife. Early in August he appeared in Paris before a council of war. His crime was as notorious as the influence which he had exercised. The Ultras let loose their passions against him whom they regarded as a renegade from their cause. The journal *l'Indépendant*, which took up his defence, was suppressed; the accused defended himself, pleading his own cause nobly and simply. "I have been deceived regarding the true interests of France," he said; "some glorious memories, my warm love of the fatherland, some illusions have been able to mislead me, but the greatness even of the sacrifices I have made in breaking off the dearest of ties proves that no personal motive entered into my conduct. I declare that I had no hand in any plot which may have preceded the return of Napoleon. I shall say more; I am convinced that there was

---

* Guizot, *Mémoires pour servir à l'histoire de mon temps.*

no express conspiracy to bring Napoleon back from Elba." Labédoyère was condemned, and his wife threw herself in vain at the feet of the king. "I know your sentiments and those of your family, madame," he replied, "never was it more painful for me to pronounce a refusal." Benjamin Constant drew up a memorial in his favor. But, on the 19th of August, the young general died courageously, himself commanding the soldiers to fire.

Five weeks later, on the 27th of September, the twin brothers Faucher, both generals of the republic, both carried away by the enthusiasm of the hundred days, without having ever served under the empire, expiated, in their turn, the insurrection which had taken place in their little town of Réole, and which, it was said, they had instigated. The public prosecutor, like the magistrates, displayed towards them the most disgusting violence. A decree of the Court of Orleans condemned Lavalette to death.

A more illustrious culprit attracted all attention at this time. Marshal Ney had been arrested on the 5th of August in a friend's house, where he was hiding. A rare weapon, left inadvertently on a table, had betrayed his whereabouts. "He does more harm to us in letting himself be arrested than he has ever yet done," said King Louis XVIII., rightly foreseeing the evils which he knew not how to avoid. Immediately brought to Paris, the marshal was transferred to a council of war, which declared itself incompetent; the accused, belonging to the Chamber of Peers, was to be tried by it. The case was opened in the Chamber with a speech by the Duc de Richelieu, composed, it was said, by Lainé, and stamped unfortunately, by the strong passions which then prevailed among the Royalists. The indictment bore the same character. It was not till the 4th of December that the marshal appeared before the court.

The ambassadors of the four great powers signatory to the capitulation of Paris, had refused to interpose on behalf of the culprit, who claimed the benefit of this act. Meanwhile, the defenders of the marshal recurred in the first place to the article guaranteeing personal safety. The king, having signed this convention, found himself, they contended, bound by such signature not to investigate past acts. Dupin and Berryer were equally desirous of making the best of the clause which sheltered from prosecution all the inhabitants of the ceded countries: the marshal belonged originally to Sarre-

louis. He himself protested against this advocate's quirk.
"I was born French," he cried, "I wish to live and die French;
I thank my generous defenders, but I beg them rather to
renounce my defence than to present it incomplete; I am
accused, contrary to the faith of treaties, and they would not
have me invoke them. From them, I appeal, like Moreau, to
Europe and to posterity!"

The court interdicted the argument on the subject of the
bearing of the capitulation of Paris; the acts of Marshal Ney
were notorious, and the hearing of witnesses was only capable
of conveying hope to the accused himself and to his friends.
The deposition of General de Bourmont drew from the marshal a reply which transferred to him, in turn, the weight of
culpability. "It is seven months since the witness prepared
his evidence," Ney exclaimed; "he has had time to do it well.
He believed that I should be treated like Labédoyère, that we
should never find ourselves face to face; but it is otherwise.
I come to the point. The fact is that, on the 14th of March, I
asked for the signal with Marshal Lecourbe . . . pity it is
that Lecourbe is no more, but I summon him against all these
witnesses before a higher tribunal, before God, who hears us,
and who shall judge us,—you and me, Monsieur le Bourmont!
I consulted you. No one said to me, you are risking your
honor and your reputation for this fatal cause! . . . Bourmont collected the troops. He had a great command, and
could arrest me; I was alone and had not a single saddle-horse
on which to escape. When I was reading the proclamation,
Bourmont and Lecourbe were with me; the officers, like the
soldiers, threw themselves upon us, they embraced us, they
stifled us. The superior officers came to dine at my house; I
was sad, and nevertheless the table was merry; there is the
truth, Monsieur de Bourmont. You said that I should have
to take a carabine and charge at the head of my troops, who
would follow me! I was still twenty leagues from Napoleon's
columns, and I had already raised two regiments. Would
you have marched under such conditions? I believe not, you
have not strength of character enough."

Forbidden to have recourse to the capitulation of Paris, the
defenders of the marshal were completely disarmed; they
were driven to descant on the career of the accused, and on
the services which he had rendered to France. The argument
of the attorney-general, Bellart, was severe and violent. The
royal commissioners requested the Court of Peers to pro-

nounce capital sentence against Marshal Ney, convicted of
high treason. Lanjuinais alone refrained from answering the
various questions set by the court; he declared that he was
unable, conscientiously, to decide, the defence not having
been complete. One hundred and fifty-nine voices voted the
culpability. The Duc de Broglie, still very young, and sitting
for the first time in the chamber, opposed it boldly; he maintained that when a revolution has triumphed so completely as
to become temporarily the government of the country, there
results from it on behalf of the acts which have created the
government a kind of prescription which does not allow of
their being prosecuted. When they came to the application
for the penalty, seventeen voices declared on the second vote
for deportation. Five peers abstained from voting. One
hundred and thirty-nine voices pronounced for capital punishment. Among these rigorous judges, were counted many
marshals and generals, companions-in-arms of Marshal Ney.
The fatal sentence was passed on the 7th of December, at two
o'clock in the morning.

Some hours later, Marshal Ney, Duc d'Elchingen and
Prince de la Moskawa, heard in his prison of the Luxembourg
the decree of his condemnation. "Say *Michel Ney*, and ere
long but a little dust," said he, interrupting the Recorder of
the Court, Cauchy, in the enumeration of his titles. His wife
and children had hastened to join him; he spoke to them for
a long time, consoling his wife, who several times fainted.
He feigned to believe in the possibility of a pardon, in order to
put an end to these sad farewells. The lady hurried to the
Tuileries; the audience which she solicited was refused, "her
demand not having sufficient object;" already her husband
had succumbed under platoon fire at the entrance of the
Grand Avenue of the Observatoire. "Soldiers, straight to the
heart!" he cried. Before commanding the fire, he protested
against the judgment which condemned him. "I appeal from
it to mankind, to posterity, and to God! Long live France!"

It was in 1815, in the midst of the passions which raised up
the great political persecutions, the weakness and the injury
of the king and the government to allow themselves to be
carried along by the transports of the party, to which they
yielded all without resisting. "There were assuredly grave
reasons for leaving the law to take its free course: it was of
consequence that generations formed in the vicissitudes of the
revolution and in the triumphs of the empire might learn by

brilliant examples that the power and the success of the
moment did not decide everything, that there are inviolable
duties, that one may not tamper with impunity with the
forms of government and with the peace of the people, and
that at this terrible game the most powerful, the most illustrious, risk their honor and their life.

" But another grand truth must enter into the balance, and
weigh heavily in the final decision. The Emperor Napoleon
had maintained his position for a lengthened period and with
brilliance, accepted and admired by France and by Europe,
and supported by the devotion of a host of men, by the army
and the people. The ideas of right and duty, the sentiments
of respect and fidelity, were confused and in conflict in many
minds. There were, seemingly, two legitimate and natural
forms of government, and many spirits might, without per-
versity, have been troubled in their choice. King Louis
XVIII. and his counsellors could, in their turn, without weakness, have taken account of this moral disturbance. Marshal
Ney, pardoned and banished after his condemnation, by
letters royal, in which the reasons were gravely stated—this
had been royally rising up like a dam above all, friends and
enemies, in order to arrest the flow of blood, and, in this way,
the reaction of 1815 had been subdued and closed, as well as
the hundred days." *

King Louis XVIII. did not know how to seize this occasion
to place clemency by the side of justice, and to display above a
head condemned that granduer of spirit and heart which had
also its influence in establishing power and commanding fidelity. The passion of revenge which had seized the royalist
party was not yet appeased. The appeal of Lavalette had been
rejected some days after the execution of Marshal Ney. A
stranger to all public duties under the first restoration, he had
not betrayed any oath in serving the Emperor Napoleon; yet
he was condemned to death, and the most odious rage was provoked against him. At the suggestion of Decazes, the Duc de
Richelieu counselled the Duchess d'Angoulême to request his
pardon from the king, who was quite ready to grant it. Personally, and by instinct, the duchess was disposed to implore
this favor, but her friends opposed it. Marshal Marmont
vainly multiplied his efforts in order to obtain a pardon,
which Madame Lavalette begged on her knees. The culprit

---

* *Mémoires pour servir à l'histoire de mon temps.*

asked to be allowed to die by the bullets of the soldiers in place of having to mount the scaffold, but his request was rejected. His friends then concurred in a scheme to effect his escape.

On the 20th of December, Madame Lavalette arrived at five o'clock at the gates of the prison of the Conciergerie, in order to dine there with her husband, according to custom; she was accompanied by her daughter, and by an old waiting-maid. At seven o'clock, covered with his wife's dress, leaning on the shoulder of his daughter, his face concealed in his handkerchief as if to hide his tears, the criminal went forth from his prison; he crossed the halls of the Palais de Justice and the posts of the gendarmerie; delayed for a moment at the outer gate by the absence of the porters, he entered a sedan chair, and was conducted to the Rue de Harlay, where one of his friends waited for him with a cabriolet. Harbored for five days at the Ministry for Foreign Affairs, in the house of Bresson, head of the account-office, he was at last escorted out of France by Sir Robert Wilson, an English officer who generously devoted himself to saving political prisoners.* Lavalette was to turn old in exile, oppressed by the sufferings which ruined his life and his energy. The emotions which his wife had undergone affected her reason. The rage of the ultras on the subject of the escape was so violent that they made it the object of a summons against the ministry before the Chamber of Deputies. The tattle of the drawing rooms was disgusting. "Ah! the little villain!" said one lady, generally good and gentle, in speaking of Mademoiselle Lavalette, an accomplice in her father's escape. The poor child could not remain in the convent where she was being educated, many families having threatened in that case to withdraw their daughters. "It is said that they make it languish," some persons remarked, in speaking of the long interval which elapsed between the arrest of Marshal Ney and his trial; "they make us languish also. Do they think that two heads can suffice to expiate the outrage of the 20th of March?"

The public sentiment in France was not in accord with this misrule of violence, and it was with sincere satisfaction that it received the acquittal of Generals Drouot and Cambronne, and the commutation of sentence granted by the king to Generals Boyer, Debelle, and Travot and to Admiral Linois. Two months before the execution of Marshal Ney, the companion

---

* Sir Robert underwent in his turn a trial for this cause.

of his most brilliant military exploits, Joachim Murat, recently
King of Naples, had also succumbed under platoon fire (13th
October, 1815).   More fortunate than Ney, in spite of his still
graver faults, he owed not his death to French bullets.   Flat-
terred by a vain hope of recovering his kingdom, he had projected a disembarkment on the coast of Calabria, he was induced to land at the port of Pizzo; betrayed by the captain of
his vessel, he was seized and the men who accompanied him
were either killed or made prisoners.   Condemned to death by
court-martial, he was shot in a yard of the fortress.   "I have
too often braved death to fear it," said he when some one
wished to bind his eyes.   These heroes of so many battles were
still young.   Ney was forty-seven years of age; Murat had
not attained his forty-fifth year.

The period of great political trials was not yet at an end.
Generals Lefebvre-Desnouettes, Drouet d'Erlon, and Lallemand, were condemned by default; General Chartran was executed; General Mouton-Duvernet, hidden for many months
at Montbrison, in the house of M. de Meaux, an ardent royalist,
delivered himself up on seeing his protector threatened, and
was executed on the 27th of July, 1816.   Donnadieu, who commanded at Grenoble, had attributed an illusory importance to
a conspiracy directed by Paul Didier, an old constitutional,
who had been tossed from party to party, and who seemed to
plot from a natural turn for intrigue rather than from any
very definite object.   He sometimes spoke of Napoleon II.,
sometimes of the Duc d'Orléans, as the sovereign whom he
wished to give to France, and his principal plan appeared to
be a sudden military attack on Grenoble.   The attempt to
carry this plan into execution was soon suppressed by the
police of the town, who were on their guard for several days
before.   Six men were killed among the insurgents.   The
general wrote to Paris in a transport of excitement, "Long
live the king! I have just time to say to your Excellency that
his Majesty's troops have covered themselves with glory.   At
midnight the hills were illumined by the fires of rebellion
throughout the province.   The town has been attacked on all
sides at once.   I should not be able to praise too much the
brave legion of the Isère, and its worthy colonel.   Already
more than sixteen miscreants are in our power; a great number more is expected.   The court-martial is going to deal
promptly and severely.   We estimate the number of the
wretches who have attacked the town at 4000."

The exaggeration of the details was flagrant, but this was not enough, unfortunately, to enlighten the government, which was excited and suspicious. The general and the prefect, who vied with each other in zeal, had already put Grenoble in a state of siege. They were invested with enlarged powers, and the ministry believed itself obliged to refuse forgiveness, even to those of the accused who were interceded for by the most important inhabitants in the town. Twenty-five of the insurgents were executed; their chief, Paul Didier, perished on the scaffold on the 10th of May. When the truth respecting the gravity of the danger which threatened Grenoble at last found its way to light, the reaction of public opinion was so strong that it accused Decazes of having combined with General Donnadieu in getting up a mock-insurrection. Other conspiracies meanwhile received an undoubted stimulus. At Paris a popular plot cost the lives of its three leaders, Plaignier, Carbonneau, and Tolleron, poor workmen, misled by foolish hopes. The scaffold was likewise set up in the departments of Sarthe and Somme. The agitation prevails at all points. The journals fomented it with passion. In the heart even of the cabinet union was not complete. The Duc de Richelieu, ceaselessly thwarted by the whimsical independence of M. de Vaublanc, demanded and obtained his replacement by Lainé. At the same time, and to satisfy the royalists, Barbé-Marbois, who displeased them, was removed from the Ministry of Justice, and Dambray recovered the seals of office. After a prolonged and fruitless discussion on the electoral law, and the much disputed budget vote, the chamber ended its first session on the 20th of April, 1816. Notwithstanding the changes, it broke up in an excited state, still disquieted by fears of the future and of the opposition party, moderate and monarchical, which it saw in its midst. At its head those men took their place every day more distinctly who were then honored by the name of Doctrinaires. They were bold and honest, devoted to the reconstruction of society anew on wide and solid foundations, without animosity towards the *ancien cégime,* without weakness for revolutionary theories, and doing their country the credit of believing it capable of learning to govern itself, and of emerging from chaos while advancing towards knowledge. Royer-Collard was their veritable leader, and at his side fought Serre.

In 1816 it was the honor of Decazes to comprehend, and to be the first to make, the effort necessary to escape from chaos.

The schism between the country and the chamber was every day becoming greater. He felt that dissolution was indispensable, and he undertook to gain over to that idea the Duc de Richelieu, Lainé, and the king himself. He demanded from his friends—among others from Guizot, who had a short time before re-entered the Council of State as master of petitions —the notes with which he often supported his reasonings. The disturbances which had spread among the corps diplomatique were of equal service to his cause. "If the *ultras* come to power, as the Comte d'Artois is loudly declaring," wrote the ambassadors, "the ministry will not last a month; but, while waiting for its fall, he will have agitated the country, put the monarchy in danger, and rendered impossible of fulfilment the engagements into which France has entered at the instance of the foreign powers."

The king chose his side. He had hesitated a long time, and his hesitations were natural. How was he to dissolve the first pronouncedly royalist chamber which had assembled for five-and-twenty years—a chamber which he himself had qualified as *introuvable,* and in which he counted so many of his oldest friends? Meanwhile the chamber had been more than once irreverent, and almost as disrespectful towards him as a revolutionary assembly could have been. It often insulted the charter, and sometimes menaced it: now the charter was the work of the king; he held it as his glory, and considered himself bound to defend it. On Wednesday, 14th August, at the rising of the Council, the king stopped his ministers as they were about to leave. "Gentlemen," he said, "the moment has arrived for coming to a determination with respect to the Chamber of Deputies. Three months ago I had decided upon summoning it, and that was my opinion a month ago. But all I have seen, all that I see every day, proves so clearly the spirit of the party which rules the chamber, the dangers with which it threatens France and myself are so evident, that my opinion has completely changed. From this moment you may regard the chamber as dissolved."

The king had ordered this to be kept secret, which was carefully done. On the 5th of September, at half-past eleven at night, the Duc de Richelieu informed Monsieur that the ordinance of dissolution was signed, and would be in the *Moniteur* in the morning. The king's door was closed, and the wrath of Monsieur had to wait till the next day to blow itself off vainly. The preamble announced that the king had determined to revert simply to the original text of the charter. "We are convinced," said Louis XVIII., "that the wants and the wishes of our subjects will be united to preserve intact the constitutional charter, based on the public law of France and the guarantee of general peace. We have, in consequence, judged it necessary to reduce the Chamber of Deputies to the number fixed by the charter, and only to summon men of the age of forty years." The new Chamber of Deputies was called for the 4th of November.

The ebullition of public joy was lively and general. The anger of the ultras was equalled by the satisfaction of the moderate men. "Those who had for a long time been accustomed to shout 'Long live the king!'" kept silence. Those who had kept silence shouted 'Long live the king!'" says Montlosier in his book *De la Monarchie française.* "France breathes again: the charter triumphs and the king reigns," wrote Lally-Tollendal to Decazes. The instructions given by the latter to the prefects were as moderate as they were wise. He himself summed them up in saying; "Whether we get to the king by a charter, or to the charter by the king, our arrival shall be equally welcome." On the whole, the elections responded to this honest and patriotic appeal. The government passed henceforth into the hands of men of moderate opinions, which people came to know under the name of the Centre. The charter had placed the bases of constitutional government in their great and important aspects, and it (the Centre) occupied itself after this in defining them, and in regulating their application in detail.

The discussion of the electoral law took up almost the entire session of 1816. "I have adopted all the principles of this measure," wrote Lainé to Guizot, a few days before the opening of the debate. "The concentration of the franchise, direct election, equal rights of voters, their meeting in a single assembly in each department—I really believe these to be the best. I have, however, still some perplexities of spirit on some of these questions, and very little time to get out of them. Help me to prepare the draft of the motions." The bill introduced by the ministry, and violently attacked by the right, had a two-fold aim—to put an end to the revolutionary régime, and to put in force constitutional government. The principles on which this bill rested obtained for France thirty years of a regular and liberal government, at once seriously sustained and controlled. Tossed since then on the heaving

surface of universal suffrage, we turn with respectful sorrow
towards that quiet harbor which the tempest of 1848 compelled
us to leave, without other storms having brought us any
nearer to it.

The electoral law was succeeded by the law of enlistment, a
wise and far-reaching conception of Marshal Gouvion St. Cyr,
who had replaced the Duc de Feltre as minister of war. The
martial insisted from the first on the principle that all classes
of the nation were called upon to assist in forming the army,
without getting into the way, as Germany did then, of making
military service compulsory for all. This idea had always
been strange to the organization of the French army, but it
was to be imposed upon us by the unforeseen reverses. In
accordance with the equality established in the military nation
by Marshal Gouvion St. Cyr, those who entered by the lowest
rank had the right of promotion to the highest; and this was
partly assured to them by the ascending scale of the middle
ranks. Those who aspired to enter by a higher grade, were at
first bound to show by competition some merit already acquired, then to acquire by hard study the special instruction
for their duty. The obligations imposed upon, and the rights
recognized by all, were upheld by law.

The supreme test of legislators is the long result of their
labors. More than one has succumbed; others have not had
time to find out by experience the merits or defects of their
conceptions. Marshal Gouvion St. Cyr created for France a
strong and faithful army, religiously preserving the memory
of past glory, and animated by a severely military spirit.
Other circumstances have enfeebled this salutary influence,
and we have gathered the bitter fruits of the lax system which
was introduced under the second empire into both the morals
and the interior organization of the army. When, at the
opening of the session of 1818, the illustrious warrior came
himself to the tribune, to defend at once the new army he
wished to create and the old army which he wished to attach
to the new one as a glorious reserve, he moved the chamber
by his grave and firm language in recalling to its memory the
sufferings of the soldiers who had recently been unhappily
disbanded. This speech assured the passing of the bill.

The elections of 1816, and the partial renewing of the chamber, had brought into it elements which scarcely existed in
that of 1815. The Left was brilliantly represented. Lafayette,
Benjamin Constant, and Manuel attacked the press laws which

were introduced by the cabinet in 1818. The ministry had undergone several changes. Pasquier had replaced Dambray as keeper of the seals, and he was in his turn succeeded by Serre. It was he who projected the measure which did away with the exceptional régime under which the press lived for three years, and which henceforth regulated its rights and obligations. Serre has left upon those who heard him, the impression of an eloquence unapproachable even in such a time of eloquence. "He sustained general principles as a magistrate who applies them, not as a philosopher who explains them. His speech was profound and not abstract, colored and not figurative, and his arguments were actions. As strong in impromptu as after cogitation, when he had surmounted a slight hesitation and timidity at first he went to his point firmly and impressively, like a man ardently sincere, who sought nowhere personal success, and who only occupied himself in making his cause to triumph, while communicating to his audience his sentiments with his conviction."*

During the discussion of the press laws, Guizot ascended for the first time—as commissary of the king, and to defend some articles of the measure—that tribune which was to become so familiar to him. His age not yet permitting him to take part in the assembly, he took an active and ardent part in the discussions which were carried on outside the chamber by the polemics of the newspapers. Independent friends of the government, whom they sometimes annoyed even while defending it, the doctrinaires eloquently advocated their ideas in the *Globe,* the *Courier,* the *Archives philosophiques et politiques,* and the *Revue française.* Animated by the noblest hopes for the future, and every day engaged in the arena, they carried into the contest a devotion equal to their pride, and a pride which for the most part surpassed their ambition.

Their influence had increased, and became more direct and efficacious at the time when the press laws were brought before the chambers. The chambers, then renewed for the fifth time, had seen new members join the opposition; the ultras, agitated amongst themselves, plotting in their turn in a small assembly which took from the place where it held its meeting the name of *Terrasse du bord de l'eau.* Secret notes, drawn up by Vitrolles, were addressed to the foreign powers, warning them of the dangers which menaced the restoration, and of the

---

* *Mémoires pour servir à l'histoire de mon temps.*

powerlessness of France to keep to her engagements with them
if she again fell into the hands of revolutionaries.   The culpability of this communication was all the more flagrant, inas-
much as our relation towards the allies had already been improved in several ways: the army of occupation had been
reduced, a contract had been accepted for the payment of the
war indemnity, and the Duc de Richelieu was preparing to go
to the Congress of Aix-la-Chapelle in the hope of obtaining a
complete liberation of the territory.   Vitrolles was expelled
from the Privy Council on the 24th July, 1818.   Already in
1816, for his book *La Monarchie selon la Charte*, in which he
had personally offended the king, the name of Chateaubriand
had been erased from the list of the ministers of State.

Richelieu succeeded at Aix-la-Chapelle, and had the pleasure
of returning to Paris as bearer of the convention, signed on
the 9th of October in the Congress, which settled the 30th of
November as the date of the withdrawal of the foreign troops.
The days of grace which had been granted to France for its
payments were doubled.   Meanwhile the allies had cemented
their union by a protocol which was destined to perpetuate it,
and the Emperor Alexander—instructed by Pozzo, who had
joined him at the Congress—warned Richelieu against the
dangers which were menacing the government of the king.
Every one was finding fault with the electoral law.   The Duc
de Richelieu was strongly in favor of modifying it, and he
arrived at Paris with that idea on the 28th of November, 1818.

The electoral law was unjustly attacked, and the inconveniences which resulted from its application flowed inevitably
from the violent strife of parties, equally ardent and inexperienced.   The Duc de Richelieu met in the very heart of his
cabinet an opposition which he could not put down, and he
decided to break with Decazes, who had become a count and a
member of the Chamber of Peers.   The latter retired at first
before the fury of the right; but Richelieu having vainly
endeavored to form a cabinet, Decazes became the directing
minister, at the head of an enfeebled and divided majority,
confronted by the ultras, more and more irreconcilable, and
by the left, more numerous and animated than in the past.
The enterprise was beyond his powers, and all the eloquence
of Serre, who had become keeper of the seals, did not suffice to
carry it out.

He alone represented in the government the friends from
whom he was to separate with *éclat*.   Decazes pressed Royer-

Collard to enter the cabinet. He hesitated, accepted for a moment, then at last refused. "You do not know what you would do," he said to Decazes. "My way of treating matters is entirely different from yours. You evade the questions, you twist them about, you gain time. As for me, I should attack them in front, produce them in public, and turn them inside out before everybody. I should compromise, instead of aiding you."* Royer-Collard was right. He was more fit to counsel and control power, than to exercise it; he was a great spectator and a great critic, rather than a great political actor. General Dessoles had become minister of foreign affairs, and Baron Louis minister of finance. The electoral law remained still intact.

It was destined soon to undergo new attacks, for the always precarious existence of the ministry was not to last long. "There was in the parliamentary arena a cabinet brilliant with integrity, and in the country a loyally constitutional government. But it possessed more rhetorical than political power, and neither its care for personal safety nor its successes in the tribune were sufficient to rally the great government party which its formation had divided. Discord was kindling between the chambers themselves. The Chamber of Peers accepted the proposal of the Marquis Barthélemy for the reform of the law of elections. The attacks of the right as well as the left were still more efficacious in shaking the power, than the latter's victories were in consolidating it. The constant favor of the king sustained uneasily a friend whose downfall he foresaw with sadness. Two sinister events—the one long prepared by the directing committee of the affairs of the left, the other unforeseen by all—gave the fatal blow to the ministry of Decazes. Grégoire, formerly a constitutional bishop, regicide by his approval of the condemnation of Louis XVI., and senator under the Empire, at once pious and revolutionary through every phase of his existence, was returned to the Chamber of Deputies by the assembly of Grenoble (11th September, 1819), and, on the 13th of February, 1820, the Duc de Berry was assassinated by Louvel, on coming out of the Opera.

The election of Grégoire was not long in being invalidated by the chamber itself; but it appeared none the less a sign of the times, and caused a lively feeling of uneasiness, not only

* Mémoires pour servir à l'histoire de mon temps.

in France, among the moderate spirits which were occupied with the progress of reaction towards the left, but in Europe, among the sovereigns and ministers menaced with revolution. Risings had taken place in England, and Parliament had voted laws of repression. The democratic fermentation was daily increasing in Germany. A celebrated dramatist, Auguste Kotzebue, accused of betraying the national cause, had been assassinated on the 28th of March, 1819, by a fanatic called Charles Sand, who cried out, as he struck his victim, "O God, I thank Thee that Thou hast permitted me to do this deed!" Prussia and Austria united to repress the progress of the evil. They did not let the fears be unknown in Paris with which they were inspired by the state of France, always destined to assure or to disturb the world's repose. The king inclined henceforth to the proposed reforms in the electoral law. "Well, brother, you see what they are driving you to!" said the Comte d'Artois, who for a long time had abstained from talking politics in the royal circle. "Yes, brother, and I will provide for it," replied Louis XVIII. A draft of the law of legislature was prepared by Serre, with the consent of the Duc de Berry.

The minds of men were at the same time troubled by other causes of agitation. There was ever since the first days of the restoration the constant effort of the Catholics, eager to establish between Church and State those ties which they deemed necessary to the independence and the dignity of the clergy. An attempt had been made at Rome to modify in this sense the Concordat of 1801, but the negotiations, badly entered upon, were abortive, and the new Concordat, for a moment accepted in 1817, was abandoned in 1819. Almost at the same time, and in spite of the overwhelming influence which he exercised over the great Council of Public Instruction, Royer-Collard resigned the presidency, uneasy, it was said, at some hostile tendencies towards the university which he came upon when in power. "We shall perish; this is a solution," he replied to Decazes, who was seeking to reattach him to the government. Marshal Gouvion St. Cyr, General Dessoles, and Baron Louis refused to touch the electoral law. The Duc de Richelieu had not consented to charge himself with the formation of a new cabinet. Pasquier, Roy, and La Tour-Maubourg replaced in the council the retiring ministers, and Decazes became its president.

More than ever was the cabinet lacking in force and unity; more than ever was it attacked by all parties, abandoned by a part of the doctrinaires, and sustained by the younger and more ardent, who inspired measures of pacification and liberalism. Seven of the peers who had been excluded after the hundred days were reinstalled; and Marshal Grouchy and General Gilly were comprised in the amnesty. The Duc de Rovigo, tried for contumacy, was acquitted. The projected electoral law remained in suspense in consequence of the illness of Serre; what was known or guessed as to its nature roused the violent indignation of the left, well satisfied up to that time by the law of the 5th of February, 1817. The cabinet had entered upon *pourparlers* with the chiefs of the right, and appeared disposed to make important concessions to them; when, on the night of the 13th of February, 1820, the rumor ran through Paris that the Duc de Berry, after conducting his wife to her carriage on coming out of the Opera, had been stabbed as he was re-entering the hall. The princess hearing the cry of her wounded husband, threw herself from the carriage at once, and was covered with his blood. Some months before (after two miscarriages) she had given birth to a daughter, and was again looking forward to become a mother, when, to the sound of the joyful music, she received in her arms the lifeless body of the duke. From the first there was but little hope. Already, around the couch of the dying man, sinister rumors and incredible suspicions were circulating. The grief and marked concern of Decazes as chief of the cabinet were arousing an evident distrust. The examination of Louvel, who declared that he had acted of his own accord and without any accomplice, did not allay the excitement. The prince bade farewell to those who surrounded him, beseeching the king to forgive the man who had stabbed him. The Duchesse de Berry, mad with despair, asked permission to return to Sicily. King Louis XVIII. himself closed the eyes of the nephew whom he called his son.

The storm broke forth in the chambers before they had been officially informed of the death of the Duc de Berry. Clausel de Coussergues, a member of the Court of Cassation, and a fanatical royalist, rushed into the tribune, robed in mourning, "Gentlemen," cried he, "there is no law defining the method of making an accusation against ministers, but the debate upon such a question ought naturally to take place in public sitting. I propose to the chamber to vote an indictment against M. Decazes, minister of the interior, as an accomplice in the assassination of the Duc de Berry, and I ask leave to speak in support of my proposition." Silence was imposed on the orator, by cries that were almost unanimous; but his idea had taken root in many minds. A proposal by Bourdonnaye for an address to the king, veiled the same accusation in more guarded forms of speech. General Foy protested. "Let it be simply a question," said he, "of the tears that we shall all shed over a prince regretted by all Frenchmen, and especially regretted by the friends of liberty, because they know that advantage will be taken of this frightful occurrence to seek to destroy the liberties and the rights which have been recognized and sanctioned by the wisdom of the monarch."

Immediately, and with justice, Louis XVIII. instinctively felt himself menaced by the odious attack upon his minister. "The royalists gave me the finishing stroke," said he; "they know that the policy of M. Decazes is also mine, and they accuse him of having assassinated my nephew. It is not the first calumny that they have hurled at me. I wish to save our country without the ultras, if it is possible. Let us seek for a majority outside the circle of M. Clausel, and M. de la Bourdonnaye and their friends." In the Chamber of Deputies, Ste. Aulaire, father-in-law of Decazes, hearing Clausel de Coussergues repeating, with a slight modification, his denunciation of the previous day, cried out, "I do not oppose M. Clausel's proposition being consigned to the minutes. I content myself with asking that the reply which I make to it may also be included. This reply will not be lengthy: You are a calumniator!"

The current of excited passions was too violent to yield to the beneficent wishes of the monarch, and the patriotic efforts of sober-minded men. Sinister projects were being agitated amongst the men of the right. They had dared to propose to the Duke de Bellune to use force towards the president of the Council if he persisted in retaining power. In the chambers, the two parties in opposition, equally excited, inveighed against the measures abridging personal liberty and the freedom of the press, such measures having been immediately proposed by the minister. It was indispensable to the government that these measures should be adopted. The left centre would only consent to support them on condition of the abandonment of the new electoral law "It is necessary for the ultras to be once more in power," said Royer-Collard; "they will not keep it three months. What do I say? They will not ascend the tribune three times. There is a sword of Damocles suspended above our heads, and it is necessary to take measures to dispel the danger."

Once more in possession of power, the ultras were to retain it much longer, and to use it with more vigor than Royer-Collard had foreseen. Decazes, however, could not deceive himself as to the dangers of the situation in which he found himself placed, and he begged the king to sanction his retirement. The royalists did not cease repeating that only one victim was necessary to them, and that they were ready to support the Duc de Richelieu. The latter persisted in remaining in his retreat; the king refused to intervene. "I have too many times sought in vain for the co-operation of M. de Richelieu," said he; "my dignity does not permit me to try again." The violence of the journals against the president of the Council continued to increase, and the threats respecting his liberty and his life grew more serious. Vitrolles apprised Monsieur of these things. "In the interest of the king, as well as in that of the monarchy," said he, "a voluntary retreat would be more advantageous than a defeat accomplished by violence." Monsieur repaired to the king, accompanied by the Duchesse d'Angoulême, pleading earnestly for the abandonment of the favorite. "We make this request of you in order to escape a fresh crime." "Ah!" cried the king, "I will brave the daggers; and there is a greater distance than you think between the assassin's steel and the heart of an honest man." "Ah! sire," replied madame, "thanks to God it is not for your majesty that we fear, but for one who is very dear to you." "I defy the crime on my friend's account, as well as on my own," proudly responded Louis XVIII. Decazes, who arrived a few moments later, obtained, however, permission to retire. Richelieu yielded to the entreaties that were made to him in the name of the monarch. Monsieur wished to have his share in the settlement, and went to the house of Richelieu who was ill. "Only one thing in the world do I ask of you," said he; "one man more, that is yourself; one man less, that is M. Decazes. Form your ministry as shall seem good to yourself, and be certain that I shall approve everything and support everything. Your policy shall be mine, and I will be your foremost champion."

Monsieur promised for himself and his party more than he was able, and more than he was destined, to fulfil. The Duc de Richelieu foresaw this when he saw himself compelled once more to accept power. The new *Duc Decazes*, minister of state, member of the Privy Council, set out for London in the capacity of ambassador. The Duc de Richelieu having refused to take a portfolio, there had been some difficulty in finding a new minister of the interior. Count Simon was at last called upon to undertake this difficult charge. An advocate at the bar of Aix before the revolution, banished on the 18th Fructidor, he had been councillor of state under the empire. Appointed a representative during the hundred days, and since then a member of the Chamber of Deputies, he had gone through all *régimes* with a tranquil complaisance which did not promise to strengthen the government he consented to serve. Mounier, son of the celebrated member of the Constituent Assembly, replaced Guizot in the direction of the departmental and communal administration, which had been entrusted to the latter under Decazes.

The first acts of the minister soon gave opportunity for judging what would be the direction of his policy. Serre, always absent, but resolved upon supporting the Duc de Richelieu with all his influence, and with the venerated brilliancy of his eloquence, retained considerable irritation against his old friends, who had been in alliance with Decazes. "It is M. Royer-Collard and his friends," wrote he to the fallen minister; "it is their intractable pride which has done you most harm, and which has precipitated your fall by placing you in the power of the ultras." He hastened to satisfy immediately his animosities and his fears: Royer-Collard, Camille-Jordan, Barante, and Guizot were struck out of the list of the Council of State. "I was expecting your letter," replied Guizot to the keeper of the seals. "I ought to have foreseen it, and I did foresee it, when I proudly manifested my disapprobation. I congratulate myself on having no change to make in my conduct. To-day, as yesterday, I shall belong only to myself, and that completely." Decazes vainly labored to effect a reconciliation between his friend and the government.

The outburst of royalist violence against him did not cease with his fall. For a long time an enemy to Decazes, Chateaubriand dared to write in the *Conservateur* these words, of mournful celebrity. "Those who still struggle against public hatred have not been able to resist public sorrow; our tears, our sighs, our sobs have terrified an imprudent minister; his feet have slipped from under him in a pool of blood; he has fallen." The importance of the victory of the ultras was estimated by their passionate attacks upon liberty. "The assassination of the Duc de Berry," wrote Charles Nodier, in the

Drapeau Blanc, "is a clause of the ordinance of September 5th.
It is asked whether the knife which killed the Duc de Berry
was a poniard, a dagger, or what: I have seen it; the instrument is a liberal idea."

During the trial of the assassin (whose crime had furnished
the occasion, but was not the origin of the outburst of political
passions) the discussion upon the "laws of exception" was exciting in the chambers violent storms, which were re-echoing
far beyond, creating in Paris and in the departments an ever-
increasing agitation. Honestly but vainly desirous of maintaining a moderate line of conduct, the government inclined
more and more towards the right, and found itself every day
more effectually and more eagerly attacked by the liberals.
"Whilst even the ministers are sometimes led astray," said
Benjamin Constant, "the representatives of the nation have
walked in the lines of the constitution. Do you wish to depart
from them? Will you re-enact the 'laws of exception?' The
Convention, the Directory, Bonaparte, governed by laws of exception! Where is the Convention? Where is the Directory?
Where is Bonaparte?" General Foy was roused up to exclaim,
"Do you think that without the presence of foreigners, and the
terror that they inspired, we should have ingloriously submitted
to the outrages and insults of a handful of wretches whom we
despised, and whom we have seen in the dust for thirty years?"
Corday, a member of the left, rose in his place, and loudly
cried, "Monsieur, you are an insolent fellow!" A duel took
place the next day, followed by a reconciliation; but the public
fervor was less easily calmed than private quarrels; the people
increasingly gathered in crowds outside the chambers. The
voting of the laws of exception was followed by the suppression
of several journals. A national subscription was opened at the
house of Lafitte in favor of the victims of the new legislation.
The electoral law was destined to arouse more violent and more
dangerous attacks. It was modified in order to satisfy the
right. After the discussion it was found almost assimilated to
the project elaborated in 1819 by Serre. He supported it on
several occasions with an eloquence which the state of his
health rendered sorrowfully effective. Adversaries the most
formidable were roused up against the various articles of the
project. Twice Royer-Collard spoke with that unanswerable
authority which his character as well as his mental superiority
merited. Corbière accused him of upholding the sovereignty
of the people. The illustrious defender of a wise liberty thus

proudly expounded its eternal basis. "Privilege, absolute power, the sovereignty of the people, are, under diverse, and more or less unfortunate forms, the empire of force upon earth. There are two elements in society—the one material, which is the individual, his power and his will; the other moral, which is right, resulting from the true interests of society. Will you form society out of the material element? Then the majority of individuals—the majority of wills, whatever they may be, is sovereign. If voluntarily, or in spite of itself, this sovereignty blindly or violently places itself in the hands of a single person or of several persons, without changing its character, it is a force more wise and more moderate, but it is still only force. This is the root of absolute power and of privilege. Will you, on the contrary, form society with the moral element, which is right? Justice is the sovereign, because justice is the rule of right. Free constitutions have for their object the dethronement of force and the accomplishment of the reign of justice. It is force if your government represents persons; it is justice if it represents rights and interests."

It was the glory of Royer-Collard, and the secret of his influence over the distinguished men who surrounded him, that he always raised to the highest regions of thought the questions upon which he spoke. This was also the cause of his isolation even in the midst of his brilliant renown. Lafayette more effectively declared war against the government by a threatening manifesto. "I flattered myself," said he, "that the different parties, yielding at last to the general need for freedom and repose, were by mutual sacrifices, and with no mental reservations, about to seek these benefits in the exercise of the rights which the charter has recognized. My hopes have been deceived. The counter-revolution rests with the government, but they wish to fix the blame on the chambers. It has devolved on my friends and myself to declare it to the nation. Thinking also that the engagements of the charter were founded on reciprocity, I have loyally denounced the violators of their sworn faith."

In developing his thought, Lafayette manifested his fear lest the younger generation, threatened with the loss of all the fruits of the revolution, should themselves seize once more upon the sacred fasces of the principles of eternal truth and sovereign justice. The struggle, in fact, was already commencing in the streets, between the young royalists from the barracks of the body-guard (as it was said) and the students, ardently liberal,

MARSHAL FOY

grouped round the chambers or escorting popular deputies.
On the 3rd of June a pupil of the school of law, the young
Lallemand, was killed by a pistol-shot. The agitation lasted
for several days, maintained by the funeral obsequies of the
unfortunate victim as well as by the trial and execution of
Louvel. On August 19th, after the closing of the session and
the passing of the electoral law, an important conspiracy was
suddenly discovered, hatched by a few Bonapartist officers,
and by the young leaders of the democratic party. The day
had arrived for carrying out the enterprise. Several arrests
were effected; the accused, numerous and important, were sent
before the Court of Peers.

The popular and political emotion which was reigning in
France, and which was re-echoing afar, was, in its turn, excited
and encouraged by the blasts of revolution which had again
begun to blow across Europe. In England, King George III.
had just died, tenderly regretted by his people, who had constantly loved and respected him through his long madness: the
scandalous trial instituted by the new monarch, George IV.,
against his queen, Caroline of Brunswick, excited the most violent and contrary passions. The revolution having broken out
in Spain, King Ferdinand VII. was obliged to accept the constitution voted in 1812, by the Cortes met at Cadiz during the
national war against the Emperor Napoleon and King Joseph.
The reaction was immediately felt at Naples; the sovereigns
found themselves compelled to proclaim the Spanish Constitution, though ignorant of its conditions. Portugal was affected
by the same contagion. The Diet of Warsaw rejected the laws
proposed by the Emperor Alexander; a regiment mutinied at
St. Petersburg. The European sovereigns became so uneasy
that a congress was convoked at Troppau, and afterwards at
Laybach, for the purpose of taking the measures necessary for
maintaining public order. Metternich, one of the most able
and skilful amongst diplomatists, succeeded in separating the
Emperor Alexander from alliance with France, as well as from
the liberal ideas which had brought them together. A protocol
of Russia, Prussia, and Austria laid down the principle of
armed intervention in the case of States in a state of revolution.
It was also decided to apply the principle to the kingdom of
Naples. England had urged Austria to interfere alone in the
affairs of the two Sicilies, and refused to adhere to the declaration of the absolutist powers. France placed restrictions upon
her adhesion. The King of Naples was called to take part in

the congress, but the Neapolitan Parliament would not agree to his appointing his son, the Duke of Calabria, regent, till he had sworn that he would make no change in the constitution. The conciliatory appeals issued from Laybach by the monarch who had thus recovered his liberty, produced no result; the Austrian troops entered the kingdom of Naples. At the same moment a military insurrection broke out in Piedmont, and the king having refused to accept the Spanish Constitution, a model approved by all the revolutionaries, found himself obliged to abdicate. An Austrian army was at once directed against Piedmont, with the support of those troops who had remained loyal. Both in Turin and Naples the Austrian forces were completely successful, the Neapolitans scattering like cowards. After some serious resistance, the Piedmontese insurgents were beaten at Novara. The fears of the congress were removed, though some indignation was still felt. Piedmont, as well as the Two Sicilies, was now placed under Austrian occupation by diplomatic convention; there was some display of absolutist reaction at Naples; at Turin, a severe repression was brought to bear upon the revolutionists, and even the liberals. Lombardy and Modena were agitated by the political trials of some prominent public men; and the legations were also much disturbed. The Pope excommunicated the "carbonari," who had, for the most part, a share in the disorders of the Italian peninsula. Metternich triumphed at Laybach: he at first succeeded in influencing the Emperor Alexander, and secured his assistance in declaring against the revolutionary spirit, which he was too apt to confound with the spirit of liberty. "The allied sovereigns were not ignorant of the fact that they had to resist a devastating torrent," said the circular adopted by Austria, Prussia, and Russia; "to preserve whatever legally exists, was the invariable principle of their policy. The changes useful and necessary to the legislation and administration of States should emanate only from the free will, the well-considered and enlightened impulse, of those whom God had rendered responsible for the power. All that exceeds that limit must necessarily lead to disorder and social overthrow—to evils much more insupportable than those pretended to be remedied."

Neither France nor England adhered to this frank declaration of absolute power, and the coalition of European states was thus virtually dissolved. The ultra-royalist party were none the less delighted because this distant success succeeded the fears caused by the rising tide of revolution. All seemed to conspire to urge the government towards that right side, which alone offered it enthusiastic support. On the 29th September, 1820, the Duchess of Berry gave birth to a child, whose birth caused transports of joy not only to the extreme royalists, but to the mass of the population. None but a few men of foresight were apprehensive of seeing the imprudent partisans of power derive additional arrogance from that certainty of direct succession. Every day the separation between the ministry and liberals became more complete. Serre entirely abandoned his former friends, who opposed him with increasing vivacity. In his pamphlet entitled, *The Government of France since the Restoration,* Guizot severely attacked him. Next year, 1821, he endeavored to direct his friends in the way of legal opposition, and regular government offered them by the charter. His work *On the Present Government and Opposition in France* was entirely devoted to this purpose.

The partial renewal of the chamber was an indication that the royalists were being visited by a return of favor. A large number of the members of the "lost chamber" were again elected. Richelieu and Pasquier began to feel uneasy as to a success exceeding their hopes and desires. The king thought the same:—" Why, we are now like the poor knight who had not agility enough to leap on horseback," said he; "he prayed to St. George with such fervor that St. George gave him more than there was need for, and he jumped to the other side."

The result of the increase of power on the right was inevitable. Richelieu resolved to gain over the principal leaders. After long hesitation, mixed with some dissension, Villèle and Corbière, moderate leaders of the excited party, accepted the title of ministers without office, which was also granted to Lainé, who had long refused the office of president of public instruction. This duty was entrusted to Corbière. Chateaubriand was appointed minister at Berlin, and had great influence in securing the admission of his friends into the cabinet. "It is true that in the cabinet we are only two against seven," said Villèle, "but we rely upon a compact mass of one hundred and sixty deputies, whereas our seven colleagues have not more than a hundred behind them. With such support it will be our own fault if we have not the preponderance."

It was in fact the preponderance of the ardent and combative right which was every day becoming obviously more perma-

nent. The moderate right, approximating to the centre, both
in their views and interests, still rallied round the Duc de Richelieu and Pasquier, though tacitly beaten. Still the peaceful
alliance of the two parts of the right could not last, and the
declarations of Villèle and Corbière in favor of an efficacious
and practical government having been repelled by Richelieu,
the two leaders of the right withdrew, one starting for
Toulouse, and the other for Rennes. Their friends in the
chambers redoubled their attacks upon the ministry, and when
Richelieu complained to Monsieur, reminding him of his
promises, which had been repeated since his entry into the
ministry; "The fact is, my dear duke," replied Monsieur, "if
you allow me to say so, you have taken my words too liter-
ally: and then the circumstances then were so difficult." The
president rose abruptly, and hurrying to Pasquier's house
threw himself into an arm-chair, exclaiming, "He has broken
his word of honor! He has broken his word as a gentleman!"
"What would you have me to do?" said the king to Richelieu.
"He conspired against Louis XVI.; he conspired against me;
he will conspire against himself." The explosion of a barrel
of gunpowder in the king's apartments gave room to suspect
another attempt to renew the painful circumstances preceding
the fall of the Duc Decazes. The king himself shared this opinion. "These attempts are Protean," he wrote to Decazes, "every
day assuming a new form. It is quite probable that at the
bottom of the sack there may be found an infamous intrigue,
instead of an execrable wretch."

Nevertheless Richelieu succumbed to the attack directed
against him. He had refused to sacrifice several of his colleagues, and his colleagues in their turn refused to take share
in the new ministry. When the ultras made some advances,
Serre replied, as Royer-Collard had recently done: "You have
not enough for three months." Montmorency, Villèle, Corbière, Peyronnet, Bellune, and Clermont-Tonnerre, now composed the government. Ravez, president of the Chamber of
Deputies, belonged to the right. Chateaubriand was sent to
London as ambassador. The power passed entirely, and for
several years, into the hands of men who had scarcely the
slightest experience of it in the chambers, without having
ever really exercised it. Villèle, "moderator" of the right,
who was frequently unaware of the ideas, passions, and plans
of his friends, nevertheless found himself at the head of the
government as a party man, where he was to remain for some

time as a party man, although he strove to make the government spirit have more influence with his associates than the party spirit. He reached this result by the great and natural way: the head of the parliamentary majority became head of the government.

At the moment when his cabinet was being formed his position was one of the greatest difficulty. "It was no longer stormy discussions in the chamber, and riots in the streets: secret societies, plots, insurrections, an enthusiastic resolution to overthrow the established order, were everywhere fermenting and manifesting themselves in the eastern, western, and southern departments; at Belfort, Colmar, Toulon, Saumur, Nantes, Rochelle, even at Paris before the eyes of the ministers, among both military and professional men, both in the royal guard and the regiments of the line. Within less than three years the restoration was attacked and endangered by eight serious plots." *

The general excitement and alarm was excessive. The public liberty was not seriously endangered, and those who defended it were not disarmed. To struggle against the tendency of a government which displeased them, they had numerous adequate legal resources. They were nevertheless sincere in their patriotic prejudices, convinced that all means were not only permitted, but necessary, to protect the great liberal institutions recently secured to the country. The three leaders of the different parties in the opposition in the Chamber of Deputies, Lafayette, Manuel, and Argenson, brought to the conspiracies their characteristic habits of thought and natural disposition. With obstinate fidelity to the principles of liberty which he had adopted when young, Lafayette could, at certain periods of his life, meet the arguments of demagogues with unswerving firmness. A man of noble birth, liberal and popular, with no natural disposition to be revolutionary, he was blindly induced to be urged and to urge others to repeated revolutions. Manuel was the docile son and able defender of the revolution which had been accomplished since 1789, capable of becoming in her service a government partisan, but determined in any case to support her at all risks. Argenson, a melancholy dreamer, passionately devoted to the cure of the evils afflicting the human race, plotted with much hope of success, but always with untiring energy.

---

* Guizot's *Mémoires*, etc.

The Court of the Peers showed great moderation with respect
to the accused of the 19th August. It had pronounced the
charge inapplicable to most of the principal men who were implicated, and acquitted many of the others. The plots which
afterwards were divulged towards the end of 1821, at Saumur
and Belfort, seemed to be more skilfully contrived. Carbo-
narism had made great progress in France, and the leaders
were resolved not to abandon their accomplices. An accident
led to the discovery of the Saumur conspiracy, the centre of
which was the military school. The movement which soon
after declared itself in Alsace and delivered up Colmar to a
provisional government, proved abortive, like that of Saumur,
on account of repeated blunders.

On the 1st of January, 1822, Lafayette reached Belfort, to
put himself at the head of the insurrection. He found the plot
had been discovered, and several of the leaders arrested. On
January 7th, Arnold Scheffer and Courcelles went to Marseilles, where they expected to find preparations made for a
rising; the same disappointment attended them, their accomplices were either arrested or in flight. Several weeks afterwards, on the 24th of February, a more serious attempt at last
broke out in the west, Saumur being the centre, and General
Berton the principal leader. The town was attacked by bands
of men from Parthenay and Thouars; but the hesitation of the
inhabitants, and the determined attitude of a certain number of
the pupils in the military school, put a stop to that unimportant manifestation. There was at the same time great excitement in the 45th regiment of the line, then garrisoned at
Rochelle: four young sub-officers were accused of taking a
leading part in the insurrection. Almost simultaneously a
rising was attempted at Colmar, to deliver those accused of
conspiring at Belfort. In all parts of France, under the influence and auspices of the Carbonari, there was an outburst
of attempts, which were both serious and silly, followed up
step by step by the authorities, and sometimes even encouraged eagerly by interested agents. During two years these
men procured from various parts of the kingdom nineteen
condemnations to death, twelve of which were carried out.
Imprisoned after the Rochelle plot, the four sergeants, Bories,
Raoulx, Goubin, and Pommier, were on the point of undergoing their sentence, to escape which attempts had been in
vain made in their favor, though they were ignorant of it, and
probably thought they were abandoned. The magistrates

urged them to save their lives by giving some information as to the chief instigators of their fatal attempt. They all replied that they had nothing to reveal, and died without a word. Such devotion deserved leaders of more foresight.

Such noisy but powerless attempts at a rising were of service to the new government rather than a cause of weakness. The violence of the parliamentary debates increased, but the protection granted to the conspirators by those who did not conspire was necessarily prejudicial to the latter. Press censorship now brought many to trial: Béranger being twice already condemned for his outspoken songs, Benjamin Constant also was prosecuted.

The elections of a fifth of the chamber strengthened the ministerial majority. The power had really passed from the king's hands to those of Monsieur and his friends. Richelieu died on the 17th May, regretted and respected even by those who had most keenly opposed him. On his return from Aix-la-Chapelle, after the evacuation of the territory, he at first, with quiet simplicity, refused the national recompense offered him, and made over to the Bordeaux hospitals as a gift the income of 50,000 livres which was finally settled upon him. The king had always more esteemed him than loved him; habit had great influence in his personal affection, which the Duke Decazes had seen decrease with his removal. Henceforward other influences bore upon Louis XVIII., which were favorable to the predominance of the ultras.

From this time the tendencies of the government were clearly manifested. On the 1st of June the Abbé Frayssinous was appointed grand master of the university. An eloquent orator, honorable and candid, weak in character and narrow-minded, he was sometimes alarmed at the violent acts to which he found himself driven, without resisting or blaming them. The reorganization of the school of medicine, and school of law, and the suppression of the normal school were succeeded by stringent measures against individuals. In the preceding year Cousin's philosophical lectures were closed. Guizot's lectures in modern history were attended by a multitude of lads, who were diligently occupied in more serious studies; the tendency of the teaching was as moderate as it was liberal, but the professor was well-known to be strongly opposed to the government, and the lectures were suspended. It was in reviews and newspapers that independent minds now found

expression, not having yet attained their natural development
in the parliamentary arena.

The government were now triumphant in France, the effer-
vescence of the opposition being less eager without losing its
earnestness; and conspiracies ceased. Villèle had to struggle
against the interior difficulties of his party and foreign embar-
rassments. The Italian revolutionists were easily beaten by
the Austrian armies. The Spanish revolution remained triumphant, and was said to threaten the life of King Ferdinand
VII., as it certainly hampered his liberty of action. Men's
minds were anxiously expecting a European intervention in
Spain, a congress at Verona having been invoked to deliberate
upon it.

When Villèle, in forming his cabinet, proposed to the king
to appoint Mathieu de Montmorency as foreign minister, Louis
XVIII. made several objections. Eagerly devoted to good
works of every kind, president of those powerful associations
consecrated to that end which were known by the name of
"the Congregation," and with great influence naturally among
the earnest Catholics of the right, Montmorency's intellect was
not in proportion to his virtue. "He will betray you without
intending it, from weakness," said the king: "when away from
you, he will act according to his inclinations, not your directions; and instead of being served, you will be thwarted
and compromised." The penetration of Louis XVIII. had not
deceived him. When Villèle sent Montmorency to the Verona
congress, the head of the ministry wished France to remain a
stranger to any armed intervention in Spain, and instructed
his representatives to undertake no engagements to that effect.
Chateaubriand accompanied Montmorency to the congress;
sharing secretly the views of the foreign minister rather than
those of Villèle, he at first withheld his views and kept himself
in the background. Metternich had resolved to draw France
into the policy of intervention, contrary to that of England,
and thus at one blow destroy the Spanish revolution by French
arms, and the alliance between Paris and London, which was
annoying to him. Montmorency easily gave way to his influence, and Chateaubriand was seduced by the flattering attentions of the Emperor Alexander. France found herself engaged to a course suitable to the purposes of the three great
northern powers, which would necessarily lead to a war with
Spain. The king refused to recall at once his ambassador from
Madrid. "Louis XIV. destroyed the Pyrenees," said he; "I

shall not allow them to be raised again. He placed my house on the throne of Spain; I shall not allow it to fall. The other sovereigns have not the same duties as I; my ambassador must not quit Madrid till the day when 100,000 Frenchmen march to replace him." In reality, when thus speaking Louis XVIII. had tacitly accepted the part assigned him by Metternich in the European intervention in Spain, but he was lending his ear to the proposals made by the Duke of Wellington on the part of England. The two powers were to treat with the Spanish government in a friendly manner, in order to obtain such constitutional concessions as would preserve a state of peace. Montmorency believed his policy was condemned, and resigned, being replaced by Chateaubriand as minister of foreign affairs.

The war, nevertheless, became imminent. The Spanish government, proudly resolving to maintain the national independence, would make no concession. The French ambassador, Lagarde, was recalled, and on the 23rd January, 1823, at the opening of the chambers, the king himself announced the resolution he had formed. "I have ordered the recall of my minister," said he; "100,000 Frenchmen, commanded by a prince of my family whom I fondly call my son, are ready to march with a prayer to the God of St. Louis, that they may preserve the throne of Spain to the grandson of Henri IV., save that fair kingdom from ruin, and reconcile it to Europe. Let Ferdinand VII. be free to give to his people the institutions which they can have only from him, and which, while securing tranquillity to Spain, will remove the well-founded uneasiness of France; from that moment hostilities will cease, as I now, gentlemen, in your presence solemnly promise."

On the 15th March, 1823, the Duke of Angoulême and his staff left Paris, much liked and respected by the army on account of his moderation and justice. He soon gave a double proof of his strength of mind. On account of the loyalty of several officers being doubted in Paris, the Duc de Bellune, then minister of war, resolved to take the post of major-general at the head of the Spanish army; but the prince firmly resisted, and the Duc de Bellune was recalled. At the same time the Duke of Angoulême, being with good reason dissatisfied with the administration of military supplies, entrusted the management to Ouvrard, already celebrated for his daring speculations, but of great skill and foresight. On the 7th April, the French advanced-guard crossed the Bidassoa, and the duke entered Irun, already thronged with his allies, the insurgents and royalist juntas. Almost at the same moment the Cortes left Madrid, taking with them to Seville, King Ferdinand VII.

On the morning of the 24th May the prince entered the Spanish capital, without having met any serious resistance. He at once appointed a regency under the presidency of the Duke of Infantado. He had great difficulty in restraining the violent opposition of the royalists to the constitutionalists, and was perpetually hampered himself in his sensible procedure by the instructions sent from Paris. Chateaubriand showed great favor to the Spanish royalists, in the hope of gratifying in France the passionate enthusiasm of the right, who alone supported the armed intervention, generally disapproved of by the country. The three great powers of the north sent accredited representatives to the regency. King Louis XVIII. sent to Madrid as ambassador the Marquis of Talaru. The Cortes withdrew to Cadiz; and, on the king refusing to accompany them, they suspended his powers, and appointed a regency to compel the monarch's obedience. The Duke of Angoulême gave orders to begin the siege of Cadiz.

Spain was delivered to all the horrors of civil war. Don Miguel, second son of the King of Portugal, who was then captive, had excited a counter-revolution at Lisbon; everywhere guerilla bands of opposing factions hindered the movements of the armies, while taking an active share in the war. General Molitor, however, defeated the constitutional General Ballesteros, at Campillo de Arenas. The duke of Angoulême left Madrid to conduct personally the siege of Cadiz; and with the hope of mitigating the violence and vengeance which his presence was not sufficient to restrain, he published at Andujar, on the 8th August, an order which enjoined that political prisoners were to be set at liberty, and no arrests were to be made without instructions from the French commandants. Journalists and newspapers were subjected to the same authority.

This order offended both the good and the evil passions of the Spanish royalists, their national pride, and their thirst for vengeance. Its publication was stopped in Madrid, and it was severely blamed in Paris. Villèle wrote to the Duke of Angoulême that it was a breaking of the engagements entered into with Spain that we should not interfere in her home affairs. Every day aggravated the dissension between the Spanish regency and the powerful ally that had established it, and protected it with her arms. This was frequently painful to Angoulême's honorably sincerity. His success in carrying the Trocadéro fort before Cadiz led to a commencement of negotiations with the Cortes. "What most worries them," said the prince, "is the question of guarantees; for they know that the king's word is utterly worthless, and that in spite of his promises he might very well hang every one of them."

No guarantee could restrain the vindictive and angry passions of the victorious royalists. The war was still carried on in several parts, but Cadiz succumbed to our attacks by sea and land. On the 30th September, the Cortes declared themselves dissolved, and King Ferdinand VII. now free, embarked next day with all his family, to meet, at port St. Marie, the Duke of Angoulême, and the principal members of the regency of Madrid, who had just arrived at head-quarters. The shouts of the populace already hailed the monarch, and threatened his enemies. Angoulême insisted upon a general pardon; but the King of Spain pointed out with his hand the ragged crowd gathered under the windows of the palace, and replied, "You hear the will of the people." "This country is about to fall back into absolutism," wrote the prince to Villèle. "I have conscientiously done my part, and shall only express my settled conviction that every foolish act that can be done will be done."

The reaction was already setting in with unparalleled violence. All the acts of the constitutional government were annulled. Even before reaching Madrid, Ferdinand VII. banished for life to fifteen leagues from the capital all who had had a share in it. Angoulême refused absolutely to wait for the king at Madrid, and wrote to him with severity, boldly demanding the fulfilment of his engagements with France for the good government of Spain. "I asked your Majesty to give an amnesty, and grant to your people some assurance for the future. You have done neither one nor the other. During the fourteen days since your Majesty recovered your authority, nothing has been heard of on your part but arrests and arbitrary edicts, measures opposed to all regular government and all social order. Anxiety, fear, and discontent, begin to spread everywhere."

The Duke of Angoulême returned to France thus dissatisfied and anxious, in spite of the successes he had gained, and the honor he had acquired. "The war was not popular in France:

in fact, it was unjust, because unnecessary. The Spanish
revolution, in spite of its excesses, exposed France and the
restoration to no serious risk; and the intervention was an
attack upon the principle of the legitimate independence of
states. It really produced neither to Spain nor France any
good result. It restored Spain to the incurable and incapable
despotism of Ferdinand VII., without putting a stop to the
revolutions; it substituted the ferocities of the absolutist
populace for that of the anarchical populace. Instead of confirming the influence of France beyond the Pyrenees, it threw
the King of Spain into the arms of the absolutist powers, and
delivered up the Spanish liberals to the protection of England.
France though victorious was there politically defeated; in the
eyes of all who could clearly judge, the general and permanent
effects of that war were no better than its causes." *

At home it was considered a great success by the leaders of
the royalists, who had imposed it upon Villèle, and with him
upon King Louis XVIII. A certain coolness reigned between
the prime minister and Chateaubriand. The latter had taken
no share in the parliamentary government, but joined in the
stormy debates in the chambers. He proudly showed his
delight at the success of his war in Spain, as he termed it, and
the favors showered upon him by foreign sovereigns. On the
Emperor Alexander sending him the cross of St. Andrew, the
king took offence, and wrote to Villèle, " Pozzo and La Ferronnays have just made me give you, through the Emperor Alexander, a slap on the cheek, but I shall be even with him, and
give him a Roland for his Oliver. I now make you, my dear
Villèle, knight of my orders, and they are worth more than
his."

Villèle was then fully occupied with an important campaign.
On the 26th February, 1823, in a keen discussion on Spanish
affairs, Manuel laid the blame upon foreign intervention of
the evils that formerly desolated England and France. When
violently interrupted by the royalists, whose anger he constantly provoked, he replied, " Can any one be ignorant that
what caused the misfortune of the Stuarts was nothing but
the assistance granted them by France—an assistance foreign
to the parliament—a clandestine assistance, which compelled
them to place themselves in revolt against public opinion?
They were precipitated by public opinion. It is certainly a

misfortune, but that misfortune would have been avoided had
the Stuarts sought their support within the nation. Need I say
that the moment when the dangers of the royal family of
France became most serious, was when France, revolutionary
France, felt it necessary to defend herself by strength and
energy of an entirely new character?"

The orator had not finished, but no one heard the rest. The
right had risen in a body with violent protestations, demanding
the expulsion of the defender of regicide. Manuel remained in
the tribune, apparently unmoved by the indignation which he
took pleasure in exciting. In the midst of the tumult, Ravez,
the president, suspended the sitting without restoring order.
Neither a letter of Manuel, explaining his words, nor the moderate and manly speech delivered next day, was sufficient to
calm the fury of the right. Though perhaps rather imprudently, it had determined to use its power in taking revenge of
this most daring opponent. The discussion lasted several
days, conducted with great keenness in the chamber, and commented upon passionately by partisans of both sides without.
Manuel was saluted in the streets with loud shouts, and the
police felt it necessary to close the gates of the gardens of the
Tuileries.

Bourdonnaye made a formal proposal to exclude Manuel from
the chamber, which was agreed to by the commission appointed to consider it. Royer-Collard eloquently contested the
assembly's right to pronounce that exclusion. "I know something more hateful than the violation of the laws," said he;
"and that is, to give that violation fine names in order to le-
gitimatize it and summon sophistry to the assistance of force.
The revolution has only too abundantly shown this scandal.
Supposing force is produced, we are sometimes powerless to
prevent it: but let us at least compel it to keep its name and
character, so that it may retain its responsibility. When I
consider one after another the various necessities which rule
human affairs, I dare not lay it down absolutely as a fixed
principle that recourse to force can always be avoided. It
holds a great place in every history, and receives various names
according to its origin. When it comes from the government
or the powers, it is called *coup d'état;* when it comes from the
people, it is called 'insurrection;' when employed by a state
against a state, it gets the name of 'intervention.' The recourse to force in the present case is of the first class, it is a
coup d'état that is being directed against M. Manuel. . . . As a

matter of fact, M. Manuel has not justified regicide. He is only accused of having wished to do it; and that cannot be proved against him when he affirms the contrary. There is therefore no real reason for the exclusion; and the *coup d'état* does not fulfil the first of its conditions, which is that it be necessary."

In spite of all those efforts, an amendment of Hyde de Neuville, that Manuel should be excluded from the chamber during the remainder of the session, was carried by a large majority. Manuel boldly declared that he would not submit to such exclusion. "I acknowledge the right of no one here to accuse me or judge me," said he. "I look for judges, and I only find accusers. I do not await an act of justice; it is an act of vengeance to which I resign myself. I profess respect for the authorities, but I have much greater respect for the law which established them; and I fail to acknowledge their power as soon as, in spite of that law, they usurp rights which it has not conferred upon them. In such a state of things, I know not if submission is an act of prudence, but I know that whenever resistance is a right it becomes a duty. Having entered this chamber by the will of those who had the right to send me, I am now about to leave it only because compelled by those who have not the right to exclude me; and if that resolution on my part is to bring down on my head more serious dangers, I reflect that the field of liberty has sometimes been fertilized by noble blood!" Manuel's friends announced their intention of sharing his lot.

Next day, on the 3rd of March, a large crowd assembled round the Palais Bourbon. Manuel entered in his deputy's dress, accompanied by the whole of the left. Ravez protested officially against his presence and suspended the sitting, announcing that he was about to give the orders necessary for executing the decision of the chamber. "M. le President," said Manuel, "I declared yesterday that I should only yield to force; to-day I shall keep my word."

The members of the majority had left, and the deputies of the left with part of the left centre remained alone, motionless in their places. The first summons of the chief usher producing no result, a group of national guards appeared, with a detachment of veterans. "It is an insult to the national guard!" exclaimed Lafayette. The officer commanding the battalion advanced towards Manuel, and repeated the orders he had received for his expulsion. Then, after some hesitation, he left to go for fresh orders. Furnished this time with written instructions, he summoned Manuel to go out. On his refusal, he ordered the national guards to use force against the recalcitrant deputy. The national guard moved not a step. Showing the same impassibility when a second order was given, the applause of the deputies burst forth, and was repeated by several persons in the gallery. At last a detachment of gendarmes appeared on the threshold, and their colonel advancing a few steps said, "Gentlemen, I have just received official orders to compel M. Manuel to leave the chamber, since he resists the summons already made, and the efforts of the national guard." There were immediate shouts of recrimination: "Give orders to charge, as on the 18th Brumaire!" The colonel advanced towards Manuel, and seized him by the arm, while two gendarmes laid hold on his collar. His friends rushed towards him. "That is sufficient, gentlemen!" said Manuel, after being moved a short distance. He went out of the hall accompanied by all the members of the left, and allowed himself to be conducted to his carriage.

On account of this violation of the privileges of the chamber, and the excitement which resulted from it, Villèle understood the necessity of another appeal to the country. He calculated to derive from that source influence enough at length to rule according to his own ideas, or that of those whose will he followed. Immediately after the Spanish campaign the success of the elections was great for the government, and their power thus confirmed for a long time. Seventeen opponents alone were re-elected. Villèle resolved to present at once two proposals, which the deputies of the right were in favor of. By the one, a general election of all the deputies septennially was substituted for the partial yearly election; that was a guarantee of power, as well as duration to the new chamber. By the second proposal, a great financial measure, the conversion of five per cent. stock into three per cents.—that is to say, paying up the stockholders in full, or reducing their interest, announced a great political measure, an indemnity to the emigrants, and prepared to carry it out. The two laws were voted without difficulty by the Chamber of Deputies; but the second was violently opposed in the Chamber of Peers. Chateaubriand spoke not a word in favor of the project: he was reported to have said, "I have seen a good many break their heads against a wall, but people who themselves build a wall to break their heads against, I never saw yet." Villèle's anger at his colleague was constantly increasing, and when the Chamber of Peers rejected the law, Chateaubriand went up to the president of the council and said, "If you withdraw, we are ready to follow." "Villèle's only reply," says Chateaubriand, in his *Mémoires*, "was to honor us with a look, which we still see. Next day, Whit-Sunday, the 6th June, 1824, I went to the Tuileries, at half-past six, to pay my respects to Monsieur. The first drawing-room of the Marson pavilion was almost empty, only a few persons entering, and all with an air of embarrassment. One of Monsieur's aides-de-camp said that he did not expect to see me there, and asked if I had not received any message. 'No,' said I, 'what message could I receive?' 'I suspect you will soon know,' he replied. Then, as no one came to conduct me to Monsieur's room, I went to hear the music in the chapel; and when fully intent upon the beautiful chants, an usher came to say that I was wanted. It was my secretary, Pilorge, who handed me a letter and official note, and told me I was no longer a minister. The Duc de Rauzan, who had charge of the political department, had opened the letter, but had not the courage to bring it to me. It was from Villèle, as follows, 'M. le Viscomte, in obedience to the king's command, I at once transmit to your Excellency an order which his Majesty has just given: 'Count Villèle, president of our ministerial council, is appointed interim foreign minister, replacing Viscount Chateaubriand.' "

The insult was of the grossest character, and showed the extreme imprudence of Villèle! There are some allies who are necessary, though unpleasant; and Chateaubriand, in spite of his assumption and caprice, was less dangerous as a rival than as an enemy. Now all at once become a distinguished and powerful leader of the opposition, he launched incessant attacks at the ministry, from the tribune, which was eagerly supplied to him by the *Journal des Débats*. At one time, in spite of their friendship for him, the Bertins were on the point of quarrelling with Villèle. They requested that Chateaubriand should be appointed ambassador at Rome. The minister refused, alleging the king's dislike of Chateaubriand. "In that case," replied Bertin de Vaux, "remember that *les Débats* have already overthrown the Decazes and Richelieu ministries, and can soon overthrow the Villèle ministry." "You overthrew the two first by stirring up royalism," replied Villèle; "but to overthrow mine you must first stir up a revolution."

It was from the bosom of royalism itself that the *Journal des Débats* and Chateaubriand were about to excite the keenest opposition to Villèle. He had driven from the chamber most of his enemies; and others, like Camille-Jordan, were dead: Serre, also dead, no longer checked him by his attacks or his assistance. Chateaubriand, however, attacked him in the Chamber of Peers, and Bourdonnaye in the Chamber of Deputies; and round them were grouped the grievances of every sort which are quickly begot by power. Resolute opponents seconded attacks, the tendency of which they sometimes disapproved. Thus Villèle found himself entirely at the mercy of his friends, compelled to husband them, and accept their wishes in order to retain their support. He had just given Monsieur and his pious advisers the satisfaction of seeing Monseigneur de Frayssinous, already grand master of the university, raised to the new functions of minister of public instruction. At the bottom of his heart, and while reckoning upon the toleration of the ultras, who were masters of the power, Villèle principally depended on the king's good will. Louis XVIII. was old and sickly, and died on the 16th of September, 1824, surrounded during his last moments, and after his death, by all the ancient pomp of royalty. Several years previously, on receiving Barbé-Marbois in his room, he said, as he pointed to his bed, "My brother will not die in that bed!" Among those sovereigns who had immediately preceded him, as well as those soon to succeed him on the throne, Louis XVIII. was to be the only one to die peacefully in his palace.

CHAPTER XIX.

KING CHARLES X. AND THE REVOLUTION OF 1830 (1834—1830).

AFTER succeeding Louis XVIII., King Charles celebrated his succession by suppressing the censure of the press, though it was soon afterwards restored. On his return to Paris (27th September), after spending several days at St. Cloud, the new monarch showed a genuine desire for conciliation, and was well received by public opinion, the only favor asked from him being dismissal of the ministry. Charles X. refused. Like his brother and his children, he looked upon Villèle as the most able and useful of all his servants. Nevertheless the president of the council soon learnt that he had changed mas-

ters, " and that there is little to be counted upon in the mind
and heart of a king, however sincere, when the surface and interior are at variance.   Men are much more governed than is
generally believed, or than they themselves believe, by their real
thoughts.   Louis XVIII. and Charles X. have been much compared for the purpose of distinguishing one from the other; the
distinction was much more profound than has been indicated.
Louis XVIII. was a moderate of the old *régime*, and a free-
thinker of the eighteenth century.   Charles X. was a faithful
'emigrant,' and a humble devotee.   The wisdom of Louis
XVIII. was full of selfishness and skepticism, but earnest and
genuine.   When Charles X. acted as a wise king, it was by his
sense of honor, by uncalculating kindness, by momentary impulse and the desire to please, not from conviction or taste.
Through all the cabinets of his reign—Montesquiou, Talleyrand, Richelieu, Decazes, and Villèle—the government of Louis
XVIII. was always consistent and similar to itself, without bad
intention or false purpose.   Charles X. shifted about, from contradiction to contradiction and inconsistency to inconsistency,
till the day when, restored to his real faith and real intention,
he committed the fault which cost him his throne." *

From the beginning of the new reign, and in spite of the
kind words or isolated acts which cleverly calmed the anger of
the liberals, Villèle faithfully served the king's personal instincts and the wishes of his advisers.   He made no effort to
correct the inconstancy and fickleness of the king, but limited
himself to making him accomplish, whenever circumstances
admitted of it, so many acts of moderate and popular policy
that he should not seem exclusively devoted to the party who
really held his heart and faith in keeping.   The first measures
presented by the ministry at the opening of the session clearly
proved sovereign will.   The law of indemnity to "emigrants,"
that of communities of women, and that of sacrilege, were
really the manifesto of the new kingdom.   The intelligent
effort invariably made for the advantage or pleasure of the
spirit of progress, was always due to Villèle, and to him the
honor must be ascribed.

It was Villèle who in 1825 resisted the exclusive application
of the reparatory measure brought before the chambers in
favor of the victims of the revolutionary confiscations.   Those
condemned or banished at the successive crises of the revolu-

* Guizot's *Mémoires*, etc.

tion were to have their share in that indemnity, which the "emigrant" party tried to appropriate entirely to themselves. Public opinion has in fact retained the recollection of their pretensions, and the measure presented on the 3rd of January, 1825, has by succeeding generations been termed "the emigrants' indemnity." It provoked violent attacks; it caused great anxiety to those who had acquired the national property, and seemed to open a dangerous path. The right supported it with a passionate bitterness, which Villèle and Montignac tried in vain to modify. The law had been proclaimed as one to heal up the remaining wounds of the revolution; it bitterly revived its most painful recollections. The creation of stock to the amount of a milliard, by a law voted on the 15th of March by the deputies, and 23rd of April by the peers, continued to be unpopular in spite of its evident fairness. But this unjust criticism was soon falsified by the good effects whcih were produced in the provinces, and beneficial influence upon men's minds.

The proposal of a law on sacrilege was opposed both in the peers and deputies on higher grounds, based on earnest and profound liberalism. Royer-Collard and Broglie were more hostile to sacrilege than any man, but they boldly stood up against the application of extreme penalties to a crime which the law had no power to punish. "This bill now before the chamber," said Royer-Collard, "is of a special order, hitherto unknown in our deliberations. Not only does it introduce into our legislation a new crime, but what is much more extraordinary, it creates a new principle of criminality—a class of crimes which are, so to say, supernatural, which do not fall under our senses, which human reason cannot discover or understand, and which are only manifested to religious faith enlightened by revelation. Thus the penal law brings under discussion both religion and civil society—their nature, end, and respective independence. . . . The law has a religious belief, and since it is sovereign it must be obeyed. Truth in the matter of faith belongs to its domain; truth in its turn takes possession of the law, makes its constitutions both political and civil, that is to say, it makes everything. Not only is its kingdom of this world, but this world is its kingdom, the sceptre has passed from its hands. Therefore, just as in politics we are shut up between absolute power and revolutionary sedition, in religion we are confined between theocracy and atheism. Let them beware; the revolution has certainly been impious even to cruelty, but it is this crime especially that has destroyed it; and it may be predicted for the counter-revolution that reprisals of cruelty, even if only written, will bear witness against her, and shatter her in turn." The law was voted without amendment, including the first article, which pronounced capital punishment against profaners of sacred objects. "It is only referring them to their natural judge!" exclaimed Bonald in an impulse of fanatical violence which was blamed even by his friends: this sentence of his speech was not inserted in the *Moniteur*.

Such procedure only the more embittered the dissension, already so profound, which divided the men who had produced the revolution from those who underwent it. The struggle became as keen in the religious arena as in the political arena. In the foremost ranks of the hottest partisans of a return to the faith and practice of the past, there fought the Abbé Lamennais, soon destined to turn his arms elsewhere. The opposition journals, the *Courrier*, *Constitutionnel*, and the *Globe*, eagerly brought before the public the numerous questions discussed in the Chambers. Everything supplied material for fiery discussion—a curé's sermon, the representation of a new piece at the theatre, the recognition of the independence of Haiti, or the conversion of public stock. King Charles X. was consecrated on the 19th May, 1824, with all the pomp necessary to such a ceremony. The numerous acts of clemency which signalized the consecration assisted to appease the popular excitement for some time.

Before the session was reopened, 21st January, 1825, General Foy had died—still young, passionately regretted, and with numerous proofs of public admiration heaped upon him even till after his death. The Emperor Alexander was also dead, having left still pending the question of the independence of Greece, which had been recently raised by the insurrection of the Christians against the oppression of the Turks. The serious and resolute opposition of the Chamber of Peers to the imprudent procedure of the government was daily manifested with great notoriety. Villèle submitted against his will to the demands of his party for a law in favor of primogeniture and the substitution of property. He himself was by no means deceived as to its success. "Should the government propose to restore the law of primogeniture," he wrote in the preceding year to Prince Polignac, then ambassador in London, "they would not find a majority to obtain it, because the evil is more deeply-seated; it is in our manners, which still all bear the impress left by the revolution. The bonds of subordination are so relaxed in our families, that the father is often compelled to consider the wishes of all his children." In his eloquent speech in the Chamber of Peers, Broglie did not criticise so severely the state of manners and families, but boldly resisted what he considered an ill-timed and useless return towards an antiquated legislation. "What is now preparing," said he," is a social and political revolution, a revolution against the revolution which took place in France nearly forty years ago. If I had the right of advising the councillors of the crown, I should say to them, 'Give way while there is still time, to the pressure of public opinion. Perseverance is a virtue, but not when in excess.' There are certainly circumstances under which a statesman ought to resist public complaints however general, raise his solitary voice against public opinion if led astray, and remain alone on the breach to defend the interests of truth; but it is only then that the truth is of such an order that higher minds can alone reach it. Here, on the contrary, where the point at issue is the peace of families, the relationship between fathers and children, the ties between brothers and sisters, the rudest workman or simplest artisan knows as much as the greatest philosopher. Here we deal with some of those truths which God is sometimes pleased to hide from the wise in order to reveal them to the simple and ignorant. It is one of those occasions when the legislator can resign himself blindfolded to go with the stream, exclaiming with confidence, 'Vox populi, vox Dei!'" The law was reduced to a single clause, which gave permission to extend to a second generation the "substitution of the disposable part of the successions;" and was passed in that form by both chambers.

The bill on the press, presented in the end of the year 1826, was not to obtain even that meagre success. Intended to satisfy the claims of the clergy as well as the ultras, it did not please Lamennais, who, with his usual violence, characterized it as a "monument probably unique of hypocrisy and tyranny," and roused to their highest pitch the wrath and indignation of all the liberals. Peyronnet had announced it as a "law of justice and love;" Chateaubriand termed it a "law of the Vandals." "It is a censorship!" exclaimed Benjamin Constant. "It would amount to the same thing as a proposal in these terms: 'Printing is suppressed in France for the profit of Belgium,'" declared Casimir Périer, then become one of the leaders of the opposition in the Chamber of Deputies. The French Academy drew up an address to be presented to the king, to protest against the painful position in which literature should be placed by the new legislation. The address was not received, and many of the academicians were deprived of the offices they held. The *Courrier* was prosecuted. In spite of this display of power and resolution on the part of the government, the bill as amended by the Chamber of Deputies received so decided an opposition in the peers that the ministry found themselves compelled to withdraw it (17th April, 1827).

The public excitement constantly increased. It was notably exhibited when the king was reviewing the national guard on the 29th April, abusive terms being shouted in various places, not only against the ministers, but against the princesses. On being informed by some of his *cortège* of circumstances which had escaped his notice, the king resolved to discharge the national guard (30th April). On the 24th June, the day after the closing of the session, he issued an order restoring the censorship of periodicals and newspapers. The ill-advised severity of its application answered to the arbitrary violence of the act of power. Eloquent and outspoken pamphlets supplemented the enforced silence of the newspapers. Chateaubriand, always a consistent advocate of the liberty of the press, was one of the foremost combatants in this arena, and a society was formed for the gratuitous dissemination of his writings. There was at the same time a strong antipathy formed against the clerical "congregations" and the order of Jesuits. A petition of Montlosier to the Chamber of Peers was the occasion of a long and brilliant debate. In spite of the eloquent defence of the Abbé Frayssinous, minister of public instruction, the chamber sent the petition to the president of the council, demanding the application of the laws which interdicted Jesuitical establishments in France.

The home difficulties were not the only ones then weighing upon the cabinet. The death of King John VI. of Portugal led to the abdication of his son Don Pedro, the first Emperor of Brazil, on condition that his daughter Maria should marry her uncle Don Miguel, and both should occupy the throne of Portugal. Pedro at the same time granted a constitutional charter to Portugal. Several provinces revolted, and declared Miguel an absolute monarch. Conquered in Portugal, the insurgents retired to Spain, where they were well received; and on an invasion into Portugal being attempted, the diplomatic relations between the two kingdoms of the peninsula were broken. The French Government disapproving of the King of Spain's conduct, recalled Moustier, their ambassador. The Portuguese constitutionals having claimed the support of England, the cabinet sent an army. "To those who blame the government for delay," said Canning in Parliament, "the answer is very short: it was only last Friday that I received the official request from Portugal; on Saturday the ministers decided what was to be done; on Sunday, the decision received the king's sanction; on Monday it was communicated to both houses; and at this very moment the troops are on their way to Portugal." The English minister of foreign affairs declared his policy of opposition to French intervention and occupation in Spain. He had already recognized the republics in South America, those old Spanish colonies which revolted against the yoke of the mother country. "Should France occupy Spain," said he, "was it necessary to blockade Cadiz to restore the situation of England? No, I looked to the other side of the Atlantic, and sought for compensation in another hemisphere. I thought of Spain as she was known to our ancestors; and determined that if the French should have Spain, it would not be Spain with the Indies. I called in the new world to redress the balance of the old. I have left to France the unpleasant burden of her invasion, which I am convinced she would gladly be rid of."

Several months afterwards Canning died, succumbing in his turn like Pitt, Fox, Castlereagh, and Romilly under the weight of a government which had long exceeded human strength. But Spain had at last yielded to the pressure exercised upon her by England and France. The government of Charles X., after some violent attacks by the right, recalled the Swiss brigade sent to protect the royal family in Madrid.

After friendly relations between Spain and Portugal were restored, the affairs of Greece became the object of a European arrangement. Supported from the first by England, the Greek insurgents asked without success from the Duke of Orleans the honor of placing his son, the Duke of Nemours, on the new throne of Greece. The Duke of Wellington was instructed by Canning to offer the mediation of England, between Russia and Turkey, and between Turkey and Greece. By a protocol of the 4th April, the cabinets of St. Petersburg and London agreed together to guarantee to Greece a semi-independence. The Emperor Nicholas absolutely refused to admit of any intervention from Europe in his quarrels with Turkey. He said to Wellington, with Oriental exaggeration, "I have just been making reductions in my army, and have now only 600,-000 men to place at the disposal of my friends, and 1,200,000 to oppose my enemies." While showing favor towards Greece, France did not adhere to the Anglo-Russian protocol. On the 6th July she undertook with those allies to put a stop to the "bloody struggle which delivered the Grecian provinces and islands of the Archipelago to all the disorders of anarchy, brought every day fresh hindrances to European commerce, and occasional piracies demanding onerous measures of surveillance and repression." The Porte having rejected the friendly proposals offered by the three powers, and General Ibrahim having violated a provisional armistice demanded by the allies, the combined English, Russian, and French fleet, under the orders of Admiral Codrington, the senior commander, forced the entrance of Navarino harbor, and the Turkish fleet defending it was almost completely destroyed. The struggle between the Turks and Greeks was still keenly contested. The ambassadors of the three powers left Constantinople. The proclamations of Turkey formed a reason for Russian armaments. France wished for a peaceful arrangement, but without success. The disorder continued to reign in Portugal, and a serious insurrection broke out in Catalonia, yet the English ministry, now under Wellington's direction, seemed resolved to maintain the policy of non-intervention; France found herself joined to Russia, and separated both from Austria and Prussia. Some preparations were also being made to punish the Dey of Algiers, who had encouraged the Mediterranean pirates.

In the midst of this fermentation and these foreign distractions, the opposition to Villèle was steadily increasing; he was blamed for evils of every sort. "Even in the Palais Bourbon and the Tuileries, its two strongholds, the cabinet was visibly losing ground. In the Chamber of Deputies the ministerial majority became smaller and more depressed, even when victorious. At court, some of the king's most trusted servants, whether from party-spirit or from monarchical anxiety, wished for Villèle's fall, and were already considering who should succeed him. The king also, on learning some fresh indication of the public feeling, said with a tone of annoyance as he returned to his private room, "Always Villèle! Always against Villèle!" *

---

* Guizot's *Mémoires*, etc.

In reality such judgment was grossly unjust. If the right enjoyed power for six years, and had so exercised it as to be able to retain it; if Charles X. not only succeeded peacefully to Louis XVIII., but ruled without trouble, and even with occasional popularity—it was Villèle especially they had to thank for it. He had kept his party and power within the general limits of the charter, and for six years conducted the constitutional government under a prince, and with friends who were supposed not to understand it, and to have accepted it against their wills. He was wrong in yielding to the king or his party when he disapproved of their plans, and thus accepting the responsibility of faults committed under his name, and with his consent, though against his will. Taking the whole burden on himself, he asked the king for a dissolution, 5th November, 1827. The elections were fixed for the 17th and 24th November.

The liberal movement became, not only more animated, but more concentrated and more powerful in its efforts towards a common aid. Men of extremely different general views and special intentions were brought closer together. A public association, with the motto, "Heaven helps those who help themselves," was formed by the opposition to organize in the elections; and by rallying both liberals and royalists who were disgusted with the ministry, its success exceeded all expectation. The more moderate friends of the government had been much afraid of this test. Lainé refused for a long time to believe a dissolution possible. "In any case," he wrote to Decazes, in the beginning of October, "I shall give you my hearty assistance to secure the exercise of the public rights of election and the liberty of the press. Whatever may be the evils of the latter, they are not to be compared to the advantages which result from it, in a nation where no right is fixed, and which, after the horrors of the revolution, the prostration of the empire, and the ebb and flow of the restoration, remains hesitating and uncertain, without being really indifferent. The people of France are treated like a people of puppets, and what is worse, they themselves laugh at it."

"What actually produces the elections," says Guizot in his *Mémoires*, "is the wind that blows and the impulse impressed on men's minds by events. The elections, considered as a whole, are almost always more true than is believed by interested or silly distrust. However anxious and adroit, the government's influence over them is for the most part only

secondary." In 1827 the government left no means untried to
influence strongly the electoral results. Seventy-six new
peers were added to the Upper Chamber, in the hope of weakening its independence; and opposition writers were vigorously repressed. Even the tribunals, however, were sometimes free from administrative pressure. At Manuel's death
his funeral obsequies were the occasion of a great public
demonstration. Mignet, then a very young man, one of the
most ardent colleagues of Thiers in the management of the
Constitutionnel and *Globe*, wrote an account of the ceremony
in a pamphlet, which was prosecuted. On Mignet's acquittal,
"Paris celebrated the verdict as a counterpoise to the press
censorship," wrote Salvandy, always anxious to note the
progress of liberal opinion." "Frenchmen of the charter,"
exclaimed the *Journal des Débats*, "prepare wings to fly to
the combat! Frenchmen of the restoration, make haste to
give us a royalist chamber which will not blast that name by
servility. Frenchmen of honor and truth, purge your country
from the scandal of a perverse and dishonored administration."

The coalition of liberals with the royalists opposed to the
ministry had a brilliant triumph, and seemed certain of a
majority. Villèle and his colleagues offered to resign, but
King Charles X. was undecided and alarmed. Various
schemes were devised for changing the ministry while retaining the president of the council, but the force of circumstances was too great. Villèle withdrew in favor of Martignac, to be actual chief of the cabinet without bearing the
title. Count Portalis became keeper of the seals; Count Ferronnays foreign minister, and Count Roy chancellor of the
exchequer. Royer-Collard, chosen by seven colleagues, was
appointed president of the chamber. Though but little favorable to Villèle, the princess royal had been opposed to his dismissal. "You are deserting M. de Villèle," said she to the
king; "it is your first step downwards from the throne."

"Thus began a new attempt at government by the centre;
but with much less energy or chance of success than that
which from 1816 to 1821, under the simultaneous or alternate
direction of Richelieu and Decazes, had protected France and
the crown against the domination of the members of the right
and those of the left. The centre in 1816, while the country
was in pressing danger, had derived much energy even from
that force, and had to deal, both on the right and left, only with

resistance which, though resolute, was still in the opinion of the public too inexperienced and badly organized to be capable of governing. In 1828, on the contrary, the right having only left power after a possession of **six** years, believed themselves both sure of soon recovering it and capable of exercising it, and therefore eagerly and hopefully attacked the unexpected successors who had snatched it from them. Threatened in the chambers by ambitious and powerful rivals, the new-born power only found there allies who were lukewarm, or hindered in their good intentions; and sensible men were much more paralyzed or compromised by the violent or thoughtless, than successful in directing or restraining their troublesome companions. Another point was that, whereas from 1816 to 1821, King Louis XVIII. gave genuine and practical assistance to the government of the centre, in 1828 King Charles X. considered the cabinet which took the place of the leaders of the right as a disagreeable experiment which he had to undergo, but to which he lent himself with anxiety, without confidence in its success, resolving not to test it more than was strictly necessary. "The ministry resulting from the first conflict will be necessarily rather insignificant," wrote the Duc de Broglie after the elections, "but we must support them, and try to prevent any one being alarmed. Should we succeed, after the fall of the present ministry, in getting through the year tranquilly, it will be a triumphant success."

Martignac's ministry was not to last long, and the hope of seeing it establish itself and become permanent was still more ephemeral. In vain did the cabinet try to find fresh support. Notwithstanding his fall, Villèle kept up with Charles X. a constant correspondence, which had no favorable influence on the mutual and confidential relations between the king and his ministers. Chateaubriand rejected the overtures made him, as they had no bearing on the ministry of foreign affairs, which alone he coveted. He still kept up a bitter opposition in the *Journal des Débats*. Vatimesnil, who formerly stood in the ranks of the ultras, now more moderate than he avowed, was appointed minister of public instruction, and made all haste to reopen the professional courses of lectures which Villèle had closed. Guizot and Villemain began again their lectures to crowded classes of enthusiastic pupils, who

*Guizot's *Mémoires*, etc.

eagerly flocked to them as well as to Cousin. Guizot's principal aim at this time was to struggle against the error of superficial minds separating the past from the present, and the history of the nation from its new life. "In my lectures from 1828 to 1830," says he in his *Mémoires*, "I constantly labored to bring back my hearers to an intelligent and impartial appreciation of our ancient social condition, and thus contribute my share in restoring between the varic us elements of our social system, old and new, monarchical, aristocratic, or democratic, that mutual esteem and harmony which may be suspended by an access of revolutionary fever, but which soon become indispensable both to the liberty and prosperity of the citizens, both to the power and tranquillity of the state."

Notwithstanding the distrust with which Martignac's ministry inspired some of the liberals, it gave good assistance to the wise and prudent efforts of sensible men to secure at last the foundation of the public liberties upon strong bases. A law for the purpose of securing the annual revision of the electoral lists, a proposal for new press-regulations and suppressing the preliminary authorization of newspapers, as well as the censorship, were soon brought before the chambers, and passed by large majorities. Martignac defended his measures with that persuasive and dignified eloquence which gained for him the name of "the Syren," given him by Dupont, the Eure deputy. Benjamin Constant attacked the press law, after demanding and supporting it. "Attacked by contradictory accusations," said the minister of the interior, "we reply by our acts. We present ourselves before you with uncovered foreheads, and look you in the face without fear, because our consciences are at rest, and you are just. The declaration of war which has just been been addressed to us will only be signed, we are confident, by a small number of enemies. We have not provoked it, but we do not fear it, because we have as witnesses and judges of the conflict you, gentlemen, and France." At the same time, and as if to reduce at last to nothing the attacks directed against the "clerical" tendencies of the government, there appeared two orders regulating the private management of the small seminaries which had occasioned numerous protests, and declaring that ecclesiastical schools, managed by religious bodies who were not authorized, should henceforth be subject to the rule of the university. This measure, which really excluded Jesuits from teaching, greatly pleased and astonished the liberals, but caused much dis-

pleasure and anxiety amongst the ultras, who were very suspicious of the influence of Ravez upon the king. The journey
made by Charles X. in the eastern provinces after the close of
the session, and the enthusiasm with which he was received,
assisted more successfully in removing the alarm of the
court. The king unfortunately derived from that source
illusions which soon after contributed in drawing him on
towards ruin.

The misfortune of the liberals in 1829 was, that they disturbed with their own hands the touchy and precarious harmony which had been established between them and the moderate royalists. Martignac brought in two bills securing to
the electoral principle a share in the administration of the
departments and communes, and imposing new rules and
limits on the central power with regard to local affairs.

"These concessions might appear either too great or too
narrow. In any case they were real, and defenders of the
people's liberties could not do better than accept them and hold
by them. But among the liberal party which had till then
supported the cabinet, two spirits but slightly allied to politics,
the spirit of impatience and the spirit of system, the desire for
popularity and the rigor of logic, could not be satisfied with
conquests so incomplete and easy. The right refrained from
voting, and left the ministers to struggle with the demands of
their allies. Notwithstanding Martignac's efforts, an amendment which seemed more important than it really was formed
a sort of attack upon the bill to systematize the departmental
administration. In the king's opinion, and that of the chambers, the ministry had reached the limit of their credit, unable
to obtain from the king what would have satisfied the chambers, or from the chambers what would have reassured the
king. They themselves by suddenly withdrawing both bills
confessed their double powerlessness, and remained still standing, though dying." *

Two months previously, on account of an accident which
had compelled Ferronnays to leave the ministry of foreign
affairs, the king tried to replace him by Prince Polignac, for
whom he had a strong attachment, but not succeeding, the
office remained vacant. Chateaubriand, who had been covet-
ing it, was then in Rome: his purpose was to take revenge
upon Villèle, by forming a new cabinet himself. He was

---

* Guizot's *Mémoires*, etc.

spared, however, both the trouble and the satisfaction. On the 9th of August, the *Moniteur* announced the formation of Polignac's ministry. Bourdonnaye was appointed home minister.

What was the object in view? No one knew; Polignac and the king as little as the public. But Charles X. had displayed on the Tuileries the flag of the counter-revolution. There was a universal outburst of anger and anxiety. "There it is now again broken, that bond of love and confidence which joined the people to the monarch!" exclaimed the *Journal des Débats*, on the 10th of August. "See again the court with its old hatreds, emigration with its errors, the priesthood with its antipathy to freedom, coming to interpose between France and her king! What constituted the glory of this kingdom was the moderation in the exercise of power; now moderation is impossible. Those now ruling the affairs would like to be moderate, but they cannot. What will they do then? Will they bring to their assistance the force of the bayonet? Bayonets in these days are intelligent; they know and respect the law. Are they about to tear up that charter which made the immortality of Louis XVIII., and the power of his successor? Let them consider well: the charter now is an authority against which all the efforts of despotism should be broken. The people pay a milliard to the law; they would not pay two millions on the orders of a minister. With illegal taxes there should be born a Hampden to crush them. Hampden? Must we again recall to mind that name of alarm and warfare? Unhappy France! Unhappy king!"

The Bertins were prosecuted for that article, and condemned by the lower court, though the judgment was quashed by the Cour de Cassation. The new ministers were extremely astonished at this manifestation of public opinion. It was more serious and sustained than such popular impulses generally are in France, because the danger seemed still greater to enlightened men than to the mass of the nation. Guizot and Berryer had just taken their seats as deputies, being at last qualified by age to enter the chamber; one representing Calvados, the other Haute-Loire. Both were already known; both destined to join together in political combat, not without mutual respect and liking; both eager for the fray. The struggle was everywhere concealed and threatening, and had not yet burst forth at any point. Societies were publicly formed, both in the provinces and in Paris, to refuse payment of taxes, should the government attempt to raise them without legal sanction of the chambers. "We shall not make a *coup d'état*," said Polignac to Michaud. "What, your highness! you won't! I am sorry for that," replied the historian of the crusades, who had formerly been insulted by Villèle. "Why?" asked Polignac. "Because all your party wish for *coups d'état*, and if you don't make one, you will have nobody." Polignac had not yet understood. The prejudice against him astonished the king and his new minister. Polignac had recently, in the Chamber of Peers, declared his attachment to the charter. "His declarations are sincere: he believed the charter compatible with the political preponderance of the ancient nobility and the definitive supremacy of the ancient royalty. He flattered himself that he could develop the new institutions by making them subject to the rule of influences which they had been created for the very purpose of abolishing or limiting. It is impossible to estimate the extent of the conscientious illusions which may deceive a weak mind, of some ardor and elevation, but mystically vague and keen. Alarmed at his unpopularity, and afraid to increase it by his actions, Polignac did nothing. The cabinet formed to subdue the revolution and save the monarchy remained motionless and fruitless. They prepared an expedition to Algiers, and summoned the chambers, with constant declarations of their devotion to the charter. They hoped to get rid of the difficulty through a majority and a conquest!" * Henceforth it was as president of the council that he had to keep up the struggle. After some dissension within the cabinet, Bourdonnaye withdrew, Montbel replaced him as home minister, and Guernon Ranville was appointed minister of public instruction.

The king and ministers thought to find a useful diversion from the agitation of home affairs in general European politics, at that time difficult and complicated. After being urged by Russia, and without receiving much support from England, the French government promised pecuniary assistance to the Greek insurgents, and entered upon some negotiation with President Capo d'Istria as to the future organization of the new state. It was intended by the intervention of a corps of the French army, supported by the English fleet, to assist the operations of the Russians, and compel Ibrahim Pacha to return to Egypt. This expedition was delayed through the Duke of Wellington's

* Guizot's *Mémoires*, etc.

objections and Metternich's diplomacy, but on the 17th August, 1828, the French troops set sail at Toulon, under the orders of General Maison. On the 6th October the last Egyptian division evacuated the Morea, all the strongholds were delivered up to us, and the Peloponnesus was freed from it enemies. The conference of allied powers, by arrangement with Capo d'Istria, offered the crown of Greece to Prince Leopold, of Saxe-Coburg, widower of the Princess Charlotte, heiress to the English throne. After some discussion of the conditions of acceptance, the prince definitively refused the crown. The English ministry, who had supported him, lost their hold on the public confidence. The state of Europe was not reassuring. Don Miguel and the absolutists triumphed in Portugal over the rights of Queen Maria. In Spain, Ferdinand VII., on the occasion of his young queen's confinement, issued a pragmatic sanction, restoring the ancient order of the Spanish monarchy admitting females to the royal succession. The Dey of Algiers refused the satisfaction demanded in France, on account of the consul having been insulted; and on the failure of a blockade to reduce the town, an expedition, commanded by Bourmont, set out for Africa, on the 16th May, 1830. The landing was successfully effected on the 14th June; and soon news of the taking of Algiers (4th July) came to fill all hearts with joy and pride.

This public satisfaction was not diminished by the discontent of England. George IV. had just died; and the Duke of Wellington, who was still retained in power by William IV., demanded from the French government an engagement to retain none of the territories they had just conquered. Polignac refused. "Never," said Lord Aberdeen to Laval, the French ambassador, "never did France, under the Republic or under the empire, give England such serious ground of complaint as she has been giving us for the last year." "Polignac is considered a man of worth and honor," said Wellington; "I look upon him as one of the falsest and ablest men that exist."

Wellington did Polignac too great injustice and too great an honor at the same time. In his foreign as well as in his home policy, he was animated by perfidious intention; and his ability was merely the imprudent daring of a lofty but confused mind. The liberties of the people were not yet violated, but they were felt to be seriously endangered. Anxious not only for the safety of his throne, but for what he considered the inalienable rights of his crown, King Charles X. assumed, to maintain them, an attitude which was most offensive to the nation. He braved her more than he defended himself against her. The nation in her turn felt angry and haughty. There were hints of *coups d'état* on the people's side, ready to reply to those on the king's. Without directly attacking the reigning power, legal measures were used against it to their utmost limit; too openly to admit of a charge of hypocrisy, and too adroitly to be hindered in their hostile work. Press trials might follow each other, and the hostile acts of the government clearly show their tendency, but they also, like the opposition, kept within legality. The constitutional royalists, who had sincerely accepted and supported the restoration, felt more than any other section of the party the difficulty and danger of the situation. The address, called that of the 221, inspired by Royer-Collard and his political friends, was the last and supreme effort of those men of honor and foresight, then apprehensive of the overthrow of the monarchy which their hands had helped to raise. The speech from the throne contained one threatening sentence:—

"Peers of France, deputies of the departments, I am fully confident of your assistance in producing the good which I wish to do. You will repel with scorn the base insinuations which malevolence is seeking to propagate. Should guilty intrigues stir up against my government obstacles which I cannot, which I wish not to anticipate, I shall find power to surmount them in my determination to maintain the public peace in the well-grounded confidence of the French people, and in the affection they have always shown to their king."

"Don't urge the king too eagerly," Royer-Collard sometimes said. "Nobody knows what stupid blunders he may be guilty of." It was such blundering due to the royal illusions that the Chamber of Deputies tried to prevent in 1830. The address of the peers was embarrassed and hesitating; that of the Chamber of Deputies was both firm and modest, inflexible as to the basis of constitutional principle, sympathetic and respectful in its desire to warn the monarch of the dangers to which he was exposed. "They tell us that France is in peace, that there is no disturbance of order," said Guizot, mounting the tribune for the first time as a deputy, to speak on behalf of the address. It is true that the material order is not disturbed; all move about freely and peacefully; business is not interfered with by uproar. The social surface is tranquil, so tranquil that the government may well be tempted to believe that the bottom is in perfect security, and thus consider themselves un-

threatened by any danger. Our words, gentlemen, the candor
of our words, alone can inform the government at the present
moment; they are the only voice that can reach up to them
and dissipate their illusions. Let us beware of weakening its
force; let us beware of enervating our expressions. Truth has
already too much difficulty in reaching within the palaces of
kings; let us not send it weak and colorless; let us leave no
possibility of its being misunderstood, or of the loyalty of our
sentiments being mistaken."

On the 18th March, the address of the chamber was carried
to the Tuileries. A large number of the opposition deputies accompanied their president. Royer-Collard showed considerable
emotion, even in the tone of his voice; that of the king was dry
and abrupt, though his attitude was dignified, without either
hesitation or haughtiness. "Sir," said he, "I had the right to
expect the assistance of both chambers in effecting the good I
intended. My heart is pained to see the deputies of departments declare that, so far as they are concerned, there will be
no such assistance. I announced my determination at the
opening of the session—that determination is unchangeable.
The interests of my people forbid me to relinquish it; my ministers will let you know of my intentions." Next day, the 19th
March, the prorogation of the chamber to the 1st September
was announced in the *Moniteur*. The triumphant delight of
the ultras broke forth everywhere. "These people did not
know what a king was," said the *Universel*, Polignac's journal;
"they know it now: a breath has scattered them like chaff."
The more clear-sighted among the ecclesiastical party were not
so mistaken. "As the ministry have laid it down, the question puts us between the republic and an arbitrary court
party," said Lamennais. "Considering everything, I prefer
the former, because I prefer fever to death or paralysis causing
death."

The republicans, till then few and timid, held the same
opinion as Lamennais. At a banquet on 1st April, in honor of
the 221, Godefroy Cavaignac refused to drink to the king's
health. Odilon Barrot reproved him with intelligent firmness. They drank to the harmony of the three powers, the
constitutional king, the chamber of peers, and the chamber of
deputies. On the 16th May, the chamber was dissolved by
royal order; the electoral colleges being summoned for the
end of June and first weeks of July.

Two days afterwards, Courvoisier and Chabrol gave in

their resignation. Peyronnet became home minister and Montbel chancellor of the exchequer. Chantelauze, first president of the court of Grenoble, replaced Courvoisier. When consenting to join the cabinet, the latter said he should leave it the first day the liberties of the people were endangered. Those who knew him considered his withdrawal very ominous. Montbel and Guernon-Ranville retained their posts against their real will. "I consider the favor bestowed upon me by the king the greatest misfortune of my life," said Chantelauze.

Villèle had hitherto kept in retirement, living in the country since the abortive proposal of Labbey to bring an accusation against his cabinet. He returned to Paris in March, when Polignac offered him a seat in the cabinet, but the former president refused, and returned to Toulouse. He advised Montbel to agree to no new change in ministerial arrangements. "The importance which they attach to it proves the determination to get rid of the difficulty by a *coup d'état*," he remarked with penetrating foresight; "and that is a game you are not fit for."

The whole of France was now waiting for the *coup d'état*, and Europe was waiting as well as France. "Your two weakest points are the electoral law and the liberty of the press," said Metternich in Vienna to Rayneval; "but you cannot touch them except through the chambers. A *coup d'état* would ruin the dynasty." At St. Petersburg the Emperor Nicholas spoke in the same manner to the Duc de Mortemart, the French ambassador. "If they leave the charter it is certain ruin; if the king attempts a *coup d'état* he must bear the whole responsibility alone." His ambassador at Paris, Pozzo di Borgo repeated this to the members of the council, and to the king himself with all the authority due to the great influence he had formerly exercised in the affairs of the restoration. He one day found King Charles X. seated at his table, with his eyes fixed upon the charter, open at Article XIV.* The king read and re-read that article, sincerely anxious to discover the meaning and bearing which he wanted to find in it. In such cases one always finds what he is looking for; and the king's remarks, though vague and indirect, left

---

* "The king is supreme head of the State; commands the forces on sea and land; makes treaties of peace, alliance, and commerce; appoints all the functionaries in the public administration, and makes the rules and orders necessary for the execution of the laws and the safety of the State."

no doubt in the ambassador's mind of what his intentions
were.

All the thoughts, efforts, hopes, and fears of the nation were
absorbed by the elections, which proved to all the world that
the constitutionals were right in resolutely opposing the ministry. With very few exceptions, the 221 were re-elected, and
the opposition reckoned a majority of more than a hundred
votes. Nearly everywhere the elections passed without disturbance; the nation being ready to accept unhesitatingly the
supreme test, neither anticipated it nor hurried it by any
violence. On the 10th July, at a meeting of the leading men
of character who were friends of liberty, it was resolved that,
should there be a *coup d'état*, the payment of taxes would be
refused. People still asked if it should take place. The peers
had received their invitations to be present when the king
visited the chamber. The deputies who arrived from all parts
were as a body animated by an ardent and sincere desire to
maintain peace while obtaining justice and preserving their
liberties.

Charles X. showed no hesitation. Before the elections he
had in principle decided what course to follow should the
government receive a check. Henceforward the only question
was with reference to the action to take for vindicating the
rights of the throne. Two fatal mistakes had taken firm hold
of the monarch's mind: he believed that he was much more
endangered by the revolution than he really was; and entirely
disbelieved in the possibility of defending himself, and governing by the legal course of the constitutional *régime*. France
had no wish for a new revolution. The charter, in the hands
of a prudent and patient sovereign, supplied the means of
safely exercising the royal authority and protecting the
crown. But Charles X. had lost confidence in France and the
charter; and when the address of the 221 triumphantly resulted from the elections, he believed he was driven to his last
entrenchments, and compelled to save himself in spite of the
charter, or perish by the revolution.

"There are only Lafayette and I who have not changed
since 1789," said the king one day. True enough he had not
changed: he remained candid and fickle, trusting to himself
and his surroundings, with little observation or reflection,
though active-minded; attached to his ideas and friends of
the old *régime* as much as to his faith and his flag. All
through the profound changes undergone by France during

the uprooting of the ancient bases of society, she had experienced a transformation which influenced the most noble minds, modifying their views as well as the inborn moral sense. "Devotion to one's country, duty towards one's country, are certainly not new sentiments, which our fathers were ignorant of; yet between their ideas and ours, in this respect, there is a profound difference. Fidelity towards persons, towards superiors or equals, was in former French society the ruling principle and sentiment; personal ties were social ties. In the new social system sprung from the revolution, among various classes now brought together and mixed, duty and devotion towards one's country have assumed an empire superior to that of the ancient devotion and duty towards persons. It was owing to social facts of extreme importance that in 1789 the two parties spontaneously and instinctively called themselves the royalist party and patriotic party respectively. In one, duty and devotion to the king, head and representative of the nation; in the other, duty and devotion towards the nation itself directly, formed the principal bond of union, and ruling sentiment." * King Charles X. was so unfortunate as not to understand this change in the national sentiment. He believed himself deserted and betrayed by his servants, and ranged against himself in battle all the patriotic fears as well as hopes. This was soon afterwards proved in a striking manner by the attitude of a large number of devoted and sincere royalists.

The king determined not to unite the chambers, and not to wait till they had acted before acting himself. He also intended to keep in the most absolute secrecy the measures he was preparing. The idea of a *coup d'état* was everywhere denied emphatically; even the precautions necessary in case of armed resistance were sacrificed. On Sunday the 24th July, when the court was held at St. Cloud, as the king was on his way to hear mass, Vitrolles stopped Guernon-Ranville and said, "I don't ask you your secret, but I must inform you that it is the fate of the monarchy that is at stake. You are probably deceived in the difference of the times. A measure which was easy at the beginning of the ministry, even six months ago, is no longer possible in the effervescing state of public opinion to-day. It would inevitably have the most deplorable and unlooked for effects." The listener thought as

---

* Guizot's *Mémoires*, etc.

Vitrolles did, and had said the same thing in council. He passed on, and found the ministers met in the king's room.

After all had spoken, Charles X. took the pen to sign the orders placed before him. He stopped and held his head in his hands. "The more I think of it," he said presently, "the more I am convinced of being in the right, and that it is impossible to do otherwise." He signed; all the ministers signed also, bowing before the king as if by a tacit engagement which linked their fate to his. "For life and for death, gentlemen," said the king; "count upon me, as I count upon you."

So faithfully was the secret kept, that Marshal Marmont, placed on active service as governor of the first military division, was still ignorant of his nomination, the king having undertaken to tell him himself. The orders in council appeared in the *Moniteur* of Monday, 26th July, preceded by a long report drawn up by Chantelauze. On receiving from the keeper of the seals a copy of the official publication, Sauvo, the editor of the *Moniteur*, looked to the minister with an emotion which he could not restrain, and said, "May God protect the king! God protect France!"

All France was thunderstruck on learning that morning the king's fatal resolution. Convinced that a vast conspiracy threatened both the tranquillity of the country and the rights of the crown, Charles X. believed he had a right to attempt a *coup d'état*, and moreover that it was not contrary to the letter of the charter. The four orders in council thus announced suspended indefinitely the liberty of the press, dissolved the Chamber of the Deputies, modified the electoral law, and summoned the electoral colleges to meet from the 6th to the 18th September, the chambers on the 28th. Such was the arbitrary and imprudent act against which burst forth all at once the protestations of an indignant nation.

The first protestation, as it ought to be, was that of the journalists, ably drawn up by Thiers. It was immediately followed by the seizure of the printing-presses of the leading journals. The agitation, however, had yet led to no active results: the disturbance in men's minds was yet undeclared in action. The king went to hunt at Rambouillet, and on his return to St. Cloud he asked Marshal Marmont, who was still ignorant that he had been appointed to the command of Paris, what was the news. "Great alarm, sire; there is great depression, and an extraordinary fall in stocks." "How much?" asked the dauphin. "Four francs, monseigneur." "They will rise again."

Next day the marshal was at last informed. "It seems there is some doubt as to the tranquillity of Paris," said the king to him; "go and take the command there, calling first at M. de Polignac's. If everything is in order by the evening, you may return to St. Cloud." The choice of the Duc de Ragusa was unpopular, as had also been that of Bourmont as war minister, because both were blamed for their "treason" under the empire.

While the marshal was being installed at head-quarters, and crowds were already gathering in the streets, a certain number of deputies met in the house of Casimir Périer, Rue de Luxembourg, and discussed a proposal to protest in the name of the illegally dissolved chamber. That drawn up by Guizot was adopted next day, but in the meantime the troops had several times charged the crowd, several shots had been fired, and some barricades raised. The night passed quietly; but in the morning every eye was struck by the formidable aspect of a rising of the people. The soldiers had resumed their positions; against them a certain number of the national guards had just joined the crowds. The Polytechnic school broke open the gates, and the tricolor flag floated on the towers of Notre Dame. The columns on march were shot at from some of the houses. In the morning Marshal Marmont had written to the king: "Sire, I had the honor of reporting to your Majesty the dispersal of the crowds which disturbed the tranquillity of Paris. This morning they are again collecting, more numerous and more threatening. It is no longer a riot, but a revolution. There is urgent need for your Majesty to take means of pacification. The honor of the crown may yet be saved. To-morrow probably it would be too late." Paris was placed in a state of siege, the order having been signed on the previous evening. The Duc de Ragusa agreed to command the arrest of several deputies. Amongst those indicated by Polignac, General Gérard and Lafitte were members of the deputation who went to the Tuileries, the ministers having installed themselves there under the protection of the governor of Paris. The deputies brought to the Duc de Ragusa a general protest, and were authorized to ask him to cease firing, and to interpose between Paris and St. Cloud.

"The undersigned," said the protest, "chosen regularly as a deputation, consider themselves to be absolutely compelled in duty and honor to protest against the measures which the advisers of the crown have recently put in force for the overthrow of the legal system of elections and the ruin of the libery of the press.

"The said measures, contained in the orders of the 25th, are, in the eyes of the undersigned, directly contrary to the constitutional rights of the Chamber of Peers, the common rights of Frenchmen, the privileges and decisions of the tribunals; and are calculated to throw the state into a confusion compromising both the present peace and our future security.

"The undersigned, therefore, being inviolably faithful to their oath, protest with one accord, not only against the said measures, but against every act which may result from them.

"And, considering that, on the one hand, the Chamber of Deputies not having been constituted could not be legally dissolved; on the other hand, the attempt to form another Chamber of Deputies, in a new and arbitrary manner, is in formal opposition to the constitutional charter, and the acquired rights of the electors, the undersigned declare that they still consider themselves as being legitimately elected to represent the arrondissement or department whose suffrages they obtained; and that they can only be replaced by means of elections made in accordance with the principles and forms appointed by law. And if the undersigned do not effectively exercise the rights or fulfil all the duties which they hold through their legal election, it is because they are prevented by physical force." Sixty-three signatures were affixed to this vindication of the legal rights of the nation.

While the deputies, who were numerous in the morning, and easily counted towards the evening, were thus discussing in Audry's house, the place was surrounded by workmen, boys and young men, combatants of every sort, who filled the court, and besieged the doors, speaking to the deputies at the drawing-room windows—ready to defend them if, as was rumored, they were presently to be arrested by the police or military, but demanding at the same time their immediate assistance in preparing a revolution. Among the deputies various opinions and expectations were manifested, in some minds still vague, in others steadfast and decided. "Several wished to carry resistance to the last limits of legal order, but not further. Others were resolved upon a change of dynasty, wishing for no further revolution, but considering that necessary, and that the circumstances seemed favorable for it, and flattering themselves that they might stop there or thereabouts. Others again, more revolutionary without being aware of it, were

sanguine as to all sorts of undefined reforms in the institutions
and laws, commanded as they imagined by the interest and
wish of the people. Others again, had a decided aspiration for
a republic, and considered as abortive or deceptive any other
result of the struggle maintained by the people in the name of
liberty. Those who declared they would not become revolutionary while making a revolution, already found themselves
overwhelmed and urged forward—by the enemies of established
order, the regular conspirators, the secret societies, and the anarchical dreamers who had thrown themselves into the movement, and were every hour becoming more powerful and more
exacting. The tide still rose, reaching the elevated regions,
and spreading noisily amid the lower regions of society." *

Polignac, however, refused to understand the position of
affairs in Paris. On being informed that at certain places the
soldiers apparently shared the sentiments of the populace, he
replied, "Very well! if the troops fraternize with the people,
let the troops be fired upon." The Duc de Ragusa made a report to the king of his interview with the deputies, and the
ultimatum which they brought in the name of their colleagues
—withdrawal of the orders, and a change of ministry. "In
my opinion there is urgent need that your Majesty should
without delay take advantage of the overtures made." "Let
your Majesty not be deceived," added the colonel appointed to
carry the marshal's letter; "it is not the populace, but the entire population who are rising." Charles X. confined himself
to replying to the Duc de Ragusa. "My dear marshal, I have
great pleasure in hearing of the good and honorable conduct of
the troops under your orders. Convey to them my thanks,
and grant them a month and a half's pay. Bring your troops
together and hold your ground; wait for my orders to-morrow."
"We must treat only with large bodies," was his message on
another occasion.

The army had in fact begun to fall back; for the insurrection
had gained too much ground to leave Marmount the hope of
again occupying Paris. The Hôtel de Ville was in the hands
of the rioters; 600 barricades intersected the streets everywhere; the troops surrounding the Tuileries and Louvre were
everywhere attacked during their march; provisions began to
fail them; and many soldiers wavered on account of the repeated appeals made to them by the people. "But where do

* Guizot's *Mémoires*, etc.

the insurgents get their powder?" asked the ministers in astonishment. "They get that of the soldiers," replied Bayeux, then acting as procureur-general; "and often the soldiers themselves give them cartridges."

The government of Charles X. no longer existed in Paris. The ministers had resigned the power into the hands of the Duc de Ragusa, and now contemplated, like sad and persistent spectators, the ruins they themselves had made. "What a misfortune to have my sword broken in my hands!" said Polignac; "a little more patience and determination, and I was about to establish the government and charter upon immovable bases."

The same illusions reigned at St. Cloud, strengthened by the respect and alarm of the courtiers. On the 28th, Vitrolles tried to enlighten the king, but he was still confident of victory. "Let the insurgents lay down their arms," said he; "they know my kindness sufficiently to be certain of the most generous pardon." The evening passed in the usual courtly ceremonies. "Not a guard more, not a guard less," we are told by an eye-witness. "The windows of the drawing-rooms being open, several persons went on the balcony, listening to the firing and the tocsin, and then retiring without remark, as if they had merely been to breathe the fresh air after a day of burning heat. In the royal drawing-room the king played whist and the dauphin chess, without speaking of anything else. During the game, which thus seemed to engross their whole attention, several discharges of artillery shook the windows. The most frightful news kept constantly arriving, but without crossing the threshold of the royal drawing-room. The Duc de Duras left the room, and returned full of excitement; but as he approached the whist-table the courtier resumed his attitude and silence."

The Duc de Mortemart, who had come from Paris, could not receive an audience of the king till next day. He declared that the orders must be withdrawn. "They exaggerate the danger," said Charles X.; "I know the truth," and on the duke appearing to doubt it, the king said eagerly, "You were born in the midst of revolution, and, without knowing it, have acquired its prejudices and false ideas. My old experience is above such illusions. I know what the concessions asked of me would lead to; and I have no wish to ride like my brother on a cart." James II. had spoken thus in 1688.

Meanwhile the ministers arrived at St. Cloud, preceded by

Sémonville and Argout, who had been sent by the few peers then present in Paris. The dauphin was appointed commander-in-chief of the army; and Marshal Marmont's political opinions appearing as doubtful as his military movements, an order was sent him to retire immediately upon St. Cloud with his troops. When the royal messenger reached the Duc de Ragusa he had been obliged to abandon his positions and fall back as far as the Arc de Triomphe. Two line regiments had joined the revolution; the Louvre, the Tuileries, and all the quarters of Paris, were in the hands of the insurgents. Joubert, who was the first to enter the Tuileries, ordered the tricolor flag to be planted on the clock-tower.

The principal point now was to secure order in Paris. Lafayette was naturally appointed to the command of the national guard. "The security of Paris depends on the general's determination," said Guizot in a meeting of deputies; "but we have also our duties. It is absolutely necessary that we establish, not a provisional government, but a public authority that, under a municipal form, will undertake to restore and maintain order." A municipal commission was at once formed, composed of Lafayette, Casimir Périer, General Lobau, Schonen, and Audry de Puyraveau. It installed itself at the Hôtel de Ville. General Gérard was appointed to command the active troops.

While the revolution was being organized, the despairing servants of the tottering throne vainly strove to save it. After Mortemart had been rejected, Vitrolles and Sussy, assisted by Sémonville and Argout, attempted to obtain for the country legal satisfaction, and bring about some arrangement between the effete monarchy at St. Cloud and the revolution boiling in Paris. But on asking to see the king they were refused on account of the hour, the etiquette, military orders, sleep; and when at last admitted, found the king calm and yet angry, obstinate yet hesitating. With great difficulty they succeeded in forcing from him the dismissal of the Polignac cabinet, repeal of the orders, and the appointment of Mortemart as first minister. But, that being agreed upon, the king still hesitated, and kept Mortemart waiting for the necessary signatures. He at last gave them to his new minister, thus impelled by his patriotism to accept a task which he hated. Mortemart, ill of a consuming fever, started for Paris without having obtained the necessary passports from the displeased dauphin; and being delayed at every step on his journey, by the royal

troops or the volunteers guarding the barricades, he did not
reach the meeting of the deputies, who had been informed by
Argout that he did not bring the necessary powers. It was
with great difficulty that Mortemart succeeded in transmit-
ting to the parliamentary meeting and the municipal commission the orders of which he was the bearer. It was too late.
Nowhere were the concessions accepted; and at the Palais-
Bourbon and Hôtel de Ville it was with difficulty that any
notice was agreed to be taken of them. Lafayette had the
courage to write to Mortemart to acknowledge the receipt;
and two men on horseback having shouted on the Boulevard,
"All is finished; a peace is concluded with the king; Casimir
Périer has arranged everything!" it was with great difficulty
that General Gérard and Bérard, who were on the spot, rescued
them from being massacred by the angry crowd. There was
no longer at St. Cloud any power, not only to act, but even to
speak to the country.

Lafayette had just issued a proclamation to the national
guard, and the municipal commission addressed the French
army. On the 30th July the deputies left off the vague and
purposeless meetings they had held, and assembled at the
Palais-Bourbon, in the hall of their sittings, and invited their
absent colleagues to join them, and raise again the great public power of which they were the scattered members. The
peers then present in Paris also assembled in the Luxembourg.
The deputies entered into communication with them, and the
same day, at the close of the morning sitting, on hearing that
the Duc d'Orleans—who had hitherto kept himself aloof, inac-
tive and invisible—was disposed to come to Paris, the assembly
in the Palais-Bourbon adopted the following resolution:—

"The deputies now met in Paris feel the urgency of requesting H.R.H. Monseigneur le Duc d'Orleans to come to the capital, to exercise the functions of lieutenant-general of the kingdom, and to give expression to the desire of preserving the
national colors. They have also felt the necessity of striving
without intermission to secure for France, in the ensuing session of the chambers, all the guarantees indispensable for the
full and entire execution of the charter."

It was M. Thiers who brought from Neuilly Madame Adelaide's promise, given in the name of her absent brother, that
he should agree to receive the delegates from the chamber.
The Duchess of Orleans, affectionately anxious, though so
high-minded a royalist both in principles and habits, had per-

suaded her husband to go to Raincy to avoid the arrest which
some said was impending. As soon as Thiers introduced the
subjects he exclaimed, "All my happiness is ended!" Lafayette feared lest the deputies were too hasty in concluding an
alliance with the Duc d'Orleans and bringing the revolution to
a close. He instructed Odilon Barrot to insist beforehand on
guarantees of liberty and the revision of the charter. His
grandson, Rémusat, on going to see him at the Hôtel de Ville,
said to him: "General, if they make a monarchy, the Duc
d'Orleans will be king; if they make a republic, you will
be president. Do you take the responsibility of the republic?"

"Lafayette seemed to hesitate, though he really did not.
Generously disinterested, although fully conscious of his importance, and with almost as much anxiety for the responsibility
as desire for popularity, he was much more disposed to treat
for the people and in name of the people than ambitious of
ruling. That a republic, and a republic under his presidency,
should be thought of as a possible chance, was sufficient for
his satisfaction, I will not say his ambition. Lafayette had no
ambition: he wished to be the popular patron of the Duc
d'Orleans, not his rival.

"The Duc d'Orleans was equally unambitious. Self-re-
strained and prudent, in spite of his mental activity and the
mobile vivacity of his impressions, he had long foreseen the
chance which might carry him to the throne, but without trying to find it, and rather disposed to be afraid of it than to
long for it. After the protracted sorrows of exile and the
recent experience of the hundred days, one thought especially
occupied his attention—the wish being again necessarily entangled in the faults which the elder branch was liable to
commit, and in the consequences which might result from
these faults. On the 31st March, 1830, a few days after the
arrival of his brother-in-law, the King of Naples, at Paris, he
gave him a banquet in the Palais-Royal, at which Charles X.
and all the royal family were present. 'Monseigneur,' said
Salvandy to the Duc d'Orleans, as he passed near him,
'this banquet is quite Neapolitan; we are dancing over a
volcano.' 'That the volcano is there,' answered the duke, 'I
believe as well as you. At least the fault is not mine. I cannot reproach myself with not having tried to open the king's
eyes. But what is the use? He listened to nothing. Heaven
only knows where they will be in six months! But I know

where I shall be. Whatever happens, my family and myself
will remain in this palace; whatever danger there may be, I
shall not move a step from here. I shall not separate my lot
and that of my children from the lot of my country: that is
my fixed resolution.'

"That resolution held more place than any other intention
in the Duc d'Orleans' conduct during the whole course of the
restoration. He had also resolved to be neither conspirator
nor victim. He was devoted to the country which he had
served since his infancy. If the definitive consolidation of
the restoration had depended upon him he would, without
hesitation on his own and his family's account, as well as that
of France, have preferred the certainty of that future to the
prospects which a new revolution might afford him. In the
bottom of his heart, and without perhaps fully weighing the
fact, he felt from that time that, for the present, and in a
future which he could not fathom, he remained the actual and
all important 'reserve' of France.

"Chateaubriand, after arriving in Paris, and being carried
in triumph to the Luxembourg, said 'As lieutenant-general,
yes; but for king, Henry V.' The words of deputies and
peers did not yet go beyond that, however free their thoughts
might be. The municipal commission having declared that
the government of Charles X. was deposed, Casimir Périer
refused to sign the proclamation, on the ground that it exceeded their powers. Twelve members of the Chamber of
Deputies were chosen as delegates to go and offer the Duc
d'Orleans the appointment of lieutenant-general of the kingdom. He had just arrived in Paris from Neuilly on foot, and
not without difficulty, and when the deputation presented
itself at the Palais-Royal the prince asked for several hours
to consider. Time was pressing; he accepted, and the following proclamation was at once issued:—

"'Inhabitants of Paris! the Deputies of France now assembled in Paris have expressed the desire that I should come into
this capital to exercise the functions of lieutenant-general of
the kingdom. I have not hesitated to come to share your
dangers, to place myself in the midst of your heroic population, and use every effort to preserve you from civil war and
anarchy. On my return to the city of Paris I bore with pride
those glorious colors which you have resumed, and which I
myself have long borne. The chambers are about to assemble;
they will consider the best means of securing the reign of the

laws, and the maintenance of the rights of the nation. The charter will henceforth be a reality.'"*

The proclamation did not satisfy all the violently excited passions and hopes of the people, but it corresponded to the earnest desires and deeply felt wants of all enlightened men who were anxious to bring disorder to a close. After the delegates made their report, the Chamber of Deputies adopted the following declaration, addressed to France, which was drawn up, and read from the tribune, by Guizot:—

"Frenchmen!

"France is free. Absolutism raised its flag, and the heroic population of Paris put it down. Paris, when attacked, has by arms caused the triumph of the sacred cause which had just triumphed to no purpose in the elections. A power which had usurped our rights and disturbed our repose, was threatening both liberty and order: we resume possession of order and liberty. No more fears for acquired rights; no more barriers between us and the rights which we still want.

"A government which will at once ensure for us those advantages is what the country to-day demands above everything. Frenchmen! those of your deputies already in Paris have met together, and, until the chambers shall formally interpose, have invited a Frenchman, who has never fought except for France, the Duc d'Orleans, to exercise the functions of lieutenant-general of the kingdom. That, in their eyes, is the mode of promptly securing without war the success of the most legitimate defence.

"The Duc d'Orleans is devoted to the national and constitutional cause, and has always defended its interests, and professed its principles. He will respect our rights, for his own he will hold from us; we shall secure by law all the guarantees necessary to render liberty sure and lasting."

When this proclamation, which concluded by enumerating the guarantees necessary for liberty, was read, the chamber replied by acclamations, and at once went to the Palais-Royal. The lieutenant-general made ready to go to the Hôtel de Ville, whither he was accompanied by the deputies. Several hostile shouts were heard in the streets, some repeating, "No more Bourbons!" The general crowd, however, cried, "Long live

---

* Guizot's *Mémoires*, etc.

the charter!" "Gentlemen," said the Duc d'Orleans as he mounted the staircase, "it is an old national guard paying a visit to his former general." Viennet read the proclamation of the chamber, which was rather coldly received by the populace. General Lafayette soon came to pay his respects to the prince. "You know," said he, "that I am a republican, and consider the constitution of the United States as the most perfect that has ever existed." "So do I," replied the duke; "but do you think that in the present condition of France, and according to general opinion, it would be advisable for us to adopt it?" "No," answered Lafayette; "what the French people must now have is a popular throne, surrounded by republican institutions—entirely republican." "That is just my opinion," said the duke.

The republicans did not reckon upon such princely declarations, though they also had resolved to interview the lieutenant-general. "To-morrow you will be king, monseigneur," said Boinvilliers; "perhaps it is the last time you will hear the truth: allow me to tell it you." On the prince referring in severe terms to the convention, Godefroy Cavaignac quickly exclaimed, "Monseigneur forgets that my father was a member of the Convention!" "And mine also, sir," returned the Duc d'Orleans in a sorrowful tone; "and while cherishing his memory, I may be allowed the desire to save my country from the procedure to which he was a victim." Lafayette's conversation with the prince led to the engagement which was called the programme of the Hôtel de Ville. It promised a revision of the charter. "I am condemned to propose nothing," said the duke. "I shall not take the crown; I shall receive it from the Chamber of Deputies on the conditions it may suit them to impose. The modifications of the charter, whatever they may be, must therefore be made by that chamber alone." The popular feeling had already strongly protested against the phrase, "*The* Charter will henceforward be a reality," which was contained both in the declaration of the Duc d'Orleans and the proclamation of the chamber. The *Moniteur* of the 31st July contained this absurd correction, "*A* charter will henceforward be a reality."

While the Duc d'Orleans was being appointed lieutenant-general by the deputies, a preparatory step as it proved to his becoming king, Charles X., still at St. Cloud, saw Marshal Marmont arrive with his troops, discontented, ill-fed, and much reduced by desertion. The marshal advised the king to retire upon the Loire, to Blois or Tours, and summon there the great functionaries and the diplomatic body. The dauphin flew into a passion, having been opposed to the withdrawal of the orders and discharge of the ministers. "My father is the master," said he, "but I am far from approving of all that he has done." The quarrel with the Duke of Ragusa was so violent, that the marshal was conducted to his apartment as a prisoner, and the old king had great difficulty in restoring an appearance of friendliness. During the night, yielding to the alarms of the Duchess of Berry, who believed the safety of the palace was threatened, the king set out for Versailles, and thence went to Rambouillet—the first sad stage of a new journey into exile. The dauphin attempted to take Sèvres, but some of the corps refused to fire, and others laid down their arms.

The royal princess just then returned from Vichy. She had constantly opposed the idea of a *coup d'état*, from a conscientious regard to a sworn promise. The king threw himself into her arms, exclaiming, "How will you be able to pardon me?" Always heroic in misfortune, the daughter of Marie Antoinette had been persecuted by the mob all the way from Dijon. "I shall never again leave you," was her reply. The king had just sent the Duc d'Orleans his powers as lieutenant-general of the kingdom. The latter respectfully refused them. "You cannot receive them from everybody," said Dupin.

A new idea was now being originated among those about the king, who consulted Marmont. "What is your opinion of an abdication?" he asked. It was the only means of safety still left for the tottering throne. "Let your Majesty not allow yourself to be deprived of the crown," said the Duke of Ragusa; "but take it off your head yourself, to place it on the head of your grandson." No objection being now made to this proposal by the dauphin, who was sad and disheartened, the act of abdication was at once drawn up, and addressed to the Duc d'Orleans as lieutenant-general:—

"Rambouillet, 2nd August.

"My cousin, I am too deeply pained by the evils now afflicting and threatening my peoples, not to have sought for some means of preventing them. I have, therefore, taken the resolution to abdicate the throne, in favor of my grandson the Duc de Bordeaux.

"The dauphin, who shares my sentiments, also renounces his rights in favor of his nephew."

"As lieutenant-general of the kingdom you will therefore have to proclaim the accession of Henry V. to the throne. You will, moreover, take every measure in your power to conduct the forms of government during the minority of the new king. At present I confine myself to the announcement of my dispositions, as a means of still avoiding many evils." The small fugitive court at Rambouillet already began to address the little duke as "sire."

The abdication of the king and dauphin came too late, as the recall of the orders and change of ministers had done. A monarchy under the Duc de Bordeaux, with Orleans as regent, would have been not only the legal solution, but the more politic one. On the 2nd August, 1830, it seemed to the most moderate statesman more impracticable even than reconciliation with the king himself. At that time neither the liberal party nor the royalists would have had sufficient discretion, nor the regent sufficient power, to conduct and maintain a government so complicated, divided and agitated. The masses were giving way to revolutionary passion, and the leaders were yielding to the pressure of the masses. The state of men's minds, and the circumstances, allowed no choice but a new monarchy or a republic. Amongst the lower orders and most young men the latter was every moment becoming more popular and threatening. Of their own accord, or under orders, some in confused bands, others commanded by the chiefs of the national guard, 50,000 or 60,000 men were marching to Rambouillet. The old king was soon to understand the startling message conveyed by this demonstration. At the same time, three commissioners —Marshal Maison, Barrot, and Schonen—were appointed to protect the safety of the royal family, and impress upon them the necessity for departure. "I have abdicated," said Charles X., "but it is in favor of my grandson; and we have resolved to defend his rights to the last drop of our blood." The Parisian columns were already surrounding the château. "Sire," said Barrot, with emotion, "I have no right to express an opinion upon the rights spoken of by your Majesty, or the hopes depending on them. But whatever may be the future reserved by God for your grandson, prevent his name from being the signal for the catastrophe now at hand; let him not be stained by the blood now about to be shed." Charles X. paused, full of thought and emotion. He consulted Marshal Marmont. "They have there 60,000 or 80,000," said the Duke of Ragusa;

" with those who are gone, and those who refuse to march, we do not muster 1300 men." "That is sufficient," said the king, and he agreed to set out. At four o'clock in the morning, the royal fugitives reached Maintenon, constantly informed of new desertions. The king declared to Marmont, who had accompanied him, that he renounced all idea of maintaining a useless struggle, and that he would make for Cherbourg by the way of Dreux.

Those troops who had remained faithful withdrew. A small body of the guards and picked gendarmes followed the royal carriages through towns with the tricolor flags hoisted everywhere by the contagion of the Parisian revolution. The commissioners did not display their cockade before the fallen monarch. "We are not jailers," said Odilon Barrot; "our mission is one of humanity and respect." The wretched journey was much prolonged, rendering the revolutionist leaders in Paris uneasy and impatient. "What answer can be given to an old man who tells you that he is tired?" wrote the commissioners to those who urged them. It was not till the 16th August that the royal family embarked at Cherbourg, on the American vessels the *Great Britain* and *Charles Carrol*, which had been hired for them by Captain Dumont d'Urville. The king had announced his intention of going to England, and the English government consented. At one time the diplomatic body expressed a design of joining the king at Rambouillet, but Pozzo di Borgo and Lord Charles Stuart entered a formal protest. The Russian ambassador soon after warmly espoused the cause of the new dynasty. "The Orleans family wish to reign," said he; "they are right, they must reign! I am with them, to life or death!" King Charles X. was abandoned by Europe as well as by France, when he went on board at Cherbourg to seek refuge in that England which had so long sheltered his family, and which was one day to shelter in their turn those who were now replacing him on the throne. As he passed through the country the populace had received him without any welcome; at the moment of embarking, there were tears in every eye. The princess royal, dressed in mourning, and holding her children by the hand, cast a last look upon that country which was for a second time sending her to exile.

Meanwhile a new government was constituted at Paris, and the whole of France was, without resistance, passing under new laws. In every ear seemed to resound the grand saying of the psalmist, formerly repeated by Bossuet before Louis

XIV. : *Et nunc, reges, intelligite; erudimini, qui judicatis terram.*

The new-born power in Paris felt much joy and real relief when they at last learnt, on the 17th August, that the royal family had left France without danger and insult. The mass of the population were fully engrossed with other interests. On the 1st August the municipal commission had transferred their powers to the lieutenant-general. Provisional commissioners were appointed to manage the public departments; Dupont to the ministry of justice; General Gérard, of war; Guizot, of the interior; Baron Louis, of finance; Girod, of the police. A privy council, including Broglie, Laffitte, Casimir Périer, Dupin, and Sebastiani, assisted the Duc d'Orleans in his first attempts of government. On the 3rd August the chambers assembled to discuss the revision of the charter, noisily demanded by some enthusiasts, both republican and monarchical. The inheritance of titles of nobility was the object of the most violent attacks. The still excited populace seemed on the point of again imposing their wishes by force. The duke was disposed to let them have their way, but through the persistent efforts of some of his principal friends the question was deferred till next session.

The prince opened the session with much of the usual ceremonial. "Attached both by feeling and conviction to the principles of a free government," said he, "I accept all its consequences. The past is for me a source of pain, I deplore misfortunes which I should have wished to prevent; but in the midst of that magnanimous impulse of the capital, and all the French towns, a well grounded pride fills my heart with emotion, and I look forward with confidence to the future of our country. Yes, gentlemen, she will be happy and free, this France so dear to me; she will show to Europe that, being solely occupied with her home prosperity, she cherishes peace as well as liberty, and wishes only for the happiness and tranquillity of her neighbors."

Three days later (7th August), on the formal request of the two chambers, who had declared the throne vacant, the Duc d'Orleans solemnly accepted the crown; and on the 9th August, at a "royal sitting," he took, in presence of the whole country, the oaths which he was so long and faithfully to keep.

CHAPTER XX.

PARLIAMENTARY GOVERNMENT. KING LOUIS PHILIPPE.
(1830—1840.)

" IT is neither wise nor honorable to overlook, when the ex. citing stimulus is no longer felt, the true causes of events," says Guizot in his *Mémoires.* "The necessity, a necessity which weighed equally on all, royalists as well as liberals, the Duc d'Orleans as well as France, the necessity of choosing between the new monarchy and anarchy, such was in 1830, for men of honor, and independently of the part played by revolutionary passions, the cause which determined the change of dynasty. At the critical moment, this necessity was felt by every man, by the most intimate friends of King Charles X. as well as by the most ardent members of the opposition. Several of the royalists retired from public life. Others, and of the highest character, swore fealty to the new *régime.* One single conviction ruled all earnest men: by monarchy alone could France escape the opening abyss, and only one monarchy was possible." The establishment of the new reign was a deliverance for all. "I, too, am amongst the victorious," said Royer-Collard, sad in the general rejoicing.

France had hastened to throw off a yoke which had neither long nor heavily weighed upon her shoulders. Jealous of the liberties she had gained through so many shocks and crimes, she revolted as soon as she saw them endangered, without employing that steadfast patience which experience has taught nations exercised in self-government. She did not yet feel the difficulties of the enterprise she was attempting by founding a new dynasty in the face of numerous and keenly hostile parties. She seemed to take pleasure in aggravating those difficulties, by changing the charter as well as the dynasty. For that there was certainly no necessity. The charter had just undergone the most severe tests successfully and honorably. King Charles X., to escape from its rule, had been compelled to violate it, yet it survived that violence. Both in the streets and the chambers it was the flag of resistance and vic-

tory. It came into their imagination to pull down and tear
that flag.

Resolute hands, however, were not wanting in its defence.
As soon as a decidedly revolutionary tendency was manifest,
the men who were engaged in the great event then being accomplished acknowledged how much they differed from each
other, and separated. It was from the revision of the charter
that the policy of resistance takes its date. The party of the
government began to be formed, still without unity, inexperienced, and feeling its way, but determined to make an earnest
experiment of a constitutional monarchy, and defend it boldly
against the revolutionary spirit.

Representatives of the two opposing tendencies were brought
together in the new cabinet formed by King Louis Philippe on
his accession. Dupont, the deputy for Eure, and Laffitte, led
the progressionists, assisted by General Gérard and Bignon;
Casimir Périer, General Sebastiani, Baron Louis, Molé, and
Dupin were all more or less obstructionists. Broglie and
Guizot pursued their path in constant harmony, which continued, with a shade of disagreement, through their long
career. "Though different in origin, position, and character,
we were united not only by a friendship already of long standing," says Guizot in his *Mémoires*, but by sharing ultimately in
the same principles and generous "sentiments, the most
powerful of ties, when (as rarely happens) it really exists."
Broglie, in his will, gave such witness of this close union as
afterwards touched the friend destined to survive him, to the
bottom of his heart. "Our long friendship," he wrote, "I consider one of the most precious blessings that God has granted
me."

Louis Philippe's personal liking, if not his intimate confidence, was reserved for those of his ministers who inclined to
the left. That side above all was then to him a source of danger and difficulty. The work of administrative reorganization
absorbed the strength of those appointed to carry it out, who
had at the same time to struggle against revolutionary attempts everywhere secretly in action. Lafayette's appointment
to command the national guard was confirmed. The radical
passion for effacing the past was manifested, both in qualify-
ing the charter as that of 1830, and in changing the seal of
state, which was now decorated with tricolor flags, behind
the arms of the house of Orleans. In their turn the lilies were
soon to disappear from the emblems of France.

The elections for the purpose of replacing the deputies who had resigned, or confirming the titles of those called to public functions, gave striking evidence that the people were in favor of the new royal establishment. The Chamber of Peers, seriously reduced in numbers by a good many resignations, as well as by the unreasonable expulsion of those peers who had been appointed under the reign of Charles X., was moreover threatened in its fundamental principle of hereditary descent. Having obtained the right to choose its own president, Pasquier was appointed to that important post, which had already been entrusted to him by the Duc d'Orleans in his quality of lieutenant-general of the kingdom. Many important bills were at once brought befor the chambers. On the 29th August the king held his first grand review of the national guards of Paris and the suburbs, and was received with enthusiastic shouting. The repression of rioting, caused by the unsettled state of the popular mind, and the closing of the political "clubs," reassured all lovers of order, and restored hopes that trade and industry would speedily revive. "France has made a revolution," said Guizot to the chamber, "but she had no intention of placing herself in a permanently revolutionary state. The prominent features of a revolutionary state are, that all things are being incessantly put in question, that the claims are indefinite, that constant appeals are made to force and violence. Those features exist in all the present popular societies, in their action and tendency, and in the impulse they are striving to impress upon France. That is not progress, but disorder: it is aimless excitement, not advancement. Since the government is armed with legal power against the dangers of popular societies, it not only must not abandon it, but it must make use of it. It has already done so, and is resolved to do so as often as is demanded by good order in the country and the steady development of its liberties."

It was against King Charles's ministers that the popular rage and rancor stirred up the most violent and almost uncontrollable hatred. "What would you have done to M. de Polignac if you had caught him?" said Odilon Barrot to an old woman, who persisted in searching the carriage of the commissioners on their return from accompanying the old king to Cherbourg. "Ah! sir," cried she, "I should have strangled him with my own hands!" Those ministers who had been arrested could scarcely understand the reason of their imprisonment or the fury of the populace. It had to be explained to them that their captivity alone protected them from the mob, who were perpetually threatening them. They were charged on the 27th September, on the motion of Salverte, and on the 17th October they found that they were threatened even in the Château of Vincennes by a mob that had already proceeded to frightful excesses. The crowd blocked the streets of Paris, shouting loudly for the heads of the ministers, and after being driven back from the garden of the Palais-Royal, rushed eagerly along the roads leading to the fortress. General Fabvier, who had the military command of Paris, having felt anxious about the prisoners' safety ordered General Pajol to make the necessary arrangements. The mob had already arrived before Vincennes. Awoke by their cries about eleven o'clock at night, the imprisoned ministers saw them through their narrow windows, crowding by torchlight in front of the fortress, and demanding entrance. General Daumesnil, who commanded the guard of the prison, ordered the gate to be opened, and presented himself alone to the crowd. "What do you want?" "We want the ministers." "You won't get them; they belong only to the law. I shall blow up the powder-magazine rather than give them up to you." His looks were as full of energy as his words; and the crowd, surprised and cowed, after pausing for a moment began to return to Paris, shouting "Long life to the Wooden Leg!" During the night the rioters forced their way into the Palais-Royal, which was still badly guarded, declaring that they wished to see the king; and some were actually going up the staircase, when some of the national guards arrived and arrested the ringleaders.

The king and his ministers acted together in repressing the violence of the populace, and opposing the hateful excesses of a vengeance which was as useless as it was cruel. To lay down the principle of the application of the penal laws, Tracy had already proposed the abolition of capital punishment. In 1822, in the midst of the plots and political trials which were then causing much agitation, Guizot published a pamphlet *On Capital Punishment for Political Offences,* to show clearly that it was inexpedient and immoral. An address of the Chamber of Deputies supported an amendment to the same effect in place of Tracy's proposal. The king's reply gave grounds to hope that the question would soon be decided; but from the report of riots the discussion was considered dangerous, and therefore adjourned, and the revolutionists grew bolder. The latent discord in the cabinet broke forth on the occasion of a proclamation issued by Odilon Barrot, prefect of the Seine; and the conservative ministers, Périer, Molé, Louis, and Dupin resigned, as well as Guizot and Broglie. Laffitte and Dupont were, like their former colleagues, resolved to use their power equitably and gently in the great question of the trial of the ministers; and their connection which the party of progress rendered this more easy of accomplishment. Montalivet, still quite young, when summoned by the king to become minister of the interior, shrunk from accepting the heavy burden. "Then you will not assist me in saving the ministers?" asked the king. It was to the honor of the young minister that he successfully and courageously responded on this occasion to the confidence of which he was the object.

The trial of the ministers began on the 15th December, 1830. They had been brought with a good escort to the Little Luxembourg. More than a month previously, just after quitting the cabinet, Guizot had openly declared his opinion, and that of his friends among the deputies. "When going to the tribune," says he in his *Mémoires*, "as I passed in front of Casimir Périer, he said in a low voice, 'All you can do is in vain; you will not save Polignac's head!' I had better hopes of the public feeling, and I expressed my own in a few words: 'I have no interest in the fallen ministers, nor has any communication passed between them and me; but I have the profound conviction that the honor of the nation, the honor of her history, forbids that their blood be shed. After changing the government and renewing the face of the country, it is a wretched thing to proceed with a mean judicial act, side by side with that vast judicial act which had struck, not four men, but a whole government, a whole dynasty. As to blood, France desires nothing unnecessary. All the revolutions shed blood from anger, not from necessity; three months, six months after, the blood so shed turned against them. Let us not to-day enter upon a path in which we did not march even during the struggle."

Martignac made it a point of honor to defend Polignac, who had formerly overthrown him. Chantelauze's counsel was Sauzet, still young and little known, but most successful. There was still immense danger and difficulty. For eight days the cabinet with all its power, Lafayette with all his popularity, and King Louis Philippe with his experienced and wise tact, and the Peers' Court with a bold discretion, consumed themselves in efforts, ever nearly failing, to restrain the revolutionary intrigues and that imprudent rage which sought, in the death of the prisoners, to find satisfaction and success respectively.

On the last day of the trial, a carriage was in attendance in a side door of the Little Luxembourg, into which the four prisoners stepped as soon as the court was dismissed. Montalivet, minister of the interior, and Lieutenant-Colonel Lavocat, rode on horseback, one on each side, General Fabvier, having wished to take charge himself of the escort posted in the Rue de Madame. The horses galloped off, and soon the procession reached the outer boulevards. As it entered into the court of the fortress of Vincennes, a cannon-shot fired from the donjon, reassured many anxious minds in Paris. The prisoners were now safe from the fury of the populace. The baulked hopes of the mob sought vengeance in the streets of Paris. At one time the Louvre was threatened. The national guard grudgingly restrained an indignation which many of them shared. Polignac, Peyronnet, Chantelauze, and Guernon-Ranville, were condemned to imprisonment for life, a sentence of "civil death" being added in the case of the president of the council; and almost before the verdict was pronounced, the ministers were secretly, though not without difficulty, conveyed to the state prison of Ham by the courage and foresight of those to whom they were entrusted, and thus freed from the dangers with which their lives had been so long threatened. The fury of the populace cooled down, and the satisfaction soon become general. The danger was now past, and their self-love satisfied. Lafayette and his friends alone remained dissatisfied and dejected: they had boldly and honorably compromised themselves. The office of commandant-general being suppressed by the new law as to the organization of the national guard, the king had an offer made to Lafayette to retain the honorary title, with the effective command, of the national guard of Paris. Lafayette, laying down political conditions to his acceptance—namely, a chamber of peers chosen from candidates elected by the people, a chamber of deputies elected in accordance with a new electoral law, and a large extension of the right of suffrage—with an expression of regret the king accepted the general's resignation; and Count Lobau replaced him as commandant-general, without any public manifestation of great excitement. "Don't trouble me," said the old soldier to Montalivet. "I know nothing about the national guard." "What! you know nothing about it, when the question, this very day, perhaps, is one of battle and danger?" "Ah! if that is what is the matter, all right! Come what may, I accept."

The street-fightings were not finished in the streets of Paris, and the most deplorable excesses soon occasioned some rigorous repression. Abroad, owing to the universally agitated state of Europe, the nation generally wished earnestly for peace. The world was tired of the troubles and suffering caused by war: the passionate longing for peace had taken possession of the nation. The revolutionist partisans and dreamers still sometimes stirred up the popular emotion. The explosion which had turned France upside down resounded all around: in Belgium, Switzerland, and Spain, revolutionary disturbances shook Europe from its centre to its extremities. In Germany, Poland, Italy, all the questions and international complications which are stirred up by revolution were raised, as well as other questions, not revolutionary but politically important and difficult. The Ottoman Empire, more and more tottering; Asia, more and more divided up and disputed over between England and Russia; France conquering in Africa; then in the New World, France and England, England and the United States, the United States and France, engaging in keen contests about territory, money, influence and honor. Formerly war, many long wars, had sprung from all these questions; from 1830 to 1848 there were only a few partial and temporary threats of war. Everywhere men hastened to deal with events in a summary manner. The world remained motionless in the midst of the storms, recovering from its rest strength to endure fresh harsh shocks.

It was the good fortune of the monarchy of 1830, from its very beginning, to meet in England and amongst the English people with a sincere and earnest sympathy, which influenced the English government. The Duke of Wellington had assisted with no good grace in Polignac's reckless proceedings, though by personal taste and habit he had favored the fallen and proscribed dynasty. His good sense and impartiality led him to understand the change of opinion in France, and the serious consequences which had followed from it. "That means a change of dynasty," he at once said. The English government was the first to acknowledge the new monarch of France; and the choice made by King Louis Philippe of Talleyrand as his ambassador at London, strengthened this good understanding from the first. Frequently impatiently desirous of recovering

his share of power and influence under the government of the
restoration, Talleyrand kept himself ill-naturedly aloof from
it. He accepted the difficult duty of placing the French government in confidential communication, and, when, necessary,
in common action, with the principal European governments.
It was a work of reparation analogous in some respects to that
which in 1814 he accomplished at Vienna. " He was well
suited to succeed in it, for he brought to it the very qualifica-
tions necessary—a combination of liberal intelligence and
aristocratic habits, impassiveness and daring, cool patience
and prompt tact, and the art of acting and waiting with a
certain lofty manner." *

One important question brought together in London all the
representatives of Europe, now jealous and anxious. In the
midst of the revolutionary risings caused by the revolution
just accomplished in France, that of Belgium against the
hated yoke of Holland was the first and most serious (25th
August, 1830). A provisional government was organized on
the 26th September, and on the 3rd October the new state declared its independence, which was soon confirmed by the national congress. A conference was already open in London,
for the purpose of determining the situation of Belgium in
Europe. It was a difficult and protracted undertaking, complicated by the claims and thoughtless defiance of the Belgians,
by the unmanageable obstinacy of the King of Holland, by the
irritation and distrust of the northern powers. King Louis
Philippe personally contributed to these delicate negotiations a
disinterested prudence which raised and simplified the question. " The Low Countries have always been the stone of
stumbling in Europe," said he; " none of the great powers can,
without anxiety and jealousy, see them in the hands of another. Let them be by general consent an independent and
neutral state, and that state will become keystone in the arch
of the European order." In 1814, England wished to place the
independence of the Netherlands as a barrier between France
the conqueror, and threatened Europe. In 1830, King Louis
Philippe wished in his turn to found peacefully a barrier of
neutrality and pacification. He refused to allow his son, the
Duc de Nemours, to be placed on the throne of the new state.
In 1832, in agreement with England, he supported by arms the
resolution of Europe, against the obstinate and triumphant

* Guizot's *Mémoires*, etc.

Dutch. Subsequently, he continued in constant harmony with the able and wise prince whom Belgium had the good fortune to receive as her first king. The family alliance which was concluded between the two monarchs by the marriage of King Leopold with the Princess Louise d'Orleans served to bind closer together the natural ties arising from their similarity in sound judgment and foresight.

Italy was agitated without results, through the intrigues of her refugees, who had been cast on the French frontiers by the successive shocks of her internal revolutions. Spain was still more so, with that ardor and persistence which characterized all her political movements. The Spanish refugees, who were very numerous in France, and had long been actively encouraged by the French liberals, offered King Louis Philippe to unite the Duc de Nemours to the young queen, Donna Maria, of Portugal, and combine the whole peninsula under one sceptre, by overthrowing the throne of Ferdinand VII. and disregarding the claims of Don Miguel. The king refused to second the proposed insurrection. The procedure of Ferdinand VII. with regard to him was bad, inconsistent, and disloyal; but the French government confined themselves to granting the Spanish refugees full liberty of action on the frontiers. When they came back to France after their reverses, beaten and dispersed, they were brought together and supported, on condition of remaining at some distance from the frontiers in places assigned to them. Ferdinand VII. now assumed a conciliatory attitude. "France is, and desires to remain, at peace with all her neighbors, notably with Spain," such were the government's instructions to its agents.

France wished also to remain at peace with Russia, and was grieved to see (29th November, 1830) a Polish insurrection break out under the most noble leaders, which was to end only in redoubling the woes of Poland. The first attempt of Joseph Chlepecki, as well as of General Skrynecki, only aimed at obtaining from the Emperor Nicholas just and honorable concessions in favor of Poland, such as the Emperor Alexander intended to reconstitute her. The passions of the people, imprudent from the ardor of their patriotism, paralyzed those efforts, squandered the influence, and then the lives, of their bravest and most intelligent leaders, and delivered up Warsaw and Poland to the horrors of unrestrained popular factions, to let them then fall again under the heavy Russian yoke. The Poles had reckoned too much upon the promises of French revolutionists, and their influence with the French government. There had been no engagement entered into: nor did France fail towards them in a single duty, as was proclaimed by Sebastiani with inconsiderate bluntness. "Order reigns at Warsaw," he announced to the chamber, at the very time when the Polish insurrection was expiring in a sea of blood. France alone had tried to interpose with Russia in favor of Poland, before the last days of the struggle; and she for a long time generously received the wretched fugitives.

The foreign policy of France, though everywhere really peaceful, was not one of inaction or indifference. "It is necessary," said the king, "to weigh the interests, and measure the distances, far from us. Nothing obliges us to engage France. We can act or not act, according to French prudence or interest. Round about us, at our gates, we are engaged before hand; we cannot permit the affairs of our neighbors to be directed by others than themselves, and without us."

It was on this principle that we soon after took arms against the citadel of Antwerp; and this principle also suggested in July, 1832, the expedition commanded by Admiral Roussin against the exactions of Don Miguel in Portugal upon the Frenchmen domiciled in his states. There had been delay in redressing our grievances, and England had obtained satisfaction analogous to that which we were demanding. The Tagus was forced, the Portuguese fleet captured, and the compensation insisted upon was paid at a convention signed on board of the French admiral's ship. In England the indignation was intense. "A blush rises to my brow," said Wellington in the House of Lords, "when I think of the treatment which our former allies are undergoing with impunity." The tories had been replaced in power by the whigs; Palmerston and Grey did not ask France to give an account of the chastisement which she had inflicted upon Portugal. At about the same time the French government were acting in Italy with the same vigor which they displayed in Portugal. Austria had promptly repressed the insurrections which agitated the states possessed by the princes of his house. She in the same way assisted the papal troops against the revolutionary risings in the legations. As soon as the Austrian forces retired the agitation recommenced, and the European powers felt it their duty to address a common appeal to the Pope, to induce him to undertake in earnest some system of political and administrative reform. Promises had proved of little value, and indignation reappeared in the pontifical states. Cardinal Bernetti boldly announced to the foreign powers an intention to renounce the proposed changes, and have recourse to energetic repression. The Austrians returned from all parts to the papal states. The French government resolved not to leave them in sole possession, after having, without success, expressed this desire at Rome. The occupation of Ancona being resolved upon, "the small French squadron, commanded by the captain of the ship *Gallois*, arrived opposite it on the 22nd February, 1832, having set sail from Toulon on the 7th, and carrying the 66th regiment of the line, under the orders of Colonel Coombes. At two o'clock in the morning the frigate *Victoire* entered the harbor in full sail, and the troops were landed in silence. The gates of the town were burst open, and without a drop of blood being shed the town and citadal were occupied the same morning. Our soldiers mounted sentry everywhere together with those of the Pope, and the French and Roman flags floated side by side. "If we succeed," wrote Barante, the ambassador at Turin, to Guizot, "we shall displease Austria, without her wishing to quarrel with us, a very desirable result. We shall have shown to the Italian governments that we do not agree to their making themselves vassals to avoid granting their subjects anything. We shall have actually shown our strength, to the great joy of all the French-liberal party, who will be encouraged and strengthened by the presence of our flag in Italy. The carbonari themselves will begin to set more value on our ministry than on Lafayette."*

All Europe was beginning to know the powerful hand which had just taken hold, for too short a time, of the helm of our vessel, beaten about by the waves. When the occupation of Ancona was known in Paris, the representatives of the great powers hastened to call upon Casimir Périer, who had been home minister since 13th March, 1831, and found him in bad health, but excited and proud. On hearing the Prussian minister, Baron Werther, ask if international law still existed in Europe, he rose from his couch, and going up to him exclaimed, "The international law in Europe, sir, I am now defending. Do you think it easy to maintain treaties and peace? The honor of France must also be maintained; and it enjoined what I have just done. I have a right to the confidence of Europe; and I reckoned upon it."

* Guizot's *Mémoires*, etc.

Casimir Périer was not naturally disposed to reckon upon other men's kindness, but his daring resolution was never hindered by his prudent distrust. The occupation of Ancona did not disturb our friendly relations with the court of Rome. Through our ambassador, St. Aulaire, they accepted it as a temporary act, the conditions of which were fixed by a convention (16th April, 1833). Peace was maintained in Europe, as well as the honor of France. The determined and important experiment was perfectly successful.

Abroad, however, as well as at home, the efforts of the French government were constantly weakened and hindered by the revolutionary fermentation. It had fatally caused the fall of Laffitte's cabinet, though they really and in majority belonged to the left, but proved powerless and inefficacious against the disorderly fury of the demagogues and rioters, who were perpetually stirring up new agitations in the streets of Paris. This weakness was soon to declare itself in a painful and striking manner.

There was much alarm beforehand in the anticipation of a popular manifestation on the 14th February, the anniversary of the murder of the Duc de Berry, which was to be commemorated by religious services. The Archbishop of Paris, and the curé of St. Roch refused to allow the celebration in their churches by solemn mass, as was demanded by the legitimists. It was at St. Germain l'Auxerrois that the ceremony took place. The government did nothing to prevent it, and took no precautions against revolutionary excesses. Several days previously, on the 21st January, the death of Louis XVI. was brought to recollection without any insult to disturb its majesty; but on the 14th February, the populace proceeded to the most frightful excesses. The church of St. Germain, with the presbytery and archbishop's palace, were sacked with a savage fury. "Like everybody else," says Guizot in his *Mémoires*, "I saw floating in the river and dragged in the streets sacred objects, priests' robes, the archbishop's furniture, paintings, and books; I saw the cross thrown down; I have visited the archbishop's palace, or rather the site of his palace, and the vicarage, and church of St. Germain l'Auxerrois, that ancient parish church of our kings, since they were destroyed. Those sudden ruins, that naked desolation of the holy places, formed a hideous sight; less hideous, however, than the brutal delight of the destroyers, and the mocking indifference of the spectators who crowded round."

The same spectacle, under various aspects, was reproduced in many other towns, sometimes provoked by similar manifestations of attachment to the fallen monarchy. Not only did Laffitte allow anarchy to display itself freely, without any earnest attempt to repress or punish it, but he took advantage of these disorders to ask King Louis Philippe to efface from the coins and escutcheons the traditional arms of France; and unfortunately was too easily successful.

So much lack of energy and foresight could not suffice for the government of the country, or the confidence of honorable men, in the midst of times so disturbed. Without much personal liking, but from a necessity which he clearly perceived, the king asked Casimir Périer to form a cabinet, at the same time summoning Marshal Soult to sit in it. "I must have that grand sword," said Louis Philippe. Casimir Périer, however, claimed the right of being president, to which the marshal did not dare offer opposition.

It is a rare occurrence for a man in a single year of government to impress his seal upon a whole policy, and establish his glory forever. Those leaders of men who remain powerful in the memory of their contemporaries and successors have generally long borne the burden of power, and learned to exercise it with a steady hand. Casimir Périer deserved and obtained success of a more striking kind. Devoted in his youth to financial affairs, he was elected in 1817 to the Chamber of Deputies, and constantly sat there, acquiring every year greater influence, without taking any part at any time in official duties. Borne to the front from the first days of the revolution of 1830, he refused to be made a minister, saying, it was too soon. In 1831, he was elected President of the Chamber of Deputies, when he found it necessary to accept power. "Do you not see that everything is crumbling about us?" he had for some time been saying to his friends; "and that the government is about to become impossible?" It was upon him that the duty devolved of showing the nation that it must be governed, and the revolutionists that a government had at last seized the authority.

"He had been created by God for a wild and excited period. Some expression of his mental earnestness was constantly reflected in his countenance, gait, look, and tone of voice. His physical vigor equalled his moral. "How can you expect a man of my build to yield?" he frequently asked. Eager and restless, he always seemed to be defying his opponents, and implicitly trusting his friends. From the latter he exacted a never-failing devotion. "I laugh at my friends when I am right," he exclaimed one day; "it is when I am wrong that I require their support." In private conversation he listened coldly, disputed little, and almost always showed that his mind was already made up. In the chamber, he seldom showed eloquence, and sometimes want of tact, but he was always successful and powerful. Both in private and in the tribune, he sometimes allowed himself to be carried away by violent fits of anger. He terrified his partisans somewhat as well as his friends, but possessed the confidence of the one in spite of their doubt, and compelled that of the others in the midst of their annoyance. This was due to the power of the man, much superior to that of the orator." *

When he entered into power, on the 13th March, 1831, Casimir Périer formed a just estimate of the difficulties of the task which he undertook in undertaking to rescue the country from anarchy; but he was not at first conscious of all its tremendous import. "After all," said he, when the revolutionary press was let loose upon him, and every day giving a distorted view of his conduct and intentions, "after all, what does it matter to me? I have the *Moniteur* as a record of my acts, the tribune of the chambers to explain them, and the future to judge them.

For the moment Casimir Périer had scarcely strength enough for the task. With dignity as well as enthusiasm and ability, he made use of all the resources at command. He exacted and obtained from his agents perpetually renewed efforts; but the evil was more deeply-seated than he had believed, and constant proofs of it were manifested. There were frequent fresh riots in the streets of Paris, sometimes with violence, at other times in secret, but always stirring up the passions of the populace by various means, and under various pretexts, in the name of the Polish insurrection or some trials of obscure conspirators. Open or secret associations everywhere exercised their fatal influence. On the occasion of the commercial and industrial crisis which weighed upon the whole of France, serious insurrections in Lyons and Grenoble in 1831 revealed the wretched slavery submitted to by peaceful and sensible workmen, who were induced to actions and crimes at which they themselves were afterwards

---

* Guizot's *Mémoires*, etc.

shocked. The juries too often were under the same influence, and magistrates were therefore put to the pain of seeing their pression powerless or insufficient. The audacity of prisoners at the bar was redoubled; "we have still some bullets in our cartridges," exclaimed several amongst them.

Périer persisted in struggling, however great might have been his real dejection and doubt. Brave to audacity in the foreign relations of France and Europe, he showed himself not the less obstinate in resisting insurrection, disconcerting the offenders sometimes by a word or look. Stopped one day in his carriage with General Sebastiani, in the Place Vendôme, he stepped out without hesitation, walked up to the rioters, and addressing the row in front, who were shouting "Long live Poland!" on account of the news received that very morning of the fall of Warsaw, he asked what they wanted. "We wish for the rights of man and our liberties!" "Well, I give you them! What will you do with them?" And, shrugging his shoulders, he quietly passed through the crowd, who made way for him as well as the soldiers, then leaving the sentry-post of the treasury. At the same time, in spite of the serious troubles then beginning to show themselves in several provinces, he obstinately refused to propose any exceptional laws or rigorous measures. "The law should be sufficient for everything," said he. "Order in Paris and Vendée by the maintenance of law, peace in Europe by respecting sworn promises, that is enough to serve as an answer to much reproach, to calm much anxiety, and rally many convictions." He repelled, both for himself and the country, every sign of weakness, proudly claiming the confidence and support of his friends. "I do not accept your indulgence," he exclaimed from the tribune; "I only claim justice and my country's esteem."

There was at that time no threatening danger, whatever may have been said, in the visit made to Paris by Queen Hortense with her son Prince Bonaparte, destined to become the Emperor Napoleon III. The king and queen showed the exiled princess a kindness and respect, which never interrupted their relations with the Bonapartes, and the memory of which must have produced certain results. Queen Hortense's visit was unknown to the public. In spite of the shouts, "Long live the Emperor!" sometimes heard in the mobs, the recollections of Napoleon was then dormant, and Bonapartism in complete abeyance. There was, however, a proposal made to the

Chamber of Deputies, asking that the ashes of Napoleon
should be brought back to France. "It is true," said Charles
Lameth, "that Napoleon suppressed anarchy, but there is no
need for his coffin coming to increase it in these days." The
cabinet had ordered the emperor's statue to be re-erected on
the column in the Place Vendôme, and made no objection to
referring the petition to the ministers. It was destined to
produce some result nine years later.

Throughout the incessantly recurring noise of insurrection,
heard even at the gates of the Palais Bourbon, the legislative
work was bravely and consistently pursued. Seventy-eight
bills, successively presented by the cabinet on the 13th March,
1831, disposed of a mass of pending questions, and political or
administrative reforms. By some of them several painful
duties were imposed upon the head of the government. He
found himself compelled by the pressure of public opinion to
propose the abolition of hereditary peerage, which he considered useful, and create thirty-six new peers in order to
oblige the chamber to weaken itself with its own hands. His
most determined supporters, Royer-Collard and Guizot, supported on this occasion by Thiers, were opposed to the bill, and
boldly attacked it. "You are very fortunate to be able to say
what you think," Périer sometimes said to them.

The struggle meanwhile was prolonged, and while being
prolonged gradually undermined the strength of the resistance. Périer, however, though bravely supported by his
friends, felt weary and isolated. "No one does his duty completely," said he; "no one comes to the assistance of the government in moments of difficulty. I cannot myself do everything. Though a good horse, I cannot without assistance get
out of the rut; yet, if need were, I shall kill myself at the
task. But let everybody do his honest endeavors, and pull
along with me. That is our sole chance of saving France. I
hope soon to obtain the disarming of the great powers. This
warlike fermentation will then subside; and as for me, I shall
retire, my task being terminated. The burden is already too
heavy, and when the danger is gone it will be intolerable."
From his confidence in Guizot, he chose the latter to continue
his work, and expound his parliamentary doctrines. "All
those discussions do not suit me," said he; "I am a man of
active struggle."

His struggling was now drawing to a close, and precursory
signs of eternal rest soon after caused even him some anxiety

Cholera broke forth in Paris during March, 1832, being predicted some months previously from scientific observation, although no remedy had yet been discovered to cope with its terrible ravages. The alarm of the populace soon produced disorder and absurd charges. The horrible scenes which had taken place during the epidemics of the middle ages seemed at one time destined to be renewed in Paris; several men were massacred on the charge of poisoning. Casimir Périer unfortunately had an attack of it when already weak from ill-health. "I shall only leave this place feet foremost," he said to Montalivet, who called to see him. As danger increased, men's courage revived. The noble side of human nature was shown in deeds of kindness, multiplied everywhere, for the assistance of the sick and unfortunate. The courageous devotion of trustees, doctors, and priests, was equalled by that of the women. The Duke of Orleans, then quite young and already popular, visited the Hôtel-Dieu hospital with Casimir Périer, and Barbé-Marbois, then eighty-seven years old, and president of the general council of the hospitals, offered to accompany them. Several patients died during the visit, but neither the prince nor the minister thought of hurrying it over. Three days later, Périer was ill in bed, and soon after he was, despaired of. The prince was reserved for a more tragical end, fatal to his country and his family. Death had reaped an illustrious harvest, Cuvier being of the number, his death (on the 13th May, 1832) being accelerated by the prevailing epidemic. The friends of Périer felt his case hopeless, though he still struggled with all his physical and mental vigor. During his delirious attacks, from which he frequently suffered, he was still eagerly engrossed with the dangers of the country, which he knew would soon be deprived of him. Once he rose on his bed, and throwing away everything from him, exclaimed in a ringing voice, "Alas! alas! the president of the council is mad!" "I am very ill," he said, on coming to his senses, "my wings are clipped; but the country is in even worse health than I am!" When at last, on the 16th May, he succumbed, there was a great demonstration of national grief and gratitude before his deathbed and tomb. The gap made was already felt in the foremost rank of those rare servants of the country on whom Providence has bestowed as a gift "those sublime instincts which form as it were the divine part of the art of governing." "To his last day," said Royer-Collard, in the speech spoken at his funeral, "he fought with an intrepidity which never belied itself; when his strength was overcome, his soul was not."

The most striking testimony paid to Périer's memory was the sudden increase of anarchy and conspiracy that at once signalized the disappearance of his firm and strong will. His cabinet were left mutilated when face to face with a situation becoming daily more serious, as Périer had himself foreseen. Talleyrand, whom for a moment they had thought of to appoint premier, had no wish to accept a burden which did not suit him. The difficult questions of foreign policy were nearly resolved, but the mutual animosity of parties broke out simultaneously. While a new and terrible insurrection was being prepared in Paris, the Duchesse de Berry had secretly arrived in Vendée, to place herself at the head of a legitimist insurrection which had for several months been arranged and prepared in several places.

The zeal of the royalist gentry and their impatience of exile had overpowered the wise advice of the friends of the royal family, then living at Lullworth in England. Chateaubriand, Fitz-James, and Berryer strove eagerly to dissuade the princess from her journey, and their friends from the proposed rising; but all their efforts were in vain. In April, 1832, the Duchess de Berry on her return from Italy, where, unknown to any, she had formed a new alliance, arrived secretly at Marseilles in the *Carlo-Alberto*, freighted by herself. The hopes they had formed of an insurrection in that town proving abortive, the princess, on whom Charles X. had conferred the title of regent, boldly crossed France in company with a few devoted friends, and reached the chateau of Dampierre in Saintonge. There she received secretly the insurrectionist leaders, the aged remnants of the former Vendeans, or brave inheritors of their perseverance in a path that seemed interminable. Charette, Autichamp, Rochejacquelein, and Marshal Bourmont eagerly showed their devotion. The rising was fixed for the 24th May, and the duchess travelled over the country districts in disguise, brave and untiring, full of excited delight in her hopeful activity. The royalist leaders, however, were depressed, for the warlike ardor was extinguished. The peasants did not respond to their appeals, and the hesitation of many of the country gentry on whom they had counted delayed their operations till the beginning of June. The insurrection broke out only partially and weakly, without that contagious brilliancy which attracts and strikes the lower orders. The repression was prompt and energetic; and the authorities endeavored to apprehend the Duchess de Berry, who had unfortunately persisted in her enterprise. She was obliged to take refuge in Nantes, while several trifling engagements cost her the lives of her most devoted partisans. Several gentlemen still held the Château Pénissière when the princess reached Nantes. Traced up to her last retreat, and betrayed by a man of the lower order to whom she had been entrusted, she was taken, along with her friend Miss Kersabiec, in a place of concealment made in the wall of a fireplace. Arrested on the 6th November, 1832, she was conducted to the Château Blaye, where she was kept for eight months, to the regret of all parties. On the 8th June, 1833, the duchess left her prison, without trial or condemnation, and at once went to Palermo. Her illustrious friends who had in vain opposed her project, Chateaubriand, Hyde, Fitz-James, and Berryer, had been imprudently accused by the government, but the tribunals pronounced that there was no ground for the charge; and the sentence of the Vendeans taken armed was commuted by the crown, while many of the others were acquitted. The total destruction of the hopes of the royalists led to the subsidence of their passion, and soon the only traces that remained of the insurrection were several administrative difficulties.

The stirring up of the demagogic indignation was due to two causes more serious and deep-seated. In 1830 the revolutionists again flattered themselves with the hope of definitively seizing the power; but it escaped them through that divine pity for France which has often disarmed the enemies of her well-being at the very moment of their apparent triumph. The constant insurrections in Paris during the whole of the year 1831 kept up amongst the lower orders an excitability and desire for action. Like the legitimist leaders, the republican leaders did not think the moment propitious for a great effort, but they could not restrain the undisciplined wishes of their soldiers. Some seditious manifestations had already occurred, such as the breaking of the official seals on the doors of the hall formerly occupied by the "Friends of the People." Only an opportunity was wanting for the explosion already projected and prepared; and the death of General Lamarque, well known in the army for his enlightened liberalism and rare military talent, supplied a pretext. An immense concourse of people was assembled on the 5th June, 1832, to escort the car which was to convey his body to the country, and after some speeches

were made, the tricolor flag was quickly replaced by the red
flag, with loud shouts of "Long live the republic! Down with
Louis Philippe! Down with the Bourbons!" General Exelmans was insulted. Troops began to appear, but at the same
time there appeared an organized insurrection. The gun-
smiths' shops were pillaged; several military posts were taken
possession of, and barricades were erected in various places.
There was some keen fighting, but towards evening the important positions were again in the hands of those on the side of
order. The national guards performed their duty with a courage which surprised their military chiefs, due partly to the
personal interests which were everywhere in danger. The in-
surrectionists were posted in the neighborhood of the Church
St. Merry. At the first report of the outbreak, the king had
left Neuilly, and was accompanied to Paris by the queen. At
five o'clock in the afternoon, and six next morning, the king
visited the bivouacs, and then the very spots where the fighting had been hottest. He was welcomed with shouts. "I have
a good cuirass," said he to those who advised him to be prudent;
"I have my five sons." A handful of men still resisted, repelling the successive attacks of the troops, and secretly supplied
with powder and provisions by friends whose courage did not
equal their own. The fighting lasted for two whole days, and
cost the lives of some of the bravest republicans, so enthusiastic and led away by generous motives as to lose their common
sense. "Almost at the same time, on the 6th June, 1832, 100
republicans in Paris at the Cloister St. Merry, and some fifty
legitimists in Vendée at the Château Pénissière, surrounded by
enemies, fire, and ruins, fought in utter desperation, and died
shouting "Long live the Republic!" and "Long live Henry V.!"
respectively, thus giving up their lives as a human sacrifice, in
the hope of perhaps thus one day serving a future which they
were not to see." *

So many formidable shocks proved too much for the strength
of the cabinet over which Casimir Périer had recently presided.
It was violently attacked both publicly and in the chambers by
the leaders of the opposition, and they published against it a
report, or "Manifesto to our constituents," trying to induce
the king to accept their conclusions. He replied by the partial
renewal of his ministry. Marshal Soult became president of
the council, Thiers home minister, and Broglie agreed to become

---

* Guizot's *Mémoires,* etc.

foreign minister on condition that Guizot should be appointed minister of public instruction. Constituted on the 11th of October, 1832, the new cabinet at once convoked the chambers for the 19th November, being resolved to act on their own account, and endeavor to establish political liberty in the country—in other words, trustworthy guarantees both of the security of individual rights and interests, and a proper attention to public affairs. Coming immediately after the terrible trials which had just agitated the new monarchy, it was a difficult and daring enterprise to govern with success and regularity, while at the same time leaving in every direction striking traces of their action. It was to the honor of the cabinet of the 11th October that they attempted this work, and in a large measure accomplished it, notwithstanding the obstacles which seemed certain to paralyze their early efforts.

Each of the new ministers found himself at first burdened with a delicate and heavy task. After a long alternation of hurry and delay, the London conference finished its labors on the 1st October, 1832; and the separation of Belgium and Holland, accomplished in fact, was definitely acknowledged by Europe. King William, however, still held the citadel of Antwerp. The English fleet assembled at Spithead and ours at Cherbourg; and by a convention concluded on the 22nd October, between England and France, it was demanded that the belligerents should evacuate each other's territories before the 12th November. Should the king of Holland refuse, the French army were to invade Belgium on the 15th. The evacuation not having taking place, on the 17th, at one o'clock, the Dukes of Orleans and Nemours passed through Brussels at the head of the troops, Marshal Gérard being commander-in-chief. On the 29th the trench was opened against the fortress, and it was not till the 5th December that the place surrendered. The garrison remained prisoners of war, because the king of Holland refused to abandon the forts of Lillo and Liefkenskoek at the mouth of the Scheldt. The princes had greatly distinguished themselves, Orleans insisting on superintending the work of the trenches, and scaling the parapet of the St. Laurent lunette in the midst of a storm of shot. "My sons have done their duty," said the queen, with modest pride. "I am glad they have proved that they may be relied upon." The kingdom of Belgium was now founded.

Thiers was at that time engaged in the pacification of the western provinces. He also undertook the completion of all the great public monuments commenced by the empire and languidly continued by the restoration. The chamber unhesitatingly voted him large supplies. It was the pacific honor of King Louis Philippe to accomplish grand works of which he had not had the initiative, and to reduce to practical action principles of order and public utility which had been noisily professed by his predecessors. The public instruction was a striking instance. The legislative assembly and national convention proposed to give France a grand system of public instruction. Three men of distinguished and very different mental qualities, Talleyrand, Condorcet, and Daunou, were successively appointed to present to their respective sovereigns reports on this important question. There was much discussion without result. On emerging from the French Revolution, after some unsuccessful attempts, the only higher schools were the "Polytechnique" and the "Normale;" and the "Institut" was the highest stage for literary or scientific ambition. By organizing the lycées, and then founding the university under the fertile management of Fontanes, the Emperor Napoleon provided for the great and important wants of secondary education; but the modest and vast career of primary teaching, the necessities of popular instruction, were still persistently neglected. The revolution decreed that instruction was to be public, gratuitous, and obligatory. According to the principles of Napoleon, the education of youth belonged exclusively and entirely to the state.

No one passed from words to deeds. The expense of primary instruction was left absolutely in charge of families and communes, which was enough alone to strike all the statutes with sterility. In fact, since the various religious bodies ceased to exercise their pious duty of instructing the people, schools and teachers had disappeared throughout the greater part of France, without being successfully replaced. Guizot undertook to fill up this gap, and at last satisfy this want. He conceived the idea of extending his reforms farther, and laid before the chambers the proposal of a law at once liberal and protective, conserving to the university her dignified right to the foremost rank in secondary instruction, without denying to her natural rivals, the Catholic Church and free thought, the perilous honor of free contest. He also endeavored to resolve the question of intermediate instruction by higher primary schools; but the opposition encountered, and rapid changes of power, rendered abortive those fair hopes, which have been repeatedly

aimed at since by generous endeavor. Several months previously, Montalembert, Lacordaire, and Lamennais, united by
a sympathy of ideas and beliefs which was destined soon to
disappear, had boldly defended that liberty of instruction
under whose color they were afterwards long to fight on various principles. To the close of his life, Guizot never ceased to
regret the fate of the great enterprise which he had been the
first to attempt, though unsuccessfully, and to which he was
afterwards to consecrate all his remaining strength.

A special satisfaction to Guizot as minister of public instruction was being able at least to found in France a complete and
prospective system of primary education, which, though often
modified in its details, has remained the basis and starting
point of all the advancements which in the last forty-five years
have been made in popular instruction. It is the seal of inferiority impressed on human works, that they are necessarily slow
in their effects, and only produce light in the midst of chaos
after long efforts. The results of the law of 28th June, 1833,
were thenceforward patent to all. The impetus which it gave
to popular instruction has never slackened. In the midst of
much sorrow, it will be to the honor of the present time that it
has supported it with fresh ardor.

The powerful development of higher education under eminent teachers selected with the greatest care, the foundation of
new chairs in the great public schools, the appointment of a
class of moral and political science in the institute, the en-
couragement everywhere granted to literary and scientific
bodies, the grants procured with great difficulty from the
chambers for the moderate endowment of study and research,
and finally the great attention bestowed upon the improvement
of historical studies in France,—such were the special labors of
Guizot during the three and a half years that he held office as
minister of public instruction. The toils and combats of parliamentary life left to the ministers but little leisure for the noble
enterprises with which they anxiously aspired to have their
names associated. Hostile passions were not yet entirely appeased, and frequently the storm was heard on the horizon.
It burst out afresh after two years, which had caused hopes of
some repose.

Sincerely and resolutely liberal, the cabinet of the 11th October did not renounce the policy of courageous resistance which
it believed compatible with the full exercise of every public
liberty. Compelled by the violent language of the newspapers

to institute some press trials, it was most of all anxious about the fatal influence exercised by perpetually urging the people to form associations, as if the profuse publication of incendiary articles were not enough. The *Catéchisme republicain, Catéchisme des Droits de l'homme* and *Le Pilori* gained much additional influence by being cried in the streets—a new abuse against which the courts afforded no remedy. In order to notify clearly the right thus claimed, Rodde, the manager of a popular journal *Bon Sens* stood in the Place de la Bourse, dressed in a blouse and cap, and began distributing a packet of sheets, declaring his intention of repelling violence by violence should the police attempt to interfere with his liberty. "Let them take care," said he, "I am on the ground of legality, and I have the right there to appeal to the courage of Frenchmen; I have the right there to appeal to insurrection. In that case, if ever, it will be the most sacred of duties." Two bills for restricting the rights of public criers and those of voluntary associations were laid before the chambers by the cabinet. The first became law without difficulty, and the second had undergone some keen attack when some practical difficulties came to overthrow many optimist illusions. On the 5th April, 1834, there was a violent outbreak in Lyons, soon accompanied by bloodshed.

This insurrection, organized by Mazzini, the chief of the Italian carbonari, had long been in preparation. It was to be combined with an invasion of refugees upon the territory of Savoy, and a strike of the Lyonese workmen. The refugees, however, failed in their attempts, and the workmen resumed their work, in spite of all that their leaders could urge. A second time, but merely by accident, they were induced to revolt. The Parisian leaders of the party, including Godefroy Cavaignac and Garnier-Pagès, had come to Lyons to rouse the revolutionary passion. On the occasion of the trial of several leaders of the Rights of Man Society, on the 5th April, there were several violent scenes in court. "No bayonets!" shouted the workmen when they saw the soldiers arrive. The president adjourned the court to the 9th, and on that day all was in readiness. At daybreak any doubt was no longer possible: Lyons was undergoing, not a tumultuous and disorderly agitation, but a movement which was both violent and systematic. Resolutions had evidently been made, orders given, time fixed. The court was to open at eleven o'clock, and before its doors the Place St. Jean remained, the whole morning, empty and deserted. The insurgents wished to appear in a body and act all at once. The secret agents of the Rights of Man Society were waiting collected in their respective quarters. At half-past eleven, when the court had opened, the first band arrived, and then the others. Barricades were quickly thrown up at the four corners of the place, others being at the same time erected in all parts of the town. An ultra-republican proclamation, conveying the grossest abuse of King Louis Philippe and his ministers, was distributed in great numbers. The attack began in all parts, and was everywhere repulsed courageously. For five hours, a civil war, premeditated and organized against the existing government, caused blood to flow in the streets of Lyons. It was kept up by the insurgents with skilful audacity and fanatical keenness and determination; by the authorities with steady firmness; by the troops with a fidelity to their colors and a vigor which towards the end almost passed into fury. A similar outbreak was prepared in the same way at St. Etienne, Vienne, Grenoble, Châlons, Auxerre, Arbois, Marseilles, and Lunéville. In the streets of Lyons, during the fighting, bulletins, dated like the proclamations the year XLII. of the republic, were incessantly publishing news, which was almost all false, amongst the insurgents to keep up their courage. "At Vienne," said one of those bulletins (22 Germinal, 11th April), "the national guard is master of the town; they have stopped the artillery coming against us. The insurrection is breaking out everywhere. Patience and courage! The garrison must of course become weak and demoralized. Even should it hold its positions, we have only to keep it in check till our brothers arrive from the departments." The garrison did not become demoralized; the brothers from the departments did not come; and on the 13th April, in the evening, all over the town, the beaten insurgents gave up fighting. When authority was everywhere restored, men were astonished to find, among the dead, the prisoners, and the wounded in the hospitals, scarcely one tenth of the workmen belonging to the silk-mills, and six strangers for one Lyonnais!

In Paris as well as Lyons the republican party had announced, and made preparations for, their victory. A Breton gentleman, Kersausie, an eager partisan of the carbonari, took the leadership of the "Society of Action," by whom the movement was to be commenced. He was arrested, as well as all the leaders of the Rights of Man Society, Godefroy Cavaignac alone escaping. The news of the definitive check suffered by the insurgents at Lyons excited the rage and shame of the masses enrolled under Parisian revolution. On the 13th April, at five o'clock afternoon, the outbreak took place in Paris. Barricades started from the ground with inconceivable rapidity, several officers were wounded, others killed. As in 1832, the insurgent operations seemed to be concentrated in the St. Merry quarter. General Bugeaud commanded the troops, and Thiers accompanied him when he went by night to take observations. "They passed along close to the houses, at the head of a small column, without any light but that from some candles in several windows falling upon their arms and uniforms. A shot fired from a cellar struck the captain of the troop dead, and another wounded mortally a young auditor of the Council of State who had come with a message to Thiers. As they advanced forward, new victims fell, and they looked in vain to discover the murderers. The soldiers' hearts boiled with anger, and as soon as daylight appeared a general attack was directed against the insurgents. There was a perpetual firing kept up from the houses and barricades. In the Rue Transnonain some soldiers were carrying their wounded captain on a litter, when several musket-shots from a house they were passing were fired at them, and killed their captain in their hands. Wild with rage, they burst open the doors of the house, rushed headlong over all the floors, into all the rooms, and a cruel and indiscriminate massacre blindly avenged savage assassinations."* This deplorable scene procured among the people for General Bugeaud, the sinister surname of butcher of the Rue Transnonain. It put a sad end to the struggle, the insurgents either hiding themselves or effecting their escape. A great many were arrested, shortly to appear before the Court of Peers. Admiral de Rigny, and Guizot announced to the chambers that the insurrection was subdued in Paris as well as in Lyons. After having provided for the evident necessities of legislation by passing a law respecting the possession of arms and ammunition, the Chamber of Deputies was dissolved on the 24th May, 1834.

The elections went almost everywhere in favor of the government, and testified strongly to the fears and repugnance which the revolutionary attempts inspired in the minds of honest people. Meanwhile the cabinet had suffered some loss of strength, and further embarrassment was impending.

* *Mémoires pour servir à l'histoire de mon temps.*

Following on an adverse vote of the chamber on the subject of the indemnities long due to the United States, the Duc de Broglie gave in his resignation. Guizot did not follow his example, and at this there was some astonishment in the chamber among those near Thiers. Thiers turning to those about him, said smartly, "Guizot has not retired with De Broglie, in order to make him return." The result was soon to justify Thiers' perspicacity. The question of the government of Algeria at that time gave rise to some dissensions within the cabinet. Marshal Soult, a very capable commander, was much less suited to treat with politicians, and often caused embarrassment to his colleagues. Not without difficulty he was replaced by Marshal Gérard, who in his turn retired some months later, accompanied by most of the other ministers. They were all determined to put the government of the country into the hands of the third party, which was increasing in the chambers under the influence of Dupin. A ministry which lasted for three days was the only success of this experiment. Again power was accepted by Thiers, Guizot, Duchâtel, Humann, and Rigny. Marshal Mortier became president of the council. Old, weary, and restless, Talleyrand quitted the embassy in London. The veterans of the great struggles of the past were disappearing from the arena, either retiring from active life, or being removed by death. Lafayette died peaceably at La Grange, surrounded by his children, and recalling piously in his enfeebled memory the recollection of the admirable wife whom he had recently lost. He wished to be interred by her side in the cemetery of Picpus, consecrated to the memory of the victims of the Terror, and no political demonstration disturbed the solemnity of the funeral rites. After the ardent struggles but recently extinguished, the populace, once so easily excited, had become indifferent; moreover, the leaders of the insurrection had entered on a course in which the patriotism of Lafayette prevented him from following them.

Before the Court of Peers burst forth the audacity of the numerous conspirators put on trial for complicity in the rising which took place in the month of April. The conflict was removed from the streets to the palace of the Luxembourg; it was boldly proclaimed, and systematically pursued by the launching of invectives, declamation, and theories, instead of the discharge of arms. Lying letters and insulting proclamations circulated everywhere among the people, seeking at the same time to sow erroneous impressions and artificially to excite the public passions. The courage and calm resolution of the Court of Peers was not relaxed, in spite of the provocations constantly being launched by the accused and their friends. "You wish 164 heads; take them!" cried one of those at the bar. "You have brought me here by force, you have ruined me, you have butchered me; here is my breast, strike me, kill me!" But only one condemnation to death was pronounced. Transportation was the most serious penalty inflicted. Guizot was soon obliged, however, in the presence of the chamber to support the necessity of the repression with a firmness for which he was accused of cruelty. "They forget constantly in this debate," said he, "what is the aim of all punishment, of all penal legislation. It is not only to punish and to repress the guilty, but to prevent the repetition of similar crimes. Preventive and general intimidation, such is the principle, the dominant aim, of the penal laws. It is necessary to choose in this world between the intimidation of the just and of the unjust, between the security of rogues and of orderly citizens; the former or the latter must stand in fear; there must be a sentiment, profound and lasting, of a superior power, always capable of overtaking and punishing. In the bosom of the family, in the relations of man with his God, there is something of dread, and this is so naturally and necessarily. He who fears nothing, ere long respects nothing."

M. de Broglie supported the same cause with a courage and an elevation of thought and language that strengthened him in the position which he had newly accepted in the cabinet. After tedious struggles within, and repeated effort on the part of the king to re-form a ministry, Marshal Mortier retired, and the Duc de Broglie replaced him as president of the council. The laws of September, 1835, intended to furnish the government with the weapons suited for an efficacious repression of the ceaseless attacks arising out of the revolution, bore by no means the character of exceptional measures. They maintained the essential guarantees of justice, while providing for the present and accidental wants of society. They were defended by the leaders of the conservative party with profound conviction; violently attacked both in the chambers and in the country by the opposition, they were nevertheless voted by a great majority, and were favorably received by the impartial and honest onlookers, who felt themselves effectively protected without oppression.

The tendencies and the events which broke out at the

moment when the cabinet presented the laws of September justified by anticipation their anxiety for the peace of society. For some days vague rumors, which seemed mysteriously to herald the fact as a secret that had escaped from numerous confidants, threatened the king and the royal family with some unknown danger. Already seven projects of assassination had been discovered, when a grand review of the national guard was convoked for the 28th July, 1835. At the moment when the royal procession arrived on the Boulevard du Temple, the king, who was bending over the shoulder of his horse to receive a petition, suddenly heard a noise as of platoon firing. He recovered himself instantly. "Joinville, this is for me," said he to the son who was nearest him: "let us go on." Meanwhile a crowd of dead and dying already surrounded him, including Marshal Mortier, General Lachasse de Vérigny, Captain de Vilate, many officers of the national guard, and several soldiers and women. The Duc d'Orleans had received a contusion, and a spent ball had penetrated the cravat of the Duc de Brogle. Cries of horror at the crime committed, and enthusiastic acclamations for the king, resounded on all sides. At the Chancellery, where were assembled the queen, the princesses, and those of his ministers who had not accompanied the king, there prevailed the greatest consternation and a terrible uneasiness. They did not yet know the number and quality of the victims, nor the circumstances of the attempt.

One man attempted to make his escape by means of a rope suspended from a window on the third floor of the house No. 50, on the Boulevard du Temple. Wounded himself by the explosion which he had effected, he was easily arrested. The "infernal machine" was presently seized; it consisted of twenty-five gun barrels supported on a scaffolding of oak, and the discharge of these was rendered stimultaneous by the employment of a single train of powder. Several of the guns had burst, while others had not gone off, and it is to this circumstance that the safety of the king may be attributed. It was soon ascertained that the author of the crime was a Corsican named Fieschi. Already guilty and condemned, dissatisfied with his social position, he had been urged on the path of villainy by three Parisian workmen, who were ardent demagogues and affiliated to the Society of the Rights of Man. The latter were also arrested, and were tried and condemned some months subsequently by the Court of Peers. Hardly had they suffered the reward of their crime (26th of February, 1836) when another attempt to assassinate the king was made by a young southern, Louis Alibaud, who was formerly a soldier, and had taken part in the revolution of July. On six other occasions, either against Louis Philippe or his sons, were similar attempts renewed without ever once having shaken the calm courage of the king. On the other hand, he had great difficulty in ratifying some of the sentences pronounced against the criminals.

Meanwhile order was re-established; the dread and terror which the attempts had caused had assisted rather than shaken the prudent, resolute policy practised by the king and his ministers. A military expedition in Algeria under the Duc d'Orleans and Marshal Clauzel met with distinguished success; the French army occupied Mascara, to the great honor of its commanders. The discussion on the financial laws then absorbed the chambers; Humann, able and bold, suddenly rose, and proposed, without preliminary discussion in the Council, the measure which De Villèle had tried without success in 1824, and which was based on the reimbursement or reduction of the rentes. Humann, who had formerly supported the ministry of the restoration, attached great importance to his enterprise. "What would you have?" said Royer-Collard. "Guizot has his law on primary education, Thiers has his on the completion of the public monuments, and now Humann wants a share of fame." The cabinet refused to allow itself to be entangled thus; the king was personally opposed to the measure; and Humann was replaced in the financial department by D'Argout. The fallen minister and his proposition meanwhile reckoned on numerous partisans in the chamber, who challenged the government to explain its ulterior intentions respecting the conversation of rentes. They accused the Duc de Broglie of not being sufficiently explicit on the subject; he repeated the reasons for his reserve, returning to the very terms of reproach which they had addressed to him. "Is this clear?" he asked as he ended his speech. The chamber was offended; the Duc de Broglie was not popular, partly because of his defects, partly because of his very gifts of mind and character. Certain propositions were formerly presented for the prompt conversion of rentes; the cabinet demanded an adjournment, but was defeated, and resigned immediately.

Thiers shared the opinion of his colleagues on the question

that had arisen; but he was not at all equally at one with them in his convictions and political views, and although often fighting by their side for the same objects, he never entertained much liking for the doctrinaires. When, therefore, Humann, Molé, and Gérard refused to form a cabinet, and when Dupin and Passy also declined the honor in the name of the third party, the king charged Thiers with the difficult function. The new ministry was definitely constituted on the 22nd of February, 1836, under his presidency. The harmonious union and action of men properly trained in the work of free and monarchical government had vanished; henceforth the wishes of leaders were diverse, if not antagonistic; the powers and efforts that were put forth after the revolution of 1830, for the purpose of establishing and sustaining the throne, were ruined absolutely and forever.

The country found itself at this time in a delicate situation with respect to the great powers of the north, who had remained suspicious and defiant even after they had ended by accepting the government sprung from the revolution of July, and the conclusion of the English alliance, which had displeased and embarrassed them in their relations with France. The combination of narrow views and egotistical passions had prevented the King of Prussia as well as the Emperor Nicholas and Metternich from rendering to the sound foreign policy of the country the justice which it merited. The revolutionary movements which had disturbed Germany were attributed to the contagion of French ideas, and to the protection which France granted to political refugees. A conference of the sovereigns at Münchengratz in 1833, and near Töplitz in 1835, had been followed by protests addressed to France; while the cold, determined attitude of the French discouraged such attempts at intimidation, without improving the existing relations. The complication of affairs in the east, and the aspirations of the Pasha of Egypt, Mehemet Ali, towards independence, were a continual source of disquietude to Russia, ambitious, with all her patience and ostentation—to England, decidedly Turkish in her proclivities—and to Prussia, disinterested but anxious. The attitude of France was shifting and contradictory, fettered as she was by revolutionary memories, by the traditions of the Egyptian expedition, by the desire to maintain the Ottoman Empire, while serving the ambition of the pasha. At different times Russia had already intervened for the protection of the Porte, which she was desir-

ous of holding at her mercy. The convention of Kutaieh, concluded under her auspices on the 5th May, 1833, had temporarily appeased the difference between Turkey and the Pasha of
Egypt, without calming Turkish uneasiness. On the 10th of
July, the treaty of Unkiar-Skelessi gave the sultan the assurance of Russian protection, on the sole condition that the Dar-
danelles should be closed to all foreign vessels of war. The
Black Sea should thus be a Russian lake, while Russia preserved the full liberty of her maritime operations in the Mediterranean. Great was the displeasure of England and France.
In spite of his personal dissatisfaction, Metternich applied
himself to arrange matters. The relations meantime remained
difficult and strained between the Porte and Mehemet, and
between France and the Emperor Nicholas, who was naturally
prejudiced against Louis Philippe and his government. England herself was somewhat affected by the good-will which
France had evinced towards the Pasha of Egypt. But the
agreement of the policy of the two countries on another point
contributed strongly to maintain a good understanding between the French and English governments.

King Ferdinand VII. died in September, 1835, and left the
succession to the throne contested, in spite of the definitive act
sanctioned by the Cortes, which had guaranteed the crown to
his eldest daughter, the Infanta Isabella. Long distracted between his family affections and his absolutist tendencies, the
monarch had sown the seeds of the Carlist insurrection, which
burst forth immediately on his death. A numerous and
resolute party supported the claim of Don Carlos to the throne
in the name of the Salic law, established in Spain by the Pragmatic Sanction of Philippe V., which Ferdinand VII. himself
had for the moment recognized. Those wise and moderate
Spaniards who aspired to give their country a free constitution naturally supported the title of the young queen. Zea
Bermudez, who was placed at the head of the ministry of the
Queen Regent Christina, was known and esteemed in London
as well as Paris. The English and French cabinets did not
hesitate, but recognized the rights of Isabella II., in conformity
with the old Spanish law accepted by the nation. Civil war
already prevailed in Spain; it began in Portugal, where the
usurper Dom Miguel declared in the name of the same principle the exclusion of the young Queen Donna Maria from the
throne. Don Carlos had sought support from Dom Miguel, but
the latter was defeated, and the new governments of the two

sovereignties appealed to the great liberal and constitutional powers for assistance. On the 13th of April, 1834, a triple alliance was concluded in London, between England, Spain and Portugal. A month later the French government protested against the exclusively English policy of Lord Palmerston; but while it chose to adhere to an existing treaty, it declined, in agreement with England, all armed intervention. The civil war continued to rage, but Don Carlos embarked for England, while Dom Miguel, taking a lasting farewell of Portugal, retired to Italy. Henceforth it ₄was against the revolutionary Spaniards, her allies at one moment, that the Regent Maria Christina had to struggle.

Some months before the government changed hands in France, without seriously modifying the existing policy, the power in Spain passed to Mendizabel, the leader of the radicals, who were resolved to restore the constitution of 1812. He immediately manifested a marked preference for the support of England, and that country testified towards him a feeling of great friendship. Hardly had Thiers become president of the council, than Lord Palmerston announced his intention of intervening in the affairs of the Peninsula, and proposed to us to act in concert. "France could occupy," he said, "the port of Passage, the valley of Bastan, and Fontarabia. For the rest, she shall trace at her will the line within which she shall be willing to limit her occupation."

King Louis Philippe had constantly been opposed to all thought of intervention in Spain. "Let us aid the Spaniards from a distance," said he, "but never let us enter the same boat with them. If once we are there, it will be necessary to take the helm, and God knows where we shall find ourselves." Thiers sustained the contrary principle with a settled conviction; he had, however, flatly refused intervention at the beginning of his ministry, but the situation had become aggravated in Spain. In the Basque provinces, the Carlist bands and the royal troops, fighting with a fury that was of little effect, abandoned themselves to revolting cruelties, which were everywhere tolerated, and sometimes commanded by their leaders. At the same time the intrigues of the secret societies, and the passions stirred up by the demagogues, burst forth in the provinces of the South—Barcelona, Valencia, Malaga, Seville, Cordova, and Cadiz — making the cry, "Long live the constitution of 1812!" re-echo on every side, and causing innumerable scenes of bloodshed. A military in-

surrection in Madrid was resolutely repressed by General
Quesada, the captain-general of Castille. The government
passed from the hands of Mendizabel to those of Isturitz, who
was more moderate, and less attached to the English alliance.
He claimed afresh the effectual aid of France. The services
indirectly accorded to Spain were multiplied, but the king remained absolutely opposed to intervention. The French ambassador at Madrid was ill, and De Bois le Comte was commis-
sioned to carry thither the reply of the French government.
"The Spaniards," he wrote to Thiers, on the 12th August, 1836,
"have been so accustomed to see us intervene in their affairs,
and to see us decide their questions of succession, from the
time of Henry of Transtamare downwards, to Philip V., Ferdinand VII., and his father and the Queen Isabella, that the
idea that we shall end by intervening now is profoundly believed, and it is hardly possible to root the belief out of the
country. They think that they must leave us to speak, and
that we shall always conclude by coming to direct intervention, being unable to support in Spain either revolutionary
anarchy or the restoration of Don Carlos." A successful military insurrection at St. Ildefonso had forced Queen Christina's
hand by an invasion of the palace of La Granja. She accepted
the constitution of 1812. General Quesada was murdered by
the insurgents, and a new cabinet having been formed, the
Cortes were dissolved and a general election was decreed.
The king wished to testify with emphasis his neutrality in the
affairs of the Peninsula; he demanded the retirement of the
corps of the French troops on the frontier. Thiers opposed
this, and the majority of his colleagues coincided with him.
"Nothing can bring the king to intervention," said he, "and
nothing can make me renounce it." The cabinet of the 22nd
of February resigned, and Comte Molé was charged with the
duty of reconstituting the ministry.

The prudent, sensible, and moderate policy prevailed in
foreign relations; as far as concerned the interior, it remained
both firm and clear, although without much _éclat_ or success.
An unfortunate expedition against the town of Constantine, in
pursuance of the schemes of conquest which at this time appeared too vast, had caused the retirement of Marshal Clauzel
as governor-general of Algeria. The sentiment of misfortune
weighed painfully on all minds in spite of the heroism of
which the troops and their leaders had given proof in the retreat. Commander Changarnier at the head of his battalion

disputed with the Arabs each step as they followed up the pursuit with fury. He descried the cavalry of Achmet Bey, disposed so as to make a general charge. As soon as he saw them approaching the commander formed his battalion in square. "Soldiers!" he cried, "look, these people, they are 6000, and you are 300; you see that the game is equal." The courage of the soldiers did not falter at this youthful explosion of an heroic soul, which continued to be worthy of himself even in extreme old age. The glory of General Changarnier began on that day.

A new source of disquietude, prophetic in its vague unrest, began to alarm the king and his counsellors. On the 30th of October, Prince Louis Napoleon Bonaparte arrived at Strasbourg, where he maintained certain secret relations. With no other support than that of Colonel Vaudrey and a major, gained beforehand to his cause, he paraded the streets of the town, and presented himself at the barracks of the 4th regiment of artillery, where he was received with cries of "Long live the emperor!" He then tried to gain the soldiers of the second barracks, but the officers were not favorable to him, and remained faithful to their duty. The general in command, and the prefect, whose hotel had been surrounded by the insurgent soldiers, made their escape. They caused the arrest of the prince and his followers; Persigny, his most intimate confidant, alone contrived to get away. The attempts at insurrection immediately ceased, and order was restored. The king denied himself the thought of using severity towards a young man, who was haunted by the visions of grandeur associated with his name, and by the conviction that he was destined to retrieve that name. The embarkation of the prince for the United States was resolved upon before the prayers of Queen Hortense were heard, imploring on his behalf the royal clemency. He departed, loaded with tokens of the thoughtful kindness of the monarch, and not without engaging himself never again to set foot on French soil. His adherents were taken before the court at Colmar, and were all acquitted by the jury. More than one of these have reappeared in the history of later years. Providence has impenetrable secrets; the fiasco of Strasbourg prepared the way to the second empire, by making ring once more in the ears of France the name of Napoleon, the power of which on her soul has withstood so many mistakes and so much of suffering.

Insignificant in itself, the attempt of Prince Louis Napoleon

indicated in the minds of the people and in the army a fickleness and a tendency to waver that was disquieting. A slight
insurrection had also taken place in a regiment at Vendôme,
this time to the cry of " Long live the Republic !" The ministers proposed three legal projects, designed to complete the
penal code, in order to prevent the recurrence of similar disorders. At the same time, and by an unfortunate combination
of circumstances, two measures, announced long before—the
one fixing the payment of the dowry of the Queen of the Belgians, the other confirming the endowment to the Duc de
Nemours—required to be presented in the course of the same
session. The Chamber of Deputies had never given proof of
liberality in its relations with King Louis Philippe. They
exaggerated in public the personal fortune of the king; they
attributed to him an avidity assuredly very foreign to his
spirit and his conduct, although the memory of his past dis-
tresses had occasionally left him disturbed as to the future fortune of his children. The projects of endowments were unpopular, while the plans of penal repression were cleverly attacked
by the opposition, the first article presented being rejected.
The government felt itself checked; the public was convinced
of the impotence of the cabinet; and the king inclined towards
a policy of concession and conciliation. After several days of
internal crisis, Guizot and his friends retired, and Molé recon-
stituted the ministry, immediately allowing the unpopular
measures to drop. A general amnesty was announced.
Already, some months previously, the grace of the king had
set free from prison the four ministers of Charles X. A certain
appeasement of passions made itself felt, a little superficial
perhaps, and soon destined to suffer fresh shocks, but it procured for the ministry of Molé some years of calm and of governmental freedom. The marriage of the Duc d'Orleans on the
30th May, 1837, with the grave and intellectual Princess
Hélène of Mecklenburg-Schwerin, who was subsequently to
bear her great sorrows nobly, seemed a pledge of stability, and
was favorably received in public opinion. Some months later,
on the 17th of October, the Princess Marie d'Orleans was mar-
ried to Duke Alexander of Wurtemburg. In her adopted
country she continued her artistic labors, in which she had
shown rare talent, modelling, after her statue of Joan of Arc,
the figures of the two angels which were one day to shelter
with their wings the tomb where she lay beside her brother,
the Duc d'Orleans. The happy issue of the second expedition

to Constantine, and the distinction which the Duc de Nemours gained in the siege, contributed to invest the Molé ministry at its outset with a certain amount of popularity. Several important laws, which had long been in course of preparation, including those respecting the general and municipal councils, and the closing of the gambling-houses, were readily voted by the chambers. The left and the third party supported the amnesty and the policy of conciliation. In the conservative party many of the leaders were dejected and uneasy, but still they supported the policy of the ministry.

Abroad, a short and brilliant expedition, under Admiral Baudin and Prince de Joinville, secured the fort of St. Jean d'Ulloa and the town of Vera Cruz, forcing the Mexican government to sign a treaty of peace, on the 9th of March, 1839, making allowance to France for the injury inflicted on her national interests. The complicated affairs of the small South American republics at the mouth of the Plate, and the injuries done to us by the republic of Haïti, afforded opportunities for skilful and resolute management. At the request of France, Switzerland interdicted its territory to Prince Louis Napoleon, who had returned to Europe on the occasion of his mother's death. The last difficulties of Belgium disappeared before the kindly interposition of the great powers, and the King of Holland agreed to accept the conditions of separation fixed upon in twenty-four articles drawn up by the conference. The citadel and town of Ancona was evacuated on the oft-repeated demand of the Pope, at the moment when the Austrians themselves quitted the Papal territory. The cabinet renounced in Italy the policy of daring interference, liberal, and at the same time conservative, which had been inaugurated by Casimir Périer.

The very persons who had recently opposed Casimir Périer saw with regret the abandonment of his foreign policy. The declarations which Molé made in the chambers against absolute governments offended those governments, without reassuring the liberal party in France. Every day the schism between the ministry and the left manifested itself more clearly, the latter having been sued for its help by the cabinet from the beginning; every day also the ministry unfortunately drew away from that portion of the conservative party which wished to found in order a *régime* of liberty, and to establish amid the powers of the state the preponderance of the Chamber of Deputies. Guizot combined with Thiers and Odilon Barrot against

the cabinet, which neither satisfied the ultra-liberal aspirations
of the first, nor the test of the others for stable authority side
by side with fearless liberty. The coalition was necessarily to
be temporary, like the union which had allowed Molé himself
to supersede the co-operation of Guizot and Duchâtel in order
to get his measure accepted by the Chamber of Deputies. The
present union had the grave disadvantage of presenting to the
country the problem of an alliance which was difficult to understand, and which was opposed to its common sense. It accomplished the dislocation of the great government party,
recently founded for the purpose of re-establishing order after
the revolution of 1830; it drove to the side of Molé that party
formed more recently in a less liberal direction, astonished and
displeased to see its natural leaders temporarily joined to
strange allies.

The dissolution of the chamber, called for in 1838 by Molé,
modified the composition of the assembly, without acting profoundly on the state of parties. The ministry zealously struggled against a certain number of the particular friends of the
doctrinaires. The address of 1839, drawn up by a committee
favorable to the opposition, was skilfully discussed and amended
by the cabinet, which carried it with a majority too weak to
ensure success. A ministerial crisis, and some efforts on the
part of Marshal Soult to constitute a new cabinet, terminated
in confirming Molé in power, and in another dissolution of the
chamber. This time, and in spite of the little favor which the
coalition met with in general among sensible honest men, who
were friends of order, and spectators rather than actors in the
political struggle, the weakness of Molé's situation appeared
undeniable. The majority was still too small to render government possible, and the ministry retiring, the coalition was
immediately placed at the head of the affairs of the country.
The radical vice of its principle soon made itself felt. Guizot
and Odilon Barrot were not able to govern together, as Guizot
and Thiers had done, and were still able to do. The opposition
evinced some natural enough distrust of Guizot and his friends;
it expected the less influential posts to be assigned to them,
and these they declined on account of their personal dignity
and the honor of their cause in the common victory. The
crisis was prolonged, and business suffered in consequence.
The king resolved to form a provisional ministry which wielded
authority for six weeks in the midst of growing excitement.
Supported by the conservatives, Passy was elected president of

the chamber over Odilon Barrot, who had the support of the left. In this disorder of parties and minds the important members of the centre and left centre, who by agreement had separated from their unpopular or incompatible leaders, prepared with great exertion the constitution of a new conciliatory cabinet, when on the 12th of May an insurrection broke out in the most populous quarters of Paris, crowds attacking simultaneously the Hôtel de Ville, the Palais de Justice, and the Prefecture of Police. Vigorous measures of repression put a stop to this frantic attempt, which was inspired by the feebleness and irresolution of the authorities. On the same day the ministry was definitely formed, under the presidency of Marshal Soult; the centre properly so called was represented by Duchâtel, Villemain, and Cunin-Gridaine, while Passy, Dufaure and Teste shared with them the political sway. Thiers was nominated by his friends for the presidency of the chamber, the cabinet having supported Sauzet, who only obtained a majority of seven votes. Meanwhile the political party of liberal order, so often and so seriously shaken, rallied with a dawning of confidence around the cabinet, which was composed of confused and contradictory elements, but which began by securing a victory under its colors.

The internal business of administration and organization, and the movement of commercial and industrial development which began to make itself felt, absorbed public thought more, and occupied the government more than the evident and advancing decadence of the Ottoman Empire, and the covetousness and ambition which that decadence excited in Russia and Egypt. The Porte had determined to make one more vigorous effort, which it believed itself capable of accomplishing under the protection of Russia. On the 21st of April, 1839, the Turkish army passed the Euphrates, for the purpose of attacking that of the pasha, which was commanded by his son Ibrahim. Some days later the European powers convoked a conference at Vienna, and on the request of the two aides-de-camp sent to Egypt and to Constantinople by Marshal Soult, the sultan and the pasha ordered the suspension of hostilities, when it was learned that the two armies had met, and that the Turkish forces had been completely destroyed, on the 21st of June, 1839. The Sultan Mahmoud died on the 30th of June, and a few days later Pasha Achmet-Feruzzi, commander of the Turkish fleet, conducted the whole fleet to Alexandria, in order to deliver it up to Mehemet Ali. The young Sultan Abdul-Medjid evinced an inclination to make larger concessions to the Pasha of Egypt. Such was not, however, the tendency of the great powers, who were desirous of maintaining their influence in eastern affairs. In the fear of finding herself condemned in Europe to a position of troublesome isolation, Russia felt constrained to adhere to the resolutions of the projected conference of Vienna. On the 27th of July the representatives of the five courts assembled at Vienna addressed the following note to the Porte: "The undersigned have received from their respective governments this morning certain instructions, in virtue of which they have the honor to inform the Sublime Porte that harmony on the eastern question is confirmed among the five great powers, and to engage the suspension of all definitive settlement without their concurrence, in consideration of the interest which they take in his affairs."

It was a great deal to say, and a great deal to promise; the cabinets of London and Paris were agreed to maintain the Ottoman Empire, but they were not of one mind regarding the extent of the concessions which were necessary to secure to the Porte the partial submission of its troublesome vassal. Lord Palmerston said to De Bourqueney, "It will be necessary to open at Constantinople and Alexandria a negotiation on the double basis of the constitution of the heredity of Egypt in the family of Mehemet Ali and of the evacuation of Syria by the Egyptian troops." The French government, on the other hand, claimed with emphasis the hereditary possession of Syria for Mehemet Ali. The cause of the pasha was popular in France, where the people had conceived a very exaggerated idea of his forces. Moreover, no one expected to see Russia adopt unconditionally the policy of Lord Palmerston, and the hope still remained that England could be brought to our way of thinking. General Sébastiani, who proceeded to resume his post in London, did not long allow these illusions to exist. He was convinced that the resolution was unalterable in the minds of the ministers of Great Britain; besides, it was suspected that she was at heart favorable to Turkey. The friends of Guizot in the cabinet urged the king to despatch him to London on this difficult mission; he had recently handled the question in the chamber; "Lord Chatham once said, 'I would not discuss with any one who tells me that the maintenance of the Ottoman Empire is not a question of life or death for England.' As for myself, gentlemen, I am less timid; I do not think that for such powers as England and France there may be thus in the distance, and with certainty, any questions of life or death. But Lord Chatham was passionately convinced of the importance of maintaining the Ottoman Empire; and England still thinks so strongly with him that she devotes herself to this cause even with a touch of superstition, in my opinion. She has often shown herself somewhat hostile to the new states which have formed themselves, or which are inclined to form themselves, from the natural dismemberment of the Ottoman Empire. Greece, for example, has not always found her friendly; Egypt still less. I will not enter into an examination of the motives which may have influenced on similar occasions the policy of England. I believe that she is sometimes deceived, that she has sometimes sacrificed the great to the minor policy, the general interest of Great Britain to some secondary interests. The first interest that concerns Great Britain is that Russia shall not dominate in the east."

It was this idea which Guizot was charged to represent in London, when he accepted, in the month of February, 1840, the mission of ambassador. King Louis Philippe had not been favorable to this choice, on which the ministers had insisted unanimously. The new ambassador had hardly arrived at his post, when the cabinet from which he held his powers found itself compelled to retire, in consequence of a new and painful check, suffered for the second time, on the project of endowment in favor of the Duc de Nemours. Thiers was called by the king to the presidency of the new ministry, which from the beginning published its resolution to demand neither electoral reform nor dissolution. Under these conditions of a government which in advance protected itself against its characteristic tendencies towards the left, Guizot believed it to be his duty to remain at his post. " I here occupy the decisive position on the question of war," wrote he to his friends. " It is only here that the policy that would force on war, or would lend itself to that purpose, or to whatever would bring about war, may find a basis. As long as this position is ours we are in a position to forewarn and arrest. It is here that we must and can defend the policy of peace."

Peace was from that time seriously manaced by the growing ill-humor of England and by the illusions of France. Guizot applied himself to calm the one and dissipate the other. He diverted his government from certain intentions which he suspected. " It is possible," he wrote to Thiers on the 17th of March, " that we may return to the policy of waiting, amid endless difficulties, as the outcome of which we foresee in the east the maintenance of the *statu quo ;* but it may be also that events will be precipitated, and that we may soon find ourselves obliged to take a side. If that comes to pass, the alternative in which we shall be placed will be this: either to put ourselves on a footing with England, acting with her in the question of Constantinople, and obtaining from her in the Syrian question some concessions for Mehemet Ali, or to retire from the affair, and leave it to be concluded between the four powers, we in the meantime standing aloof and waiting the course of events. If we do not make an attempt to bring about between France and England an arrangement with which the pasha may be satisfied on the question of Syria, it will be necessary to await the other issue, and to hold ourselves prepared." Some days later he wrote to General Baudrand, aide-de-camp to the king: "I wish much I had the same security that the king has granted to you. I hope that they will do nothing without us, and I work for it; but this is only a hope, and the work is difficult. The English policy is occupied sometimes lightly and very rashly in foreign questions. In this affair, besides, all the Powers except France flatter the inclinations of England, and show themselves ready to do whatever she wishes. We alone, her particular allies, say, no! The others never dream of anything but pleasing; we want to be reasonable at the risk of displeasing. The situation is neither very comfortable nor perfectly certain. We can achieve success by good management and with time. I believe that we would be wrong to confide in ourselves in the matter; it is always necessary to fear a hasty and sudden stroke."

Meantime, and while the situation remained in this serious and delicate state, good services were redoubled between France and England: the French government helped to arbitrate between England and the King of Naples on a commercial question which had failed to become a political one; soon the negotiation of a commercial treaty, and the question of extending the right of search for the abolition of the slave-trade, were to be the objects of diplomatic correspondence. England responded with readiness to the desire manifested by the French ministry to obtain the restitution of the ashes of the Emperor Napoleon. Lord Palmerston wrote on this subject to Lord Granville, his ambassador at Paris: "My Lord, the government of her Majesty having taken into consideration the request of the French government to obtain authorization to transport from St. Helena to France the remains of Napoleon Bonaparte, I request your Excellency to assure M. Thiers that the government of her Majesty will accede with pleasure to this request. The government of her Majesty hope that the promptness of this response will be considered in France as a proof of their desire to efface all traces of those national animosities which, during the life of the emperor, armed against each other the French and English nations. The government of her Majesty is confident that if such sentiments still exist anywhere, they will be buried in the tomb in which the remains of Napoleon are to be laid."

The Minister of the Interior, Rémusat, repeated these words to the Chamber of Deputies when he announced the negotiation and its results. "Henceforth France, and France alone, will possess all that remains of Napoleon. His tomb, like his fame, shall belong to none but his own country. The monarchy of 1830 is the only and legitimate inheritor of all the memories of which France is proud. It was for it—for that monarchy which for the first time has rallied all the forces and conciliated all the aims of the French Revolution, to raise, and to honor without fear, the statue and the tomb of a popular hero. For there is one thing, one only, which dreads not comparison with glory, and that is liberty."

Liberty was still to be more than once menaced by the great name of Napoleon I. and by the influence which it exercised in France. In 1840 the nation, king and people alike, were eager with a generous improvidence to raise a monument anew to him. The most illustrious among those of whom France was proud had already put their hand to the work; Lamartine, and Victor Hugo, as well as Beranger, continued to nourish the new generations from the story of the Napoleonic legend. Other and more able hands were to work in turn at the same task.

The enthusiasm which manifested itself in France on the occasion of the transference of Napoleon's remains did not carry away all minds, and the chamber refused to vote more than a million francs for the cost of the expedition and sepulture. It was then occupied with great domestic projects, the first serious enterprises in railways, a law on the labor of children in factories, and many important questions of commercial administration. The anxiety and interest was not inclined to lessen respecting eastern affairs, which were still as obscure on the spot as in London.

A Turkish plenipotentiary had arrived in London. For the original proposals of Lord Palmerston, assuring to Mehemet Ali the hereditary possession of Egypt, and a title during life to the pashalic of Acre, the representatives of Austria and Prussia—Neumann and Von Bulow—seemed disposed to substitute the relinquishment for life of all Syria, and the hereditary cession of Egypt. At Paris there was hesitation over these overtures. The grand vizier, hostile to the Pasha of Egypt, was dead; Mehemet Ali sent an emissary to Constantinople, charged with direct proposals to the sultan. The cabinet of the Tuileries desired to wait the result of this negotiation, to which it attached some value. On the other hand, Lord Palmerston was resolved to break it off; and he succeeded. An insurrection of the Druses, cleverly fomented by England, broke out against Mehemet Ali. "They will rise to the last man provided they are furnished with arms and ammunition," wrote Wood, the dragoman, to Lord Ponsonby, the ambassador at Constantinople. "There has never, perhaps, been a movement more favorable to the separation of Syria from Egypt, and to the accomplishment of the political views of Lord Palmerston regarding Mehemet Ali."

Guizot remained uneasy respecting the future, but the danger was nearer than he believed. Two drafts of treaties had been officially communicated to him—the one common to the five Powers, and containing the maximum concessions which they could make to France; the other, to be concluded between the four Powers in case of France refusing the first arrangement: they showed her concurrence should be dispensed with. The French ambassador reckoned on a final delay, before the lapse of which he could make a definitive resolution; but Lord Palmerston had decided otherwise. On the 15th of July, without calling afresh for the participation of France, the quadruple treaty was signed in London, to be executed immediately. Orders were already given to have presented to the Pasha of Egypt the resolution taken to impose on him the conditions which he had already peremptorily repelled. Only on the 17th of July, Lord Palmerston communicated to Guizot a memorandum, carefully prepared, full of apologies and flattering expressions towards France, claiming her good services at Alexandria with Mehemet Ali. "The sultan," said he, "will propose in the first place to the pasha to concede to him, always under the title of vassalage, the possession of Egypt hereditarily, and the portion already offered of the pashalic of St. Jean d'Acre, including the fortress, but only during life. He will grant him a period of ten days in order to accept this proposal. Should the pasha refuse, the sultan will make a new proposition, which will not comprehend more than Egypt, always granted hereditarily. If, after a fresh delay of ten days, the pasha still refuses, then the sultan will address himself to the four powers, who undertake towards him, and among themselves, to force his vassal into obedience."

It was probable war at short notice, supported by Europe, against a prince whom we had imprudently covered with our protection; we should find ourselves isolated from Europe, and condemned to a situation at once humiliating and dangerous. The wrath and indignation in Paris were great; the feelings were legitimate, and found expression in Guizot's note to Lord Palmerston in answer to the memorandum. "France," the cabinet said, "has not received in these latter circumstances any positive proposal on which she might give an opinion; it isnot necessary therefore to impute to a refusal that she has not been able to make the determination which England communicates to her in the name doubtless of the four powers."

Lord Palmerston having protested against this phrase, Guizot commented upon it with a grave and impressive dignity. "This phrase surprises you, my Lord; the fact which it expresses has much more astonished the government of the king, and myself as well. When you communicated to me last Friday the memorandum to which I responded, intimating that, unknown to us, without our having either been definitely told or asked anything, a definitive resolution had been taken by the four powers, a convention signed, perhaps execution actually begun, I was profoundly astonished—I must say, hurt. When you come to the end of a negotiation in which we have constantly taken part you owe it to the government of the king to invoke it, and to say to it: 'Since we have not been able hitherto to put ourselves in harmony so as to act together as five powers, we are unable to put off any longer, and we have resolved to act on that basis and by that means. Will you join us? This is all that we desire. If decidedly you do not wish it, we shall be obliged to act as four powers, on the basis and by the means which we have indicated.' That was the natural course. On the contrary, without informing us, while preserving secrecy towards us, you have resolved to act without us. This is not, my Lord, the proper

proceeding for an old and intimate ally, and the government
of the king has every right to take offence at it. The alliance
of France and England has given ten years of peace to Europe; the whig ministry, allow me to say, was born under its
colors, and it has drawn from it during ten years some of its
energy. Canning, if I am not deceived, was your friend and
the leader of your political party. In a great and celebrated
speech he portrayed England as one day taking into her keeping the cave of storms, and possessing herself of the key.
France also has this key, and hers is perhaps the larger. She
has never wished to help herself by its use. Do not render
this policy more difficult and less sure for us. Do not give
serious reasons for, and a redoubled impulse to, the national
passions in France. This is not what you owe to us, what
Europe owes to us, for the moderation and prudence which we
have shown during ten years!"

This was indeed, and in spite of the eager protestations of
Lord Palmerston, the first result of the treaty of the 15th of
July, the effect being to excite outbursts of passion, and of
that warlike feeling which is always easy to awaken in our
minds. The revolutionaries profited immediately by it in
order to advance towards their aim, careless of the fresh em-
barrassments which confronted the country in a moment of
national crisis. Everywhere agitation was stimulated on the
subject of electoral reform, by means of petitions and banquets. Important industrial strikes took place at various
points. At home as well as abroad the attitude of the government continued resolute and composed. Armaments were
being prepared in the meantime; all the soldiers of the classes
of 1836 and 1839 still disengaged were called out, and the fortified places were put into a state of defence. Threatened by
serious dangers, France held herself ready for any event, and
made this known to Europe. Her representatives maintained
their reserve, and were distant and gravely dissatisfied. The
powers were disquieted thereby, but without ceasing to pursue
the resolutions which had offended France. Count Walewski
was charged by Thiers to bear to Mehemet Ali counsels of
moderation and prudence; he urged his futile efforts even at
Constantinople. Lord Palmerston had skilfully succeeded in
explaining his conduct before Parliament and to the public,
which was at first very divided regarding the real nature of
the Eastern question, as well as the diplomatic proceedings of
the government. Henceforth the English feeling was carried

away by party dissensions, which tended to strengthen the
ministry.

Meanwhile events were precipitated in the east, and the
powers seemed to seize the opportunity of discarding in advance all means of pacific solution. The first interval of ten
days had not expired, and already, by order of the government, Commodore Sir Charles Napier began hostilities, by
capturing the Egyptian merchant-ships in the harbor of Beyrout, and by exciting the uprising of the Syrian insurgents.
Twenty years afterwards he himself pronounced upon the
part which he had then played in Syria. "I was ashamed
for my country and for myself," he said in Parliament, on the
17th of August, 1860. "The government had sent me there to
perform a mission; I acquitted myself of it, but against my
will. Under Mehemet Ali, Syria was quiet and peaceable. If
Lord Ponsonby had not sent agents to stir up the population,
it would have been impossible for us with the weak forces at
our disposal to put to flight an army of three or four thousand
men." A few days later this army, under the orders of Ibrahim Pasha, drifted miserably into the hands of a force composed of English, Austrians, Turks, and Albanians, disem-
barked at Beyrout by the Anglo-Austrian fleet. Beyrout
succumbed on the 11th of September, and Sidon on the 21st,
giving up vast supplies of provisions to the victors almost
without resistance. On the 14th of September the sultan, supported by the allied powers, pronounced the deposition of
Mehemet Ali.

In France the astonishment and dismay were great; all
hope of maintaining peace was now at an end. The possession
of Egypt alone had been guaranteed to the pasha; on the
advice of the wisest councillors the ministry resolved to make
a *casus belli* of an attack upon this point, and to continue
warlike preparations, concentrating in the waters of the Isle
d'Hyères the fleet which was then anchored in the neighborhood of Salamine. "If you want to take Egypt from the
pasha," declared Guizot to Lord Palmerston, "the cannon
will decide between us." The attitude was resolute without
being provocative; it was unfortunately too often contradicted by rash words, and by that outburst of revolutionary
passions which had been so long unchained amongst us. In
England as well as in Germany the public feeling responded in
patriotic demonstrations, which were also ardent and inconsiderate. "We are returning to 1831," wrote Guizot on the

13th of October, to the Duc de Broglie, "to the revolutionary spirit, making use of the national power, and urging on war without legitimate motives, and without reasonable chances of success, in the sole hope, and with the sole purpose, of creating revolutions. The question of Syria is not a legitimate case for war. This I hold as undeniable. France, which has not gone to war to liberate Poland from Russia and Italy from Austria, cannot reasonably go to war in order that Syria may be held by the pasha and not by the sultan. No other question has hitherto been raised in principle by the convention of 15th July. In fact, by its execution no great French interest is attacked. Enterprise in the east may bring about something different from what is aimed at: questions may be born there, events may arise to which France could not remain indifferent. It is a question of arming, of holding herself ready; it is not a reason for herself raising in the east events and questions still more grave, and which are not born naturally."

At home the natural results of the warlike agitation found expression in revolutionary agitation; a strange attempt happened which serves to show its effects on excited spirits ruled by a fixed idea. On the 6th of August, at two in the morning, a small English packet-boat, the *City of Edinburgh* landed on the French coast, at Vimereux, near Boulogne, Prince Louis Napoleon, accompanied by some accomplices, who had either come like him from England or joined him on the shore. For many months, in spite of the sentiments of gratitude which he had formerly testified towards the king, the prince had labored to gain over officers in various regiments occupying the northern departments. He had purchased the *Commerce*, and its principal editor, Maugin, a passionate Jacobin in the Chamber of Deputies, too corrupt to refuse the means of making money. They had tried to spread the conviction that the Bonapartist pretenders had experienced kindness at the hands of several great powers. On embarking in the Thames, Louis Napoleon announced to his companions the object of his enterprise. "We proceed to France," he said. "There we shall find powerful and devoted friends. The only obstacle to victory is at Boulogne; once that point is carried, our success is sure. Numerous auxiliaries await us; and if I am seconded as they have promised me, as sure as the sun shines on us, in a few days we shall be in Paris, and history will say that it was with a handful of brave men such as you that I accomplished this great and glorious enterprise."

Three accomplices only awaited the prince on the coast; one of these, Aladenise, a young lieutenant of the 42nd regiment of the line, reckoned to carry along with him all his comrades. They marched on Boulogne, to which the packet-boat had just returned. The barracks were naturally the first object of attention. The lieutenant preceded the conspirators, announcing to the assembled soldiers the downfall of King Louis Philippe, as it had been decreed by Prince Louis in a proclamation which he had brought from England; they were then chosen to march on Paris in order to re-establish the empire. Surprised, and excited by a speech by Louis Napoleon, the soldiers cried "Long live the emperor!" But some officers had already hastened to the spot; the captain, Colonel Puygelier, with sword in hand, struggled against the conspirators by whom he was surrounded. "Prince Louis or not!" exclaimed the captain, "I only see in you a conspirator. Clear the barracks!" The soldiers advanced in order to protect him in the struggle, which was prolonged. The brave officer had just exclaimed, "Help, grenadiers!" when unfortunately a bullet from a pistol which the prince held struck a soldier in the neck very near where the captain was standing. Disconcerted by this accident, the insurgents retired in disorder, addressing themselves on their route to the people, and directing their course to the magazines of arms in the upper town. The gate of the arsenal resisted their efforts; the national guard began to assemble; the small force took in all haste the direction of the shore, casting themselves pell-mell into the long-boat of the packet. Pursued, summoned to stop, the victims of some stray shots, they saw their hopes betrayed by the waves as well as by man; the boat capsized, and those on board had some difficulty in saving their lives. Perhaps they believed themselves threatened by the rigors of a government which they had twice gratuitously offended. Honest people reproached King Louis Philippe with the generous attitude which he had maintained towards him whom they then called an adventurer, but whom, by the strangest coincidence, they were one day to call upon to reign over France. Condemned by the Court of Peers to perpetual confinement, and imprisoned within the walls of Ham, from which he was to escape at the end of six years, Prince Louis acknowledged subsequently the justice of his sentence. Finding himself, during a tour as President of the Republic, under the walls of the fortress which had held him a prisoner (22nd July, 1849), he expressed surprise that he had not been impeached for twice violating the laws of his country. " To-day, when elected by all France, I have become the legitimate head of this great nation, I shall not glorify myself for a captivity which had for its cause an attack upon a regularly constituted government. When one has seen how the most just revolutions draw evils in their train, one understands fully the audacity of having wished to take on one's self the terrible responsibility of a change. I do not therefore compassionate myself for having expiated here by an imprisonment of six years my temerity against the laws and against my country."

The attempt of Prince Louis Napoleon excited more curiosity and raillery than apprehension. A fresh outrage against the king, committed by a miserable fellow named Darmès, on the 15th of October, 1840, caused more uneasiness, and seemed to indicate a growing state of revolutionary agitation. The government suffered insensibly from the contagion of restlessness. Anxious as it was, it became more and more warlike. Thiers proposed a fine plan for the fortification of Paris; he claimed the augmentation of the effective army; and the chambers were convoked to respond to these wants. The cabinet presented to the king a plan for the speech from the crown; its language was firm and dignified, but it was conceived in the prospect of war, and for the purpose of demanding from the country the means of putting it in a state of preparation. The king declined to place himself in such jeopardy. He believed that peace was possible and desirable. From the heart even of the cabinet he received advice to seek elsewhere for other ministers, "Discharge us, sire," said Cousin, "we drive you to war." For the second time in a month the cabinet offered its resignation, which was accepted by the king. Guizot was still in London, ready to take part in the session of the chambers; the king and Thiers wrote to him at the same time, pressing him to return to Paris. A few days later, on the 29th of October, 1840, he formed, under the presidency of Soult, and as minister of foreign affairs, the last cabinet which was for many years to govern France under the constitutional monarchy by the noble and peaceable alliance of liberty and authority.

It was a heavy burden which the new councillors had accepted from the crown in a situation of which they knew all the dangers. "Why has the cabinet of 29th October taken the place of that of the 1st of March?" said Thiers in the discussion of the address. "Because the cabinet of the 1st of March thought that in a certain case it was necessary to make war. Why has the cabinet of the 29th of October come? It has come with certain peace." Guizot at once replied, "The honorable gentleman has only uttered a moiety of the truth; under the ministry of 1st March war was certain." The preparations for war had not ceased, and the attitude of France remained resolute in its isolation. The question of the fortifications of Paris was brought before the chambers in agreement with Thiers; and in spite of the doubts of the preservers of peace at any price, and in spite of the secret discontent of the abettors of disorder, the law was voted, and the great work commenced. The Duke of Wellington said on this subject to Guizot: "Your fortifications of Paris have closed that era of wars of invasion and of rapid marching on capitals which Napoleon opened. They have almost done for you what the ocean does for us. If the sovereigns of Europe believe me, they will all do as much. I know not whether wars will be thus rendered shorter or less murderous, but they will infallibly be less revolutionary. You have rendered by this example a great service to the security of nations and the order of Europe." Even at the present time, after a double and grievous experience—of enemies besieging the capital of France with success, and of a triumphant insurrection retaining it for more than two months against the efforts of the regular government—the words of the Duke of Wellington remain true, and have been justified by events. The resistance of France during the war of 1870 and 1871 concentrated almost entirely in Paris; only the fortifications of Paris rendered that resistance possible.

Meanwhile the change of the French ministry weighed on the diplomatic deliberations. It was known in Europe that the new ministry was favorable to peace, without relaxing anything of the quiet dignity of its attitude. The German powers began then to manifest the desire of putting an end to a situtation which with good reason disquieted peaceable spirits. Despite the deposition pronounced by the sultan against Mehemet Ali, it was the general opinion that the heredity of Egypt had been guaranteed to the pasha on certain conditions which he could still execute. On the spontaneous advice of Sir Charles Napier, Mehemet Ali sent back to Constantinople, the Turkish fleet which still remained in his harbors, and ordered the evacuation of Syria by his troops.

Henceforth, the treaty of the 15th of July was executed, and
it was left to the four powers to overcome the tardiness and
malice of the Porte. They employed themselves actively in
this, not without meeting obstacles on the part of Mehemet
Ali as well as on that of Lord Ponsonby. At the same time,
and in order to signalize the return of France into the European concert, a special convention, accepted by all the
powers, ruled the question of the closing of the Straits in the
Black Sea. The two treaties were signed on the 13th of July,
1841. Eventually, and in spite of the errors, the faults, and
the disquieting griefs which had for France marked the great
eastern question, the European peace had been maintained.
In the midst of peace the armaments of precaution raised by
France in 1840 had been maintained also; the fortifications of
Paris arose; and Europe, feeling the void which the absence
of France made in her councils, showed herself eager to make
her return to her place. France did not return till Europe
asked her, after having caused the Porte to make the concessions claimed by the pasha, while declaring that the treaty of
15th July, 1840, was finally extinguished. Mehemet Ali,
driven from Syria, threatened even in Egypt, was established
hereditarily and under equitable conditions, not on account
of his own forces, but in consideration of France, and in the
firm desire of maintaining peace in Europe. By the convention of 13th July, 1841, the Porte found herself withdrawn
from the exclusive protection of Russia, and placed in the
sphere of the general interests, and of the common deliberations of Europe, while this sensible and wary policy removed
from her the grave dangers which had so long menaced her.

The re-establishment of good relations with England soon
manifested itself with heartiness. The ministry of Lord
Palmerston had been replaced by that of Sir Robert Peel and
Lord Aberdeen, both of whom were animated towards France
with kindly intentions. The difficult negotiations relative to
the repression of the slave-trade had been renewed with the
new cabinet; public opinion in France claimed the abolition of
the reciprocal right of search among the vessels suspected of
trading. Prolonged and lively discussions took place in the
chambers. Immediately after these discussions, and while
the question was still pending, Queen Victoria came to pay to
King Louis Philippe, at the Château d'Eu, a visit of friendship and good neighborliness, which the king returned to her
some weeks later at Windsor (2nd September, and 7th October,

1844). At the beginning of this exchange of royal courtesies, the Duc de Broglie, entrusted with carrying out in London the negotiation with reference to the right of search, inaugurated, by mutual arrangement with the English commissioners, a new system of watching and repressing the slave-traffic. And, on the successful result of a transaction which had been conducted on both sides with dignified sincerity, Broglie was able to say to Lord Aberdeen: "I hope, my Lord, that on this occasion, as on many others, it will be your good fortune to say to your opponents what the Lacedemonian did to the Athenian, 'What thou sayest, that I do.' It is to you that the definitive overthrow of the trade in negroes is due."

This good understanding between France and England, so long disturbed, so necessary to the peace of Europe, had to resist all the difficulties and daily jealousies of diplomacy. The two governments acted together upon the Porte in favor of the Christians of Lebanon; and Lord Aberdeen's instructions to Sir Edward Lyons at Athens prescribed the same moderation as Guizot invariably recommended to Piscatory, who was then our minister in Greece, powerful and influential in the midst of the difficulties of a government which was new, and therefore much exposed to the suspicions of the English minister. In Spain nothing could destroy that ancient rivalry between the two nations which was produced by remote recollections, as well as recent struggles. A dread of the ambitious designs and preponderance of France in Spain greatly and permanently influenced, and still influences, the mind of England. The revolutions which continued to agitate Spain, the fall of Queen Christina as regent, and elevation of General Espartero to power, conferred for a short time upon the English agents a predominating influence, which was moderated in its effects by the good sense and justice of the cabinet in London. The same moderation, mixed with some display of ill-temper, signalized Lord Aberdeen's attitude on the occasion of the great commercial treaties concluded in 1843 and 1845 between France and Belgium. In the distant seas no difficulty was raised by the establishment of our stations in the Gulf of Guinea, and on the islands Mayotte and Nossi-Bé on the east coast of Africa. France was still hindered in her progress by the prejudice and distrust of England, though certain of her earnest good-will and her unswerving loyalty. Happy times, when the politicians of both countries did not speak all they thought, but never spoke anything but the truth!

The same harmony did not everywhere reign in our diplomatic relations. The Emperor Nicholas persisted in his systematic reserve towards King Louis Philippe. On the 1st of January, 1842, Count Pahlen, the Russian ambassador, when about to become senior member of the diplomatic body, whose duty was to pay their respects to the king, was recalled by the emperor, and set out for St. Petersburg. The French ambassador in Russia, M. Barante, was already in Paris, but the French legation were indisposed on St. Nicholas' day, and did not appear at the emperor's reception. Neither of the two ambassadors returned to his post.

It was from abroad that in 1840, when the new cabinet was summoned, the most serious dangers and urgent difficulties came upon us, but a resolute and wise policy kept us clear of their effects or weakened their power. With reference to home affairs, France seemed stronger, and every day more prosperous. Immediately after Guizot and his friends came to power, it was their duty to render to the emperor that homage of funeral rites which was then universally considered the last of his triumphs. On the 2nd December, 1840, Prince Joinville landed at Cherbourg, bringing back from St. Helena Napoleon's remains; and the chaplain of the hospital gave expression to the general sentiment, when, with the deepest emotion, he said to the prince, " Will your royal highness allow a ploughman's son, who has become a navy chaplain, to offer his respectful homage to the son of his king? You will perhaps pardon me for joining my feeble voice to the great voice of France, and anticipating the judgment which posterity will form of your expedition to St. Helena, when engraving your name beside that of the king, your august father, on the tomb of the great man?"

The same confiding and sympathetic generosity which had sent so far the son of the king to bring back the Emperor Napoleon's remains signalized the whole of the ceremonial of the 15th December, when King Louis Philippe, accompanied by all his family and court, received the funeral procession at the Invalides. The popular emotion and curiosity remained quite peaceful, in spite of some attempts to produce disorder. A great memory and spectacle had attracted the multitude, and nothing more. "The friends of the *régime* of liberty and peace were justified in believing that the imperial *régime* was

entirely contained in the emperor's tomb. No fault of theirs
led to the events which revealed it. It is not because King
Louis Philippe and his councillors again raised Napoleon's
statue, and brought back his coffin from St. Helena, that the
name of Napoleon had such power amid the social disturbances
of 1848. The monarchy of 1830 would not have gained a day
by showing itself jealous and suspicious, eager to crush all
recollections of the empire. And in such subordinate attempts
it would have lost the glory of the liberty which it respected,
and the generosity which it displayed towards its enemies—a
glory which remains to it after its disasters, and which is also
a power that death cannot injure." *

In their noble efforts to secure that difficult glory for their
country, the leaders of the liberal-conservative party frequently met with painful deceptions and serious difficulties.
The passionate manifestations of revolutionary excitement
were succeeded by revolutionary theories, which secretly undermined amongst the masses those remains of moral and
religious principles which had survived the protracted shocks
in our recent history, or were slowly reappearing with peace
and order. The St. Simonians had recently undertaken to
renew society by their principles; a famous trial exposed and
combated their tendencies, and the society was dissolved; and
the many distinguished men who had yielded to the attractions
of Père Enfantin's theories, resumed, like him, the duties of
practical life. Victor Considérant and Fourier in their turn
had their dreams of overthrowing or regenerating the social
state. Auguste Comte reduced to a philosophy the lower instincts of human nature, and in the name of positivism explained away our consoling hopes of eternity. The results of
those theories acted vaguely upon many minds who believed
themselves free from their influence. The revolt against
divine and higher order necessarily begat a revolt against
human and material order, as was daily proved by the abuses
of the liberty of the press. The government felt this, and
were fully conscious of the present and future danger; they
allowed the institution full liberty of action, while endeavoring
to prevent or repress abuses. Several press trials resulted, on
the part of the juries, in dangerous acquittals. A new and
utterly abominable attempt was made upon the life of the Duc
d'Aumale, colonel of the 17th regiment of light infantry, as he

entered Paris at the head of his troops, with his brothers the
Dukes of Orleans and Nemours, who had gone to meet him.
The horse of the officer beside the prince received the ball intended for the latter, and fell dead instantly. The people were
deeply moved. Quénisset, the assassin, was not an isolated
fanatic; there was a clearly proved conspiracy. The Peers'
Court shared in the excitement, and the debates were brilliantly conducted by Hébert, who was formerly for several
years a member of the Chamber of Deputies, and had just
been raised to the post of procureur-general at the royal
court, to which new position he was called till the king
should entrust him with the difficult functions of keeper of
the seals.

Whilst the legal authorities of the country labored to defend
its peace, so constantly menaced, the chambers discussed and
adopted the more important measures of administrative and
social progress. A law referring to the work of children in
manufactories, the works necessary for the development of
national defence, the navy, and roads and bridges, the network of the principal lines of railway, were all voted in the
session 1841–42. After a discussion marked by much keen
discussion, the Chamber of Deputies rejected Ganneron's proposal to exclude official men from the Assembly, as well as
that of Ducos on electoral reform. The mind of the government, in accordance with the real want of the country, was in
favor of the consolidation of the gains of liberty, so dearly
bought, and not in favor of new and dangerous enterprises.
"Be careful," said Guizot, "not to take up all the questions
they may be pleased to raise, or any business they may ask
you to enter upon. Do not so easily undertake whatever
burdens the first comer may fancy to lay on your shoulders,
when the burden which we must bear is already so heavy.
Decide the necessary questions, perform well the duties which
fall to be performed in due course, rejecting those which are
wantonly and unnecessarily thrown in your way."

The general elections of 1842 had just given the sanction of
the country to that firm and prudent policy, when a great
misfortune, sent directly by the hand of God, suddenly struck
the royal family and France. All could not say, as did Queen
Marie-Amélie, when prostrate in her pious grief, "My God! it
is not too much, but it is a great deal!" All felt like the
mother, that it was a great deal, and that the new foundations
of the national repose were shaken, when, on the 13th July,

1842, the Duc d'Orleans was thrown from his carriage, only to survive a few minutes. Young, handsome, and of the most attractive and amiable disposition, and well qualified to address and please the people, the Duc d'Orleans by degrees had learned the lessons of wise government. He had become the firm stay of the throne, and a source of consoling hope, at the moment when an untimely death removed him from his family and country. "I have no information to give you," wrote Guizot to all the French representatives at the principal foreign courts; "the details of our misfortune are known everywhere. I was for three hours in that wretched room, opposite that prince as he was dying on a mattress, his father, mother, brothers, and sisters on their knees around him, holding their breaths to hear him breathe, keeping back everybody that a little fresh air might reach him. I saw him die. I saw the king and queen kiss their dead son. As we left the house, with the prince's body on a litter, and the king and queen on foot behind him, a long-continued shout of "Long live the king!" burst from the crowd, composed of people of the lower orders who had assembled round the house. I have just seen the king. Yesterday, during that agony, he showed admirable courage, presence of mind, and self-possession. To-day he is tired, and gives way more than yesterday to sorrow, but with a physical and moral strength that surpasses everything. We have hastened the assembly of the chambers by a week, and they will now meet on the 26th, the obsequies taking place only a few days after. Everything is, and will be, perfectly quiet. Good order is indispensable, and everybody feels it. I hope also that it will be continued, and produce its proper result."

"In France the king never dies," said the Duc de Broglie to the House of Peers, on the 27th August, 1842. "An excellent point in monarchical government is, that the supreme authority never undergoes any interruption, that the supremacy is never disputed; that between two reigns there cannot even be a thought of detecting the least interval of delay or hesitation. It is by that means especially that this government rules the minds of men, and restrains their ambitions. The monarchy is the empire of right, order, and law. Everything must be regulated in the monarchy; everything which can be reasonably foreseen must be so; nothing ought to be left by choice or forgetfulness to the uncertainty of events. Under such a government, in fact, the monarchy is the support of the State;

when that support begins to fail everything falls to pieces; everything is shaken as soon as it appears to totter. This we have recently had experience of. At the moment when the hand of God weighed upon us—when that infinite Wisdom whose ways are not as our ways, struck the nation in the person of the first-born of the royal house, and reaped our dearest hope in full flower, all hearts felt frozen with secret terror. Public anxiety manifested itself through the accents of grief; there was uneasiness on every brow, as well as tears in every eye. All mentally considered how many years still separate the heir of the throne from the age when he can with a firm hand seize the sceptre of his grandfather and the sword of his father. All asked themselves what should in the meantime happen if the days of the king were not numbered according to his people's prayers and the State's wants. All sought for an answer in the charter, and regretted its silence."

It was to supply this omission in the charter, and calm the well-founded anxiety of the country, that the chambers were summoned to legislate regarding the regency. "The law as proposed is very simple," wrote Guizot to the diplomatic agents. "It is an application to the regency of the essential principles of our constitutional monarchy—heredity, the Salic law, the unity and inviolability of the royal power. The guard and tutelage of the king in his minority are entrusted to his mother and grandmother. The proposal does not aim at the anticipating or providing for all imaginable hypotheses or possible chances. It decides the questions, and provides for the necessities, imposed upon us by present circumstances."

The discussion in the chambers was more ambitious and theoretical than were the deliberations in the ministerial council. All the characteristics of the different systems of regency were laid down, with their respective advantages and inconveniences. The opposition defended the principle of an elective regency—in practical application, a female regency; but Thiers on this point abandoned his friends, and eloquently spoke on behalf of the ministerial proposal. The extreme left, through Ledru-Rollin as their mouthpiece, demanded an appeal to the people, who, they said, were the only really constituent power. Guizot and Thiers were of one mind in rejecting this theory. "The constitutional government is the sovereignty of society organized," said the former. "Beyond that, there is only the social mass, moving about at hap-hazard, struggling with the chances of revolution. Revolutions are not organized; they have not assigned to them a place and legal procedure in the course of the affairs of nations. No human power governs such events; they belong to a greater master. God alone disposes of them; and when they break out God makes use of the most various instruments to reconstitute shaken society. In the course of my life I have seen three constituent powers; in the year VIII., Napoleon; in 1814, Louis XVIII.; in 1830, the Chamber of Deputies. This is the real and actual state of matters. All that you talk about— those votes, voting-papers, open registers, appeals to the people —all that is fiction, imagination, and pretence."

"I do not believe in the constituent power," said Thiers. "It did exist, I know, at different epochs in our history; but allow me to tell you that if it was the real sovereign, if it was above the constituted powers, it would, nevertheless, have had a wretched part to play by itself. In fact, it was in the French assemblies in the wake of the factions; and under the consulate, and under the empire, at the service of a great man. It then assumed the form of a conservative senate, who, on a signal given by a man who made everything bend under the ascendancy of his genius, made all the constitutions which he asked of them. Under the restoration it took another form. It concealed itself under Article XIV. of the Charter: it was the power of conceding the charter, and modifying it. Those were the different parts played by the constituent power for the last fifty years. Do not say it is the glory of our history, for the victories of Zurich, Marengo, and Austerlitz have nothing in common with those wretched constitutional comedies. I therefore have no respect for the constituent power."

Thus defended by most lofty and powerful arguments, the law was passed by a great majority in both chambers. The Duke of Nemours, who was respected and esteemed by all, was appointed to exercise, in case of necessity, the powers of that temporary monarchy which is called the regency; and the bereaved Duchess of Orleans bravely undertook the charge and education of her two sons, Louis Philippe, Count of Paris, born 24th August, 1838, and Robert, Duke of Chartres, born 1st November, 1840. She afterwards nobly prepared them for a future more sad and troubled than could then be anticipated.

The government also resumed their course, really weakened, though in the long vistas of the future apparently strengthened by the harmony of thought and feeling which was manifested immediately after the catastrophe. Affairs of great complexity and importance were now in preparation, which were exaggerated by the agitations of parliamentary rule, and produced very serious results on the minds of the people. Afar off, in the regions of the Pacific Ocean, the storms were gradually gathering which were soon to burst upon London and Paris, in the chambers and the diplomatic communications of both nations. All was the natural result of events which appeared unimportant.

French sailors had long felt the want of finding in the southern seas a landmark and secure refuge under the national flag. In 1844 this want seemed to be met by an establishment on the Marquesas Islands, made by the advice of Admiral Petit-Thouars, who had just returned from those countries, and was now appointed to take possession in the name of France. The ambition of the brave sailor was not limited by these precise instructions; he thought he might extend our protectorate as far as the Society Islands, and more particularly Tahiti. The native queen, Pomare, afraid and anxious, unresistingly accepted a rule which was speciously disguised, and the French flag floated over Tahiti, as well as the Marquesas.

No political power had till then taken possession of the Society Islands, and our occupation was regular. The religious power, however, of some English missionaries had been there in exercise alone, with a devotion which was at first attended with danger, but afterwards uninterrupted and powerful. At the thought of a possible invasion of apostles from another Christian communion, the convictions and jealousy of the English missionaries quickly took alarm. Mutual susceptibilities led to troublesome procedure. The influence of the English missionaries was naturally great; and Admiral Petit-Thouars believed that the interests and dignity of France were injured by the action of Pritchard, the English missionary-consul, as well as by the conduct which he had suggested to Queen Pomare. In 1843, on returning to those countries after a long absence, the admiral declared the sovereign of the island had forfeited her rights, on account of the infraction of a treaty voluntarily concluded with France. He then boldly took possession of the Society Islands, without, at first, any resistance.

When in February, 1844, this distant news reached Paris, the government considered the admiral's action violent and

irregular, and at once disavowed it by restoring our simple
protectorate, in spite of the excitement and indignation of the
opposition, who charged the ministers with a cowardly complaisance towards England.   Meanwhile the anger of the
Tahitians and uneasiness of the English missionaries had
borne their fruits.   A sedition broke out in the Society Islands,
which was firmly and prudently repressed by Admiral Bruat,
recently appointed governor of our possessions in Oceania.
His subordinates, however, were not so moderate; and, on the
occasion of an attack on a French sailor, Commandant d'Au-
bigny ordered Mr. Pritchard to be arrested and imprisoned,
and declared Papeiti, the capital, to be in a state of siege.   Admiral Bruat set at liberty the former consular agent, just appointed by Lord Aberdeen to the Friendly Isles, and placed
him on board a small English vessel, which took him away.
The missionaries gladly assisted our governor in his efforts to
appease the rising of the natives, though the struggle at Tahiti
still lasted for some time.   It broke out also in London on a
question put to Sir Robert Peel in the House of Commons,
when the irritation of the ministry was clearly shown from
his reply.   The resulting negotiations were long and intricate.
England thought her national honor was wounded; and anger
was stirred up by religious prejudices.   The good sense and
friendly intentions of the ministers on both sides, who had
been specially appointed to treat the affair, succeeded in avoiding complications it might have involved.   England agreed to
acknowledge the French protectorate of Tahiti, without protesting against the expulsion of Mr. Pritchard, only asking on
his behalf a moderate indemnity for the losses he had undergone.

In his speech from the throne, at the opening of the session
1845, King Louis Philippe responded to the sentiments expressed by the Queen of England at the prorogation of Parliament: "My government," said he, "took part with that of
the Queen of Great Britain in discussions which might have
occasioned a doubt lest the relations between the two States
were altered.   A mutual feeling of good will and equity has
maintained between France and England that happy harmony which is a guarantee for the peace of the world."

In Paris there was an extremely keen discussion upon the
paragraph of the address which approved of the conduct of
the ministry.   Both in France and England public opinion
was excited.   The concessions strictly indispensable to the

peace of the world seemed enormous, and humiliating to the
pride of our country. It was the first time for four years that
the parliamentary opposition felt itself borne by a current adverse to the ministerial policy, and they lost no time in
taking advantage of it. The government boldly accepted the
challenge. "I thank the commission for the frankness of
their adhesion," said Guizot. "We are convinced that our
four years' policy has been sound, honorable, advantageous to
the country, suited to its interests, and morally great. But
such a policy is difficult, very difficult: it has many prejudices, passions and obstacles to surmount on these benches,
beyond these benches, in public, everywhere—great and small
obstacles. To succeed, it requires the well-defined and steady
assistance of the great powers of the State. If that assistance,
I do not say entirely fails us, but is not so steadfast that that
policy can be continued with success, we should not remain in
charge of it. We should not allow what we consider a good
policy to be disfigured, enervated, and degraded in our hands,
or that it should become common-place by weakness. All that
we ask for is, that the decision be perfectly clear and intelli-
gible to every one. Whatever it is, the cabinet will be glad of it."

The discussion rallied several hesitating minds, but disturbed others who were already influenced by stupid or mis-
leading reports in some of the newspapers. The majority of
the chamber approved of the conduct of the cabinet, but it
was seriously reduced in number, 213 having voted for the
paragraph, against 205. The cabinet resolved to resign.

It was an impressive scene, not easily forgot by those present, the excitement suddenly pervading the Chamber of Deputies on the comparative check of the ministry and the news
of their proposed resignation. Two hundred and seventeen
conservative deputies, in solemn assembly, resolved to make a
formal request to their parliamentary chiefs not to abandon
the helm of government at such a moment. Touched and
strengthened by this sympathy and confidence, the ministers
again accepted the burden. The deserters returned to the
flag; and the government soon found a new occasion of showing their independence of action with regard to foreign powers. Amongst the more ignorant classes, the conservative
deputies who had supported the cabinet through that formidable crisis received and kept the name of "Pritchardists," as
an insulting memorial of a silly and groundless public irritation.

The confidence and sympathy as well as the spirit of justice and moderation of the French and English governments could alone produce a peaceful result from a puerile quarrel, aggravated and increased by the difficulties inherent to parliamentary *régime*. The good intentions of the English minister were at almost the same moment put to another test. The Duc de Bordeaux had left the peaceful abode where he had grown up in exile with his grandfather and uncle, his early education being piously directed by the dauphin. He undertook several voyages, first in Germany, and without any protest on the part of the French government, no political character being attached to the courtesy naturally paid by the sovereigns to an exiled prince. When the duke seemed about to direct his steps towards England, the attitude of the legitimists in France became aggressive. They declared their intention of making a brilliant gathering round the prince. Queen Victoria showed her desire to remain a stranger to any manifestation, and not to receive the illustrious traveller; and the French government expressed a similar opinion. The Duc de Bordeaux came to London in November, 1843, and lived there several weeks, receiving many people at Belgrave Square, and noisily hailed as king by several thoughtless persons; but the Queen did not receive him, and her government referred in severe terms to facts which they could not prevent. The prince left London, but the agitation caused in France by the provoking conduct of the legitimists soon came to a head. During the discussion on the address at the opening of the session of 1844, the commission used the phrase "the public conscience branded by criminal manifestations." The expression was harsh and awkward, and went too far. The stiff and somewhat embarrassed defence and protest of the legitimists produced no great result; but the left took advantage of the attack, and some violent scenes took place in the chamber, Guizot being the principal object of attack. Without approving entirely of the address drawn up by the commission, the government supported it loyally and bravely. The paragraph was voted by a large majority; and the deputies who had visited the Duc de Bordeaux in Belgrave Square got the name of "the branded," as the conservative deputies that of the "Pritchardists." Thus were embittered the internal animosities, which were soon to aggravate the political situation, and deliver France up to revolution and absolute power. "You are trying to govern against the head and the tail," said

Royer-Collard formerly to Guizot; "it is too difficult an undertaking, and you will not succeed."

However faithful and reasonable the English minister proved himself more than once in our regard and in the European complications and agitations, he frequently showed a personal impatience and suspicion when acted upon by the national prejudices. The English had always shown interest in our Algerian settlements, and the extension of our power in the north of Africa. Since Marshal Bugeaud succeeded to Marshal Vallée as governor of Algeria (December, 1840), such fears were redoubled. Bold and determined, passionately engrossed in the work he had undertaken and the means of accomplishing it, Bugeaud ardently strove to realize his ideas as to our African settlements, the complete conquest of the Arabs, and the system of military colonization. His convictions and ideas being generally well-founded, if sometimes exaggerated, he expressed them with the frankness of a soldier of honor and the courage of a good citizen. As Governor of Algeria, however, he had faults which naturally flowed from those qualities. His zeal and spirit of initiative frequently urged him to speak and act too quickly. His speeches to the chamber and his pamphlets sometimes offended and embarrassed Marshal Soult in Paris. His success in Algeria was undoubted, and he proceeded to carry his success further. In the spring of 1844, Abd-el-Kader was pursued and beaten over the whole interior of Algeria, most of the tribes, now decimated and discouraged, having abandoned him, or only supporting him secretly and with hesitation. The surprise and capture of Smalah, on the 16th May, 1843, by the Duc d'Aumale, was a serious blow to his prestige even among the Arabs. Our repeated expeditions into the least accessible parts of the regency, from the defiles of Jurjura to the frontiers of the great desert, and the permanent occupation of Biskra and several other important points, spread abroad everywhere the conviction of our superior strength, and our resolution to establish our empire on a firm basis. It might be said that the conquest was complete; but Abd-el-Kader was one of those who never give up hope or the struggle. He took a position on the west of the province of Oran, on the doubtful frontier of Morocco, and thence pursued or recommenced the war incessantly. Sometimes, with his roving bands he made sudden raids upon the regency; sometimes he inflamed the natural fanaticism of the Moorish population, and brought them with him against us, being always sure of a refuge with them. He had great influence over the Emperor Abd-el-Rhamman himself, at one time getting him to share in his Mohammedan antipathies, at another terrifying him with accounts of us or of his own projects. He stirred up between that prince and us a dispute as to the possession of certain territories between the course of the Tafna and the frontier of Morocco. On the 30th May, 1844, a numerous body of Moorish horse invaded our soil, and came ostentatiously to attack General Lamoricière, in his camp at Lalla Maghrania, two leagues from the frontier. The explanations demanded by Marshal Bugeaud from the chiefs being unsatisfactory, and the fanatical enthusiasm of the Mohammedans becoming more and more excited, the government ordered that compensation should be insisted upon by arms; and the Prince de Joinville was at the same time placed in command of a squadron on the coast of Morocco. This caused in London much excitement, and a political anxiety partly due to commercial interests. England had much communication with Algiers, and the port of Tangiers supplied Gibraltar with most of its resources. Men were alarmed at the thought of a French conquest. Guizot lost no time in reassuring Lord Aberdeen, who in his turn used all endeavors to act diplomatically upon the Emperor of Morocco. His action remaining unsuccessful, Bugeaud entered the Moorish territory with 10,000 men, and on the 19th August, at Isly, gained an easy victory over 25,000 enemies assembled against him. The marshal took possession of their camp, artillery, colors, and all their baggage. At sea, on the 15th, Prince Joinville bombarded, at the northern extremity of Morocco, Mogador, Abd-el-Rhamman's favorite town, took possession of the small island guarding the entrance to the harbor, and stationed there a garrison of 500 men. Thus in five days the war was finished, before the eyes of an English squadron, who were following at a distance the movements of ours. The news of our two victories increased the English dissatisfaction: the government took this suspicious distrust into consideration when imposing upon the emperor their conditions of peace, which he had much difficulty in agreeing to. Abd-el-Kader was to be expelled from the territory of Morocco, and henceforward deprived of the assistance which had been granted him. An exact limit was to be assigned to the territories of Algeria and Morocco; "beyond, nothing is known exactly," said the old Turkish generals shortly before, "it is the country of guns."

Guns lost their dominion when, on the 18th March, 1845, the treaty between France and the Emperor of Morocco was signed. Abd-el-Kader, nevertheless, still continued to infest our frontiers, and frequently made sudden attempts to surprise our soldiers, assisted by a wide-spread conspiracy of the Arabian chiefs. One of the insurrections in the Dahra tribes induced a struggle with a tribe till then unsubdued; and on the Mohammedans taking refuge in a cave when pursued by Colonel Pelissier, he summoned them several times to come forth, promising them their liberty if they delivered up their arms and horses. The Arabs refusing, the colonel had bun dles of wood heaped up at the entrance of the cavern, and threatened to set fire to them. The Arabs fired upon our soldiers from within the cavern; the flames rose, and most of the obstinate wretches perished, choked by the smoke. In this deplorable alternative of the necessities of war, which put in the balance humanity towards the enemy and the safety of the soldiers whom he was commanding, Colonel Pelissier (after, Marshal Duc de Malakoff) acted as Ludlow did in Ireland against the peasants in revolt, as Napoleon did at Auster- litz against the Russian battalions when crowded on the ice, which he broke under their feet by cannon-shot. This act of Pelissier was fiercely attacked by the journals of the opposition. Guizot alone defended him. Marshal Bugeaud was greatly offended, thinking that his attempts at military colonization were not sufficiently encouraged; and without being authorized, addressed a circular to the chiefs of the Algerian corps, ordering the application of his views. The government's embarrassment in Algeria was increased by their authority being thus perpetually harassed. Bugeaud had already several times announced his intention to retire, but the renewal of hostilities with the Arabs, and the distinction of the campaign in the plains of the Mitidja against the insurrection excited by Abd-el-Kader, delayed the accomplishment of this resolution. Marshal Soult, now old and weak, withdrew from the practical direction of affairs, soon to rest altogether with the title of Marshal-General of France, which had been borne only by Turenne, Villars, and Saxe. General Molines St. Yon, who succeeded him as war minister, drew up a scheme for military colonization which confirmed Bugeaud's views, though the latter considered it weak and colorless. The chambers objected to the proposal, and the ministry, in accordance with the decision of a special committee, rejected it. Marshal Bugeaud immediately resigned.

The king had long thought of placing one of his sons at the head of the government of Algeria. The Duc d'Aumale served there with distinction, and Bugeaud wrote, "I wish to be replaced here by a prince, not in the interests of the constitutional monarchy, but those of the matter in hand. He will be granted what would be refused to me. The Duc d'Aumale is, and will daily more and more be, a man of ability. I shall leave him, I trust, the office in good working order; but there will still be much to do for a long time. It is a labor of giants and of ages." On the 11th September, 1847, the Duc d'Aumale was appointed Governor of Algeria, as the most natural successor to Marshal Bugeaud, and best fitted to exercise upon the army there, as well as the native races, a happy and powerful influence. Only a few months, however, were to elapse before the tempest of new revolutions tore him away from a life and duty which were dear to him. Before that sad day the young prince had at last forced Abd-el-Kader to his last entrenchments, compelling from the hero of that religious and national resistance a submission which he was no longer able to refuse. In spite of several further attempts at insurrection, the conquest of Algeria was finally completed in February, 1848.

It was no doubt to our success in Africa and the prudent firmness of our attitude that we must attribute the development of our influence with the Mohammedans. From 1845 to 1847 the representatives of the great Mussulman powers flocked to Paris—the Morocco ambassador, Sidi-ben-Achache; Ibrahim Pacha, eldest son of Mehemet Ali; the Bey of Tunis; an envoy from the Shah of Persia. Turkey had at last agreed to give the various races of Lebanon the natural chiefs whom they demanded, especially the Druses and Maronites. In spite of the opposition of the Pachas and their slow compliance, the European diplomatic demands obtained a certain amount of satisfaction. From 1845 to 1848 the state of the Syrian Christians was sensibly improved, and gave them hopes of a happier future. The same protection over the Christian populations extended throughout the Ottoman Empire. By a convention of 21st March, 1844, the lives of Christian converts who had been seized with remorse and abjured Islam were assured. France's influence had now regained in the east much of her ancient empire.

She exercised the same influence, enhanced by recollections of earnest and practical sympathy, in the small Christian kingdom lately founded on the limits of the east. Greece knew how genuine and disinterested were the good wishes of France in her behalf. "France has but one thing to ask from Greece in return for all she has done for her," wrote Guizot to Piscatory, on sending him as minister to Athens; "that she may learn to develop the infinite resources contained in her bosom; that by a skilful, prudent, and active administration she may gradually, without any shock, without encountering dangerous risks, rise to the degree of prosperity and power necessary to occupy in the world the place to which she is destined by the natural process of politics. We shall then be amply satisfied, and never think of claiming from King Otho any other proof of gratitude."

Greece asked from the king whom she had chosen for herself resolutions which his conscientious hesitation could not give; and differences among the foreign powers at Athens fomented the popular discontent. "The question of king cannot be laid down," said Piscatory; "he is already there, and must remain. Yes, some reform is necessary to give the country assurance, but more than that amounts to a revolution; and it is not the business of governments to protect them."

The revolution, however, did break out (15th September, 1843), and compelled King Otho to accept a liberal constitution. After some party struggles and disturbance, Colettis assumed the reins of government in his country. One of the foremost and most able of the patriots who conspired against the Turkish rule, chief of the Palicares in the armed struggle, and ardently devoted to the national cause, Colettis had learned much during the seven years he was Grecian minister in Paris, but he remained Greek to the bottom of his soul. He was at the same time full of respect and love for France, sometimes suspicious of England, and distrustful with regard to Russia and Austria, who had looked with an evil eye upon the new revolution of Greece.

The harmony which had recently reigned between the diplomatic instructions of France and England was now quickly disturbed. The ministry of Peel and Aberdeen was replaced by that of Lord Palmerston, and Sir Edward Lyons resumed that course with which he had been so closely identified. The interior troubles of Greece, which Colettis had firmly repressed, were again fomented by foreign influences. The financial difficulties of the small and poor state were increased by England's demands for the payment of interest due on the loan formerly guaranteed by her together with France and Italy. Colettis met all these difficulties with unconquerable courage; and it was to his wisdom and devotion that the Greeks and their friends trusted, when he fell ill, and died on the 10th September, 1847, still humming with his trembling lips the old national songs which had delighted his youth. His loss was a dreadful shock to his country, and was felt long after, through disorders that were perpetually reappearing. "Colettis is gone to join the battalion of Plutarch's heroes," was the sad remark of those who had known and loved him.

It is the honor as well as the special difficulty of free governments that they live in the full light of day, and are constantly subjected to the complications which public discussion too often brings upon the solution of questions still undecided. Probably no government was ever more habitually struggling with this difficulty than that of Louis Philippe. Born of a revolution, it was, both in Europe and France, perpetually undergoing the consequences of its origin. It was long suspected, when no longer disputed; and at the very moment when a temporary lull of interior excitement and passion allowed it a glimpse of order in peace, it found itself dragged into European complications which momentarily threatened its repose and supplied new material for parliamentary attacks. From 1840 to 1848 the discussions in the chambers bore constantly upon foreign affairs. The ministry had undergone various internal changes. Humann's death was largely due to the difficulties and disgust which he had involuntarily excited by ordering a new census. He was replaced, first by Lacave-Laplagne, and then by Dumon, who had long been one of Guizot's intimate friends. The departments of war, the navy, and public works had been under various heads; but the chiefs of the cabinet remaining the same, the opposition continued to attack the same names. They were constantly losing strength in this protracted attack, and the elections of 1846 returned to the chambers a larger conservative majority than ever. Still the effect of a continued persistence began already to be felt in that majority itself. In the midst of the debates referring to foreign affairs, as well as during questions of business, only the proposals relating to electoral reform constantly reap-

peared, occasioning a silent agitation which was beginning to
stagger many minds. In their intimate and continual communication with the members of both chambers, the cabinet
were soon convinced of this fact. The fundamental policy of
the conservative party since the revolution of 1830, had as its
object the establishment of a free government under the preponderating influence of the middle classes, an influence
acknowledged and accepted in the general interest of the country, and submitted to every test and all the influences of general liberty. It was this very conception of the governmental
régime in France which the opposition attacked by demanding
electoral reform, the results or tendency of which they had not
even themselves estimated.

It is the frequently burdensome, but always glorious cost of
public liberty, that all its conditions are incessantly discussed.
The French Government were not astonished at this, but they
found it necessary to calm, even among their opponents, the
dissatisfaction caused by the natural development of liberty.
In accordance with men's natural tendency to refuse to their
adversaries rights which they claim for themselves, those who
loudly professed the most advanced liberal opinions were
doubtful about allowing liberty of teaching to the University,
and showed great anxiety at the free development of religious
bodies. The charter secured to new France all the liberty
advisable; and she had taken her share in freeing education.
"With reference to public instruction," said Guizot (31st
January, 1846), "all the rights do not belong to the State;
some of them are, I do not say superior, but anterior to her
own, and exist with them. Such are the rights of the family.
Children belong to the family before belonging to the State.
The State has the right to distribute instruction, assign it to
its proper institutions, and overlook it everywhere, but has
not the right to impose it arbitrarily and exclusively upon
families without their consent, and perhaps against their conviction. The *régime* of the Imperial University did not admit
this primitive and inviolable right of families. Moreover it
did not admit, at least to a sufficient degree, another order of
rights, the rights of religious belief. Napoleon well understood the greatness and power of religion; he also equally well
understood its dignity and liberty. He often misunderstood
the right belonging to men who are the depositaries of religious
belief, to maintain them, and transmit them from generation
to generation by education and teaching. That is not a privi-

lege of the Catholic religion; that right is applicable to all
creeds, to all religious bodies, Catholic or Protestant, Christian
or non-Christian. It is the right of parents to rear their children in their faith, by ministers of their faith. In organizing
the University, Napoleon took no account of the right of families, nor the right of religious beliefs. The principle of liberty
of education, the only real security of those rights, was
foreign to the University *régime.* To the charter and the
government of 1830 must be referred the honor of having
brought this principle to light, and attempted its practical realization. It is not only an engagement and duty, but the interest of the constitutional monarchy, to keep this promise
strictly. How remote originally from the principles of liberty,
the great creations of the Empire—those at least which are
really conformable to the genius of our social system—may admit those principles, and thence derive new power. Liberty
may enter into that mighty apparatus created for the restoration and protection of power. What is more strongly imagined
in the interest of power than our administrative *régime,* by
prefects, their Councils, and the Council of State? Yet into
that *régime* we introduce the principles and instruments of
liberty. The Councils-General elected, the Councils-Municipal
elected, the mayors necessarily chosen from the elected Municipal Councils; those institutions, of great reality and vitality,
which will from day to day be developed and play a greater
part in our society, have all come to adapt themselves to the
administrative *régime* which we have from the empire. The
same thing may take place with the great institution of the
University, and the government will thereby gain advantage
and liberty. In order that the present power may become
stronger and more durable, liberty must come to its aid. In a
public and responsible government, it is a too great burden
which monopolizes them, whatever be the shoulders supporting it. There is no strength or responsibility sufficient for it;
the government must be discharged of part of the burden, and
society must display its liberty in the service of its affairs, and
be itself responsible for the good or bad use to which it is put,"

Few people dared to protest seriously against the general
laying down of the principles of liberty; but in practice and in
the daily application of the principles, the chambers and great
mass of the people were opposed to liberty of education.
Twice, in 1841 and 1844, Villemain proposed without success
some schemes which, without fully deciding the question, pro

duced notable progress in the principle of liberty. Salvandy
made fresh attempts, which also remained fruitless. Indignation and anxiety took possession of the partisans of liberty of
education. As it extended and became warmer, the struggle
changed in character, and became violent and aggressive. The
University found itself unjustly attacked, and several bishops
imprudently threw themselves into the struggle. In the eyes
of the public the question of the liberty of instruction became
a case of war between the University and the Church, that is
to say, the State and the Church. Then moderate and sensible
men who were indifferent believed themselves threatened in
their personal liberty by the increasing influence attributed to
the Jesuits. Founded in the sixteenth century for the defence
of absolute power in the spiritual order, and perhaps the temporal too, the Society of Jesus, in spite of the immense services
rendered by her to the propagation of Christianity and the development of instruction, had remained constantly suspected
by the partisans of liberty, who looked upon her as still faithful to the first idea with which she started. The legislation as
to religious bodies bound down the Jesuits to rules which they
did not observe. The number of their schools was constantly
increasing, and their influence being boldly displayed, the public alarm demanded that the laws should be enforced against
them. The government conceived the idea of a procedure
which was more efficacious and more moderate. They asked
Pope Gregory XVI., the natural and supreme head of the
order, to dissolve in France the Society of Jesus. Rossi was
appointed to carry out this negotiation at Rome.

An Italian, of extremely liberal views, who had taken refuge
first at Geneva and then at Paris on account of his opinions,
Rossi was at the same time daring with self-control, patient
and persevering, endowed with a keen subtlety, and an influence
over men which was acquired gradually and quietly. After
long and complicated negotiations, Rossi was at last successful.
The court of Rome really laid down for the Jesuits the conduct
demanded from them by the French government and people;
though the court of Rome and the French government apparently allowed the Jesuits the honor of a spontaneous and voluntary withdrawal. On the 6th July, 1845, the *Moniteur* contained this official notice: "The government has received news
from Rome. The negotiation with which M. Rossi was entrusted has attained its object. The body of Jesuits in France
will cease to exist in France, and is going to disperse of its own

accord. Its houses will be closed, and its novitiates dissolved."
At Rome, Rossi laid special stress on the Holy See adhering to
its engagements. "I shall yield nothing," he wrote to Guizot,
"to party-spirit or a foolish hostility. No attack upon the
liberty of individuals; no obligation to leave France or sell
property; and no harassing interference in purely religious
functions; but the dispersal of the body, the closing of the
houses where they lived together, and the dissolution of the
novitiates; that has been promised, and that is indispensable."
Rossi had just been officially appointed ambassador at Rome,
when Pope Gregory XVI., already very old, died, on the 1st
June, 1846. Three days afterwards, Cardinal Mastai Ferretti,
who was piously devoted to his diocese, and personally unknown to the majority of the members of the Sacred College,
was elected Pope, and proclaimed under the name of Pius IX.

During a period and in a country still entirely filled with
noble hopes, it was a beautiful and consoling sight to see the
new pontiff commence, after his high elevation, by a complete
and touching amnesty; and to see the Roman people, so recently agitated by secretly hostile passions, eagerly rush before
the Pope, who promised them reforms ardently desired.
Thiers as well as the French government and their Roman ambassador strove to encourage Pius IX. in those popular measures. During his first conversations with Rossi, the Pope referred to everything, "both temporal and spiritual affairs—
the chance of his presiding over an Italian league, and his relations to the foreign powers; to his Swiss guard, and a civic
guard; finance and commerce, administrative abuses and judicial reform. His mind evidently dealt with every subject,
and considered every question, with glimpses at every possible
reform, sometimes with a simple confidence, sometimes with a
half-official anxiety; keenly enjoying his popularity, and, in
spite of his first generous impulses, with some hope of adhering to the aspirations without passing to the practical applica-
tions of the theories. 'That is not the ideal of government,'
said Rossi, somewhat uneasy on seeing the promised reforms
go off into smoke; 'it is government in an ideal state.'"*

Fear and anxiety were soon added to the natural sluggish-
ness and hesitation of an old government which men wished to
draw from its long-continued paths and routine. Cardinal
Gizzi, appointed secretary of state, soon exhausted himself in

---

* Guizot's *Mémoires*, etc.

his efforts to act without displeasing anybody.   A latent struggle was engendered between old and young Italy, and the
inertia of the government chafed men's minds.   The French
ambassador urged the Pope to give his people some proofs of
his liberal intentions.   The efforts of Pius were sincere in spite
of their weakness.   The ill-managed rule of the Austrians
weighed heavily on all the Italian States, and in all minds there
was now rising the thought of freedom from the foreign yoke
by the glorious effort of national unity.   The Pope shared in
this thought and desire common to all the Italians, his accession and early reforms having impressed new energy upon
them.   In Tuscany the grand duke entered upon a path of administrative, financial, and judicial improvements.   Piedmont
was about to receive a constitution.   Even at Naples the popular agitation became intense, and the king had already granted
some commercial reforms.   The whole of Italy was now ready
for action, and soon Pius IX. was induced to join thoroughly
in the national effort against foreigners.   The Pope was still
advancing as leader of the generous effort for social and political reform.   He had just formed a civic guard, armed with
French guns .The budget was published; the municipal organization of the city of Rome was improved; liberty of the press
extended; while railways were decreed, schools and asylums
founded.   The Pope convoked at Rome an Assembly of the
Notables for the 15th November.   He wished to find support
from those liberal and moderate men in the laity who wished
like himself for reform without revolution.   Both he and they
were destined to succumb under the blows which the rival and
extreme parties aimed at each other.   The projects of reactionary plots and threats of popular insurrections were already crossing each other in all directions, causing anxiety and
annoyance to the Pope and the friends faithful to his policy.
Rossi had already formed a friendly intimacy with Pius IX.,
which was soon after to engage him definitely in his service,
at the cost of his life, and to his own lasting renown.   The
thought of the independence of the Italian States, delivered
from the presence of foreigners, and united in an Italian confederation, together with a thoroughgoing reform of their internal condition, constituted the basis of the Pope's fond hopes,
which his future minister had a clearer conception of, and the
French government steadily supported.   " Peace and liberty,
progress without war or revolution"—that grand motto of the
monarchy of 1830—had constantly directed its policy abroad

as well as at home. At Rome, as well as in France, revolution was destined to obtain the mastery. The cause, however, was still good and great. In 1847, and the first months of 1848, there were still hopes. The Pope had honestly commenced the reforms, and then accepted the idea of having a lay minister. "Your holiness has awoke Italy," said Rossi, "it is a glory, but on condition that the impossible is not attempted." The attitude of the French government protected the action of the Holy See. The Austrians had evacuated Ferrara, having occupied it without good reason. Appearances seemed to promise well, but excited minds still retained their antagonism. "In Italy," said Mazzini, " there exists no moderate party."

There was good reason for believing there was no moderate party in Switzerland. The political struggles envenomed by religious ones, divided the cantons, and threatened to break the federal treaty. In presence of the radical movement, which was eaily becoming more defined in Berne, Geneva, and the Vaudois country, the cantons which were really Catholic believed that their religious liberty and independent action were threatened, and formed a special alliance (Sonderbund) binding them to defend each other's independence and rights of sovereignty. The Helvetic Diet urged by their demands, ordered the expulsion of the Jesuits, who had been invited by the canton of Lucerne to superintend the schools. Several armed fights had already taken place at various places, and a civil war was in preparation. The French government were somewhat anxious about this disturbance in a neighboring country, whose federal treaty was under the protection of the great powers by the very fact of its neutrality. In the interests of liberty, thus threatened, as well as peace, France believed it her duty to stir up on the part of Europe a diplomatic intervention, which might dispense with a material and violent intervention. For that purpose a memorandum from the five great powers was addressed to the Diet; but it had been with great difficulty forced from Lord Palmerston against his inclination, and he secretly informed the Swiss radicals of it. The latter precipitated their operations; the troops of the Diet marched against the free corps of the Sonderbund, who were speedily dispersed. Friburg capitulated without great resistance. The struggle was more severe at Lucerne, but it also yielded. The Valais alone still resisted, and the defeated Sonderbund had now no hope except in foreign intervention. King Louis Philippe and his cabinet had no natural inclination for that, although resolved not to allow Austria to make use alone of that last resource. "Let us beware of interfering in Switzerland as well as in Spain," said the king; "let us prevent others from interfering. A great service is already done. Let each people perform its own business, and bear its burden by the use of its rights."

There was then a fermentation throughout all Europe, and everywhere from the bosom of a long peace there burst forth that violent uneasiness which generally presages the terrible blows of fate. An old and dangerous element had reappeared in the situation of Europe: England and France were now divided and hostile. To the difficulties which had in various points broken out between the two powers, to the struggle of influences which had succeeded the "cordial understanding," there was now added a wounding of national pride. Lord Palmerston measured himself in Spain with the French government in an important question, and was beaten. The annoyance of England was great, and anger succeeded the annoyance.

Revolutionary changes, in a country of perpetual agitation, had brought Queen Christina to be regent of Spain. Having the intention of marrying her daughter, Queen Isabella, she and her friends of the moderate party strongly desired a union with the royal family of France. The king loudly and resolutely repelled that idea. "Our policy is simple," wrote Guizot to Flahault, the ambassador at Vienna. "At London, and probably elsewhere, they would not wish to see one of our princes reign in Madrid. We understand the exclusion, and accept it in the interests of the general peace and the European balance of power; but in the same interests we return it, and allow of no prince on the throne of Madrid who is not a member of the house of Bourbon. It has many husbands to offer—princes of Naples, Lucca, the sons of Don Carlos, the sons of Don Francisco. We propose none of them; we forbid none of them. He who suits Spain will suit us—but in the circle of the house of Bourbon. It is for us a French interest of the first order; and in my opinion it is evidently also a Spanish interest and a European interest." (27th March, 1842.)

This clearly expressed policy of the French government had been loyally accepted by Lord Aberdeen, then foreign minister. It was secretly attacked by Sir Henry Bulwer, English ambassador at Madrid, who was intriguing in favor of the young queen's union with Prince Leopold of Saxe Coburg. This

manœuvre, openly condemned by Lord Aberdeen, caused complications in our official negotiations. After long hesitation
with regard to a Neapolitan candidate—Count Trapani, brother
of the king—the French government modified their intention.
The influence of France was declared more definitely. It appeared that the future spouses of the Queen of Spain and the
Infanta Louisa Fernanda must be the Duc de Cadiz, son of
Prince Don Francisco, and the Duc de Montpensier, youngest
son of King Louis Philippe. "For heaven's sake, don't let us
miss this prince!" exclaimed Queen Christina, as soon as she
saw the possibility of so desirable a union for her second
daughter. The fall of Peel's cabinet changed the relative position of France and England in Spain. Lord Palmerston now
was in favor of the Prince of Coburg as a candidate. "I lay
infinite stress upon agreement in our plans and action," wrote
Guizot to Jarnac, then our representative in London. "I
have already proved that sufficiently, and shall do much to
make it good. But in fact, France perhaps ought to have
an isolated policy in Spain; and if the initiation of an isolated
policy was taken in London, I surely ought to adopt in Paris
the policy also."

The interior policy of Spain, as well as her foreign alliances,
were at stake. The moderates, who were in power, were
threatened by the revolutionary "progressists," their constant
enemies. The support of France was certain and necessary.
After tergiversation and hesitation had uselessly prolonged
the diplomatic intrigues, Queen Christina, and her minister
Isturitz, at last decided definitely for the French alliance, and
the marriage of the Duc of Cadiz with Queen Isabella, and that
of the Duc of Montpensier with the Infanta, were officially
announced. On the 10th and 11th October, 1846, the two
unions were solemnly celebrated in the palace, and in the
church of Our Lady of Atocha, at Madrid. Unions of difficult
completion, and which were to be variously crossed by many
shocks and griefs, but which were not to exercise, either on
Spain or on European politics, the influence attributed to them
by the triumph of France and the dissatisfaction of England.
The son of Queen Isabella, reared in exile, reigns on the throne
of Spain; beside him, raised by spontaneous affection to that
elevation, is his cousin the daughter of the Duc of Montpensier
and the Infanta. God sports with human anticipations and
anxieties, just as He often, in His impenetrable designs, de-
stroys the fairest hopes and the purest happiness.

CHAPTER XXI.

REFORM AND REVOLUTION (1847—1848).

I HAVE gone over the history and policy of King Louis Philippe's government from 1830 to 1847, and after taking pleasure in showing its steadfast tendency towards the well-being and progressive development of the country under its influence, I now come with profound repugnance and sorrow to those painful days by the faults and misfortunes of which France was launched into dangerous enterprises, such that men of the greatest foresight cannot discern their end. Our country has paid, and will probably long pay, very dearly for the fatal error which overthrew the throne of the king who had for eighteen years governed it with a wisdom, prudence, and moderation acknowledged even by his enemies when they are attacking him.

"The cabinet of the 29th October, and their political friends, had a clearly defined idea and purpose. They aspired to bring to a close the French era of revolutions by establishing the free government which France had in 1789 promised herself as the consequence and political guarantee of the social revolution which she was completing." This policy, formerly the object of their youthful hopes, had become theirs, whether in power or in the opposition. "It was in fact both liberal and anti-revolutionary. Anti-revolutionary both in home and foreign affairs, since it wished to maintain the peace of Europe abroad, and the constitutional monarchy at home. Liberal, since it fully accepted and respected the essential conditions of free government; the decisive intervention of the country in its affairs, with a constant and well-sustained discussion, in public as well as in the chambers, of the ideas and acts of the government. In fact, this two-fold object was attained from 1830 to 1848. Abroad, peace was maintained without any loss to the influence or reputation of France in Europe. At home, from 1830 to 1848, political liberty was great and powerful; from 1840 to 1848 in particular, it was displayed without any new legal limit being imposed. It was this policy that the opposition—all the oppositions, monarchical and dynastic as well as republican—blindly or knowingly attacked, and tried to change. It was to change it that they demanded electoral and parliamentary reforms. In principle, the government had no absolute or permanent objections whatever to such reforms; the extension of the right of suffrage, and the incompatibility of certain functions with the office of deputy, might and must be the natural and legitimate consequences of the upward movement of society and political liberty. They did not think the reforms necessary or well-timed, and were therefore justified in delaying them as much as possible, provided they should one day allow to be accomplished by others what they thought themselves still strong enough to refuse."* " We have too much and too long maintained a good policy," said Guizot afterwards.

A frequent and formidable sign that men's minds are secretly agitated, is the anxiety by which they are seized with reference to intrigues and vices which they suppose around them. It would be a serious error to see always a symptom of moral improvement in the clamors against electoral or parliamentary corruption. Immediately after the ministerial success in the general elections of 1846, this precursory indication of storms appeared on the horizon. Guizot raised the question to its proper point of view. "Leave to countries which are not free," said he, " leave to absolute governments, that explanation of great results by small, feeble, or dishonorable human acts. In free countries, when great results are produced it is from great causes that they spring. A great fact has been shown in the elections just completed; the country has given its adhesion, its earnest and free adhesion, to the policy presented before it. Do not attribute this fact to several pretended electoral manœuvres. You have no right to come to explain, or qualify by wretched suppositions, a grand idea of the country thus grandly and freely manifested." The rumors of electoral corruptions were soon followed by rumors of parliamentary corruptions; but the majority of the chamber declared themselves "content" with the ministerial explanations. The "contents" figured in the opposition attacks by the side of the " Pritchardists."

Several improper abuses of long standing existed in certain branches of the administration; some posts in the Treasury

---

* Guizot's *Mémoires*, etc.

had been the object of pecuniary transactions between those who held the posts and were resigning, and the candidates who presented themselves to replace them. A bill, proposed on the 20th January, 1848, by Hébert, who had become keeper of the seals, formerly forbade any such transaction, under assigned penalties. Several months previously (June, 1847), M. Teste, formerly minister of public works, and then president of the Cour de Cassation, was seriously compromised in the scandalous trial of General Cubières and Pellapra. Convicted of having received a large sum of money in connection with a mining concession, he was brought before the Peers, and being led from question to question and from discussion to discussion, soon made a confession of his crime. He, as well as his accomplices, underwent the just penalty.

"It was, on the part of the cabinet, one of those acts the merit of which is only perceived afterwards, and in which the government bears the weight of the evil at the moment when it is trying most sincerely and courageously to repress it. There were several deplorable incidents—the shocking murder of the Duchess of Praslin, some scandalous trials and violent deaths following hard one upon another, and aggravating the momentary depression and the excited state of the popular imagination. The air seemed infected with moral disorder and unlooked-for misfortunes, coming to join in party attacks and the false accusations which the cabinet were subjected to. It was one of those unhealthy hurricanes often met in the lives of governments."* It was certainly culpable on the part of the opposition to try to take advantage of this disturbed state of men's minds to gain the end they were pursuing. Seven times was parliamentary reform, and three times was electoral reform, refused by the chambers, from 20th February, 1841, to 8th April, 1847; the question being then displaced, it changed its ground. The opposition made an appeal to popular passion; and parliamentary discussions were succeeded by the banquets.

"From the close of the session of 1847 to the opening of that of 1848, they kept France in a state of constant fever—an artificial and deceptive fever in this sense, that it was not the natural and spontaneous result of the actual wishes and wants of the country; but true and serious in this sense, that the political parties who took the initiative in it found amongst some of the middle classes and the lower orders a prompt and

---

* Guizot's *Mémoires*, etc.

keen adhesion to their proposals. The first banquet took place
in Paris at the Chateau-Rouge Hotel on the 9th July, 1847.
Garnier-Pagès has himself told how the royalist opposition and
the republican opposition concluded their alliance for that
purpose. On leaving the house of Odilon Barrot, the radical
members of the meeting walked together for some time. On
reaching that part of the Boulevard opposite the Foreign Office,
at the moment they were about to separate, Pagnerre said,
"Well, really, I did not expect for our proposals so speedy
and complete success. Do those gentlemen see what that may
lead to? For my part, I confess I do not see it clearly; but it
is not for us radicals to be alarmed about it." "You see that,
tree," replied Garnier-Pagès; "engrave on its bark a mark in
memory of this day, for what we have just decided upon, is a
revolution."* Garnier-Pagès did not foresee that the republic
of 1848, as well as the monarchy of 1830, should in its turn
speedily perish in that revolution, so long big with so many
storms.

For six months banquets were renewed in most of the departments—at Colmar, Strasburg, St. Quentin, Lille, Avesnes,
Cosne, Châlons, Mâcon, Lyons, Montpellier, Rouen, etc. In
many parts, there was a great display of feelings and intentions
most hostile to royalty and the dynasty. On several occasions
—at Lille, for example—the keenest members of the parliamentary opposition, Odilon Barrot and his friends, withdrew, soon
after taking their places at table, because the others absolutely
refused to dissemble their hostility to the crown and the king.
At other banquets, notably at Dijon, the ideas and passions of
1793 unblushingly reappeared. They defended Robespierre
and the reign of terror. The "red republic" openly flaunted
its colors and hopes. The attack upon monarchy and the
dynasty ranged itself, it is true, behind the parliamentary
opposition, but like Galatea running away—

Et se cupit ante videri.

It had succeeded well enough in making itself seen. The government could no longer shut their eyes. They had tolerated
the banquets so long as they could believe, or seem to believe,
that the parliamentary opposition directed, or at least ruled,
the movement. When it became evident that the anarchical
impulse was more and more gaining upon the parliamentary
opposition, and that the latter was becoming the instrument

* Guizot's *Mémoires*, etc.

instead of remaining the master, then only they forbade the banquets. It was their duty.

It was also their right, in the opinion of the most competent legal authorities, as well as according to the recent practice of other free governments, in presence of a situation full of certain danger. This right, however, was disputed by the opposition. The government, pushing the principle of legality to its farthest limit, arranged with several leading men of the opposition for the purpose of enabling the question of right to be brought speedily and methodically before competent tribunals. Just before the opening of the new session, in order to close the campaign, a new and formal banquet was being prepared in Paris, to which all the deputies and peers who had taken part in any of the preceding banquets were to be invited. This manifestation was to take place in the twelfth arrondissement of Paris. It was therefore agreed between the opposition delegates and those of the ministerial majority that the deputies invited should go to the place appointed for the meeting and take their places, so as to avoid any disturbance in the streets or the hall, and that on the police-commissary declaring that there was an order against it, the guests should protest and withdraw, to lay the question before the tribunals. The agreement thus concluded was communicated by Duchâtel to the council, who approved of it.

Meanwhile the chamber met, the session was opened, and from the very first the government could perceive a wavering in the majority. Even amongst those who blamed and feared the agitation out of doors, several believed in the urgent necessity of a concession, to remove all pretext for clamors and intrigues. On the ministers being informed of it, Guizot said, "Withdraw the question from the hands of those who now hold it, and let it be brought back to the chamber. Let the majority take a step in the direction of the concessions indicated; however small it be, I am certain it will be understood, and that you will have a new cabinet, which will do what you think necessary." It was in the same spirit that the ministry, during the discussion on the address, rejected an amendment tending to impose upon them immediate engagements with reference to reform.

"The maintenance of the unity of the conservative party," said Guizot, "the maintenance of conservative policy and power, will be the fixed idea and rule of conduct in the cabinet. They will make sincere efforts to maintain or restore the unity of the conservative party upon that question, in order that it may be the conservative party itself in its entirety that undertakes and gives to the country its solution. If such an operation in the midst of the conservative party is possible, it will take place. If that is not possible—if by the question of reforms the conservative party cannot succeed in making a common arrangement and maintaining the power of the conservative policy, the cabinet will leave to others the sad task of presiding over the disorganization of the conservative party and the ruin of its policy."

The question was not destined to be taken up again by the chambers, having escaped from the weak hands that aspired to direct it. The courtesy of the conservative reformers had no result except disquieting the government, a sort of precursory sign of the tempest. Even the parliamentary opposition found themselves baffled in their prudent efforts, A manifesto published in the *National* newspaper organized a noisy demonstration in the streets, though forbidden in the banquet-hall, the national guards being called to arms by the insurrection, and their services arranged beforehand. The convention was clearly violated, and the legal appeal to the tribunals therefore abandoned: the revolution itself declared it would decide the question. In such a situation, sorrowfully admitted by those who had negotiated the evening before, the government officially forbade the banquet. The evening papers announced that the deputies of the opposition had given up the intention of being present, and therefore the proposed manifestation was deprived of all importance. The revolutionary leaders in their turn declared that the banquet would not take place.

Disappointment increasing their irritation, the parliamentary opposition, in a momentary resistance, employed the remainder of their strength. On the 22nd February fifty-two deputies of the left laid before the chamber a bill of impeachment against the ministry, on account of their home and foreign policy during the whole course of their administration. "What would you have them do?" said to Guizot an old member of the opposition who had no share whatever in this act. "They have just rendered the banquet abortive by declaring they would not attend it, and felt compelled to do something to compensate for, and to some extent redeem, that refusal."

Weakness has a constraining power difficult to understand, which is not foreseen even by those who give way to it; and

of this the history of the revolution of 1848 offers an eloquent
and melancholy example.

The king, as well as his ministers, still hoped that the crisis
had passed, and that the disorder avoided on the occasion of
the banquet should not reappear under any pretext. The display of military forces which had been agreed upon and prepared was ordered to be suspended; instructions to arrest the
republican leaders were issued slowly, and in but few instances.
Yet a secret agitation was indicated in several parts of the
capital; there were numerous crowds; on the morning of the
23rd several corps-de-garde were attacked. As the fermentation increased, the streets were crowded with idle workmen;
people collected in knots from curiosity, or stood at their doors.
The storm was in the air, evident both to those who dreaded it
and those who were preparing to make use of it.

Meanwhile the appeal of the revolutionary leaders to the
national guard had been listened to. Many of the Parisian
shopkeepers took part in the "reform movement," without
well understanding it, and marched under the orders of their
dangerous allies. Several detachments of the 7th, 3rd, 2nd
and 10th legions appeared in the streets, some in the Faubourg
St. Antoine, others marching to the Palais Royal, or the office
of the *National* in the Rue Le Peletier, and others in the students' quarter shouting " Long live reform!" in every street.
When General Jacqueminot, the Commander-in-Chief of the
National Guard, ordered a general muster of the legions, a
large number of the guards, respectable and law-abiding men,
did not answer to the summons. They had no desire for a
revolution or reform forced from the legal powers by insurrection, but they shrunk from entering upon a struggle with soldiers wearing their own uniform, and influenced apparently
by reasonable motives. They remained in their homes dejected and anxious.

The king was as dejected as the Parisian citizens, and still
more anxious. For several months he had frequently fallen
into very low spirits, which was attributed to his grief at the
death of his only sister, Madame Adelaide of Orleans, whose
life had been always intimately associated with his, and who
had just expired (December, 1847). His most intimate friends
urged him to charm away the crisis by changing his ministry.
He still resisted, but every hour less vigorously. The cabinet
was not even informed of his perplexities. "Concessions
forced by violence from all the legal powers are not a means

of safety," said Duchâtel; "one defeat would quickly bring a second. In the revolution there was not much between the 20th June and the 10th August, and to-day things advance more quickly than in those times. Events, like travellers, now go by steam."

The truth, however, was now becoming manifest, both in the king's mind as to the tendency of his ideas, and in the eyes of his ministers as to the determination now being formed in the Palace. By the very statement of the question it was resolved upon. Guizot and Duchâtel thus expressed it to the king: "It is for your Majesty to decide. The cabinet is ready either to defend to the last the king and conservative policy which we profess, or to accept without a murmur the king's determination to call other men to power. At present, more than ever, in order to continue the struggle successfully, the cabinet has need of the king's decided support. As soon as the public should learn, as they inevitably must, that the king hesitates, the cabinet would lose all moral influence, and be unable to accomplish their task." The king seemed still in perplexity, and said he should prefer to abdicate. "You cannot say that, my dear," replied the queen, who was present at the interview with the Dukes of Nemours and Montpensier; "you belong to France, and not to yourself." "That is true," said the king, as Louis XVI. had formerly said to Malesherbes; "I am more unfortunate than the ministers, I cannot resign."

The ministers then in King Louis Philippe's cabinet had not resigned. The king, having made his decision, said, "It is with the keenest regret that I separate myself from you, but necessity and the safety of the monarchy demand this sacrifice. My will gives way; much time will be needed to regain the ground I am about to lose." There were tears in many eyes. The king sent for Molé, and Guizot himself announced to the Chamber of Deputies the change of ministry.

There was much astonishment and sorrow in the parliamentary majority, always strongly attached to the leaders they had so long followed in spite of occasional vagaries and good-natured weakness. The imminence of a great danger engrossed their minds, together with the consciousness of a great defeat. The anxiety of the chambers was re-echoed in the Tuileries; and for the last time the ministers assembled there, anxious at that last moment of their power to maintain order, now everywhere threatened. Count Molé was laboriously occupied in the formation of a cabinet. "To think that this resolution was formed in a quarter of an hour!" exclaimed the king when engaged with Jayr in some administrative details.

The excitement was great in the palace, but still greater in the streets, being skilfully kept up by several insurrectionist leaders, and spontaneously arising among the reckless portion of the populace, who are easily influenced by revolutionary clamors. Increased by those assembling from curiosity or idleness, the crowds in the squares and boulevards assumed alarming proportions. All at once, opposite the Foreign Office, there was heard, about nine o'clock in the evening, one of those fatal explosions, whether accidental or premeditated, which history often records as the origin of great popular risings.

The soldiers, who till then had remained motionless and patient, thought they were attacked, and fired in their turn. Several persons fell, some dead, others wounded, and some were knocked down and trodden under foot. The greatest disorder, caused both by alarm and indignation, broke out in the whole neighborhood. Then was the moment of action for the keen and determined insurgents. A cart which happened to be there was immediately loaded with the corpses and drawn through the streets, from one newspaper office to another, in the most populous quarters, with shouts of "Vengeance! To arms! Down with Guizot! The head of Guizot!" By daybreak Paris was covered with barricades.

Molé having failed in his efforts to form a cabinet, the king sent for Thiers. For the last time he claimed the devotion of his old ministers. "I must have immediately a military chief —an experienced chief," he said. "I have sent for Bugeaud, but I wish M. Thiers to find him appointed. Will you grant me this further service?" Duchâtel, and General Trézel, on the previous evening still minister of war, signed without hesitation Marshal Bugeaud's appointment as Commander-in-Chief of the National Guard and the Army. It was three o'clock in the morning. "It is somewhat late to set to work," said the marshal; "but I have never been beaten, and shall not make a beginning to-morrow. Let me act, and fire the cannon; there will be some bloodshed, but to-morrow evening the strength will be on the side of law, and the factious will have had their account settled."

The day had not yet dawned when the marshal was reviewing his forces. He found them demoralized, having for sixty hours remained motionless before the mob, with their feet in the mud, and their knapsacks on their backs, allowing the riot ers to attack the municipal guards, burn the sentry-boxes, cut down the trees, break the street-lamps, and harangue the soldiers. They were moreover badly supplied with provisions and ammunition. The energetic language of their new commander, and the precise orders which he gave for the march of the columns, inspired the soldiers with fresh life and courage. The movements indicated had already begun to be executed, and the troops were taking position; but the crowds again filled the streets, and at several points the soldiers were prevented from marching. One of the generals at the head of a column sent to tell Bugeaud that he was face to face with an enormous body of men, badly armed, who made no attack upon him, but only shouted "Long live reform! Long live the army! Down with Guizot!" "Order them to disperse," replied the marshal; "if they do not obey, use force, and act with resolution."

There was no fighting on either side. The staff were besieged by the entreaties of a crowd of respectable men, who in terror and consternation conjured Bugeaud to withdraw the troops because they excited the anger of the populace, and leave to the national guard the duty of appeasing the insurrection. The danger of such counsel was obvious, and the marshal paid no attention to it, till Thiers and Odilon Barrot, who had just accepted office, came to the staff with the same advice, and it therefore became an order. The marshal at first refused the ministers as he had done the citizens, and then the same order was sent by the king. "I must have a government," the marshal had recently said; and, as he was now without the government, who thus relaxed the resistance agreed upon, he in his turn gave way. His instructions for retreat were thus given to his officers: "By order of the king and ministers, you will fall back upon the Tuileries. Make your retreat with an imposing attitude, and if you are attacked, turn round, take the offensive, and act according to my instructions given this morning."

Meanwhile the formation of the ministry was posted up everywhere. A mixed crowd carried Odilon Barrot in triumph to the home office, which Guizot and Duchâtel had just left. Those round him shouted "Long live the father of the people!" but most of the notices posted up were torn. At the moment when the new ministers were about to leave Bugeaud's staff on horseback in order to pass through the city, Horace Vernet, the artist, arrived out of breath. "Don't let M. Thiers go," said he to the marshal. "I have just passed through the mob, and they are so furious against him that I am certain they would cut him in pieces!" Odilon Barrot presented himself alone to the crowd, but was powerless to calm the fury he had assisted in unchaining. "Thiers is no longer possible, and I am scarcely so, said he on his return to the staff. The king on one occasion showed himself in the court of the Tuileries, when reviewing several battalions of the national guards. There were some shouts of "Long live the king!" but the most numerous were "Long live reform! Down with Guizot!" "You have the reform; and M. Guizot is no longer a minister!" said the king; and on the shouts being again repeated, he returned to the palace.

The palace also was thronged with a confused crowd, animated by various feelings, and agitated by evident fears or secret hopes. Some urged the king to abdicate in favor of the Comte de Paris; others vigorously opposed such a relinquishment of power in presence of the insurrection. The great mind of Queen Marie-Amélie was displayed in all the simplicity of its heroism. "Mount on horseback, sire," said she, "and I shall give you my blessing." She had recently urged the king to change his cabinet; a very kind message, entrusted for Guizot to one of his most intimate friends, at the same time proved her regret.

The king sat at his writing-table, agitated and perplexed. He had begun to write his abdication, when Marshal Bugeaud entered, having just learned what was taking place in the Tuileries, and excited by the sound of some shooting which had already begun. "It is too late, sire," said he; "your abdication would complete the demoralization of the troops. Your Majesty can hear the shooting. There is nothing left but to fight." The queen seconded this advice, and Piscatory and several others were of the same opinion. The king rose without finishing his writing, and then other voices were raised to insist upon the king's promise. He sat down again, wrote and signed his abdication. By this time the troops had received orders to fall back, and Marshal Gerard took the place of Bugeaud as commandant-general. The columns were marched towards the barracks, and there was no detachment around the Palais-Bourbon, where the same disorder reigned, and the same efforts were made in vain. The Duchess of Orleans presented herself before the Chamber of Deputies as soon as the abdication of the king was known. The Duc de Nemours accompanied her, leading the Comte de Paris by the hand; and the Duc de Chartres, who was weak and ill, was wrapped up in a mantle and leaned on Ary Scheffer's arm. Before joining the princess at the gate of the chamber, the Duc de Nemours had, with his brother the Duc de Montpensier, seen the king their father take his melancholy departure, to escape the insurrection, against which he could not make up his mind to use force.

The Duchess of Orleans already knew that depriving the king of the crown was not giving it to her son. Her natural courage, however, and her maternal affection, induced her to make every effort to secure the throne for the prince of nine years whom the nation had already entrusted to her keeping. She had seen the Tuileries invaded before leaving that hall where her husband's portrait by Ingres seemed to preside over her son's destinies. "It is here one ought to die," she said, when Dupin and Grammont came to conduct her to the chamber. Odilon Barrot had gone to bring her, and succeeded in finding her in the Palais-Bourbon. The crowd showed sympathy for her, and made room respectfully, though she and her small retinue had difficulty in getting within the palace, every passage being crowded. The duchess stood near the tribune holding her two boys close to her. After Dupin announced the king's abdication, Barrot, after presenting the legal instrument, asked the chamber to proclaim at once the young king and the regency of Madame the Duchess of Orleans. Shouts of protest were heard on several benches. "It is too late!" exclaimed Lamartine, as he went to the tribune, eager to urge this difficulty, reject the regency, and demand a provisional government, so that the bloodshed might be stopped. Some others were already mentioning the word "republic." The crowd were gradually pouring into the chamber from the corriders, and Sauzet, the president, requested strangers to withdraw, and made a special appeal to the duchess herself. "Sir, this is a royal sitting!" she replied; and when her friends urged her, "If I leave this chamber, my son will no more return to it." A few minutes before her arrival, Thiers had entered the chamber in the greatest agitation: "The tide is rising, rising, rising!" he said to those who crowded round him, and then disappeared. Several voices were heard together in confusion; amongst the speakers were Larochejacquelein, Ledru-Rollin, Marie, and Berryer. The duchess had been conducted to a gallery, on account of the

threats of the insurgent battalions, who burst open the doors
after General Gourgaud had in vain tried to stop them.
Armand Marrast, one of the editors of the *National*, after
looking at the invaders, said "These are the sham public; I
shall call the real!" A few minutes afterwards shots were
heard in the court of the palace: the posts in the hands of the
national guards opened before the triumphant mob, who, after
sacking the Tuileries, hurried up against the expiring remnants of the monarchy. The Duchess of Orleans had already
twice offered to speak, but her voice was drowned in the
tumult. The new comers, stained with blood, and blackened
with gunpowder, with dishevelled hair and bare arms, climbed
on the benches, stairs, and galleries; and in every part were
shouts of "Down with the regency! Long live the republic!
Turn out the 'contents'!" Sauzet put on his hat, but a workman knocked it off, and then the president disappeared.

Several of the deputies rushed to the gallery, where the
duchess was still exposed to the looks and threats of the insurgents. "There is nothing more to be done here, madam,"
they urged; "we must go to the president's house, to form a
new chamber." She took the arm of Jules de Lasteyrie; and
on her sons being separated from her in the narrow passages,
she showed the greatest anxiety, crying "My boys! my boys!"
At one time the Comte de Paris was seized by a workman in a
blouse; but one of the national guards took him out of his
hands, and the child was passed from one to another till he rejoined his mother. No one knew what had become of the Duc
de Chartres; but he was brought to the Invalides, where the
princess went for refuge; and in the evening, after nightfall,
the mother and sons withdrew from Paris, and soon after
from France. "To-morrow, or ten years hence," said the
Duchess of Orleans as she left the Invalides, "a word, a sign
will bring me back." Afterwards, in exile, she frequently
said, "When the thought crosses my mind that I may never
again see France, I feel my heart breaking."

Wanderers and fugitives across their kingdom, after kneel-
ing for the last time beside the tomb of their children at Dreux,
and asking the hospitality of some friends who were still
faithful, and without a single attempt to recover the crown
they had lost, King Louis Philippe and Queen Marie-Amélie at
last reached the sea-coast, and set sail towards England,
that safe and well-known refuge of unfortunate princes.
Thunderstruck like them, and at their wits' end, the most

faithful of their servants and partisans waited for some sign authorizing them to protest against the unparalleled surprise to which France had been subjected. The fugitive king made no protest. His sons quietly followed him into exile. Those who were serving France abroad learned at the same time the news of their fall and the rise of a new power, and thought it their duty to bow to the national will, resolving that not a single drop of French blood should be shed in their cause. They had often unhesitatingly exposed all their own.

In bringing to a close this sketch of the history of France as it was, the cradle still obscure of new France, we leave our native land on the threshold of an unknown future, charged both with storms and with hopes. We followed it throughout the terrible acts and the pacific interludes of a long drama; we saw it delivered up to the enthusiasm of inexperience, a victim to most dangerous misconceptions, and humbling itself, throughout the intoxication and crime of the reign of terror, even to the corruption and inertia of the directory. We saw order again revive, with glory, under the powerful hand of Napoleon, as first consul, and then emperor. We saw glory in alliance with the disasters of madness; the hopes of the first restoration tarnished by the mutual distrust of the crown and the people; Napoleon's selfishness, together with the credulity of the army and nation, bring again upon us the bitter chastisement of foreign vengeance. The revolutionary tragedy demagogic or despotic, seemed at last to be nearly complete. The struggles for liberty were again limited to the parliamentary arena, and repose and hope were again reappearing. An old man's illusions might occasion this glimpse of calm, having witnessed new political disturbances, which were speedily followed by a grand attempt at government. We have seen the rise of noble efforts and fair hopes, the wisest and most steadfast minds flatter themselves that at last they had reached the haven. God did not give His permission: in His impenetrable wisdom, our country, bandied about from revolution to revolution for so many years, was not yet deemed deserving of repose. It is at the painful moment of deception and downfall that we to-day close the book of history. Under the blow of an extorted abdication and cowardly trickery, the edifice which was at last to shelter future generations disappeared, and those who had raised it withdrew for a long time into retirement. France resumed the course of her disturbed and uncertain destinies. After some new experience of republican

HF (Q)

powerlessness, she weakly attempted a second trial of imperial
government, and received a terrible fall headlong through the
want of foresight of the absolute power.   Immediately after
her most painful reverses, in one of the great intervals of
national action, she shuddered at the renewed horrors of the
demagogic fever.   Wounded, sick, humbled, borne on a raft in
the midst of the tempest, she often asked herself what hardships were yet awaiting her.   The course remains obscure, and
the nearest object remains uncertain and veiled.

France has not lost, and will not lose, courage.   She is laboring; she is hoping; and, while endeavoring to find her proper
path, she reckons upon the day when revolutions will be at an
end, and when liberty with order will forever crown the long
and painful efforts of her most faithful servants of every name
and every period!

TOMB OF NAPOLEON

France, vol. eight

SUPPLEMENTARY CHAPTER

THE revolution of February, 1848, was destined to disappoint its authors. Exhibiting at the outset strong socialistic prepossessions which led to the establishment of national workshops, it was brought to an end by a *coup d'état* which prepared the way for the restoration of the empire. As early as April, 1848, the elections for the constituent assembly showed that moderate men would soon recover their ascendency in the country at large, if not in the capital, and the apprehension of reaction against socialistic tendencies caused in June a memorable uprising on the part of the Paris workingmen, which required four days' fighting to suppress. At the election for President, which occurred on December 10 of the same year, Lamartine, who had been the idol of the men who organized the revolution, was almost entirely forgotten, and General Cavaignac, who had put down the June insurrection, and, subsequently, been placed at the head of the Executive, received only a small minority vote. Prince Louis Napoleon, who had been permitted to return to France, and who had been elected to the Assembly from several departments, was chosen President of the Republic by a majority so large that it encouraged him eventually to violate the law making him ineligible for a second term, and to overthrow the Constitution which he had sworn to obey. The legislative assembly would, probably, have been able to frustrate his design, had it not lost the confidence of the masses of the people by several reactionary measures; by restricting the franchise, for example, and by sending a French army to overthrow republican government at Rome and to bring back the Pope. The result was that, when, on December 2, 1851, the assembly was dissolved and sixteen of its members were arrested, most of the Paris workingmen declined to express disapproval of the measure, and the usurpation was ratified on December 20, by a plebiscite, no fewer than 7,439,216 out of 8,116,773 voters attesting

satisfaction at the change. The position of Louis Napoleon was that of dictator up to March 29, 1852, the
date of the first meeting of the governing bodies which,
as the elected chief of the state, he called into existence.
Even under the new Constitution established by him, he
was, practically, an autocrat, although, at first, he accepted only the office of President for ten years. On
November 21-22, 1852, however, he was declared hereditary Emperor of the French by a plebiscite in which,
again, the vote was almost unanimous, being 7,824,129
against 253,149. Almost immediately afterward, overtures for the hand of Princess Vasa and for that of the
Princess Adelaide of Hohenlohe having been repelled, he
announced his intention to marry a Spanish lady, Mdlle.
de Montijo, Countess of Teba, and, on January 30, 1853,
the marriage was celebrated in the Cathedral of Notre
Dame. For some eight years the imperial régime was
autocratic in form as well as substance, the functions of
the legislative bodies being, practically, restricted to reg-
istering the sovereign's decrees. In the autumn of 1860,
however, the parliamentary methods were liberalized, debates on the address being permitted, and other considerable advances were made toward a free constitutional
government. M. Rouher, who became the chief spokes-
man of the government, had protested against the change
and had warned his master that he would be drawn into
fresh concessions which would, eventually, deprive him
of his personal power. The prediction was fulfilled on
January 2, 1870, when the principle of a government
responsible to the Chamber of Deputies was formally
adopted, and M. Emile Olivier was appointed premier.
Thenceforth, the emperor retired from the active direction of public affairs, and confined himself entirely to the
position of a constitutional sovereign. He cannot, however, be absolved from some share of accountability for
the policy of the Olivier Cabinet, which, six months later,
led to the ruin of his dynasty and to the most disastrous
war of modern times.

In respect of its foreign policy, the Second Empire was,
at first, successful. The Crimean War, undertaken in
conjunction with England, may be said to have begun
in April, 1854, and to have, practically, ended with the
capture of Sebastopol on December 10, 1855, although it
was not until the following year that a treaty of peace

was signed by the Czar Alexander II., who had succeeded his father Nicholas I. during the winter of the great siege. In the war against Austria, which began in May, 1859, the French arms were victorious at Magenta and Solferino, but the emperor's promise to free Italy from the Alps to the Adriatic was not kept, a peace hastily arranged at Villafranca on July 11 leaving the Austrians in possession of Venetia. From 1858 to 1862, France was also engaged in distant expeditions. In alliance with England, she enforced the observance of treaties upon the Pekin government; in the course of the coercive measures, the allied troops ultimately took the Chinese capital. In Cochin China, also, a war, in which France had Spain for an ally, was brought to a close in 1862, and the foundations were then laid of the French Empire in Farther India, which has, gradually, absorbed Cambodia, Tonquin and Annam, besides making extensive acquisitions at the cost of Siam. In 1860-61, the Christian subjects of the Sultan in Syria were relieved from oppression to a considerable extent by the dispatch of a French army to that region. At this time, the prestige of the Second Empire may be said to have reached its height. Of the four European powers which had taken part in the overthrow of the great Napoleon, his nephew had humbled two: to wit, Russia and Austria; and it was believed that he only bided his time to inflict a similar punishment upon England and Prussia. The decline of the influence of Napoleon III. in Europe began with his failure to avert the dismemberment of Denmark in 1864, and his popularity at home was seriously weakened by the miscarriage of the Mexican expedition, which was brought to an end by the return of the French troops in February, 1867, their evacuation being followed, on June 19, by the execution of the Archduke Maximilian, who, at Louis Napoleon's request, had accepted the invitation to become Emperor of Mexico. The attempt of France to intervene in the so-called Seven Weeks' War of 1866 having been unwisely put off until the decisive battle of Sadowa, had no substantial results. It is true that Austria agreed to surrender Venetia to Napoleon III., who, on his part, turned it over to Italy; but Prussia, under the management of Bismarck, refused to give France any territorial compensation for the startling political change which had taken place upon her borders. The

national pride of Frenchmen was galled by the percep-
tion that their ruler had permitted the accomplishment
of a great revolution in Europe, the outcome of which
had been that France was made relatively weaker through
the great addition of strength to her neighbors. The Second Empire had witnessed the consolidation of Italy and
the formation of the North German Confederation, while
France, on her part, had gained nothing except Savoy
and Nice, which had been wrung from Victor Emmanuel.

There is no doubt that, during the first fifteen years of
the regin of Napoleon III., France enjoyed great prosperity. Railways, canals, harbors, public buildings and
churches sprang into existence under the quickening impulse of the imperial hand. The capital was almost re-
built by Haussmann, and there was scarcely an important
town that was not partially reconstructed. Arts and in-
dustries were encouraged; commerce was fostered by the
subsidizing of great lines of ocean steamers; by a treaty
with England, which was strongly tinctured with free
trade principles, the exports of France were signally increased. It must also be acknowledged that, compared
with the state of things at the present time, the weight
of taxation under the Second Empire was scarcely felt.
The French people, however, could not be expected to
realize how much better off they were than their descendants would be, and, by 1868, there were signs of growing
disaffection toward the imperial regime, especially in Paris
and the large manufacturing towns. The high price of
bread in the winter of 1868, and a coincident scarcity of
work, served the turn of the Opposition members in the
legislative chamber. Seditious cries began to be heard
in the streets; the repeated singing of the Marseillaise
provoked arrests and imprisonments. Dismay was excited by the announcement of the Finance Minister that
a new loan of seven hundred million francs was needed
in order to systematize the resources of the State, and, by
the declaration of the Minister for War, that the army,
including the first reserve, must be increased to 750,000
men, and that a Garde Mobile, which was expected to
afford 300,000 men in the course of a few years, should
be instituted as a second reserve. Thiers, who was now
a member of the legislative chamber, was listened to with
great interest when he undertook to demonstrate the hol-
lowness of the imperial finance, the burden of debt which

then seemed appalling, and the growing dimensions of the army expenditure, which, as he maintained, and as the event was to prove, was not accompanied by any real increase in the fighting strength of the nation. How unpopular the empire had become toward the close of 1868 was indicated in November by the proposal of the Opposition to commemorate the death of Baudin, a leader of the Reds, who, at the time of the *coup d'état*, had been shot on a barricade. For seventeen years, Baudin had lain in a forgotten grave, when it was suddenly remembered that he had fallen in resisting the myrmidons of Napoleon, and that he perished in defense of what was then the law and the Constitution. The assassination of the journalist Victor Noir by Prince Pierre Bonaparte, and the subsequent acquittal of the assassin, gave additional ammunition to the enemies of the imperial regime. Nevertheless, on May 8, 1870, when the nation was invited to signify by a plebiscite whether it continued to repose confidence in Napoleon III., there were 7,257,379 ayes, which constituted, of course, a great majority. Grave suspicions of fraud were current, however, and the returning officers admitted that there were 1,530,000 noes, indicating a settled hostility in Paris and most of the other large cities. The circumstance that even the army recorded nearly 50,000 votes against the sovereign was a serious matter. Within four months after the plebiscite, Napoleon III. was a prisoner, and the Second Empire was no more.

It is now known that the candidature of Prince Leopold of Hohenzollern for the Spanish crown would not have resulted in a war between France and Prussia, had not Bismarck, who believed that the time was ripe for a trial of strength, provoked the French Ministry and legislature to a hostile declaration by publishing a garbled report of an interview between King William and the French ambassador at Ems. We need not recapitulate the incidents of the ensuing contest, which began with the skirmish at Saarbruck on August 2, 1870, where the Prince Imperial was said to have undergone his baptism of fire. This insignificant success of the French arms was followed by defeats at Wissembourg and Worth, and by three great battles near Metz, on August the 14th, the 16th and the 18th, whereby, although the Germans suffered terrible losses, Bazaine was, eventually, compelled **to draw back under the cannon of the town.** On September 2, Marshal MacMahon's army, comprising more than 80,000 men, surrendered at Sedan, and the emperor, who was with the Marshal, became a prisoner of war. On September 4, the imperial regime was overthrown in Paris, and the empress, who had been discharging the functions of Regent, was compelled to fly from the Tuileries and to seek a refuge in England. A provisional government of national defense was established, the chief members of which were Jules Favre, Jules Simon, Gambetta and General Trochu. The last-named assumed the command of Paris, while Gambetta undertook the difficult task of organizing a system of national defense at Tours. Gambetta's efforts, although vigorous, proved ineffective, and the capitulation of Metz toward the close of October enabled a large German army to co-operate in the siege of Paris, which had begun on September 19. The sorties of the garrison were foiled, and, on January 30, 1871, the French capital was surrendered to the king of Prussia, who, in the previous December, had been crowned German emperor in the Palace of Versailles. On February 8, elections were held throughout France for a National Assembly convoked at Bordeaux, and, if Napoleon III. entertained any hopes of a speedy restoration, they were dashed by the outcome of the appeal to the people. Only a handful of Bonapartists were returned, and the Republicans constituted but a weak minority, the great majority consisting of Orleanists and Legitimists. The Assembly proceeded to choose M. Grevy for presiding officer, and M. Thiers as chief of the executive power, and then adjourned to Versailles. Well-founded apprehensions of reactionary designs on the part of the majority in the Assembly caused an insurrection in Paris on March 18, 1871, and the Versailles Government directed Marshal MacMahon to undertake the siege of the capital. The Commune, as the Municipal Government established in Paris was called, lasted until May 21; during its brief term of existence, it perpetrated many atrocities, and, by the assassination of the Archbishop of Paris and a number of priests, provoked sanguinary reprisals on the part of its assailants. It was a partially ruined city of which the Versailles troops took possession, the Tuileries, the Hotel de Ville and many other public buildings having been destroyed. On the 10th of May, a final treaty of peace was signed at Frankfort; by it a pecuniary indemnity of five thousand million francs was paid, and Alsace, together with a large part of Lorraine, was ceded to Germany, while, on the other hand, the fortress of Belfort was restored to France. An earnest attempt was made by the Monarchists to bring about the acceptance of the Comte de Chambord as king of France, under the name of Henri V., but, although he was recognized as the lawful sovereign by the Comte de Paris, the representative of the House of Orleans, the scheme of fusion failed, mainly because the Comte de Chambord insisted upon substituting the white flag of the Bourbons for the national tricolor. To this change, which was too obviously symbolic of reaction, the Orleanists refused to accede, and it was, accordingly, agreed that a republican form of government should be provisionally organized. On the resignation of M. Thiers in 1873, caused by a defeat of one of his measures in the Assembly, Marshal MacMahon was elected President, and, in the course of 1875, a Constitution was completed which went into operation in the following year. As this Constitution, with some amendments, is still the organic law of France, it will be well to mark some of its principal features. The organs of the State, created in 1875, were a Parliament, consisting of two branches, the Senate and the Chamber of Deputies, and then an Executive, made up of a President, the Chief Magistrate of the Republic, and of Ministers, who form a connecting link between the Parliament and the Chief Magistrate, and constitute the controlling factor in the governmental machinery. The French Senate contains three hundred members, of whom seventy-five were to be appointed for life, and two hundred and twenty-five were to be elected for nine years by the Departments. In 1884, however, the provisions relating to the mode of electing Senators were amended, and it was enacted that, as fast as the life Senators died, their seats should be distributed among the Departments, so that, eventually, all the Senators would be chosen in the same way. It is further provided that a third of the Senators shall be replaced every three years, the Senate being thus made a permanent body. The legislative power of the Senate and the Chamber of Deputies is the same, except that financial bills must originate in the latter House. It is admitted that the Senate may reduce proposals for taxes and appropriations; whether it can increase them or not is disputed, although, in practice, the Chamber has sometimes accepted augmentations. Whether Ministers are responsible to the Senate as well as to the Chamber of Deputies has been the subject of controversy; but the resignation of Premier Bourgeois in 1896, in consequence of the Senate's passing votes of censure and refusing appropriations, seems to have answered the question in the affirmative. The Senate has, moreover, two peculiar functions. First, its consent is necessary for a dissolution of the Chamber of Deputies, a provision designed as a safeguard against the President, who might otherwise dissolve the Chamber in order to attempt a *coup d'état* during its absence; and, secondly, the President is authorized, with the approval of the Council of Ministers, to constitute the Senate a High Court to try any one for an attempt on the safety of the State. This power, we may remark in passing, was used in the case of General Boulanger, who failed to appear for trial, and was condemned in his absence.

The Chamber of Deputies consists of five hundred and eighty-one members, certain seats being distributed among the various colonies, and six being allotted to Algeria. The members are chosen by secret ballot and by universal suffrage. A Deputy need be only twenty-five years old, whereas a Senator must be forty. The mode of election has varied from time to time between that of single electoral districts, a system called the *Scrutin d'Arrondissement*, corresponding to the method by which members of Congress are chosen in the United States; and that of the *Scrutin de Liste*, which consists in the choice of all the deputies of each Department on a general ticket; this latter method corresponds to that by which Presidential electors are chosen in most of our States. The *Scrutin d'Arrondissement*, or single district system, prevailed from 1876 to 1885, when the *Scrutin de Liste* was introduced. It turned out, however, that the reactionaries gained seats rather than lost them by the *Scrutin de Liste*, and the apprehensions aroused by the popularity of General Boulanger caused the Republicans to restore the *Scrutin d'Arrondissement* before the general election of 1889.

The important fact should be mentioned that the French Parliament, like the British Parliament, possesses the power of amending the Constitution. To revise constitutional laws, however, the two Chambers must meet in joint session at Versailles, and they then form what is called the National Assembly, which has one other function, that, namely, of electing the President of the Republic. This officer is chosen for seven years, and is re-eligible; the only restriction on the choice of a candidate being found in the constitutional amendment passed on August 14, 1884, which excludes all members of families that have ever reigned in France. The President is the executive head of the nation, and, as such, executes the laws, issues ordinances and appoints all the officers of the government. He has the right of initiative in legislation, but he has no veto upon the laws, and, although he may require the Chambers to reconsider a bill, the right has never been exercised. With the consent of the Senate, he can dissolve the Chamber of Deputies, but this power has fallen into disuse, no dissolution having taken place since President MacMahon's unsuccessful attempt to use it in 1877, as a means of getting a Chamber in sympathy with his views. The President has power to make treaties; but treaties of peace, of commerce, or those which burden the finances, affect the persons or property of French citizens in foreign countries, or change the territory of France, in other words, all the more important treaties, require the ratification of the Chambers. A declaration of war also requires their consent; but, as a matter of fact, the government managed to wage war in Tunis and Tonquin without any explicit consent, defending itself on the ground that the Parliament, by voting credits, had virtually sanctioned its course. Sir Henry Maine has observed of the French President that he neither reigns nor governs. It is certain that, unlike the President of the United States, the French President is not free to use his powers according to his own judgment; for the constitutional laws declare that all his acts of every kind, to be valid, must be countersigned by one of the Ministers. When, therefore, the powers of the President are enumerated, it is to be understood that these are really exercised by the Ministers, who are, at all times, responsible to the Chamber of Deputies, and who have acknowledged, three or four times, responsibility to the Senate. As a rule, the President of the Republic is not even present at the Cabinet consultations in which the real policy of the government is discussed. He has power, it is true, to select the Ministers, and, in this matter, he is at liberty to use his own discretion to some extent; but, as a matter of fact, he generally intrusts some leading politician with the formation of a Cabinet, and gives him such colleagues as he suggests. The President's duty in these cases is not as simple as is that of the English queen, for the reason that the Chamber of Deputies is not divided into two great parties, but into a number of factions or groups, several of which may unite for the purpose of forming a temporary majority, but they do not possess the elements of permanent cohesion.

Having indicated the principal organs of the Constitution which has been operative in France since 1876, we proceed to outline very briefly the principal events that have marked the course of political history. It is not needful, however, to discuss in detail each of the thirty-five Cabinets which have come into existence during the twenty-five years since the Republic began to enjoy responsible ministries; that is to say, since MacMahon's election to the Presidency in May, 1873. The first election under the new Constitution took place early in 1876, and the Republicans secured a majority of the Chamber. President MacMahon, who, previously, had placed the Duc de Broglie at the head of a Cabinet of conservative character, now deemed it his duty to select his Ministers from the republican majority, and appointed a new Cabinet drawn entirely from the Left Center. This Ministry resigned in less than a year, and was reconstructed under Jules Simon, who, presently, although he retained the support of a majority in the Chamber, was requested by the President to vacate his office, on the ground that he had not withstood the spread of Radical opinions with sufficient firmness. A new Cabinet, largely composed of Monarchists and Bonapartists, was formed, with the Duc de Broglie and M. de Fourtou in the most influential posts. This was, obviously, a violation of the fundamental principle of Parliamentary government, and the members of the republican groups joined in a protest which was answered, in June, 1877, by a dissolution of the Chamber. In the ensuing campaign, a strenuous effort was made by the reactionists to secure a triumph at the ballot-box, but, in spite of their exertions, the elections in October resulted in a victory for the Republicans, who had been marshaled by Gambetta. Upon the meeting of the new Chamber, the President found himself obliged to dismiss the Duc de Broglie and to appoint a Republican Ministry, chosen, for the most part, from members from the Left Center. The fact that, throughout 1878, the reactionists continued to be preponderant in the Senate was an obstacle to the complete triumph of the republicans, but the Senatorial elections of January, 1879, gave them a majority in that body also, and, henceforth, they assumed a more aggressive tone. MacMahon now saw no course open to him but resignation, and he, accordingly withdrew from public life. On January 30, 1879, he was replaced by Jules Grevy, a republican of Gambetta's school. For many years thereafter, the Opportunists, as the followers of Gambetta were called, remained the dominant faction in the Republican party, but they were not strong enough to avert the instability of the Ministries. Even the Cabinet formed by Gambetta himself, in November, 1881, was unable to hold office more than two months and a half. After his death, at the end of 1882, Jules Ferry was, for a time, the most influential republican politician, and the Cabinet formed by him in February, 1883, was of unusual duration. After the fall of Ferry, occasioned by the reverses which his expedition to Tonquin encountered, the people showed discontent with the Parliamentary regime by returning, at the general election of 1885, an increased number of monarchists. During the next four years, the most important event was the appearance of General Boulanger as the head of the opposition to the party in power. He had become conspicuous as Minister of War from January, 1886, to May, 1887, through his heavy expenditures on the army and his aggressive attitude toward Germany. He now proposed a revision of the Constitution, and was supported by the Bonapartists, a considerable part of the monarchists, and, also, a good many Radicals. At elections to fill vacant seats, held under the *Scrutin de Liste*, he succeeded in carrying several Departments, and was finally successful by a great majority in the Department of the Seine. At that moment, the danger of a *coup d'état* was believed to be great, and, had Boulanger been a man of capacity and energy, it is not impossible that the Republic might have been brought to an untimely end. The Republicans, however, appreciating the gravity of the crisis, drew together, and, under the vigorous leadership of M. Constant, the Minister of the Interior, they administered a severe defeat to Boulangism at the general election of 1889. Boulanger, himself, fled from France, and, in his absence, was convicted of violations of the law. He, presently, committed suicide.

Up to this time, the Catholic Church had been the bond of union between the reactionary factions. The Boulanger episode led the Papacy to doubt the wisdom of allying itself with a discredited party against a powerful republic. In the spring of 1892, Pope Leo XIII. issued an encyclical letter to the effect that the Church was not necessarily opposed to the republican form of government in France, in consequence of which declaration, afterward reiterated and emphasized, many of the reactionaries, under the name of Ralliés, have accepted the republic.

In spite of the Panama scandals, the disclosure of which in 1892 discredited a number of leading republican politicians, and, incidentally, the republican regime itself, the more conservative republicans, or Moderates, as they now began to be termed, gained a large majority of seats in the elections of 1893. On December 3 of the year named, shortly after the opening of the new Chamber, a Ministry of Moderates, or Republicans of Government, so called, was appointed, with Casimir-Perier at its head. For the first time in the history of the Third Republic, a homogeneous Cabinet was supported by a homogeneous majority. It was upset, however, in May, 1894, by an unexpected crisis, but the same conservative policy was pursued by the succeeding Ministry, which adopted a conciliatory tone toward the Church, and maintained the authority of the government against socialistic agitation.

A month later, President Carnot was murdered by an anarchist at Lyons; we should here mention that M. Sadi-Carnot, the grandson of the man who is said to have "organized victory" under the First Republic, had been chosen Chief Magistrate on M. Grevy's resignation, which, not long after his election to a second term of the Presidency, he had been compelled to offer, in consequence of the exposure of the fact that his son-in-law, M. Wilson, had been guilty of selling decorations. To the place left vacant by Carnot, the Moderates elevated Casimir-Perier, but, after passing seven months in office, a constant target for slander and insult, he resigned the Presidency, and was succeeded by M. Felix Faure, who appointed a Cabinet of Moderates, that, while showing more compliance toward the Radicals than their predecessors, adhered, upon the whole, to conservative principles. The Moderate majority, however, gradually grew feebler, until, in October, 1895, it ceased to exist, and a Radical Cabinet was formed by M. Bourgeois. He brought forward a proposal for a progressive income tax, the principle of which was adopted by the Chamber in March, 1896, but only by a majority of sixteen. The Senate, where the Moderates were preponderant, twice passed a vote of want of confidence in the Ministers, and, when they declined to resign, went so far, in April, as to refuse the credits demanded for Madagascar, thus, virtually, stopping the wheels of government. Under the circumstances, Premier Bourgeois thought it best to withdraw from office, and he was succeeded by M. Meline, who selected his colleagues entirely from the Moderates, and who remained in power until a new Chamber was elected in May, 1898. Soon after the meeting of that body, it was made evident that M. Meline did not possess the confidence of the majority, and he, accordingly, gave place to M. Brisson, who formed a Cabinet composed mainly of Advanced Radicals.

A question which has given the Brisson Cabinet much trouble was the expediency of ordering a new trial of Captain Dreyfus, a French officer who, at the close of 1894, had been found guilty of treason by a court-martial, and sentenced to imprisonment for life. It was, subsequently, disclosed that the documentary evidence upon which the judgment of the court-martial had been based had not been submitted to the inspection of the prisoner or of his counsel, and that Dreyfus had, consequently, been deprived of the safeguards which the statutory law throws about the liberty of the French citizen. A vigorous campaign in favor of a retrial was started by Emile Zola, the eminent novelist, but his efforts, for some time, seemed unavailing, and only exposed him to prosecution in his turn. A change in public opinion occurred, however, when Colonel Henry, an officer on the general staff, confessed himself to be the forger of a document which had been put forward in the Chamber as conclusive against Dreyfus, and he sealed the self-incriminating confession by suicide. Premier Brisson, soon afterward, declared in favor of revision, and persuaded most of his colleagues to adopt the same view. The papers in the case were sent to the Court of Cassation, and, if that tribunal shall decide that there is ground for a new trial, Dreyfus will be brought back to France and arraigned before a second court-martial.

In respect of colonial possessions, France has made a remarkable advance under the Third Republic. To Algeria, she has added Tunis, and has extended her dominions southward over the Sahara, to Timbuctoo, the capital of the Middle Soudan. In West Africa, she has greatly expanded her sphere of influence, and, in the spring of 1898, succeeded in securing, at the expense of England, some valuable territory in the basin of the Niger. The French Colonial Office has even contemplated the extension of French sway across the whole breadth of Africa from the Atlantic to the Nile, and Major Marchand, at the head of a small expedition, actually succeeded in reaching Fashoda, which, however, was afterward occupied by an Anglo-Egyptian force. In Central Africa, the French possess an important strip of territory next to that of the Congo Free State, and they have established a protectorate, which practically amounts to annexation, over the great island of Madagascar. In Farther India, the conquests which were begun under the Second Empire have been widened until they include not only Cochin-China and Cambodia, but also Tonquin, the whole empire of Anam and a considerable section of Siam. France has also secured from China a lease of the seaport of Kwang Chou Wan in the southern province of Kwang Tung, which port is the natural outlet for the trade of the province of Kwangsi, and she has also obtained certain exclusive rights of trade and of railroad building intended to give her the control of the markets of Southwestern China.

It seemed for many years that the gravest danger by which the Third Republic was confronted was the condition of the finances. For a time, indeed, after the war with Germany, the treasury was skillfully managed, and France astonished the world by the rapidity with which she paid the war indemnity. Subsequently, however, her Ministers were guilty of wild extravagance. They poured out money like water for roads, railroads and schools, and rolled up a huge debt to pay for them. At the same time, they built large fortifications, set up universal military service, and strove to maintain a stronger army and a more powerful fleet than her larger neighbor on the east. Meanwhile, the system of financiering prevented the French people from observing how fast they were going. A habit grew up of dividing the expenditure into ordinary and extraordinary, of which the former alone was defrayed out of the annual receipts, while the latter, as something, ostensibly, unusual, was provided for by loans. As a matter of fact, the items for extraordinary expenses reappeared every year, and became a normal part of the budget. Thus the country sank deeper and deeper into debt, with a gloomy prospect of bankruptcy before it in case of war. Fortunately, of late, the financial administration has been, to a certain extent, improved. Instead of the constantly recurring deficits, there has, more than once, been a surplus, and what is of even greater importance, many of the extraordinary expenses have been cut off. Not until they are suppressed entirely will the finances of the country be upon a thoroughly solid basis.

INDEX.

401

[handwritten note: Condé Prince & funeral oration by Boussett see 4 orations p 1558]

444

446 · INDEX.

INDEX. 447

450 INDEX.

HF (T)